T0186296

AFTER the
Y2K FIREWORKS

Business and Technology Strategies

The CRC Press
Advanced and Emerging Communications
Technologies Series
Series Editor-in-Chief: Saba Zamir

AFTER the Y2K FIREWORKS

Business and Technology Strategies

Bhuvan Unhelkar

Series Editor-in-Chief
Saba Zamir

CRC Press
Boca Raton   London   New York   Washington, D.C.

Contact Editor: Dawn Mesa
Project Editor: Maggie Mogck
Marketing Managers: Barbara Glunn, Jane Lewis,
                          Arline Massey, Jane Stark
Cover Design: Dawn Boyd

Library of Congress Cataloging-in-Publication Data

Unhelkar, Bhuvan.
    After the Y2K fireworks : business and technology strategies / Bhuvan Unhelkar.
        p.   cm. -- (Advanced and emerging communications technologies)
    Includes bibliographical references and index.
    ISBN 0-8493-9599-2 (alk. paper)
    1. Year 2000 date conversion (Computer systems).   I. Title.   II. Series.
QA76.76.S64U54   1999
005.1 ' 6—dc21   98-55541
                                                                              CIP

Foreword

Pollyannas and Doomsayers. Will January 1, 2000 be a nonevent or will hordes of mutant cannibals be ringing our doorbells at precisely 12:03 a.m.? The truth is that no one really knows. Nothing like the Year 2000 problem has ever happened before.

I first started paying serious attention to the Year 2000 problem about 4 years ago. Dr. George Schussel, Chairman and CEO of DCI, Inc. assembled a group of 20 consultants during one of DCI's Software World conferences. He asked us to suggest some themes for future conferences. Ken Orr suggested the Year 2000 problem. My immediate reaction was that the poor old chap had gone off his head. How could a simple date problem be a theme for an entire conference? Ken, however, finally did convince me to start to research Year 2000 issues. The more I learned, the more concerned I became.

What don't we know about the Year 2000?

- How severe will the problems be; how long will the problems last?
- How severe will be the effect on infrastructure (utilities, telecommunications, transportation, etc.) systems?
- What will be the impacts of Year 2000 panic reactions (bank runs, hoarding, postponed travel, etc.)?

What do we know about the Year 2000?

- We do know that the Year 2000 remediation project will be the largest information technology project to date, probably in the range of $600 billion worldwide.
- We do know that the existing software project track record is abysmal. Most software projects are delivered late and over budget. The larger the project, the larger the proportional increase defects in the delivered system. Most large software projects (in excess of 1 million lines of third generation language code) are complete failures. After all of the allocated time and budgets have been consumed, the projects are abandoned. The larger the project, the greater the rate of failure.
- We do know that for the economy as a whole the net return on information technology investments has been negative. Each dollar spent on information technology in the past has returned less than 80 cents.
- We do know that all of the resources that will be consumed on Year 2000 remediation projects will not produce any increase in productivity. The best we can expect is the maintenance of the status quo.
- We do know that we will have to wait until January 1, 2000 to adequately test if all remediation efforts have been successful. Critical infrastructure

systems, for example, can not be shut down and tested in advance. Inter-connected systems can only be tested after all remediation work has been accomplished and only within the actual operating environment of January 1, 2000 (it doesn't matter if the code works if the infrastructure has shut down).

- We do know now (1998/1999) that the only prudent approach must be to establish contingency plans for the most likely disaster scenarios facing us at work and at home.

Bhuvan Unhelkar's excellent book takes us to the next logical step in the Year 2000 remediation process, the "resurrection" of our information systems. Just keeping our largely ineffective, inefficient, uneconomical systems in operation by massive expenditure of resources is a fool's errand. Instead, Unhelkar correctly identifies that we must begin work on the new technological, methodological, and sociological processes that will be required to "resurrect" our information systems.

The Year 2000 problem may be the watershed that finally forces us to begin to effectively plan, control, and direct the resources being invested in the information economy. The Year 2000 problem maybe the event that makes us realize that our society is irrevocably interconnected. As we understand this interdependency, may-be we will begin to realize that we can no longer afford the luxury of the custom development of "islands of automation." Object-orientation promises to be a new way of thinking about information systems. Using the Object approach correctly will allow most organizations to reuse proven components to assemble systems that can seamlessly interact with the systems of their clients, suppliers, government agencies, and all of the other stakeholders of their organizations. This level of reuse will have to involve industry-wide, nation-wide, or even global reuse of components, designs, interfaces, project management activities, documentation, training, and test-ing. Unhelkar provides us with the blueprint for this object-oriented "resurrection."

I highly recommend this book for those organizations that want to look beyond January 1, 2000. I recommend this book for information technology professionals who want to plan their own careers and training beyond January 1, 2000. Finally, I recommend this book for university and technical school MIS courses as a reference of how we got into the Year 2000 problem and how the world could be *After The Y2K Fireworks*.

Richard T. Dué
Edmonton, Alberta, Canada

Preface

A Winner knows what he'll do next if he loses,
But doesn't talk about it;
A Loser doesn't know what he'll do if he loses,
But talks about what he'll do if he wins.

Eric Berne, 1970[1]

PURPOSE OF THIS BOOK

This is a prescriptive book on the "millennium bug," also known as Year 2000 or Y2K problem. Herein is discussed a detailed strategy of resurrecting your organization from a Y2K disaster, should that occur. Otherwise, it is aimed at organizations that want to reengineer themselves anyway in the new millennium.

As far as the Year 2000 bug is concerned, it is already too late to do anything about prevention if you haven't already done something about it. According to Capers Jones,[2] we are already past the date when "prevention" from the Y2K bug bite was still possible. Past January, 1998 only an extraordinary effort would have helped organizations prepare thoroughly for the Year 2000. By the time this book is in your hands, it will not make much sense to discuss prevention from Y2K hits. Although theoretically an effort can be started even on the night of December 31, 1999, the end result from this effort need not be guessed.

A recent survey of 1000 companies by Coopers & Lybrand on the millennium bug revealed that 78% of the companies regard it as a business issue. This is quite different from the earlier (circa 1995) thinking, which considered Y2K as a predominantly technological issue. Today, the Y2K problem is considered as a joint responsibility of business as well as Information Technology (IT) communities. Despite large funds set aside from the business managers, and considerable time and effort spend by the IT professionals, it is estimated that at least 50% of the organizations did not start their effort on time. If an organization started its Y2K effort after January 1998, and if it is not prepared to put *extraordinary* effort in fixing the millennium bug, then it only has a 50% chance of success. Thus, an approximate 25% of overall businesses are likely to be hit by the millennium bug in some form and with some intensity.

In the past few years, proponents of the millennium bug have spent considerable time and energy in raising the awareness of both the business and the government sectors to the potential disaster the Y2K problem can create. Today, there are hundreds of books and thousands of journal articles on the Y2K problem and newspapers report problems already faced by businesses every day. This indicates that our understanding of the issue has reached a level where we can no longer be accused of "ostrich mentality." Our heads are out of the sand, and we are staring in the direction of potential danger. The problem is that while we have been busy raising the awareness level of the issue and have remained fascinated with its prevention, it seems that both the business and the IT communities have not given enough consideration to the fact that if we are hit, what will we be doing next?

This book assumes that you are hit! It is a book that is aimed at the developments *After the Year 2000 Fireworks* have exploded in the New Year skies. It starts with a very general understanding of the type of problem we are facing, and keeps the discussion on the "preventive" aspect of the date problem to a bare minimum. This is so because prevention strategies have been outlined in great detail and indeed put in place by a large number of companies. The current literature is saturated, almost to paranoid proportions, with putting on a bullet proof vest in order to avoid being hit by the bullet. This book is unique because it aims at keeping the reader calm, cool and collected, as it works out strategies of surgically removing the bullet.

This, however, does *not* mean that you have to be hit in order to find this book useful. It is hoped that by stating the problem up front, and by assuming the worst, businesses will get a much better feel of how to rebuild if and when they crash. This book provides the equivalent of a "pre-emptive strike." Instead of prevention, which has been discussed at great length, it works at the cure. By taking this unique approach, and by being prescriptive, it is hoped that this discussion will enable a larger number of businesses to move with confidence into the next millennium. It would form part of your disaster *recovery arsenal,* from where it can be retrieved should misfortune occur.

SUMMARY OF THE BOOK

Outlined in this book is a detailed approach of how you can rebuild quickly and effectively from the ashes of a Y2K disaster. This has been called *resurrection* throughout the text — which includes an understanding of what has happened in terms of the date disaster, and how it can be converted into a situation of strategic value. Thus the book focuses *not* on a quick date fix, but on survival through resurrection. It starts by identifying the various ways you are hit, the way your organizational structure will look like and how the organization will behave after the disaster. After arguing about the strategic advantages of undertaking a resurrection process, this discussion defines and describes a detailed process discipline for resurrection. The actual resurrection process, which comprises the three essential dimensions of rebuilding, follows this. These essential dimensions are technology, methodology, and sociology. Once the process of creating the new business processes is understood, it can be applied to various types of organizations that may have been hit by the Y2K problem. Included in this discussion are simplified examples of business processes relating to banking loan applications and resurrecting a Y2K-hit payroll application. Distribution, which will be an essential architectural element of redesigning organizations in the year 2000, is discussed in the context of these redesigns. Due to the extreme importance of testing in the year 2000, especially because it has to go way beyond the traditional Y2K tests and ensure that the new system satisfies the functionality of the existing system as well as the added functionality, a separate chapter is dedicated to the topic of test planning, test designing, and execution of test cases.

Finally, this discussion accepts the fact that we are moving towards a global village. Phenomenal advances in communication and transportation have shrunk the world. Businesses will have to come to terms with these phenomena and will have to revisit their priorities in the new millennium. The sociological aspect of managing a software development, as well as managing the personality of the business in this global village, will be of utmost importance to the senior (and enlightened) management of the organization. No longer can the organization consider itself separated from the rest of the society, and no longer can it be said to be genuinely responsible towards its shareholders, if it does not consider the context in which it is operating. This context is understood and accepted by an *adwait* company. Adwait is a word derived from the Sanskrit literature, and literally means nondual. The boundaries between organizations in the next millennium will be fuzzy and undefined. Businesses will depend more on their relationships with customers, as well as with their suppliers, in order to survive and prosper. In essence, it will be difficult to look at the business as a separate entity — it will be a part of the global business — in other words it will be adwait. Creation of an adwait reengineered organization is the final goal of this exercise. The hope is that such an organization will be flexible and process-oriented enough to sustain even a Year 3000 hit — for the way IT is going today, I am sure there are a large number of "unknown" bugs that we are busily inserting in our codes and embedded chips today, that will somehow come out to bite us 1000 years from now.

LITERARY AUDIENCE

This is a business book with a technological bent. It is written in a simple descriptive style that will appeal to IT managers and senior managers who are the first point of call when an organization is hit by the Y2K problem in Year 2000. The discussion also will be of interest to those who issue the call to save the organization. These are the people ultimately responsible to the shareholders of the company — the directors, who have the responsibility of sanctioning budgets. Thus, those who have the job of providing budgets and those with the responsibility of utilizing them will together find the ideas on the resurrection process discussed in this book interesting. Finally, the people who will perform the work of creating and implementing process-based systems, the analysts and programmers, will find the technical and methodological discussions worth the time they spend away from their *real work* of programming the system.

READER CATEGORIES

For the purpose of providing relevance of this work to a large cross-section of readers, prospective readers are grouped into three categories represented by the actors: analyst/programmer, project manager, and director. These are not individual roles but *groups* of people. None of the actors are exclusive to their respective category. For example, a software engineer within the analyst/programmer category also may be performing some of the tasks of a project manager. In that case, the reading-threads relevant to the project manager may be of interest to this software engineer. Or, in a small software shop, where the CEO is the same person as the programmer, probably all reading-threads will apply. These reader groups are described in more detail below, before the reading map is presented.

ANALYST/PROGRAMMER

The analyst/programmer is not just one role, or one person. It is in fact a number of actors who are grouped together as one — for the ease of discussion as well as for the common needs of this group of readers. In reality, the analyst/programmer actor is made up of analysts who will analyze the requirements of the new system, programmers who will be involved in coding and testing the rewritten or modified system, the software engineers who will do both the jobs (analyzing and programming), team leaders providing the first level of leadership, test programmers involved in writing test cases and programming test harnesses around the 'resurrecting' code, network administrators who will be involved in revamping their LANs, and database managers who might be responsible for lower-level data conversion exercises and so on.

PROJECT MANAGER

The project manager is the person who will be responsible for the planning and administration of the Y2K resurrection. There are a number of variations of this actor that are also involved in the resurrection process at middle management level. These include the system architect who is responsible for the "grand picture" as well as the aesthetics of the system, the methodologist who takes responsibility for the discipline of development, the process consultant who may be a methodologist or who may be exclusively there to consult on the resurrection process, and the quality assurance manager who is responsible for the quality processes, documentation, standards, measurements and metrics. Once again, real people are not restricted to these actors. Any person who has the project level responsibility, or who gives input to the resurrection process at the project level, would fall in this category.

DIRECTOR

The director is an actor with ultimate responsibility to the owners or shareholders of the company. This role may be fulfilled by the Chief Executive Officer (CEO), the Chief Operating Officer (COO), the Chief Financial Officer (CFO), the Chief Information Officer (CIO), the Program Director, the Human Resources (HR) Director, or the General Manager (GM). This is an actor who, according to some authors, stands to be accountable both personally and professionally for the pending Y2K disaster.

All three reader categories mentioned above would find this book interesting, not only from the point of view of justifying, budgeting for, and promoting the resurrection process, but also converting the survival process into a strategic advantage.

READING MAP

This reading map is based on the three reader categories described above. The map shows the *reading-threads* that will be relevant to each of the reader groups. A cross-reference of chapters to reader groups follows. The reading map is based on notations and semantics, which form part of the process-discipline. It is the same discipline that will be used by us in resurrecting the enterprise. Therefore, it is described in detail in Chapter 4 of this book. For readers with the irresistible urge to make sense of each and every notation used here, it might be helpful to browse through Chapter 4. However, it is assumed that the simplicity of the notations used makes it self-explanatory, and that a small amount of deciphering may be required, not a rigorous decoding at this stage.

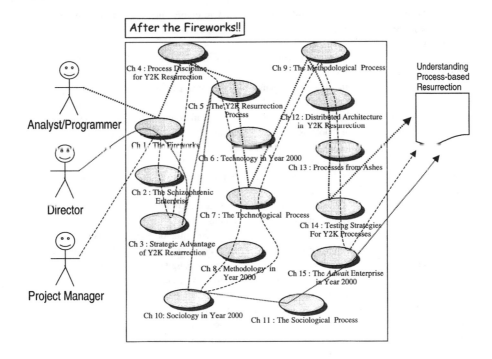

Figure P.1   Actor-based reading threads for *after the Y2K fireworks.*

ACTORS — CHAPTERS CROSS-REFERENCE

Following is a cross-reference of the actors and the possible interests they will have in reading the relevant chapters (Table P.1). The interests (in bold) are the chapters that the particular actor may read only from an "appreciating" viewpoint, as against carrying out the activities and tasks mentioned within the project. I also am aware that for some actors, some chapters will be plain boring (e.g., Chapter 3 for actor: analyst/programmer) or uninteresting (e.g., Chapter 6 for actor: director). They are marked accordingly.

TABLE P.1
Cross Reference of Actors and Relevant Chapters

Chapters	Relevance to Various Actors		
	Analyst/Programmer	Project Manager	Director
Chap. 1: The Fireworks	Nature of the problem	Review the cause	**Organizational hurt**
Chap. 2: The Schizophrenic Enterprise	**Appreciation**	Type of "hit" organization; steps in explosion; severity	Ashes of explosion; attempting redefinition
Chap. 3: Strategic Advantage of Y2K Resurrection	Boring	Kind of work that might be required during resurrection	Deriving a lot more than just a date fix; budget justification
Chap. 4: Process Discipline for Y2K Resurrection	The process-discipline and what it entails	How to enforce the discipline	**Appreciation**
Chap. 5: The Y2K Resurrection Process	Understanding the resurrection process through the discipline described	Implementing the resurrection process in the given discipline	Appreciation of the Y2K resurrection process, as put in a discipline
Chap. 6: Technology in Year 2000	Understanding the new technological advances that may be used in resurrection	Appreciation of the technological advances	Uninteresting (nitty-gritty)
Chap. 7: The Technological Process	Implementing the technological process for resurrection	Supervising the technological process for resurrection	Uninteresting (nitty-gritty)
Chap. 8: Methodology in Year 2000	**Appreciation**	Methodological advances in 2000	Uninteresting (nitty-gritty)
Chap. 9: The Methodological Process	**Appreciating and using the activities and tasks within the methodology**	Selecting and implementing the activities and tasks within the methodology	Uninteresting (nitty-gritty)
Chap. 10: Sociology in Year 2000	Boring	Personal/team processes; usability	Organizational directions; leadership
Chap. 11: The Sociological Process	Boring	Team formation; staffing	Advertising; environment; litigation
Chap. 12: Distributed Architecture in Y2K Resurrection	Design issues in distribution and their Y2K application	Architectural issues in distribution	**Appreciation**
Chap. 13: Processes from Ashes	Implementing processes in Y2K–practical scenarios	Implementing processes in Y2K–practical scenarios	**Appreciation**

TABLE P.1 *(Continued)*
Cross Reference of Actors and Relevant Chapters

Chapters	Relevance to Various Actors		
	Analyst/Programmer	Project Manager	Director
Chap. 14: Testing Strategies for Y2K Processes	Unit and system level tests of rewritten code; test tools	Test planning; test approach; test resources	**Appreciation**
Chap. 15: The *Adwait* Enterprise in Year 2000	**Appreciation**	A thought on the enterprise in the new millennium	Justifying a global village

MAPPING TO A WORKSHOP

It is envisaged that this book will provide judicious discussion topics as well as provide invaluable help to organizations that will try and rebuild after the Y2K hit. As a result, there will be a need for well-organized presentations and discussion sessions. This book can play a significant role in a 2-day (4 sessions per day) workshop on Y2K resurrection. A rough mapping of the sessions to the contents of the book is provided (Table P.2).

TABLE P.2
Mapping of the Chapters in this Book to a 2-Day Workshop

Day	Session	Presentation and Discussion Workshop Topic	Relevant Chapters	Comments
1	8:30–10:00	Causes and effect of Y2K hits	1 2	General Y2K discussion; steps in explosion
	10:30–12:00	Strategic benefits of Y2K resurrection effort; a discipline for resurrecting	3 4	Going beyond just a date-fix; a disciplined approach to any process-based development
	1:30–3:00	The resurrection process	5	Applying the process discipline to the Y2K resurrection
	3:30–5:00	Technological process (with dissection, salvage)	6 7	The languages, databases, tools used in resurrection + salvageable options

TABLE P.2 *(Continued)*
Mapping of the Chapters in this Book to a 2-Day Workshop

Day	Session	Presentation and Discussion Workshop Topic	Relevant Chapters	Comments
2	8:30–10:00	Methodological process	8 9	Applying object-orientation to Y2K resurrection process
	10:30–12:00	Sociological process	10 11	The influence of "soft factors" on resurrection
	1:30–3:00	Distributed architecture in resurrection; processes from ashes	12 13	Understanding distribution; applying the overall understanding to business processes in building the new enterprise
	3:30 — 5:00	Testing and verification in Y2K resurrection	14	Test planning, testing, and verifying the new enterprise

SEMANTICS

The author firmly believes in gender-neuter language. *Person* is, therefore, used wherever possible. However, in order to maintain simplicity of reading, *he* has been used as freely and has been balanced by equal, if not more, use of *she*. Quotes and other references have been left untouched.

Terms like *programmer* and *manager*, unless otherwise mentioned, represent roles performed by actors. These terms don't tie down real people like you and me who, in a short span of time, can jump from the role of a programmer to a manager to a director and back. Thus, when I say, "a programmer has to implement these designs," it implies the role of a programmer that might be filled by a person today, who in 5 (or 2) years time might be performing the role of a manager with significantly different responsibilities.

We throughout the text refer to the reader and the author. Occasionally, *we* refers to the general IT community of which the author is a member. *We* also refers to the teams in which the author has worked. Therefore, although this is a single author book, you may encounter *we* as a reference by the author to himself, as well as to the IT community.

Y2K means the Year 2000; YZ (pronounced as *yeez*) means Year Zero; both Y2K and YZ mean the same thing, which is the next millennium. We do not get into the debate of whether 2001 is the official start of the millennium. For the purpose of the current discussion, the first day of January 2000 is the start of the millennium.

Enterprise is the business that involves the technical people, the managers, the directors, the clients, and the suppliers. Other words that may be used interchangeably to describe an enterprise are *organization, business,* and *company.* However, enterprise is a more general word and, therefore, also encompasses *government,* which is separate from business and company.

This text is replete with repetitions. These repetitions of thoughts and concepts are for two purposes: (1) to provide links in a discussion to the previous thoughts on which it is based, and (2) to enable easier understanding of the subject matter. Please excuse the author if you are one of those *brilliant* individuals who can remember and link to everything you have read in the previous pages — the author is not.

ACKNOWLEDGEMENTS

This book aims to provide creative solutions to the Y2K problem *after the fireworks of the millennium* are over. Without proper nourishment, as well as tempering, of this creativity by a number of cherished individuals this work would not have come to fruition in a book form. First and foremost, I would like to thank my editor, Saba Zamir, who, with the option of "Y2K prevention" fast vanishing, nourished my idea of writing on Y2K prescription. Professor Brian Henderson-Sellers, my Ph.D. supervisor, encouraged me to bring in object-orientation to handle the Y2K problem, and colleagues at Object-Oriented Pty. Ltd. (OOP/L) (especially Dr. Julian Edwards, John Warner, and Stephan Meyn) who supported the effort from the practical perspective. Professor Larry Constantine and Lucy Lockwood continued to bless the idea of Y2K resurrection with relevant and constructive criticisms especially in the area of sociology and usability. Associate Professor Jenny Edwards, Head of School at the University of Technology, Sydney, was helpful in her guidance. SriPrabhat (S.D.) Pradhan, CEO, Tata Technologies, India Ltd., provided valuable insight into the business angle for resurrection, especially from the point of view of the director of one of the largest software companies in India.

A large number of professional colleagues who spared valuable time and energy in typing, drawing, proof reading, and commenting on the work include (in random order): Prashant Risbud, Rajeev Arora, Venkatesh Sanjeeva, Michael Riley, Rama Kasbekar, Pinku Talati, Ankit Shah, Amit Pradhan, Rajesh Pradhan, Yamini Kagal, Anup Badhe, Sameer Thakur, Andrew Powell, Sanjay Vaidya, Deepak Avasare, Sagar Agashe, Anant Chitale, Vivienne Counter, Subodh Deshpande, Michael Macklin, Amit Tiwary, Oskar Schlegl, Gina Sugay, Graeme Bennett, Kennith Trinh, Roy Patrao, Kelly Kimbell, Vidyanand Karandikar, Dinesh Kavthekar, and many others. My wife, Asha, daughter, Sonki Priyadarshini, and son, Keshav Raja, as well as my extended family, Girish and Chinar Mamdapur (who are budding information technologists), were all very patient and helpful in every way they could.

To each and every one of these cherished individuals that I have mentioned here, and to many more who have made indirect contributions to this work, I say with a sincerity beyond words, "Thank you!"

CRITIQUES

This work has to be criticized. It only reflects a healthy state of affairs within the IT world when a work like this gets criticized and the criticisms are accepted in a positive vein (as they will be). All comments including the good, the bad, and the ugly are sincerely welcome. To all my prospective critics whose criticisms will only add to the general wealth of knowledge of the IT professionals in handling the Y2K saga and whose criticisms will encourage me to perform better by keeping me humble, I say a big *thank you* in advance.

Bhuvan Unhelkar

REFERENCES

1. Berne, Eric, *What do you say after you say Hello?: The Psychology of Human Destiny,* Corgi, Transworld Publishers, London, 1972, 205.
2. Jones, Capers, *The Year 2000 Software Problem: Quantifying the Costs and Assessing the Consequences,* 1998, Addison Wesley Longman, Reading, MA.

Author

Bhuvan Unhelkar (MDBA, MSc, Ph.D., MACS) has over 17 years of professional Information Systems (IS) experience including consulting and senior roles in Product Development and Quality Assurance. Currently, he is the Chief Operating Officer at CASEldigital Inc., a Californian software company (with offices in India and Australia) involved in development, consulting, and training in a wide area of software activities, including Year 2000, object-oriented processes and methodologies, ERP solutions, and CAD/CAM development.

Unhelkar's experience portfolio in software development includes initiating and implementing methodological approaches to OO development with a strong emphasis on quality and reusability, as well as providing leadership and direction, staffing and budgeting, internal and external training. For the development of a financial market application, he won the Computerworld Object Developer's Awards (CODA '95) for "Best use of an object-oriented approach across the organization." His ideas on the process of Y2K resurrection derive from his experience in process-based software development, consulting to various organizations and his own research and understanding.

Unhelkar received his Doctorate from the University of Technology, Sydney. His thesis was title "Effect of Granularity of OO Design in Modeling an Enterprise and its Application to Financial Risk Management." In addition to the discussion on object granularity in designs, the thesis also discusses IT strategic planning, enterprise modeling and sociological issues in IT project management, which form the basis of the sociological dimension of the Y2K resurrection process. He has lectured in the subjects of "Object Oriented Information Systems" at University of New South Wales, as well as at University of Technology, Sydney, where he is also an Honorary Associate. He also has supervised many Master's projects at the university.

Unhelkar has participated in numerous conferences and training workshops in Australia, New Zealand, the United States, Canada, Singapore, South Africa, and India. His work has been published in *Object Magazine, ROAD,* and *Computerworld* journals, and as chapters in *Developing Business Objects* (SIGS Publications, 1997), *The OPEN Process Specification* (Addison-Wesley, 1997) and *The Handbook of Object Technology* (CRC Press, 1998). Unhelkar is a member of the Australian Computer Society, the Software Quality Association, and the Australian Software Metrics Association.

Contents

Chapter 5   The Y2K Resurrection Process

Chapter 8   Methodology in Year 2000

Chapter 9   Describing the Methodological Process

Prologue

It was New Year's eve, 1997. With barely an hour to go before the H-hour (12:00 a.m.), the spectacle of the mammoth barge with its awesome firepower, easing itself in the harbor of the Olympics 2000 city held me spellbound. Almost half a million spectators in all shapes, sizes, ages, colors and languages (not excluding C++, Cobol, Assembler, and Java) had crammed every nook and corner of the harbor. I had squeezed my way through the gaps (niche markets) to the tip of the Opera House with a hope of capturing some of the best shots of the New Year celebrations. The only thing that kept coming in between my camera lens and a clear Sydney sky, where the panorama of the New Year fireworks was to unfold, were the tiny mud-filled smelly shoes of my 2-year-old. He was comfortably perched on my shoulders for an even better view (competitive old chap). As he dug deep in my head for a better hold of my remaining hair, I wondered, "If the small fingers could reach a bit further inside, what would they find?" Through the jumbled maze of project plans for financial market's analytical products, justifications for annual bonuses, tools for object-oriented analysis and design, and thesis proposals by part-time research students, he would be sure to come across a thought or two on the state of the world as it would celebrate this mega-party in 2 years' time. *Year 2000 fireworks!* The thought sends a shudder down my spine despite the warm summer evening. Perhaps, it was going to be more than just the New Year fireworks! And if the spectacular explosions do occur, then we, especially those who coded the 2-digit firecracker, shoulder the responsibility of making a sincere attempt to come out of the chaos. For if we don't, those who sit on our shoulders today may ask us a question or two tomorrow.

My Kids

1 The Fireworks

*Come the first dawn of 00, myriad electronic morons would say to themselves,
"00 is smaller than 99. Therefore, today is earlier than yesterday."*

Sir Arthur C. Clarke

Abstract   The party of the millennium will be celebrated with two kinds of fire-works: first, the dazzling lights and the booms that will be witnessed, enjoyed, and absorbed by people all over the world; and second, the invisible and silent spectacular of the "Y2K bug" which will again be experienced by people all over the world. People will feel this potentially scary experience of the Y2K issue in various ways. They will experience the firecrackers as first-hand experience — by failure of personal gadgets or failure of social systems on which they rely for day-to-day living. They also will experience the indirect effect of the Y2K firecrackers through the organizations in which they are employed or in which they own a share. Needless to say that everyone will feel the effect of the changing face of the society resulting from this mega-advancement in the "year-field" of life. In this opening chapter, we introduce the topic of Y2K through the discussion of the millennium party, various types of "fireworks" that will explode at the Turn of the Century party and the justification for why these firecrackers are still there. The effect of the Year 2000 party is potentially a long hangover — percolating family, social, and professional aspects of life. As against the rest of the chapters in this book which are more solution-oriented, this and the next chapter are introducing the problem in a "general" chatty manner.

1.1   AFTER THE FIREWORKS

1.1.1   PARTY OF THE MILLENNIUM

On the night of December the 31, 1999 the world will immerse itself in a real-life celebration that promises to be wilder and weirder than the wildest dream. The event of my desk calendar flipping over to show 1/1/00 is certainly going to be dreamlike. Equally unbelievable, but real, will be the many millions of dollars that are expected to go up in smoke as the hopefully Y2K compliant computer-controlled fireworks explode in the skies over Earth to mark the arrival of the New Year with a difference. The purpose of these celebrations, which we have practised and rehearsed for the past 2 millenniums, is to rejoice in the birth of a spirit that can never die. The simplicity of the nativity scene — the silence of the night broken by occasional bleating of a sheep or two, the stable, the stars, the wise men, and a new-born child with a halo around his head — is so far removed from the fiery and noisy celebrations we expect to indulge in, that were it not the real reason for these celebrations, it would have been hard to establish any correlation between the two events spaced 2000 years apart. And if it were not for what we understand as the Y2K or Year 2000 Bug, it would have been hard to establish any correlation between the New Year partying with food, drinks, music, dance, and lights and the flutter in our hearts at the thought of a potential anticlimax to the whole event.

Estimates on how much the world will spend on the Y2K New Year party extravaganza can be anybody's guess, but the estimates on preventing the anticlimax of the date-related computer problem vary in the range of 12 zeroes ($1.9 to 2.3 trillion). These estimates, however, will have become irrelevant on January 1, 2000, as we will have moved from the domain of estimates, predictions, and guesses, into a real world of the *yeez* or Year Zero! And of the 3+ billion people that inhabit the Earth and celebrate the party of the millennium, many will have started feeling the bite of the real millennium bug.

1.1.2   THE PARTY GOERS

As the Earth moves on its axis on that eventful night, the cheering humanity could be divided into two groups: the Information Technology (IT) professionals and the rest. It is estimated that about 2 million of these full-time IT professionals will cheer the fireworks in the U.S., about half a million in the U.K., and about 3 million in India. These are the same numbers of professionals that would have been required if we were not to witness the "other" kind of fireworks, which have the potential of providing the dreaded anticlimax, and which is the main topic of discussion of this book. Not everyone in the IT industry has worked on the Y2K problem, but those that have given it a try have been more than adequately compensated by their business counterpart — happily and hopefully. Jones[1] in his *Year 2000 Repair Case Study* gives a detailed estimate of costs per function point, associated with searching for, repairing, and testing the Y2K problem. For corporations owning half a million function points, the costs using external contractors can go up to $187 million. At the rate of approximately $1.50 per gross physical line of code, it is difficult to discern whether the cheers going up from the IT community are for the New Year, or for a job well done, or merely for the swollen hip pocket. As for the rest of the humanity, the question will soon be answered: "Were the external fireworks the only ones that we all experienced?" Or was there an invisible firework whose effect will be felt by an unfolding of events in the days, weeks, months, and years to follow?

1.1.3   THE DAWN OF 2000

As the dawn of the new millennium breaks, at least 15% of software applications, by one estimate, will have experienced the bite of the Y2K bug.[1] If partygoers at all levels (individual, family, business) are included in the estimate, the effect of the Y2K bite is likely to be much larger. And the one thing that is certain about this "firework" is that prevention is *not* an option anymore. We have already hit the year 2000 and all the talk and discussion on prevention is a thing of the past. Today, it

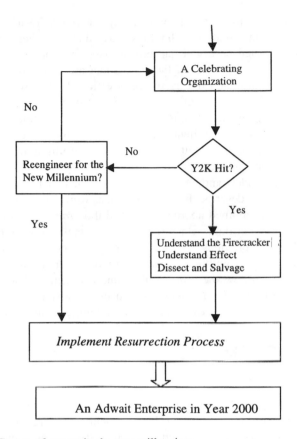

FIGURE 1.1   Course of events in the new millennium.

was already too late to start the prevention effort and only a stellar performance from the IT shops, with 100% resources dedicated to the Y2K work could have helped; on the morning of January 1, 2000, it would be quite inappropriate to discuss anything related to prevention.

If we are not the lucky ones who have enjoyed only the New Year fireworks and continued their celebrations through the night, then we are the ones who will have to work out a strategy to get out of the smouldering ashes of the other type of fireworks. The focus of the effort is no longer prevention, but on resurrection. By following the prescription of absorbing the hit and attempting to get up and get going, we will have understood a lot more about ourselves and the technology we depend on.

The likely course of action for an organization in the New Year is as shown in Figure 1.1. With prevention no longer an option, you start the day by trying to identify whether the bug has hit you or not. This exercise can last from an hour to days and months and even a year. If indeed you are affected, then before any prescriptive effort can be directed, it will be worthwhile understanding what was the nature of the bug that hit you.

Dissection is an initial, formal part of any attempt at resurrection. There is enough literature in information technology today that describes the nature of the Y2K bug. It is revisited here with an aim of dissecting the system that is hit as quickly as possible, so that parts of the system that are still good can be salvaged while the rest are redesigned during the resurrection. Herein we also develop an understanding of the effect this "hit" is going to have on your organization. It is fair to believe that the organization that is hit by Y2K will not continue to behave in the same way as it did in the past millennium. Some of the "hit" organizations are likely to make multiple uncoordinated attempts at survival, resulting in what is described here as schizophrenic behavior.

We develop an understanding of the organization that is hit, by following a disciplined approach to describe the organization, as well as the resurrection process for the same. This disciplined approach is called the *process discipline*. A process discipline is a window through which the Y2K-hit organization can be viewed. The process discipline also provides a framework when we proceed with the resurrection attempt. The hope is that within a reasonable time, the organization that has been hurt will be able to follow the process discipline and will be back on its feet — albeit as a new look organization which is capable of surviving and prospering in the new millennium. We start the effort by understanding the nature of the firecracker.

1.2 THE FIRECRACKERS

1.2.1 DOOMSAYER'S DAY

The general literature on Y2K problems discusses in gory details the spectacles of jet planes falling out of the skies and CT scan machines in large hospitals behaving erratically. Doomsayers have included anything and everything that has a silicon chip: aircraft, lifts, microwave ovens, cars, power stations, hair dryers, and so on. Will this doomsday scenario come true? If it does, then it will be the end of world, as we know it today. Discussion on resurrection will then concentrate not on the ashes from the Y2K fireworks, but on how to discover fire itself. Nevertheless, this dramatization of the possible disasters has perhaps served its purpose of drawing our attention to the Y2K issue. These issues, albeit important, are of cursory interest in the current discussion.

1.2.2 SILENT EXPLOSIONS

Of relevance to the current discussion is the fact that while the airplanes may not fall on the ground, their inability to take off will have a social impact on our day-to-day lives; while the hair drier may not explode in our hands, it may not start up, causing minor inconveniences to major disturbances within the family life; and, of course, when quite a few enterprises in which we hold an economic interest are affected by their inability to serve and deal with customers, and their listings drop significantly in value, it will have an influence on the quality of life to which we are accustomed. Thus, it appears that the firecrackers that are of interest to the current discussion are not the ones with the usual sound and light associated with them.

They are characterized more by their silence and invisibility than by the dramatic impact discussed so often. And these firecrackers are so close to our day-to-day lives that, just like the real firecrackers, the closeness of these crackers also will not be entertaining. Instead, they will hurt us and will result in the same destruction that an uncontrolled or unexpected display of fireworks can.

1.2.3 PERSONAL SITUATIONS

The personal situations of the Y2K hits are the ones in which we are personally affected by the noncompliance of date. The effect of these situations range from minor inconveniences to major problems within the household. These are the "time bombs" that the Yourdons[2] have discussed in their book.* The reaction to these situations can range from a smile on your face for minor inconveniences to stock-piling canned food and filling up the water tanks for months to come, for potentially major disasters. It is impossible to determine the things that can go wrong in the new millennium at a personal level, but all items that have a microchip in them are potential candidates for some problem. Some of these situations include:

- The security system on which you have been relying for home security would malfunction. This would either result in its being nonoperational, leaving you without the security of the alarm, or it would start off in the middle of the night, joining in the celebrations of the New Year — or ruining them.
- The microwave oven with a clock timer may not start or may not stop (if you started it at 11:58 on that fateful night to make coffee in 3 minutes), or may continue to function erratically.
- The washing machine, whose entire cycle depends on a timer, may refuse to start, stockpiling smelly clothes in the house — or it may refuse to stop.
- The embedded chip in the telephone equipment may not work, severing you from the rest of the world — which may itself not be very communicative.
- The TV and the VCR would refuse to function. The VCR would not program correctly or would not program at all. The usual source of news and entertainment would be cut off.
- The old Excel spreadsheet in which you entered your daily expenses and cross-checked your income, or entered records for the tax returns, may not accept dates in the format you want it to. Worst still, you may have last year's returns in a format different from this year.
- Cars with electronic cruise controls and other embedded objects in them may malfunction.

These are some of the situations we may find ourselves in, in the New Year. For some of us, whose VCR continues to blink "12:00" since the day it was purchased,

---

* See bibliographic notes at end of chapter.

this will be the first major brush with technology. This will be the first time when many of us will be forced to realize our dependence on technology.

In every such instance of a Y2K hit, the intensity of the hit will influence the time to recovery. The intensity of a Y2K hit (as discussed in detail in the next chapter for businesses) is a function of the level of preparedness.* Depending on the extent of the hit, we might either be able to come out of these situations with relative ease, or it could be a long drawn out process needing external help and guidance.

Another interesting issue to consider when dealing with the Y2K-hits at a personal level is the insurance policy that covers home contents for loss against theft or other damages. Home content insurance policies usually exclude large-scale disasters (such as earthquakes and floods) and also acts of war, from their insurance coverage. Should a Y2K disaster on a large scale be treated like an earthquake? Or like an act of war? Or are the gadgets that fail due to Y2K fully covered, and, therefore, can you receive compensation for them? Warranty for household gadgets also would form part of this consideration.

Needless to say that the hurts from the Y2K bite and the resurrection at a personal level will be from our "after tax income." This indicates the negligible involvement of the government in the Y2K problem at a personal level.

1.2.4 PUBLIC SITUATIONS

These are essentially the Y2K events that will take place outside the family home. Once again they have the potential of disrupting the quality of our lives but now in a social sense. An interesting "pilot run" of the possible social situations we may face came about in late February and early March of 1998, in Auckland, New Zealand. For 2 weeks, all the power cables supplying electricity to the Central Business District (CBD) failed, leaving the city area of Auckland on less than 10% power. Apart from the disturbances to many businesses — especially small shop owners and medium sized enterprises — the social life within the CBD also came to a halt. Those who were especially hurt were the restaurants, retailers, and bar owners. Warm beer and cold food served by candlelight was the norm of the day — or night. This is the social situation that can develop as a result of Y2K hits on process-control equipment that control a large chunk of our social lives. Some of the social situations than can develop in the new millennium are

- Unable to make reservations and to travel immediately due to breakdown in the reservation systems of airlines and/or hotels.
- Breakdown in the retail supplier chain resulting in shortages of groceries and other consumables.
- Errors in computer-sequenced traffic lights resulting in chaos and traffic jams. Even if traffic movements are manually controlled, and even if attempts are made to reduce traffic on the road, these efforts still are not likely to succeed. This is mainly because of psychological reasons. People

---

* The level of preparedness at a personal level corresponds to the fallback plans discussed by the Yourdons.

may *need* to just get out of the house and see what the world looks like in the new millennium.

- Inability to complete banking transactions. Since we depend more on electronic banking than on cash, the unavailability of cash is a problem of lesser degree than the inability to use our credit card or the retailer not being able to accept our EFTPOS transaction.

These are only some of the situations which will create social disruptions to our lives. They cannot be dealt with by the effort of one individual or even by a small group of people. It will require a sustained and well-directed effort from the entire society in order to resurrect from such chaos, should it occur. This is the situation that will necessitate government action. Hopefully, we will have paid for part of this resurrection exercise through the tax dollar.

1.2.5 BUSINESS SYSTEMS

What we may experience — both personally and publicly — as Y2K problems from the consumer side are likely to be the problems in the software systems that run the businesses we are dealing with. Our aim, as consumers, is to minimize the personal damage to us as we wait for others to fix the problems. These "others" happen to be the software professionals that make up the readership of this book. Therefore, we approach the problems of business systems with an aim of doing something about them so that we don't lose our clients — especially to the lucky or well-prepared businesses that have escaped the hurt of the Y2K firecrackers. Thus, when we look at business systems from a technical viewpoint, we consider Y2K problems that are likely to corrupt the data within the organization's databases. Y2K problems can cause the logic of the software systems to go wrong with results ranging from errors in the output to physical shutdown of the systems. This would bring the business to a halt. Associated issues like the press reports on the business' performance (due to Y2K crash) also will add to the firecrackers affecting the business.

1.3 JUSTIFYING THE GUN POWDER

A few years ago, I read results of a survey on teenage sex. According to the study, one of the main reasons why teenagers got involved in early sex was the fear of nuclear war. In the first half of the 1900s we, humanity, were busy building a nuclear bomb with justifiable reasons and almost unaware of the magnitude of what we were creating. During the latter half of the 1900s, we build another bomb in much the same way — unaware of the magnitude of what we were creating and with perfect justification. That we had to save two precious digits for every representation of the date provided enough justification for building the legacy software, which has the potential of bringing the world to a halt.

Another reason for the existence of this firecracker is that we grossly underestimated the life of our work. While we expected the strength of these programs to decay over years, that did not happen. Instead, programs written in the 1960s and 1970s have outlived many of their programmers. Together, these two reasons (jus-

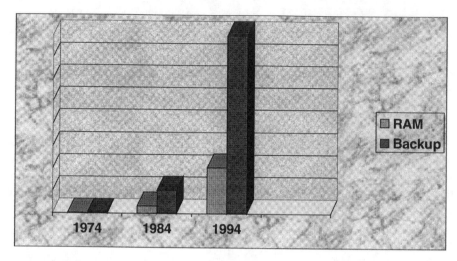

FIGURE 1.2   Phenomenal growth in computer memory in 3 decades.

tification for the use of 2-digits, and underestimating program life) have brought us where we are today, in terms of Y2K.

1.3.1   WHY WE PROGRAMMED WITH 2-DIGITS

I learned my basic programming in COBOL. Every attempt was made to make the best use of all the available resources. I wrote my first program on a coding sheet. It was punched into a deck of cards by a "responsible" data entry operator and returned to me in a box. A cultural revolution took place inside of me when I dropped the box of cards. The next quantum leap in my understanding of the computer world came when I typed my program directly on a "dumb" terminal. The "revolution" took place when I accidentally went to the NEXT PAGE without saving the typed page. Resources were stretched in every aspect of computing, and in every aspect of my job as a programmer. The floppy diskette was the size of a Frisbee, and could store a "mammoth" 320KB. A comparison of the main and backup memory in Figure 1.2 shows how the world of a programmer has changed from the miserable and miserly to plentiful and bountiful.

In 1974, the person who was to be my future COBOL trainer, had a paltry 16K main memory to play with, and a 32K backup storage. When I learned how to program in 1984, the jump in main memory was a phenomenal 40 *times* — and I almost remembered the story of the prince and the pauper as I discussed the intricacies of organizing the DATA DIVISION in my programs with my trainer. In 1994, I have no scope or desire to teach COBOL programming to my team, but as I see them discuss and organize the DATE CLASS hierarchy, I can feel the roles between the teacher and the taught have overturned. I have become the pauper. In the new millennium, I can see Year 5 school children carrying hundreds of megabytes of main memory and scores of gigabytes of backup right in the notebook placed in their school backpacks.

This over abundance of memory and disk storage was inconceivable at the time when I and people with similar background programmed in COBOL and similar procedural languages. Therefore, I offer no justification or excuses for why I programmed with a 2-byte year in my date format. That was the best way to save space, and I was proud of having achieved that saving. For example, consider the initial program I wrote for a 14,000-strong payroll system for a manufacturing organization I used to work for. Each employee record had BIRTH-DATE and a JOINING-DATE fields, which were the standard 6-digit fields, with saving of 2 bytes per field. This led to a saving of 4 bytes per record, equivalent to 56K overall storage for the payroll. However, since we had to include all the past employees for the sake of records, the personnel data ran into approximately 20,000 people, or a saving of 80K. While processing these files, the saving of 80K on a machine with main memory of 640K was a considerable 12.5%.*

I was rewarded for my "clever" work, and I saw no reason why I should not keep doing what I was doing. Year 2000 was not on the cards. And even if I had considered the far away millennium bug, I would have done nothing about it as I did not expect the system to last that long anyway. Today, it is not known to me whether the system exists or not, but assuming it exists, the scenario for its survival through Y2K is not very good. First, even in the simple example that I have provided, the system is not in a position to successfully carry out the "age" calculation. Employees born in 1960 will find themselves 20 years older than what they are (as the system may take the absolute value of the difference between 1960 and 1900) in year 2000. Second, and equally important, those of us who programmed the code have moved on to a different line of work — some of us have become professional project managers, process consultants, and directors, and at least one of us is busy writing this story. The firecracker is still alive and well, and there is no one to diffuse it.

1.3.2 UNDERESTIMATING SOFTWARE LIFE EXPECTANCY

Large numbers of Y2K-target programs were written in the 60s, 70s, and 80s.** In the early days of computing the cost of hardware was *comparatively* higher than that of the software during the same period. Therefore, it was not easy for businesses to upgrade their hardware. The life of hardware was measured in a few years and this measurement had an influence on the life expectancy of software as well. This was one of the factors why we underestimated the life of software.

Furthermore, before the advance of software engineering as a discipline, we had given no thought to the metrics and measurement aspect of software. The only early metric on measuring software was the lines of code (LOC) metric. There was no

---

* Colleagues, who have programmed in COBOL, please note that this is simply an example to explain why we did what we did. Please don't go into the intricacies of sorting the data in the main memory, or backing it up on that tape medium. Those options are all understood and accepted, but purposefully left out of this discussion.

** Yup, I am still comfortable with talking about 60s rather than 1960s — it's a psychological firecracker, all right.

sophistication in recording the user requirements and modeling the system based on those requirements. Also, there was no formal input from the user on the length of time he expected to use the software. At the end of the "lifecycle," when the system was ready, it was delivered to the user. Thus, the user, in the software lifecycle, was more like an expectant father waiting in the hospital lobby, rather than a participant in the delivery process. Indeed, many systems were there because the developers of the system (rather than the users) thought that it would be a good idea to produce such systems. Later, the cost of hardware plummeted, whereas that of the software went up. It became more cost-effective to run the same legacy system by buying more hardware, rather than by rewriting the software. Thus, the software lifetime, which was never estimated correctly in the first place, went further awry as the software continued to outlive even its rough estimations by many times. Systems that were supposed to last 3 to 5 years actually outlived this life expectancy four to five times and were fully operational 25 to 30 years or more after they were written.

This was true not only of the application software, but also of operating system (OS) and databases. Either the developers did not expect their OS to last long enough to see the turn of the century or they did not care. When the system estimation fell beyond the span of their working lives, the developers could only shrug their shoulders at the prospect of facing year 00 in 20 or 30 years time.

Finally, unlike hardware, software is not *visible* to the eye. Therefore, it is difficult to make an inventory of the software owned by the company. In any given organization, it is always easy to walk in and count the number of physical machines present. However, the job is not that easy when it comes to counting the software applications residing on those machines. The task is made more difficult by the fact that software has incremental versions, and that each version is a complete product in itself. For example, an extra memory chip does not make a new PC. The machine still remains the same physically. However, adding a new module produces a complete new version of the software and still leaves the previous software intact. This produces many versions of each software application and each is saved on tapes or other backup storage. The task of locating all this software in a large organization is so difficult that we are left with applications that remain in a "coma" for a long time. It is only when the code refuses to execute due to Y2K noncompliance, or when some other systems or databases with which it was interacting have become compliant, leaving this piece of legacy code alone and noncompliant, that we even come to know of its existence.

1.4   TYPES OF FIRECRACKERS

The two major reasons why we have so much "gun powder" were discussed in the previous section. Memory costs were higher and we did not expect the software to last this long. The result is that we programmed in 2-digit for the date and hoped that the software we were producing would fade away by the turn of the century. Well, that has not happened, and we are now left with a variety of firecrackers that have the potential of hurting us. These are the firecrackers that will appear in our dissection activities, when we start investigating the systems that are hit by Y2K

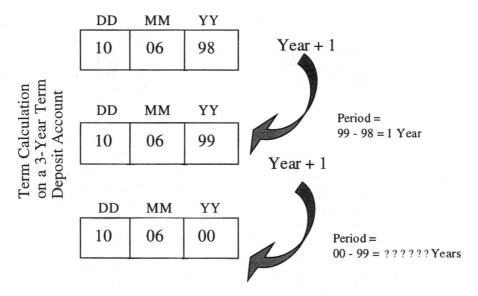

FIGURE 1.3 A simple firecracker.

within our organization. These 2-digit programming firecrackers are discussed here, followed by the fallout from their explosions.

1.4.1 THE 2-DIGIT CRACKER

Figure 1.3 shows the very basic Y2K firecracker that has been reported in all the Y2K literature. It is the classic situation of using a two-character field for storing the year (YY). The reasoning for this date definition has been described earlier on. Here is an example in which we consider the behavior of the DATE field for a 3-year term deposit account. At the end of the first year, the YY part of the DATE field has a value of 98. The interest accrued is for 1 year, but not yet paid as this is a term deposit account. At the end of the second year, the year value increases to 99, and the another round of interest is calculated for the difference in YY field (99 — 98) as shown in the Figure 1.3. At the end of the third year, when the entire interest is to be paid to the account holder, the YY field should have had a value of $99 + 1 = 100$; however, since the year in the DATE field is only two bytes, it will have a value of 00. Out of the many things that can go wrong here, three are obvious:

- The program may take the absolute value of the difference between the 2 years (00 — 99), and assume that the deposit has been with the bank for 99 years and calculate interest accordingly.
- It may maintain the negative value and calculate a *negative interest* on the term deposit, thereby debiting the term deposit account instead of crediting it.
- The system may not be able to make sense out of the result that it is getting and may behave in an unpredictable manner.

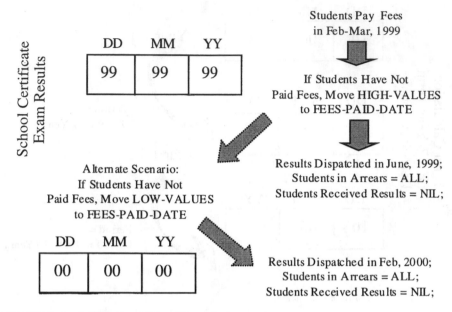

FIGURE 1.4   A High–Low-Value firecracker.

1.4.2   THE HIGH–LOW-VALUE FIRECRACKER

Another variety of the firecracker discussed here is shown in Figure 1.4. This is the case where an important result of the High School Certificate (HSC) exam has to go out by mail. The results are going to decide the career of many aspiring students. So they all wait eagerly for the mail to arrive. They have, of course, paid the fees for that semester and, apart from the amount that they paid, the date of payment also is stored in the following field described in the DATA DIVISON of the COBOL program:

```
01  FEES-PAID-DATE.
      05  FEES-PAID-DATE-DAY      PIC  99.
      05  FEES-PAID-DATE-MONTH    PIC  99.
      05  FEES-PAID-DATE-YEAR     PIC  99.
```

In this example students pay their fees in February or March every year for one of the two semesters. Consider that the fees are paid in (say) February 1999. There is a need for the system to flag the students who have not paid their fees, so that their results can be withheld until they pay their fees. Instead of providing a separate 1-byte flag to indicate whether fees have been paid or not, the programmer uses the following algorithm:

```
IF  <fees paid> THEN
      MOVE  TODAYS-DATE  TO  FEES-PAID-DATE
```

```
ELSE
    MOVE HIGH-VALUES TO FEES-PAID-DATE.
```

HIGH-VALUES, a reserved word in COBOL, inundated the received field with all '9's.

Results for the semester are usually dispatched in the month of June. When the time comes to dispatch the results, the following algorithm, which has worked for the past couple of decades, is used to verify payment of fees:

```
IF FEES-PAID-YY = 99 THEN
    <skip record>.
```

Since the above comparison will be true for all students in the Year 99, they will all be treated as if in arrears, and no one will receive their results.

Another variation of the same scenario is if LOW-VALUES were moved to the FEES-PAID-DATE field. This move would fill the DATE field with all "0"s. If the check to verify the payment of fees in this case was as follows:

```
IF FEES-PAID-YY = 00 THEN
    <skip record>.
```

Once again all students will be skipped when the results are to be dispatched for the first time in the new millennium.

This example indicates how the routinely used HIGH-VALUE and LOW-VALUE reserved words to set flags in DATE fields are going to provide the potential for the fireworks we are discussing here.

1.4.3 Amateur Date Conversion

Quite a few organizations have tried to fix their Y2K problems by undertaking a serious conversion effort before the arrival of the new millennium. We hope that their attempts have been successful. However, as shown by the example in Figure 1.5, complacency even after the Y2K bug-fixes have been completed, may provide costly and painful fireworks.

This is the situation wherein the data have already been converted from a 2-digit year field to a 4-digit year field. For a person born on August 18, 1999, the BIRTH-DATE field contains 18/08/99, as shown in the Figure 1.5. During the data (including date) conversion exercise, the DD (day), and MM(month) fields are moved to the same 2-digit receiving fields, but the YY (year) field is moved from a 2-digit field to a 4-digit field. If care is not taken in this move, and if it has not been tested thoroughly after the conversion, the resultant date field may well contain a birth date of 18/08/9900 — incomprehensible by any standards at this point in time, anyway. The behavior of the system, as a result of this date, remains unpredictable.

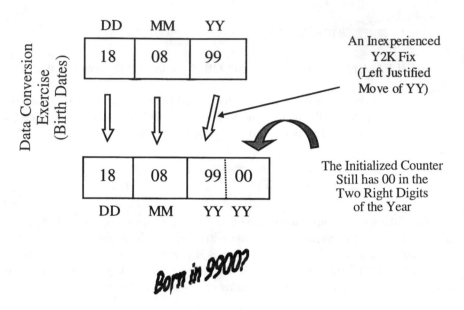

FIGURE 1.5   A complex firecracker resulting from amateur date conversion.

1.4.4   Y2K IS A LEAP YEAR

Uhlig,[3] in a recent newspaper article, reports on how at the Papworth Hospital, in Cambridgeshire, Britain (a £1 million laboratory) ground to a halt only 4 days after opening because the programmers had not considered the fact that February 29, 1996 was a leap year. Leap year is one of the many interesting scenarios expected to provide fireworks for the Year 2000. This is so because Year 2000, contrary to the previous turn of the centuries, *is* a leap year. While every 100 years is *not* a leap year, we have a leap year every 400 years, which is Year 2000 this time around.

The scenario depicted in Figure 1.6, although a dramatization, is worth considering. In a hospital system that has gone through all the hard work and careful fixing of the Y2K date bug by expanding the date field to 4 characters, a patient is asked to come back in exactly 30 days from February 15, 2000 for an important operation like open heart surgery. The hospital system skips February 29, 2000; so, when the patient arrives on March 16, as per his calendar, the operation theatre is not ready and the surgeon still has not returned from her holidays. Well, in this particular dramatization, we can argue that the hospital would have backup manual systems, and that operations can be rescheduled. However, in situations where these options are not available, the whole event can turn life threatening. And even if it doesn't, the sheer logistics of rearranging major surgeries in hospitals, and the associated social and emotional problems, are good enough fireworks to cause considerable pain and sufferings.

1.4.5   "WINDOWING" THE DATE IN THE PAST

Because of the urgency of the Y2K problem, and because of the fact that it applies to systems of all sizes, some creative companies (and individuals within the

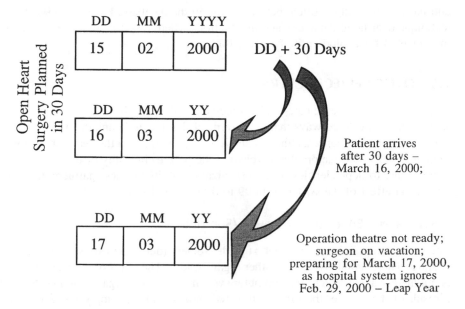

FIGURE 1.6 The "leaping" firecracker.

companies) have come up with Y2K-fixes, that promise to solve the computer date problem by simply "pushing" the current date into the past. By executing the fixes on your computers, the computer clock is moved back from the brink of 2000 to 10, 20, or more years behind. The computer BIOS (Basic-Input-Output-System) thus gains an added life of a few years. Unless the "fixing" software is accompanied by expert consultation, the solutions may not work for larger systems that have multiple modules and are running on mainframes. Furthermore, some of the "cheap" fixes would only ensure that the computer is in working order, but that will not mean that the internal date and days are correct. Simple windowing may be able to ensure that the application is running, but not necessarily in sync with the right dates. Mismatches related to the leap years as well as the days of the week and the month also would have to be considered when these fixes are implemented.

1.4.6 COMPRESSION BEYOND ENDURANCE

In order to maintain the same data layout, and thereby avoiding the need to restructure the database, compression algorithms were used as one of the many creative solutions in the prevention exercises. These algorithms maintained the same 6-digits for the overall date representation, but included an interim logic that would store 4-digits for the year in a compressed format.

This was helpful in reducing the Y2K work related to modifying the data structures that represented the data. It also obviated the need for expansion of the storage facility and, therefore, avoided the additional work required in such restructuring of data tables. However, it did put immense overhead on the processing logic to interpret and uncompress the dates stored in the 6-digit formats to an 8-digit one, and back to the 6-digit format before storing in the database. Excessive use of this technique over large databases and in situations where response time is critical has the potential for exploding in the year 2000.

1.5 OTHER FIRECRACKERS

In addition to the specific date-related firecrackers that we discussed in the previous section, there are other ways that the advent of the new millennium can hurt organizations. These influences, although derived from the fact that the year-date is going to change to 00, are factors that go beyond the pure technicality of the date. These issues relate to dependencies of the organization on its business partners, the psychological effect of the switch from 99 to 0 or 00, and so on.

1.5.1 RIPPLE EFFECT ON CUSTOMERS/SUPPLIERS

The organization exists in the context of the society (detailed discussion in the next chapter) wherein it also relates to other organizations. The effect of the Y2K problem is not merely a question of the computer systems within the organization failing. As a result of the failure, the organization will not be able to supply the goods and services it had promised its customers. Similarly, it may not be in a position to receive the goods and services it expects from its suppliers in order to carry out its production or service activities. Furthermore, when an organization's own systems are all Y2K compliant and performing as per specifications, but those of the other party with whom the company is dealing are not, then the resultant loss of orders can result in loss of goodwill. If taken to the extreme, this is a fertile ground for litigation — suing and being sued by one another.

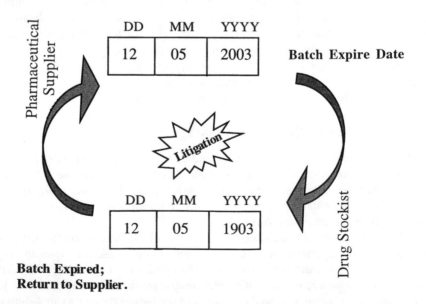

FIGURE 1.7 A ripple effect firecracker.

The ripple effect firecracker (Figure 1.7) discussed here is an example of situations where the organization is affected by the noncompliant software of the other party. The pharmaceutical company had a Y2K compliant software with a "batch expiry date" correctly stated as "12052003." When this batch of drugs reaches the drug store, the noncompliant system is not able to decipher the date on the batch of drugs received. The date is interpreted as only "03." If the receiving software had been converted to 4-digits, it may still be placing a "19" in front of the "03," and, therefore, incorrectly reading the batch expiry date as "12051903." As a result of this erroneous reading, the batch of drugs is returned back to the pharmaceutical supplier. Needless to say this firecracker will have the ripple effect of influencing the production and service of the pharmaceutical company which had a Y2K-compliant system.

The ripple effect firecracker highlights the acute need of general awareness and business partner compliance in the Y2K saga. Flint[4] reports the decision of Visa International to fine noncompliant merchant banks up to $100,000 because the result of the participating bank's noncompliance is not restricted to the banks themselves. The ripple effect will influence the entire business operation of Visa International.

1.5.2 PSYCHOLOGICAL EFFECT OF 2000

It is not that the 2-digit date is a phenomenon that is entirely related to computing. Psychologically, too, there is an apprehension about the coming of Year 2000. In my entire life I have comfortably used 2-digits to talk about years in dates. Switching over to a new style of stating the year in a date is going to be a unique psychological experience for each and every one of us. For example, rarely do I use the full four digits to tell my date of birth or to chat about my holidays with a friend. "I went to Hawaii in '98," sounds a lot more comfortable than "I went to Hawaii in 1998." Furthermore, we are so used to using 2 digits to indicate year, that for the first 10 years of the millennium, we will have an interesting time switching over to *1-digit* year in our colloquial language. I tried telling my 3-year-old son, "In '2 you will go to school," and it was quite different from telling him, "In '99 you will be 4 years old." Try reading the travel plans of a travel freak in the new millennium:

> *"In 1, I will try to visit Nepal, but that is only if I have saved enough money in 0. But I have to travel in 1, because in 2, I will be busy with the course. If I cannot make it in 1, then it will have to be 3."*

This is a social type of firecracker that can have unpredictable effect on people and their behavior. Even if it does not cause any major catastrophe, the switching over to the new millennium is expected to be stressful *irrespective* of the millennium bug.

1.5.3 THE CENTRALIZED ARCHITECTURE

The software systems that are most likely to be hit by the Y2K problem are the products of the 60s, 70s, and 80s and are usually categorized as "legacy systems." These systems were written in the procedural languages of that time — primarily COBOL. The systems usually had a heavy mainframe machine located centrally, and the users connected to these machines by using the "dumb" terminals. The only job of these terminals was to receive and display data. This architecture was the straightforward result of the availability of hardware at that time. The memory, disks, and the machines themselves were at a premium. They were physically huge machines that had to be located centrally. They had to be supported by a large operations staff, who was responsible for loading and firing off jobs around the clock, loading printer papers, mounting tapes for backups, and downloading stored jobs, changing hard disks to facilitate sorts, and so on. The debate on whether this is the best way to design systems today is still raging, with the sophistication of the distributed architecture making a genuine case against the centralized architecture's rigidity. We will discuss the distributed architecture in greater detail in Chapter 12. Here we simply note that the centralized architecture, if hit by the Y2K problem, has a very good chance of bringing the operation of the company to a halt immediately.

1.5.4 THE EURO CURRENCY CONCERN IN 1999

One of the major financial events of the world as this century draws to a close is the attempt to bring the currencies of some of the major European economies together into a single currency. This is supposed to facilitate easier and faster trade between the participating nations, and is supposed to hedge the trading companies from the unending fluctuations between the currencies. The eleven member states of the European Union that are proceeding with the merger of their currencies are Belgium, Germany, France, Austria, Finland, Portugal, The Netherlands, Italy, Ireland, Spain, and Luxembourg.

The end result of this currency merger is the introduction of a common currency called *Euro*, which will provide a medium for financial interaction for more than 300 million people in Europe. The currency exchanges between two countries are influenced by myriad factors including their balance of payment, level of trade, current interest rates, as well as the level of economic activities going on inside the countries. These result in complex calculations that need to be performed on an ongoing basis in order for the Euro to succeed.

The fact that 11 independent nations are attempting to come together as a single currency is enough to cause major concerns in the financial markets. The issue, of course, is not just financial. It is just as much a political issue as financial. Although the physical notes and coins will not come into circulation until 2002, the Union leaders have scheduled January 1, 1999 as the date for the introduction of the Euro. Some thinkers consider this date of Euro introduction, which has resulted in a major competition with the Y2K projects for resources, as the worst public policy decision in human history.[5] The paucity of resources is going to provide additional fuel to the firecracker of the millennium bug, and it will influence resurrection efforts as and when they are undertaken.

1.5.5 YEAR 2038: THE UNIX CONCERN

Thirty-eight years after the Year 2000 is a sufficiently long time to prepare for a problem that is well known to us today. However, since we don't have the history of preparing for Y2K in advance, I though it might be worth mentioning this other firecracker.

Date representation in the UNIX operating system utilizes 4-bytes of storage space. This, of course, saved "thousands of bytes" in comparison with a 6-byte or 8-byte storage. UNIX started counting date from January 1, 1970. This count is in seconds. The number of seconds that can be stored in a 4-byte internal storage will reach the maximum limit in year 2038. After January 2038, the date storage counter of UNIX will initialize to "all zeros." Considering the fact that those who retire from professional lives in 2038 were not even born in 1970, it did not cause much concern to the UNIX programmers that the date fields were set to reinitialize in 2038. If the current discussion on Year 2000 is any indication of things to come, Year 2038 is going to be another major millennium+ bug that will have to be sorted out in the coming millennium. And, hopefully, well before Year 2037.

1.6   THE FALLOUT

1.6.1   VARIETY OF FALLOUT

If only a few of the fireworks we have discussed in the previous sections explode (and we haven't discussed them all), then the effect will be similar to that of a real-life firecracker exploding next to you. It will not be entertaining, and it will hurt. This is going to be the situation with many organizations that are affected by the Y2K bug. Furthermore, as discussed earlier (and shown in Figure 1.8), the problems that will affect the organizations in the new millennium are not entirely restricted to the 2-digits of the date field on the night of December 31. The fireworks

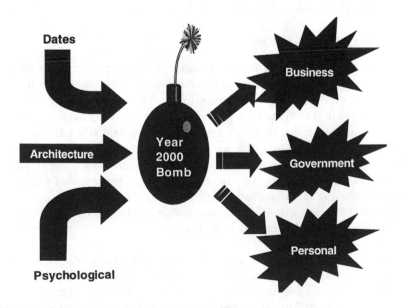

FIGURE 1.8   Various input causing a variety of fallout.

have a variety of sources and the hit is made all the grimmer because, invariably, the organizations affected by the Y2K problem will have no time to solve the problem. The types of organizations that will be affected can be categorized into the following four:

1. *Large organizations.* The main criteria for large organizations here are that they have IT professional staff on their payroll. These are usually multinational companies with many large systems and applications across a variety of platforms.
2. *Small Business.* These are essentially the people who do *not* have employed computing staff.
3. *Government.* The consideration here is to the social effect rather than plain monetary influence.
4. *Family.* Herein is considered the family, which is the basic unit of social organizational structure.

It is important to consider these organizational structures in the wake of the fireworks, because not only are they affected on their own, but their effect will continue to feed off each other. It is not only the organizations that will be affected, but also society in general, and the individuals that comprise the society. We started with the consideration that it is a technical problem that we are dealing with. Slowly, over the years, we started accepting it as a business problem. Today, it is fully accepted as a business problem, and we are discussing its effect on the business. However, what is more important is that it is now being accepted as a social problem as well. Therefore, the crises are technical, business, *and* social. The organizational structures arc discussed in the light of all these crises.

1.6.2 LARGE ORGANIZATIONS

There are many definitions of large organizations. In the context of the discussion here, large organizations are the ones that have an IT department of their own and staffed by full-time and contract IT professionals. These are the companies that will be attempting to deal with the Y2K problem inhouse. They are the ones with a large amount of legacy code that may well not be Y2K compliant. They also have a large amount of data — especially historical data — that might be lying in nonrelational databases. The multinationals within this group of companies will have the additional problem of dealing with foreign exchange conversions, made more complex due to the Euro conversion factor discussed earlier on.

Some of the factors that affect the larger organizations in dealing with the effect of a Y2K hit, and subsequent resurrection, are

- Large organizations have to consider the retention of skilled staff as their prime priority. Due to the paucity of people skilled in Y2K-related work, large organizations have to provide considerable financial benefits for the work that is vital to the business but apparently not of any strategic value.

- Many software professionals feel that concentrating on Y2K work is the case of "making hay while the sun shines." This work is not considered by many as a career-enhancing move, as it is a common belief that after the coming of the new millennium, the Y2K professionals will find themselves redundant.
- Large organizations have still not worked on the resurrection process. So far, it has essentially been a choice between prevention and nonprevention. Prescription to a Y2K disaster appears to be so scary that it has not been considered in sufficient detail. As a result, large organizations are unable to show their employees the role they will play in the future of the organization at a strategic level.
- These companies are subject to different legislation at different sites across state and country boundaries. This adds to the confusion of legal compliance and puts pressure on the legal and accounting departments of larger organizations.
- Initiative is an important strategic tool in competitiveness of large organizations. Since a large number of their staff, and 50 to 100% of their IT budget, is committed to fixing the Y2K problem, these organizations are left with no business-related IT budget. There are not enough resources for new technological initiatives which would provide new and innovative ways of conducting business. The effect of this lack of resources for new initiatives is either loss of business to the competitor or loss of business for the entire industry. For example, if large banks are unable to provide innovative solutions to their customers, borrowers are likely to look at alternative ways of financing their investments. This could include going to a building society, superannuation funds, etc.
- Many transactions of large corporations with their employees are highly automated. Salary payments, leave calculations, leave loading, bonuses, etc., are automatically calculated and credited to the respective employee accounts. Disruption of this work can influence the morale and motivation of employees at a time when this is least affordable.
- Large organizations depend on the reliability of their suppliers and retailers for movement of goods and services. Therefore, for large corporations, it is not enough to be Y2K compliant themselves. They have to consider others in their business domain in order to ensure survival.

1.6.3 SMALL BUSINESS

Small business is categorized as the type of business that usually relies on third party or packaged software in order to conduct its daily routine. These are the organizations that have either purchased information and analytical packages for their business or have effectively outsourced all of their IT activities except the core ones of specifying and verifying their systems. These include organizations like the three-people IT shops, the book store, the library, the restaurant that has a couple of PCs, or even the hotel that has a small chain of PCs connected by a network, but no software development of their own. These organizations face different problems in comparison with the larger ones. Some of these are as follows:

- They have to rely on the supplier of software to ensure that their systems are Y2K compliant.
- In the case of a Y2K hit, they are unable to solve the problem themselves since they usually don't own the code, or even understand the code.
- Although the upgrade to Y2K compliant software may be relatively easy (like upgrading to the 1997 version of the Office suite from the 1995 version), the conversion of the local data may not be that easy. This is mainly because of the limited resources and experience of small business in understanding the underlying file structures of their systems.
- They usually don't have the budget to fix the problem, or have not considered it in their budgetary process at all. They have not thought of the Y2K problem as *their* problem.
- They are unlikely to compete with the Blue Chip firms in paying beyond their capacity in getting and retaining the IT staff who can fix the problems.
- On the other hand, they have the option of running their systems manually for a short time. For example, small business would still be able to issue checks manually should the computer systems fail.
- They may find help from some of the large business partners who may have a vested interest in ensuring that the small business survives the Y2K hits.

1.6.4 GOVERNMENT

The primary concern of a government in case of war is to protect the physical wellbeing of its citizens. The situation of Y2K disaster is likened by many to that of a country being at war. In this case though, the enemy is not another country, but the 2-digit date bug. The worst case fallout from the Y2K bug for the government can be accidents due to failure of process-control equipment. At a social level, the effect of Y2K on government is influenced by the following factors:

- Social security and welfare payments by the government are a major source of survival (and in some cases the only means of survival) for a large number of families and individuals. A Y2K problem in government departments can lead to welfare payments being delayed. Wrong date and eligibility calculations also can lead to the nonpayment of welfare to people in need.
- Government has a major responsibility to legislate correctly and to legislate adequately for the possible legal battles that may ensue in the wake of Y2K hits. The current legislation is not enough to ensure that organizations take blame for their lack of Y2K compliance.
- Elected governments are different from large businesses in that the government leaders don't tend to think beyond the life of their current term.

As compared with business leaders, the government leaders are not assured that they will be around after the next election. Therefore, the government effort in fixing the problems in their systems, as well as legislating adequately, will not have started until 1996/1997, as government terms in most countries last between 3 to 5 years.

- However, government is not restricted by the same budgetary pressures that businesses are. Therefore, the government of the day can afford to spend the money needed to fix or to resurrect its systems. They also have the option of providing tax breaks to organizations and thereby encouraging them to fix their own Y2K problems.
- Government has the additional responsibility of ensuring that the community is aware of the problem. Therefore, advertisement campaigns (perhaps through newspapers and television) to update the community on the problem should be a part of government's responsibility.
- Providing uniform standards for compliance and mapping them against the actual state of systems would again have to be initiative of government or industrial bodies supported by the government.

1.6.5 FAMILY

As it comes closer to Year 2000, the family as a basic unit of the society depends heavily on the use of technology in order to remain a cohesive and functioning unit. For example, mobile phones have gone past their primary need of serving businesses and are now a part of a significant percentage of households. They are used on a daily basis for people to communicate while they commute. With the help of these technologies, the family is still able to communicate with each other and, thereby, remain a cohesive unit. People travel far and wide in search of better prospects than they ever did before. Use of technology (such as phones, e-mails, video conferencing) is able to transport families closer to each other. The effect of Y2K fireworks is likely to strain the family that depends on technology in order to keep itself together.

1.7 LET THE HANGOVER BEGIN

We have discussed the business, government, and personal/family fallout from the Y2K disaster. What was discussed was the immediate effect on these enterprises when their date-related functions fail. However, the effects of Y2K hits are not localized in time. They are likely to be felt by the world as a whole and over a long period of time. The hangover is going to be long and widespread. In this section we discuss the long-term effect of the entire Y2K saga.

1.7.1 POSSIBLE GLOBAL RECESSION

The basic premise behind any economic activity is that, in given time, I will get more in return than what I have put in. Reinvesting a part of the returns with the hopes that, in given time, that investment will provide me with further returns follows this premise. When this activity continues unhindered, the economy grows. The starting point for this activity is the fact that I have enough money to put in, in the first place. This is followed by increasing returns that can be ploughed back into the economic cauldron.

This healthy economic cycle has been severely affected by the work that has gone in, in the prevention of the Y2K problem. Information Technology has played a significant role in the growth of organizations and the society in which these organizations exist (this is discussed in detail in Chapter 2). Therefore, IT investment has been a part of the growth strategy for many organizations. However, many experts* believe that as the world moves towards the Year 2000, there is a 35% chance that the world will be plunged in a global recession due to the Y2K bug. Although we may not delve into the actual figures of the probability of recession, it is still worth considering the global hangover that can happen as a result of Y2K.

Many organizations have spent a large part of their IT budgets on trying to fix the date problem. Theoretically, it is a maintenance job. The Y2K fix takes up a large percentage of the IT budget and adds no functionality to the systems. In situations where organizations have started late, the entire (100%) of their IT budget will have been consumed by the Y2K activity and no new systems or functionality to existing systems would have accrued.

Thus, there is not going to be any return from the expenses incurred by the IT departments in fixing the date problem. Furthermore, since the budgets have been spent on maintenance, there is not much left by way of further investment. This leads towards a downward spiral of not getting returns for what has been spent and, consequently, not having more to invest. Banaghan[6] quotes from the Standard and Poor's report which states that the expected damage to the economy from the Y2K hit is of the same size as that from the turmoil in East Asia. Thus, the Y2K problem is considered to be a trigger for a global recession by many, leading to a long hangover from the New Year's party.

1.7.2 CHANGING NATURE OF BUSINESS IN Y2K

Business in the Year 2000 and beyond is likely to flourish in the abstract world of its World Wide Web. Although a business might still do so, it is no longer imperative for it to display its goods in a window by the sidewalk. Successful marketing companies are built entirely on the Web, resulting in a nature of business that is different from, say, 30 years ago. While the Y2K bug is a computer-related problem, it has not deterred the growth of the computer industry as a whole. Availability of cheap and fast hardware, and sophisticated techniques of system architecture and designs, has led to development of systems that are themselves distributed in nature, but they result in convergence and unification of business interests. This is likely to result in a closure of large number of small and medium sized businesses that can't keep up with the technology. Since they don't have enough capital in the first place,

---

* Most notably, Dr. Ed Yardeni, one of the most optimistic and bullish economists on the U.S. business scene, believes the odds of a recession in Year 2000 have increased after recent comments by official bodies, including the G10 Basle Committee on Banking Supervision, the U.S. Federal Reserve and the U.S. Internal Revenue Service. These comments deal with potential for chaos in the global banking system and financial markets unless Y2K issues are addressed by all financial institutions.

their chances of coming back in the business market are slim. The centralized businesses working on the Web do not need the same number of people that are becoming available as the small businesses shut down. This will result in a much longer hangover for those out of work than the one they might have on the morning of January 1, 2000.

1.7.3 Social Hangover in Y2K

The trade union movement has been a hallmark of this century. Never before in the industrial history could so many workers unite to become a bargaining power. However, the basic premise behind their getting together was that an employer employs them. In the new millennium, the relationship between the employer and employee is likely to be casual or contract based. Each individual wants to be a freelancer, resulting in a different definition of employment than the one we are used to. The advance of electronic commerce in the new millennium will exacerbate this "alienating" influence. For example, as mentioned before, goods and services represented by Web pages will result in reduced jobs. The developers of these Web pages can work from home if they like, reducing further the opportunities for workers to unite. Changes like these are likely to take a long time to be accepted and absorbed and, even after they are accepted, their effect will continue to be what I call a "social hangover."

1.7.4 Family Hangover in Y2K

As we step in the next millennium, we continue to rely heavily on technology in order to maintain a cohesive family unit. Satellite communication and jet travel has progressed way beyond the business need. These technologies play a crucial role in family life. Since the Y2K problems are going to influence this cohesiveness, one can expect more stress within this basic unit of the society.

Another major source of hangover is going to be the widening gap between the two generations within the home. Internet, being a part of some school curricula, provides a rich source of information for some students that the parents find scary. The speed and the method of learning in the new millennium are a likely source of personal problems in the family unit. The aging population is another reason for personal problems in the new millennium. High tech homes, the global information village,* changing business and social scene, everything is going to add to the stress of individuals living within the family unit. It is going to be a long hangover for quite a few of us.

1.8 SO WHAT?

Having discussed the various types of firecrackers and the potential effect they will have on our celebrations, the obvious question is, "So, what can we do about it?" Once an organization identifies that it is hit by the Y2K problem and that its systems

---

* Wherein a recent "real" war was touted as a "lounge room" war because of its accessibility in the lounge room.

are in disarray, it will make attempts to fix the problem. It may or may not succeed in this attempt at its first go. If not fixed, the date problem will drive the business owners of the organization to make multiple attempts to fix the problem. If tried without the disciplined approach to Y2K resurrection, these attempts are likely to lead to the schizophrenic behavior described in the next chapter. Not only are the business organizations affected by the Y2K problem but also, through the organizations, the society in the context of which they exist also is affected.

1.9   KEY POINTS

1. When the fireworks of the new millennium explode in the skies, all talks about estimations, predictions, and guesses on the Y2K bug will become a thing of the past. We will have moved in the real world of the new millennium with all its promises and all its problems.
2. The firecrackers will affect us personally and socially. Although there is a possibility of doomsday catastrophes, of more interest to us in this discussion is the invisible nature of the firecracker. The effect of this firework ranges from minor inconveniences to major problems in our personal and social lives.
3. The main reason why we programmed the dates in 2 digits is the exorbitant (compared with today's prices) cost of the memory and the permanent storage during the 1960s and 1970s. Another reason why we still sit on the gunpowder of the firecrackers is the gross underestimation of the software life expectancy.
4. Some of the firecrackers that can explode in the new millennium are (1) the standard 2-digit date, (2) moving of HIGH and LOW values as flags, (3) amateur date conversions, (4) Y2K is a leap year, and (5) compression algorithms — especially in real-time systems.
5. In addition to the pure date-related problem of a single organization, there is real concern of the ripple effect — noncompliance of one business leading to a problem with another Y2K compliant business. Psychological effect of the "0" or "00" year date, problems with centralized architecture, and the clashing of Euro currency work with the Y2K, provide the additional firepower for making the Year 2000 New Year a painful one.
6. The fall out from these fireworks will be large and small businesses, the government and its bureaucracy, and the family unit. Each will be affected in its own way, as each will have different goals in arriving at the problem.
7. The hangover from the New Year fireworks promises to be long and tortuous. As IT budgets have been consumed by the Y2K problem that is essentially a maintenance problem, there is not much left over for investment. There are no returns due to lack of investment, providing the trigger for a possible global recession.

1.10 NOTES

1. I programmed in 2-digit dates in 1980s. As a fresh engineering graduate, I was trained by TELCO — Tata Engineering and Locomotive Company — in Pune, India. The machines were Burroughs 1900s and 6800s. Some of us also worked on VAX 11/750. COBOL was the prime language for development and most of my discussion on the nature of the firecracker is based on my experience of writing COBOL code for payroll and personnel systems. By the way, in 1998, Pune was at the heart of the software revolution in India. Many software companies have made their career in identifying and fixing the Y2K problem. This is because of cheaper and highly skilled person-power available in abundance. However, this situation will have to be re-examined *after the Year 2000 fireworks.*
2. The book *Time Bomb 2000,*[2] by Edward Yourdon and Jennifer Yourdon, is a classic reference manual for prevention *and* prescription at a personal level. I had already written a few personal situations before I got hold of the Yourdons' book, which describes these situations in great detail. I left my section on personal situations anyway, as I think it sets the mood for Y2K considerations in the business environment.

1.11 REFERENCES

1. Jones, C., *The Year 2000 Software Problem: Quantifying the Costs and Assessing the Consequences,* 1998, Addison Wesley Longman, Reading, MA, 51–54, Introduction.
2. Yourdon, E. and Yourdon, J., *Time Bomb 2000: What the Year 2000 Computer Crisis Means to You,* Prentice-Hall PTR, Upper Saddle River, NJ.
3. Uhlig, R., "Countdown to the Millennium," *The Sun-Herald,* January 11, 1998.
4. Flint, J., "Banking," *The Age,* May 30, 1997, 3.
5. Jones, C., *Rules of Thumb for Year 2000 and Euro-Currency Software Repairs,* Software Productivity Research Inc., 1998, www.spr.com/html/Year_2000_Problem.
6. Banaghan, M., "Year 2000, the clock is ticking," *Business Review Weekly,* March 23, 1998, 40–48.

2   The Schizophrenic Enterprise

When a man, a business corporation, or an entire society is approaching bankruptcy, there are two courses that those involved can follow: they can evade the reality of their situation and act on a frantic, blind, range-of-the-moment expediency ... or they can identify the situation, check their premises, discover their hidden assets, and start rebuilding.

Ayn Rand, 1961, from The New Intellectual[1]

Abstract   Having considered the nature of the Y2K firecracker in detail in the previous chapter, we look here at the "effect" of the fireworks. This effect can be felt directly and personally, as in case of household PCs or microwave ovens in the kitchen; the second and more profound effect can be felt through the organizations with which we, as a society, are associated. While Y2K has effectively moved from being a technological issue to a business one, we argue in this chapter that how, with the advent of the new millennium, it is also going to be a social issue. We start the investigation of the Y2K effect on society by first understanding the relationship of technology with the organization, and that of the organization with the society. This is followed by a discussion of the characteristics of the organizations likely to explode due to Y2K, and the steps in this explosion process. The resultant ashes like "data without information" and "losses of goodwill" are discussed. The behavior of an organization that is "hit" but still exists will not be cohesive — it will represent a schizophrenic behavior, as multiple helter-skelter attempts are made at redefining the enterprise and its relationship with the external world. This abortive attempt at redefinition is described. This chapter delves into the area of the problem and its effect — subsequent chapters cover solutions to the problem.

2.1   ORGANIZATION IN A Y2K SOCIETY

The biggest surprise from the first 50 years of computers is that computation turns out to be a cultural object in its own right, with all its warts and semicolons.[2] Thus, as the information technology world moves closer to the Year 2000, it becomes obvious that it has its own culture, its own language, its own jargon, its own signs, its own music, and its own problems. Furthermore, because of its extreme importance in the profit-making goal of organizations, it has gone ahead and influenced the cultures of the organizations in which it exists. This, in turn, has had an effect on the culture of the society we live in. Just 50 years ago, it would have been inconceivable that a technological problem, such as the Y2K bug, would have any influence on our day-to-day lives. Yet today, it is influencing us directly at a personal level as well as through the organizations which exist within the fabric of the society. Thus, the Y2K problem is not limited to technology or even business, but is of concern to society in general. The discussion in this chapter starts with the link between technology, business, and society, and then discusses how the Y2K problem influences business and, thereby, society.

2.1.1 INFLUENCE OF TECHNOLOGY ON THE BUSINESS

The businesses of the 1990s put extraordinary pressures on technology — especially information technology. This required system development to respond continuously to the rapid changes in business conditions, trading rules, government policies, taxation, and other legislation, and so on. This required information technology to innovate newer techniques and approaches to developing business solutions. This positive influence of technology on business meant that business could not imagine the down side of the problems associated with simpler technology that housed the Y2K problem.

Y2K is a specific technical problem. Therefore, it continued to remain buried within the technical bowels of the organizations and the rest of business did not bother about it. Furthermore, on the face of it Y2K is a very simple problem compared with the myriad complex technical issues that the IT community has been handling for decades. Compare the challenge of creating a Binary tree and then traversing its nodes for a financial markets calculation, with that of calculating the difference between two 6-digit dates. Compare the complexities of designing a distributed architecture with that of modeling a date field and writing a stored procedure to store and retrieve it from the database. Perhaps because of its obvious simplicity, the problem remained on the back burner for years after responsible IT and business staff became fully aware of its implications. Many business executives could not easily grasp that a problem so simple as a date field would have any influence on the empire they were governing. However, as argued in the next section, we observe that technology is able to influence not only the profit making abilities of an enterprise, but also its culture and behavior. The Y2K bug is proving this impact of technology in the ability of the business to make profits as well as its ability to influence the culture of an organization.

2.1.2 BUSINESS: NOT AN INDEPENDENT ENTITY

For decades, organizations have functioned as independent entities with the sole aim of making profits. This led to a culture within the organizations that has stressed only its own survival and prosperity. Thus, it has not been considered essential for business organizations to consider the implications of its behavior in the outside world, so long as it resulted in profits for its shareholders. However, as management thinking progressed, it became clear that an organization could not function and prosper on its own. Beyond a certain limit, whatever was happening within the

The Universe

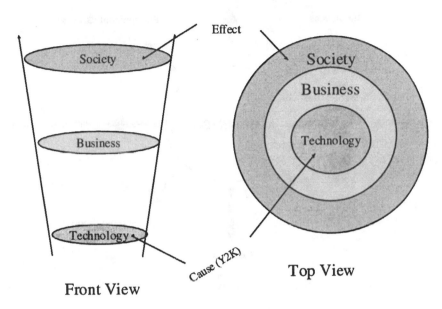

FIGURE 2.1 Business in the context of society–technology.

organization was going to have an effect on the society and vice-a-versa. Drucker[3] discusses how business leaders realized that a company cannot survive and prosper without due consideration to the social fabric within which it exists.

Thus, the notion that the organization is an independent entity has slowly been eroded. It has been replaced by the notion that business exists within the context of the society and, therefore, it has a social obligation to fulfil. With the advent of the share markets and the tools for rapid dissemination of information, it also has become a legal responsibility for the organization to inform its shareholders, and society in general, what is happening within its previously sacrosanct boundaries. At the same time, business itself continues to be influenced by the technology that it uses. Once an organization embraces technological advancements, it has the effect of changing the way in which the organization behaves — or its culture. The change in behavior of an organization in turn influences the society in which it exists. This relationship between the business embracing technology and influencing the overall society in which it exists can be understood by looking at Figure 2.1.

The top view indicates that business encompasses technology. It also indicates that business is itself surrounded by the society in whose context it exists. The front view, however, shows that there is still some gap between business and technology, and between society and business. This gap indicates that effort is required in order to smooth out technological problems that influence business, and business problems that influence society. The figure highlights the need to consider the influence of

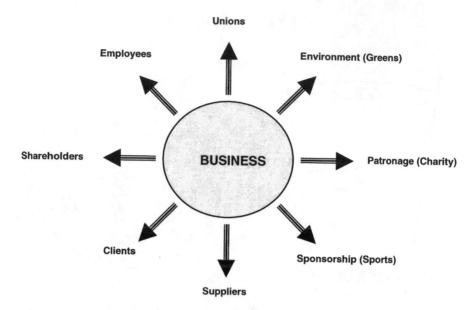

FIGURE 2.2 Influence of business on society.

this seemingly "small" technological problem of the Y2K bug on the society in general — and perhaps even beyond the society.

2.1.3 INFLUENCE OF BUSINESS ON THE SOCIETY

The gap between business and the society is inundated with various ways in which the business connects to the society (Figure 2.2). If a problem such as Y2K has influenced the business, that same influence is further carried out into the society through these various connections. Some of the ways in which business influences the society (and, therefore, a Y2K-type problem influences the society) include:

- Employment by businesses — this is the direct influence that business has on society wherein whatever happens in the business has an ability to influence the society.
- Personal shareholding of people in the various business enterprises. Since individuals are able to hold interests in businesses through the share market, they are also susceptible to the happenings in the business world.
- Interests in businesses through the superannuation funds wherein employees and the government have together contributed to make provision for the employees when they retire.
- Consumers of the produce of the business — who are influenced by the goods and services provided by the business (e.g., pharmaceutical, consumable goods, travel).

- Suppliers of raw materials or semifinished goods to business — especially if the suppliers are small businesses that depend on the large businesses for the movement of their goods.
- Recipients of sponsorships from business (e.g., sports) — as major sporting events tend to depend on the prosperity of the business that is sponsoring them for their own support.
- Recipients of patronage for social activities (e.g., charity) — as many businesses tend to support charitable organizations.
- Effect of business on environment — for example, the effect of malfunctioning of a process-control equipment that controls the flow of water in the dam or oil through a pipeline.
- Effect of relationship of business with trade unions (e.g., strikes, inconvenience, loss of pay) — this is especially important in the new millennium as the work force continues to become more literate and more conscious of its rights.

As a result of this relationship of business with society, in which the internal happenings in the business have a potential to influence the external society, the Y2K problem is going to have a direct and indirect effect on each of these relationships, and many more. Furthermore, the extent of this influence will not remain the same, but continue to grow in line with the rapid changes taking place at the technological level.

2.1.4 RATE OF THE RATE OF CHANGE

We observe that technology influences business which, in turn, influences the general fabric of the society. The influence of technology on business is further increased due to rapid advances in the field of information technology. It is interesting to note that not only is the technological world changing, but even the rate of change is *quickening*. This "rate of" the rate of change, and subsequently the rate of influence of this change on the society, has been aptly described in books like *The Future Shock*[4] and *The Third Wave*.[5] Referring back to the memory growth discussed in the previous chapter (Figure 1.2), it will be clear that not only is the availability of computer memory increasing and its prices falling, but the rate at which this is happening also is increasing. This resulted in an "information overload" in some sections of the society, further exacerbated by situations like the Y2K problem that puts an overall pressure on the society that it may not be equipped to handle. Furthermore, technologies, such as the Internet, have far-reaching implications on society by permitting not only faster or cheaper ways of functioning for individuals, but also by becoming a creative cause for a totally different type of society. Just as the influence of the Y2K issue on the organizations is going to influence the society, similarly its influence on individuals is not merely restricted to the person concerned, but has a *flow-on* effect on the society.

2.2 THE UNIT THAT EXPLODED

We have observed that the relationship between technology, business and society is concentric — business encompasses technology and it exists within the social fabric. Therefore, when something goes wrong with the technology, as is the case with the Y2K issue, it has its effect on the business and that, in turn, influences the society. The influence that technology has on business is a function of a number of factors. Certainly, technology plays its part in either advancing or hurting the cause of the business. However, the manner in which the business entity is organized is also important. Whether the organization is hierarchical, rigid, or flexible, all play an important part in determining the effect of the Y2K-hit. Thus, what we are discussing here are the characteristics of the business that make it more susceptible to Y2K explosions. Understanding these characteristics can help us understand the organizational weaknesses of the business that made it a Y2K target, and also help us to ensure that the organization is free from these characteristics in the future.

2.2.1 IGNORANT

Simply stated, the "ignorant" organization was the one that had no idea of the Y2K problem. We do not expect many organizations to fall in the ignorant category after January 1, 2000. However, it is still possible that smaller sized organizations, which were using very old systems that were performing routine jobs without any variations, may fall under this category. More important is the fact that many organizations were ignorant of the problem before it became too late to solve it. Thus, in some sense, all organizations that started their Y2K prevention effort after January 1998 fall under the category of "ignorant." This is so because, although they were aware of the problem, they were ignorant of the enormity of the task and the time it would take to fix it. Thus, it is an organization that did not know what was going to be the cause of its problems. Alternatively, it was an organization that did not know how to organize the prevention effort. Typically, it would result in the organization's Y2K effort starting as late as in 1999, or not starting at all by the time it is "hit."

2.2.2 CALLOUS

Callous organizations were not interested in listening to the reality of the Y2K problem. This would happen for two reasons:

- These organizations attributed everything to media hype. Thus, all the cautions and warning of Y2K were falling on deaf ears as those responsible for running the organization had already formed an opinion on the Y2K problem as a "hype."
- They thought that the nature of the problem was such that it would never affect them. It is difficult to imagine a business system that does not depend on date for its processing logic. Yet, some organizations that did not have intensive date-based logic could have been callous about their need to comply.

- Some math-intensive systems that were only dealing with mathematical models, or geographical systems that were dealing with the physical locations of a place and did not depend on date, probably had justifiable reasons for not worrying about the Y2K problem. These systems are not date-intensive. However, other systems to which they might interface for reporting purposes, may not have been tested because of the callous attitude of the owners of these mathematical and geographical systems.

Thus, nature of the software systems and (perhaps) excessive discussion of the Y2K problem might have led these organizations to a callous attitude. This attitude is a contributing factor to the explosions of the Y2K fireworks experienced by this organization.

2.2.3 DEPENDENT

Dependency arises as we continue to conduct business using sophisticated software systems. For example, we are able to file our tax returns electronically. Even if tax office systems are Y2K-compliant, they are likely to crash if the electronic return that is filed does not take care of the date correctly. The reverse of this situation also is true, wherein the organization filing its tax returns is Y2K complaint, but the tax office is not. Thus, a dependent organization may well be prepared for the Y2K problem, but it depends on the compliance of its business partner in order to successfully negotiate the new millennium.

Another source of possible dependency arises from situations like those in Japan. The Japanese calendar is calculated based on the reign on the emperor. The arrival of the new emperor starts a new calendar. Businesses in Japan were confident that their software systems are prepared for the Y2K change, as they thought this change as similar to the change in the dates when the reign changes. However, Japanese companies are becoming aware of the fact that, when they cross international boundaries, they have to handle dates in the format of their business partners. Thus, the dependency of the business partner plays a crucial role in the success of an organization in preventing a Y2K-hit.

Finally, a dependent organization also is one that depended on another organization to solve its problem. This organization assumes that someone else will solve the Y2K problem and they can then take the solution and implement it in one go. Alternatively, this organization depends on a business partner or an external consulting organization to solve its Y2K problems — occasionally without checking the credentials or capabilities of the other party.

2.2.4 RIGID

Rigidity of an organization is its inability to change and adapt to changing circumstances. This is an organization that is run by rules up to the last detail. Typical example is a government bureaucracy that needs to follow rules and procedures at every step of its decision-making process. When such an organization relies on its software system in order to function and if that system has suffered a severe Y2K-hit, then the organization is unable to switch over to a manual system. People within the organization are simply unable to function because of lack of the system. Thus, a rigid organization which is unable to change and adapt to manual systems is likely to explode quicker than another organization that suffers similar hits, but whose manpower is flexible enough to change. Rigidity of the organization is also reflected in the external boundary between the organization and the society (Figure 2.1). In a rigid organization, it is not only the internal functioning that is rigid, but the behavior of the organization within society also is inflexible. A rigid organization is not going to get the support that it needs from the social fabric in which it exists in order to survive the Y2K-hit. Thus, a rigid organization has much less options available when disaster strikes.

2.2.5 HIERARCHICAL

Hierarchical organizational structure supports and is supported by the rigidity of the organization. Whereas rigidity describes the inflexible rules and regulations on which the organization depends for its functioning, hierarchy is the mechanism through which this rigidity is implemented. Thus, internally a hierarchical organization would end up with many layers of management, making it inflexible when it is hit by a problem — like the Y2K. In this organization, authority flows downwards and responsibility upwards in a very formal way. The opposite of that of a process-based organization in which the flow of authority and responsibility is horizontal — between customer and the serving officer of the company.

2.2.6 COARSE

When programs were written in a way that was not modular, they ended up being large and complex. Similarly, databases were large and complex and so were the queries on the databases. These approaches to modeling and implementing the systems resulted in "coarse granular" systems.[6] Coarse granular systems have large-sized modules. These modules can range from software systems through to the way in which entire departments are organized. If smaller sized modules are selected in order to provide the same functionality, they will be required in greater numbers. There is overhead associated with a larger number of smaller sized modules. However, finer granular organizations have a much better chance of responding to situations like Y2K, which demand flexibility in the organizational structure. Thus, finer granularity provides much better ability for the organization to localize and remove the bugs (like Y2K). The finer organizational structure also is able to respond well to the Y2K-type disasters. These advantages are lost in a coarse organization.

2.2.7 BULKY

A bulky organization would be typically a large multinational organization that is still following the centralized decision-making process. This organization has kept its software systems centralized, and so also are its decision makers who operate in a centralized manner. Furthermore, because of the large size of the organization, the effect of the strategic decisions within the organization takes considerable time in reaching all parts of the organization. There are many large organizations whose head offices in New York are Y2K-compliant but whose subsidiaries in Singapore, India, or Australia are not. A severe Y2K-hit in a sensitive part of the system can bring the country operations of this bulky organization down very quickly.

2.2.8 UNHEDGED

Hedging was supposed to be the strategy used by organizations that wanted to reduce their overall risks while their IT departments were assessing and scheduling applications for Y2K migration.[7] In hedging, the Year 2000 project office shortlists the few most mission-critical applications or the organization, and start the date-compliance effort straightaway. An unhedged organization *may* have conducted its Y2K tests in a systematic and well-organized way. However, even if the organization has cleaned many of its systems of the Y2K-bug, due to its unhedged nature, the organizational cannot be sure that those systems were important from business viewpoint. On the other hand, there might be some crucial systems within the organization that may not be Y2K compliant. Unhedged organizations are the ones that approached their Y2K effort without discriminating between the mission-critical applications and the normal migration effort.

2.3 LEVEL OF Y2K PREPAREDNESS

Organizations are affected not just by the type of organizations they are, but also by their level of preparedness for the Y2K problem (Figure 2.3). At a personal level,

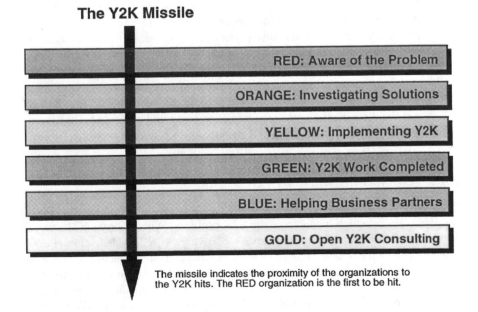

The Y2K Missile

RED: Aware of the Problem

ORANGE: Investigating Solutions

YELLOW: Implementing Y2K

GREEN: Y2K Work Completed

BLUE: Helping Business Partners

GOLD: Open Y2K Consulting

The missile indicates the proximity of the organizations to the Y2K hits. The RED organization is the first to be hit.

FIGURE 2.3 Levels of Y2K preparedness of organizations.

this preparedness is what the Yourdons[8] have been advocating in their discussion on Y2K. However, we consider here the organizations and the business systems that support these organizations, and see how their effort at Y2K prevention helps them when they are hit (despite their preparations or lack of it). While some organizations may not have even started their Y2K prevention effort, others might be attempting to help their clients and business partners to test their systems and fix their problem. Whatever might be the level of preparedness, potentially any organization that uses date in its logic is a candidate for a Y2K hit. Therefore, we consider organizations at all possible level of their Y2K preparedness with an aim of understanding the influence of this preparedness on the ability of the organization to resurrect.

2.3.1   RED: AWARE OF THE Y2K PROBLEM

This is the organization that is only aware of the fact that there is a problem out there. Either it doesn't have the financial muscle to cleanup the problem or it believes that the problem will not affect its business. Thus, a red level organization would be either "ignorant" or "callous" as described in the previous section. No serious effort has been made by this organization to tackle the problem on its own. Neither are its business partners aware of the fact that this organization has not bothered to work on the Y2K problem. Such an organization can be categorized as a "red" organization in terms of its level of Y2K preparedness for the following reasons:

- It has remained ignorant of the problem or its attitude has been callous.
- All of its systems are susceptible to a Y2K hit (thus, there are no applications that can provide the fallback plan for the business).
- It has made no attempts to identify the areas where it can be hit. Thus it does not know which of the systems are critical and which are only providing support. Thus, this organization is unable to concentrate its energies on its mission-critical systems.
- There are no manual backup plans. Therefore, the people in the organization are unprepared for a manual mode of functioning.
- Within each of the applications, the organization does not know whether it is the data, the logic or the presentation that will be affected. Thus, even if it wants to provide a manual backup, it does not know which, if any, areas of its system can be performed manually.

2.3.2   ORANGE: INVESTIGATING Y2K SOLUTIONS

Compared with the red level organization, this company has started working on the possible ways in which it can solve the Y2K problem. When hit by a Y2K bug, this organization has only a minimal advantage over the red organization. Possible alternatives that the orange organization might have considered include inhouse fixes or getting an outside consulting organization to start looking at its systems. At the time when it is hit, it is likely to have some contact with the people who have attempted some work on the problem. This organization is partly callous but it is also partly rigid, because it has been unable to carry out a Y2K prevention process that is vital to its survival. As a part of its investigations, though, this organization might have some idea of the systems that are critical to its survival, and may be able to concentrate its effort in resurrecting those particular systems.

One of the major advantages that this organization needs to leverage in its resurrection attempt is the people who have already started working on the investigation. These Y2K contacts could include the inhouse people who have started the investigations, the contractors and consultants who have worked on other Y2K projects, or the business partners who depend on the performance of this organization to provide their services.

2.3.3 YELLOW: IMPLEMENTING Y2K SOLUTIONS

The yellow color is assigned to the level of preparedness of an organization that is in the process of implementing the Y2K solutions. It is obvious that this organization started very late in its implementation of the Y2K program. Thus, it may have its priorities in the right order, but may have run out of time in handling the mission-critical systems. An organization can be said to be at the yellow preparedness level if it has done the following things at the time of the hit:

- It has investigated the problem and has considered possible approaches to the Y2K solutions.
- It has a set of priorities worked out for its critical and noncritical systems and has some idea of how it will implement fixes to the systems.
- It has a group of people who are already working on the Y2K problem. Thus, it is in a position to muster a task force for its resurrection attempt, should it decide to do so.
- It has a suite of test plans, test designs, and test cases for the Y2K problem that can be re-used in the resurrection work.
- It has basically run out of time due to a number of reasons not excluding the possibility that it was coarse and bulky, making it very difficult and complex to implement the Y2K prevention plan it had (almost) in place.

2.3.4 GREEN: Y2K WORK COMPLETED

A green organization is the one that is fully prepared for the Year 2000. This is the organization that has followed a methodical approach to testing and fixing the problems related to the 2-digit date. It is also an organization that has conducted internal (and possibly external) audits on its own systems to ensure that it is fully Y2K complaint. A green organization is the one that has not only implemented all the Y2K fixes, but also has a reasonably good idea of the amount of effort that went in, in its Y2K compliance.

Some of the characteristics of a green level organization are

- It has satisfied itself by means of its own internal auditing process that all its systems are Y2K compliant.

- It has gone through some sort of external recognition (through an audit or certification) that its systems are Y2K compliant.
- Its users are aware of the fact that their systems have been tested and certified to be Y2K compliant (this could be accomplished by means of a visible identification — like a green sticker — on each PC that has been examined) for Y2K compliance.
- It has an inventory of its databases and applications that provide information to the organization on its IT assets.
- It has hedged itself to an extend by setting its priorities right — it has concentrated on fixing the mission critical applications before working on other less critical systems.
- It has relevant insurance policies covering it in case of a Y2K hit that will enable it to proceed with resurrection with some confidence.
- This also might be an organization that may be *initiating* court actions, provided it has ensured that proper and sufficient third party contracts were in place for its business partners.

A Y2K compliant green organization can still be affected by the Y2K problem. For example:

- Small errors in data or logic have still slipped through the fixing processes.
- Some areas were investigated in a hurried way, followed by hurried fixes.
- Although the users are aware of the need for Y2K compliance, some naive users have still new written applications which are noncompliant or which are unable to read compliant data.
- Turnover of employees — joining of new employees has led to noncompliant applications being written by the end-users *after* the Y2K testing and compliance process was completed.
- More importantly, it could be because of business partners whose systems may not be compliant.
- Surprise element — if it is a coarse or bulky organization, then the hit will be felt after a while — this time delay might make the organization feel "green" for some time after the Y2K hit.
- Because of its belief that it is Y2K compliant, this organization may not be prepared for even the possibility of being hit.

2.3.5   BLUE: HELPING BUSINESS PARTNERS

A blue level Y2K preparedness indicates that the organization has gone past its own needs for Y2K compliance and is actively involved in helping its business partners with the Y2K fixes. Thus, it is an organization that is aware of the broader issues in the Y2K problem, and is able to appreciate the need for others to comply as well, for its own survival. The characteristics of a blue organization in terms of level of preparedness are

- It has gone past the green level, therefore all characteristics of green level organization apply to it.

- Perhaps its business partners are at the orange or yellow level — wherein they are investigating the solutions with the assistance of this blue level organization.
- It is legally fully prepared with all its Y2K-compliant processes documented to ensure that it can provide its attempt at compliance.
- It also is prepared to ensure that it can extract adequate compensation from its dependent organization if they have not made an attempt to fix their Y2K problem.

2.3.6   GOLD: OPEN CONSULTING IN Y2K

For an organization to be categorized at gold level of Y2K preparedness, it must be a green organization itself and providing open consulting in Y2K projects to its various clients. This indicates a very high level of preparedness of the organization itself, as it is not only fully aware of its own Y2K issues, but also those of its clients. Thus, it would typically be a Y2K consulting organization that would be quite familiar with the tools and techniques in Y2K fixes. Although it may itself be compliant, the organizations to which it has consulted (or is consulting) have not yet reached the green level.

2.4   SEQUENCE AND TIMINGS IN A Y2K EXPLOSION

2.4.1   SEQUENCE AND PROBABLE TIMING OF EVENTS

Figure 2.4 describes the sequence of events that will take place in a Y2K explosion.

The probable timings for these events are described in Table 2.1. These are typical timings for a small-to-medium sized firm. Therefore, if a good organization is affected by Y2K, it will most likely be through its clients and business partners.

2.4.2   SKEWING FACTOR

Although the sequence and timings of events are discussed here with precise dates, it is obvious that when a Y2K hit occurs in reality, it is not likely to follow the precise timings described here. For example, January 2000 is not necessarily the only time when the date problems will start biting. Some organizations will experience the problems before the event and others later. The purpose of describing the timings here is to provide a benchmark of how a Y2K hit will influence the functioning of the organization. There are a number of factors that can influence these timings. These factors can be called the *skewing factors*. These factors skew the timings shown in Table 2.1 from a few days to a few months.

As an example, consider the level of preparedness of the organization that is hit by Y2K. The more prepared the organization is (depicted by the color levels), the more time it will take for the hits to take effect. Thus, if the organization was at a green level, then it will take longer for it to reach from identification of the problem to its influence in serving the customers — as compared with an organization at orange or yellow level. In fact, one would hope that an organization at a green level (as compared with one at an orange level) would be able to use the longer time

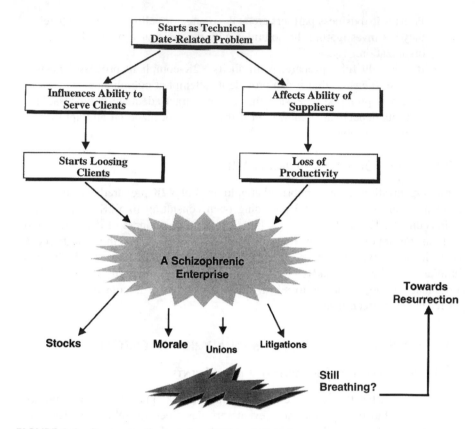

FIGURE 2.4   Sequence of events in a Y2K explosion.

TABLE 2.1
Sequence and Timings of Explosion

Sequence of Events	Probable Timings
1. Starts off as a technical date-related problem	January 2000
2. Influences the ability of the organization to serve its customers	February–March 2000
3. As a result, it starts losing business as the clients start moving elsewhere	April–May 2000
4. Technical problems start influencing the suppliers	March–April 2000
5. Starts losing productivity (service, manufacturing)	June 2000
6. Has an effect on the stocks of the company	August 2000
7. Employee morale starts going down	August–September 2000
8. Perhaps the company gets involved with trade unions for unfair sackings	October 2000
9. There are litigations in the courts	November–December 2000

window (from one step to the next one) in order to put its survival strategies in place and resurrect quickly.

In discussing the timings of the Y2K events, it is important to note that some of the Y2K firecrackers may not explode when the clock strikes 12:00 midnight on 31/12/1999. It may take a few days, months, or even years before the Y2K problems start surfacing in some organizations. In those situations, the timings described in Table 2.1 will have to be skewed appropriately in order to describe the unfolding of the events.

Finally, the timing and sequence shown in Table 2.1 also is affected by the decision to resurrect. The resurrection process need not wait until the entire explosion is complete. Astute organizations that realize that they have been hit by the Y2K problem (or are just about to be) can and should start their resurrection effort as described in this book. After a Y2K hit, it is easier to locate at least the starting point of the disaster. The Year 2000 has actually occurred. The Y2K problem that was deeply hidden and invisible during the testing also has come out in the open. This acceptance of the Y2K problem, location of the starting point of the disaster, and the decision and steps taken towards resurrection, all will contribute towards the skewing that occurs in the typical Y2K explosion timings described here.

2.5 DESCRIBING THE STEPS IN Y2K HITS

2.5.1 BASICALLY A TECHNICAL PROBLEM

The Y2K bug first shows itself as a technical problem. While the main focus in this discussion is on the business applications of the organization, problems can occur in the hardware, operating system, and other such areas of the systems that support the software. Within the business applications, the problem can occur in the data, logic, or the display of the data. Each of these types of problems has the ability to influence the functioning of the organization. Because the nature of the problem is technical, the prevention effort also concentrated on the technical aspects of the system. However, these efforts may not succeed due to a number of reasons discussed in the earlier sections of this chapter, resulting in a technical breakdown or crash of the software system.

2.5.2 INFLUENCES ABILITY TO SERVE

The effect of the technology is felt on the ability of the organization to serve its customers. The more the organization depends on its software systems to service its clients, the sooner it will feel the effect of the technical problem. And it is not necessary for the problem to be technically very complex. The logistics of detection and fixing of the Y2K problem may itself be sufficient to hamper the organization's ability to deal effectively with its customers. Examples of these situations include banks being unable to provide account details to its customers, airlines being unable to make online reservations, and insurance companies unable to accept or settle claims.

2.5.3 STARTS LOSING BUSINESS

The effects of the Y2K explosions might have been manageable if the organization's ability to serve its customers is the only effect of the Y2K hit. Such a scenario would enable the organization to retain its customers while it fixes its problem. However, it is more likely that the clients start moving to other competitors who are able to provide service because of their better preparedness for the Year 2000.

It is important to note that the organization is not moving towards a "Y2K explosion" merely because its systems are affected by Y2K or because its ability to serve its customers is temporarily affected. There is always a possibility of the business getting back on its feet from this point depending on its level of preparedness. However, when the combination of these factors continues to result in loss of current business as well as loss of future opportunities, then the organization is surely on its way to an explosion.

2.5.4 INFLUENCES SUPPLIERS

In addition to the influence the Y2K hit systems have on the organization's clients, they also now start affecting the suppliers of the organization. Thus, in addition to the loss of clients it is now the suppliers whom the organization is unable to contact and, therefore, unable to procure the raw materials or the services on which it depends for its own output. For example, in case of a pharmaceutical company, the dependence on the materials making up the medicines will be high. If the ingredients are not received in time, the company may not be able to manufacture its products. In case of service organizations, it can be an airline depending on the corresponding hotels to supply the overnight bookings.

This can happen because the organization may not be able to place orders to its suppliers, or it may not be able to receive supplies due to a breakdown in the invoicing mechanisms. It also is possible that because the organization has lost its clients it also may not be able to move its produced goods. Add to this scenario another possibility that, under the terms of the current contract, the organization may be obliged to buy raw materials and goods from the suppliers, resulting in high levels of inventory that adds to the burdens of the organization.

2.5.5 STARTS LOSING PRODUCTIVITY

The influence on the clients and the suppliers of the organization affect its productivity. The Y2K problem can prevent the organization from producing the goods and services. Once the productivity of the organization is affected, it does not serve any purpose for it to hold onto or win new clients. This is so because it may not be able to serve the existing customers in the first place. This is true especially of coarse granular organizations (the likely organizations to be hit by Y2K), where the flow-on effect of a small problem in one area of the system is immediate and profound on the remaining modules of the system. For example, because of a single date problem in the opening date of an account, a bank may not be able to put new home loans or savings products on the market.

2.5.6 DWINDLING STOCKS

Once the problems of the organization with the customer and the supplier become known it is most likely going to have an effect on the share listings of the company in the financial markets. The stock value of the company will be affected by its problems leading to further downgrading of the borrowing status of the company. A downward spiral picks up speed at this time.

2.5.7 EMPLOYEE MORALE

The cumulative effect of the loss of customers, inability of the suppliers to provide materials/services, and the loss of productivity will all have their influence on the morale of the employees. An organization will find it very difficult to turn around from this point, as it is the employees of the organization who are likely to provide the crucial stability in a technology-driven problem and a technology-driven survival. Furthermore, if the employees also hold stocks of the company (usually as a part of the bonus options), then the devaluation of the company's listings as well as its borrowing status, etc. will play its own part in further reducing employee morale.

2.5.8 DEALING WITH TRADE UNIONS

As a result of the previous steps in the Y2K explosion process, the company may now start trying desperate measures. These measures can include reduction in its number of employees — primarily driven by lack of business, loss of clients, and loss of productivity. However, because of the known lead-time in the Y2K saga, if the directors of the organization are unable to show that they had taken enough precautions to prevent the problem, they are likely to be in a position where they can't layoff the employees because of the Y2K problem. If they attempt to reduce work-force numbers anyway, then the chances of running into problems with the trade unions are high. This is a technical problem to be solved by the technological and business prowess of the organization. Any attempt to solve it by reducing the work force of the organization is likely to add more fuel to the explosions of the Y2K bug.

2.5.9 LITIGATION

Y2K is anticipated as being one of the most litigious events in the history of humanity. Never before have so many players come together with a common cause on a common date.[9] Some of the reasons why the event is expected to be litigious include:

- The fact that the problem was well known to practically the entire business world — especially towards the last 2 to 3 years before the millennium.
- It took an equally long time for businesses to recognize and accept the problem and start working on it.
- Many businesses worked on the problem for the wrong reasons (i.e., not so much to sincerely prevent the problem, but to prevent litigation). This

represented the Y2K work done by the organizations only to ensure *visibility* of compliance. Yellow or green stickers on the monitors and machines of the organization may save it from legal disasters, but not necessarily the disaster that would occur because of its systems crashing.

Litigation is almost the last step that the organization goes through before it fully explodes. It also is a step where the organization is *least* likely to be in a position to sustain a long drawn-out court battle. Thus, it is worthwhile for the organization to plan its resurrection *before* reaching litigation.

2.6   INTENSITY OF A Y2K EXPLOSION

The intensity of hit is determined by the following factors:

- The type of organization that is hit. This can be one of the organizational types described earlier on (e.g., ignorant, callous, rigid, hierarchical).
- The level of preparedness of the organization for a Y2K hit (as shown by the color combinations in Figure 2.3).
- The criticality of the systems affected. This will be determined by the way in which these systems affect the ability of the organization to serve its customers.

Together, these factors will push the financial strength of the company which will end up determining the intensity of hit (Figure 2.5). We categorize the intensity of Y2K hits as mild, medium, and severe. The intensity of the hit will be a crucial determining factor in the survival and resurrection plans of the organization. The intensity of hit will influence the timings of the explosion (how quickly does the organization go through the steps of explosion), as well as its planning and timings of the resurrection process. These timings can vary from minutes and hours in case of real-time critical systems, to days, weeks, months, and even years for support systems (e.g., batch systems providing end-of-day control totals for a bank or the tax reconciliation system). We consider the intensity of hits in more detail.

2.6.1   MILD

If the systems affected by the Y2K are noncritical or less critical systems for the organization's day-to-day functioning and if the organization had a "good" level of Y2K preparedness then the intensity of the Y2K hit will be comparatively mild. Examples of mild hits would include:

- Y2K problems only affect the less critical systems.
- Only the user interfaces of the system are affected, thus enabling the processing to go on and switching the user interface part of the system to manual mode.

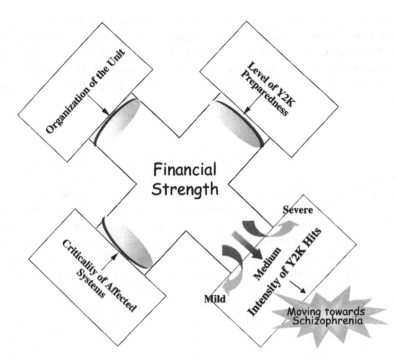

FIGURE 2.5 Intensity of the Y2K hit.

- Only the printing modules are affected, once again enabling the users to switch over the manual systems if they are prepared for the switch and if it is possible for the given system.
- Y2K conversion process during the "prevention" phase had small problems. In such situations the current problem can be localized easily and quickly.

These milder hits would require minimal resurrection or, depending on the situation, work that may not be categorized as resurrection at all. Small fixes can be effectuated straightaway restoring normal operations. These are the situations where the strategic benefits of resurrection may not necessarily outweigh the benefits of fixes. However, should the organization decide to resurrect even a mildly hit system, it will have the advantage of a larger breathing window that enables it to plan and execute the resurrection activities with relative ease.

2.6.2 MEDIUM

A medium hit would indicate either the data or the logic of a crucial system has been affected despite the attempts at prevention. Thus, at the level of preparedness, this organization could be at orange or yellow level, which will indicate that it does not yet fully know its priorities. It would, thus, not be able to appreciate the criticality of its system until it is too late. Therefore, the organization with a medium Y2K hit would find it difficult to fix the systems in a short span of time. Furthermore, it will go through the steps of explosion much faster than the milder hit organization, making the resurrection effort more urgent. A medium hit also implies that the organization will have to consider the legal issues within Y2K. It is most likely that a medium hit involves some form of legal challenge to the organization because of its lack of compliance.

2.6.3 SEVERE

This is likely to be a rigid, hierarchical, and bulky organization with coarse granular systems that have a flow-on effect. Thus, if one area of the system is affected by the Y2K problem, it influences all other modules together with the data and the logic. If the systems affected are critical to the organization's functioning then the time of explosion is traversed faster, whereas the resurrection attempt is going to take longer. This also is an organization that is at red, orange, or yellow level of preparedness — implying, thereby, that the organization will have to go through the basics of the resurrection process rather quickly. Because of the urgency of resurrection, it is also an organization that will need more funds and people to take it through the rebuilding process. A severe hit makes it imperative for the organization to abandon any plans of "quick fixing" the date. The organization will not be able to derive any strategic advantage in fixing a system that has completely crashed. Lack of preparation for the Y2K hit also means the organization is not fully aware of all the tools and techniques that were used in solving the date problem, resulting in lack of knowledge of how to fix the date. Finally, the legal issues also will play a significant role in a severe hit. As in the previously described medium hit, this organization will have to prepare for legal challenges in the courts for its lack of compliance. Alternatively, if it is the business partner whose noncompliant interfaces have caused the crash, this severely hit organization may have to prepare to sue the noncompliant partner. It is important to remember that legal effort to recover damages due to a severe Y2K hit will require considerable time and energy.

2.7   STILL BREATHING?

One essential characteristic of the unit that exploded, for the sake of this discussion, is that it is still breathing. Once it is ascertained that the company still has the financial strength to resurrect, one can go through the detailed process of budgeting, allocating the funds to various activities within the resurrection process, and hoping for a positive financial outcome. However, ascertaining the basic financial viability need not be a detailed process. If any one of the following or a combination of them have occurred, then we are not breathing.

- The company is already insolvent and probably in the hands of the receivers.
- The company has been sold off.
- The company has been purchased (at a ludicrous price) only because of its customer base.

- The company has stopped conducting all business because of collapse of its systems and its total inability to serve customers.
- The company has been sued and the pending litigation is severe enough for the company's assets to be frozen (a lockup).

These events, and events as severe as these, can result in a complete collapse and we can conclude that the company is not breathing. This is typically a "red" company with a severe hit that has provided it with no time to take any evasive action. In that event, talking of resurrection or about anything for that matter will not make sense. In such an event, discussing fixes, conversions, resurrection, and so on, is all of academic interest only.

In discussing Y2K resurrection, the hope is that despite the Y2K explosion the company has not undergone the complete disaster described above. There is still some financial life left in the organization, and it has the choice of doing something about its plight. This would typically be a yellow and above organization, with a medium-to-severe hit. Thus, in addition to the "financial oxygen," it also has a few people on its payroll that are capable of taking decisions at the board level on resurrecting the systems and, thereby, the business of the organization.

2.8 SCATTERED ASHES

As discussed before, a Y2K problem can occur anywhere in the software system. It can start with the data or the logic or the user interfaces. The more tightly coupled the software system is, the more easily the effect of the bug is felt throughout the rest of the system and then in the organization. The result of the Y2K explosions are the scattered ashes — which include mixed up data, confused logic, and the subsequent loss of contact of the organization with reality. We consider these scattered ashes of the Y2K explosion.

2.8.1 DATA WITH NO INFORMATION

A technical result of a Y2K hit is data without information. Data, on their own, are not likely to carry meaning. It is only when we analyze and present the data in a form that conveys meaning to the user, that it becomes information. Organizations, which have stopped functioning due to the date problem, still have lots of data, but they are not able to make sense out of it.

Consider for example, a financial market application that is extrapolating trends in the market for a particular set of bonds. One of the calculations that is used in arriving at the extrapolation of the trends in the future is the rate of change of price of that set of bonds over a period of time — or number of days. If the calculation of the number of days between two dates is incorrect, the resultant price extrapolations will not be right. In this example, the historical data are still there. Perhaps a conversion effort was not made or the effort did not yield correct results. The conversion was not successful, resulting in data without information. This is one of the technical ashes from the Y2K hit.

2.8.2 Schizophrenic Data

Most of the Y2K effort has concentrated on looking at dates in the future. However, once we have crossed over to the Year 2000, what is important is to look *back* and be able to see the dates in the *past century* correctly. This is called crossing over "the hump" and is discussed in the next chapter. It is mentioned here because it is one of the technical challenges of date-related work in the next millennium.

The first step associated with work in the next century is usually associated with correcting the date format to ensure day-to-day workings is carried on. This will result in a correct 4-digit year being represented in the date field (e.g., January 5, 2000). However, when the application has requirement to *mix and merge* the date from the past with the date in the next millennium, in the worst case we are going to end up with *two types* of dates. For example, in the financial market extrapolation, we may have to get the price fluctuations in the past 1 week or past 1 month from January 5, 2000. If the past date is in a 2-digit year, we have the task of subtracting 12/05/99 from 01/05/2000. When we end up with two different *types* of date representation in the same application, we have the situation of schizophrenic data.

2.8.3 Organizational Identity Crises

The ashes resulting from Y2K hits are not only technical, they also affect the way the organization is viewed by the external world. Many businesses function because of their identity in the market. This identity is essential in the smooth relationship they have with their clients as well as with their financial partners, suppliers, and so on. This identity is going to be affected by a Y2K hit, and the organization will not be able to identify itself easily in the market. This lack of identity of the organization will have an affect on all relationships of the organization with the external world.

2.8.4 Balance Sheets that Won't Balance

Balance sheets are going to be the major scattered ashes resulting from the Y2K explosions within an organization. If the Y2K hit is a severe one, as would be the case in a red or orange level organization, then the organization is in deep trouble. It will not have the systems to support its current business and at the same time it will have started losing existing business. In these situations, the effect of the hit on the balance sheets becomes more acute. We have to consider not only the need for the organization to spend, but also the *speed* with which it has to spend. For an orange or yellow organization to resurrect, it is essential to spend *rapidly* in order to resurrect from the Y2K hit. It may not be able to do so successfully if its business is already going down, resulting in a downward spiral. Furthermore, if a green level organization, which had spent a large amount of its budgets on prevention, is hit by Y2K, it will be in an equally deep trouble (as the red organization would be) as it will not be left with sufficient funds to spend on the date problem. The organization that is subject to litigation also will have to finance its court battle resulting in further crunching of its balance sheet and leaving it open for takeover bids (and, thus, total loss of identiy) by better prepared rivals.

2.9   VAIN ATTEMPTS AT REDEFINITION

Once the organization is left with the scattered ashes of the Y2K fireworks, it is likely that those responsible for running the company will attempt to redefine it based on hastily formed "plans." I believe these plans are not likely to succeed because we need a disciplined approach to redefining the organization. If proper dissection of the Y2K hit is not carried out, and the corresponding process-discipline with its methodological and sociological angle not appreciated, the chances of the redefinition becoming successful is not very high. In this section, we discuss the possible vain attempts of a Y2K-hit organization to survive. We follow this with the likely effect of these vain attempts at redefinition.

2.9.1   WHAT IS ATTEMPTED?

Since the problem is still a date-related Y2K problem, the most common approach is likely to be along the same lines as Y2K prevention. That would mean attempting to the fix the date whenever and wherever it occurs, and leave everything else the same. Technically, the exercises of date conversions and of patching the logic in the existing program will be attempted. However, this may not be the best approach to handling the Y2K hits *after the fireworks*. The reasons why this "quick-fix" approach may not be the best approach are

- Patching the entire systems and converting all the data will not provide any strategic benefits. Instead, the organization will continue to use its resources for an attempt at which it has already failed.
- More importantly though, the organization will attempt to redefine itself socially. Every attempt at redefinition will mean an attempt to reconnect the organization with the society by patching the external boundary it has with the society (Figure 2.1). Attempting to recreate the same (perhaps rigid) boundary again also will not provide any advantage from the Y2K work.

This is so because, first, we are creating the boundaries that had crashed. The defining boundary between the organization and the society was hit, and the organization folded. If we re-create the same boundaries, then the chances of being hit at the same spot are high. Second, the reality itself is moving very fast. The society within which the organization exists is moving so fast that as soon as the organization catches up with it, the reality in terms of their relationships has changed.

2.9.2   WHO ATTEMPTS THE REDEFINITION?

The CEO of the company together with its board of directors is responsible for this redefinition. Although the respective project managers and other technical people may handle the actual implementation of the technical conversion, the redefinition of the "hit" organization remains the responsibility of the board.

Depending on the severity of the hit, other members of the board of directors also can attempt redefinition. For example, a bank at green level of preparedness, with only a minor hit in one of its end-user applications, can manage a quick redefinition of its service without major involvement from its CEO. However, if the bank is at the red level and the hit is major to severe, the entire board is likely to be involved in the redefinition attempt.

2.9.3 ABORTIVE REDEFINITION

The problem with these attempts at redefinition is that they may not be well organized. A proper redefinition would effectively be the resurrection described in this book. That would entail detailed (and radical) technological changes to the systems of the organization. This may appear to be a very painful option at a time when the organization is unable to balance its balance sheets. Therefore, technically less challenging options might be tried. For example, the organization may continue to use the same databases and its corresponding data models, although the databases may be older hierarchical databases.

On the other hand, the organization may attempt radical changes to the sociological structure of the company. If, as a result of the Y2K hit, people are asked to leave the company, then the results are likely to be counterproductive. People have not caused the Y2K problem, and asking them to leave is not going to produce the solution.

2.9.4 MATCHSTICK ALLIANCES

An organization in the grip of a Y2K hit which is suffering the effects of the hit in its internal and external boundaries (Figure 2.1), is likely to look out for alliances that will help it get over the tide. However, I do not believe that this is the solution to the "definition" problem. If the organization is "hit" and its share prices are nosediving, there is no real reason why other organizations should find it an interesting proposition from business viewpoint. Therefore, the alliances that are cobbled together *after the fireworks* are likely to be matchstick alliances. If the "buying party" is interested in the data of the "hit" organization, it will have to ensure that that data is not corrupted as a result of the Y2K problem. This data can be a valuable commodity, especially if it includes the database of customers. The application logic of a Y2K-hit organization is not likely to be of much value, but the data will have to be salvaged.

2.10 THE SCHIZOPHRENIC ENTERPRISE

A schizophrenic enterprise results from everything that we have discussed until now in this chapter. It is an organization that has felt the hit of the Y2K technological problem in the way it functions. Through its business activities, it has influenced the society. Thus, its boundaries are hit. This organization was ignorant or callous, dependent, or rigid in its interpretation of the Y2K problem. Either it was unprepared for the Y2K problem and the consequences of its hit or its business partners on whom it depended were unprepared. The result of the Y2K hit is various types of ashes and the attempt to redefine itself has been undisciplined and, therefore, in vain. As a result of all this, the organization is now exhibiting schizophrenic behavior.

Some of these "disorders" are described here with the aim of identifying them as they occur within the Y2K-hit organization. These are the equivalent of the "games" within a software development project,[10] occurring at the business level. Once we can identify these behavioral patterns we will not waste valuable time continuing with them but, rather, spend the same time in undertaking the process-discipline in resurrecting the organization. Identifying information technology games and preventing their disruptive behavior within the Y2K resurrection process has been described in detail in the sociological dimension (Chapters 10 and 11) of the resurrection process.

2.10.1 MERRY-GO-ROUND ORDERS

This is the standard downward spiral of an economy, played at the organizational level. If the organization is unable to serve its customers, there is no cash flow. As a result of this lack of cash flow, it is unable to place orders for raw material. Thus, it can't produce its goods and is unable to compete in the market.

However, if it has placed orders for the raw materials and if it is the supplier that is affected, then the company can't produce its own products. If it has some orders that can't be fulfilled, it leads to a chain of orders all around that no one can complete. Thus, there is a "merry-go-round" of orders — an unhealthy cycle resulting from unfulfilled orders all around.

2.10.2 MULTIPLE CORPORATE PERSONALITIES

The organization is less likely to identify itself with its products or services. If the Y2K hit is severe and all aspects of the company's business are coming to a halt, the company would find it very difficult to identify itself with its products. If it tries to come out with a new product, and identifies itself with the new product it looses the old business. Thus, during the period that the organization is hit by Y2K and it decides to do something about it, the organization will be displaying multiple corporate personalities. The employees, business partners, and customers would all find it difficult to figure out any integrity in the behavior of the organization in light of the Y2K problem.

2.10.3 DONUT AND SAUSAGE SIZZLE CULTURE

Attempts to get out of the Y2K chaos would mean that the organization would try *all* possible means to please its customers. This can be attempted at micro and macro level. The micro level attempts may include throwing parties and hoping that it will help keep the customers while the technologists fix the problem. This can be called the "donut and sausage sizzle" culture of the organization and it is unlikely to be helpful in bringing the organization back to its feet.

2.10.4 FALSE PROJECTS

One of the major sources of further risk to the Y2K-hit organization is the attempt to start new projects in a panic mode and without the benefit of investigations and planning that a resurrection process (like this one) provides. The organization is already low on funds. It will try to start new projects with the hope of getting new business. However, the chances of starting many projects with insufficient funds and plans are likely to be high. Each Y2K-affected area of the system would provide the appeal for a new project. However, these projects may not all see the light of the day. The best approach to new work in the Y2K-hit organization is to align it with the resurrection attempt.

2.10.5 CONTINUOUS CATCH-UP GAME

The schizophrenic enterprise is likely to play a continuous catch-up game through its "quick patch" endeavors. It will spend a large amount of time and energy to re-establish its boundaries with society. However, by the time it does so, the external reality (or the society) itself has changed. For example, if an organization spends a lot of time in fixing the date problem after it is hit in Year 2000 and gets the same application back to working, the rest of the competition has moved to newer and more strategic solutions. This leaves the hit organization without the strategic systems and without the funds to produce any. Thus, if the aim is to maintain the same systems, then the organization is playing a continuous catch-up game with the external reality. This, by the way, also happens to be the problem with schizophrenia — wherein, after phenomenal effort on part of the therapist (and the client), they re-establish contact with the reality, but the reality is so dynamic that it changes and the client can't keep up with it.

2.11 INVESTIGATION

As in the case with medical schizophrenia, we start the treatment of the Y2K-hit organization by investigating the problem in an analytical way. In case of a Y2K hit, though, the investigation will be analytical at the sociological level, whereas, at a technical level, it will be a dissection. You dissect without aiming to fix the problem in a quick and dirty way. The aim is to understand the areas that are still good and salvage them while throwing away the areas of the system that don't have value. Trying to determine where the problem has hit the system, the extent of the damage, and the areas that can be salvaged, will lead to proper resurrection. This investigation is outlined as a part of the technological process of resurrection. What follows next though are the strategic advantages in resurrecting from a Y2K-hit.

2.12 NOTES

I find the influence of technology on business and that of the business on society fascinating. The debate begins with the influence of science on technology. People like Chalmers[11] ask a vital question, "What is this thing called *science*? Does science have a social responsibility or it is the technologist that puts science to its various uses that is supposed to bear the moral responsibility of the use of science?" In a remote sense, I feel morally obligated to fix (or at least discuss) the Y2K bugs I had inserted in my code, and the resultant influence of many such bugs on the society. But then I wonder at the 2-digit *enforced* test cases that passed my code. If the Y2K bug indeed ends up having the far-reaching implications on our personal lives as discussed by the Yourdons, then morality cannot be left outside of the discussion of Y2K coding.

This chapter was initially titled "Effect of the Y2K Explosions." A colleague, while commenting on the draft said, "Organizations have a personality, so the effect of an explosion within the organization will be the same as that of 'multiple personalities'." That is closer to calling the organization *schizophrenic*. The Y2K-hit organization will exhibit schizophrenic characteristics and it will need the same bold approach to solving its problems that one needs to take in treating the personality disorder. Hence, I renamed this chapter.

2.13 KEY POINTS

1. We started the discussion of the influence of technology on business and business on society.
2. This discussion provides the backdrop of the influence of the Y2K problem on the society.
3. The organizations that are hit are likely to have been ignorant, callous, dependent, rigid, hierarchical, coarse granular, bulky, or unhedged — or a combination of any of these characteristics.
4. Organizations are likely to be at different levels of Y2K preparedness when the Y2K bug hits them — understood by the different color combinations used to describe this level of preparedness.
5. The steps in a Y2K hit are described — starting off as a technical problem and going right up to possible litigation in the courts.
6. The intensity of the Y2K hit (mild, medium, and severe) also is going to play a significant role in what happens to the organization after the hit. A severely hit organization is likely to behave very erratically and will need more effort and resources in order to resurrect (if at all).
7. The erratic behavior of the organization includes undisciplined attempts at redefining itself, eventually ending up as a schizophrenic enterprise with multiple personalities.
8. All arguments in this chapter have led us to the need to investigate and resurrect.

2.14 REFERENCES

1. Rand, A., 1961, *The New Intellectual,* Random House Publishers, New York.
2. Lanier, J., "The Frontier Between Us," *Communications of the ACM,* Feb. 1997, 40: 2, 55–56. (Special Anniversary issue on 50 years of computing.)
3. Drucker, P., *Management: Tasks, Responsibilities, Practices,* Heinemann: London, 121–129.
4. Toffler, A., *The Future Shock,* 1981, Pan Books in association with Collins.
5. Toffler, A., *The Third Wave,* 1980, Pan Books in association with Collins.
6. Unhelkar, B., Effect of Granularity of Object-Oriented Design on Modelling an Enterprise, Ph.D. thesis, 1998, School of Computing Sciences, University of Technology, Sydney.

7. Hayes, I. and Ulrich, W., "Selecting and Deploying Consulting Services for a Year 2000 Project," *Am. Prog.,* 10: 6, 8–13, 1997.
8. Yourdon, E. and Yourdon, J., *Time Bomb 2000: What the Year 2000 Computer Crisis Means to You,* Prentice-Hall PTR, Upper Saddle River, NJ.
9. *Business Review Weekly,* May 1997, 46.
10. Unhelkar, B., "Transactional Analysis (TA) as Applied to the Human Factor in Object-Oriented Projects," *The Handbook of Object Technology,* chap. 42, CRC Press, Boca Raton, FL, 1998.
11. Chalmers, A. F., What is this thing called Science? University of Queensland Press, 1982.

3   Strategic Advantage of Y2K Resurrection

Every dark cloud has a silver lining.

Abstract   Resurrecting from a Y2K hit is not just an issue of correcting the date and restarting the systems. If we were to attempt the same fixes that we tried during the Y2K prevention exercise, then there would be no strategic value to it. Although the hit from the Y2K firecracker is going to hurt, it will also provide a unique opportunity to let go of the old, bulky, and rigid applications, processes, and practices that weighed down the enterprise in the past. The exercise of resurrection involves major direct and indirect benefits that far outweigh the seemingly insignificant exercise of correcting the date without any addition of functionality. To start with, resurrection leverages the benefits arising from the fact that the world is already over the Y2K hump. This implies that there is no more Y2K testing to prevent the disaster — the arrival of the Y2K event has provided the detailed testing that need not be repeated. The Y2K resurrection enables the organization to recognize and value its prime strategic asset: its information technology. This is achieved by taking inventory of all its databases and applications and prioritizing them. As the organization resurrects, it also reengineers its processes, thereby moving away from its legacy systems and introducing new technology and methodologies that enable it to survive and prosper in the new millennium. Streamlining of the organization's project management and quality assurance activities also provide major advantages. Finally, the resurrecting organization also is able to derive spin-off benefits by providing consulting to other organizations who are in trouble, or who want to resurrect anyway, irrespective of the Y2K problem. These are some of the issues discussed in this chapter with an "indicative" metrics that aims to clarify the strategic advantages but does not go into the intricacies of measurements as yet.

3.1   STRATEGIC BENEFITS FROM Y2K RESURRECTION

One of the major differences between the work related to the Y2K problem in the new millennium as compared with that in the 1990s is that in the new millennium the Y2K event has already occurred. If we were to derive any strategic benefits from the date-related work in the new millennium, then that work has to consider the fact that Y2K is not going to happen in the near future again. Therefore, it will not be worthwhile repeating the same process of testing and fixing date problems in Y2K hit systems in the new millennium. When a Y2K resurrection is attempted, the aim is to achieve a lot more than simply locate and fix the date and restart the system. The Y2K resurrection effort provides advantages of moving away from the legacy systems and replacing them with a carefully crafted architecture for a process-based organization. We discuss these advantages in light of the fact that we are now over the Y2K hump.

3.1.1   OVER THE Y2K HUMP

There was a justifiable reason to fix the systems affected by the Y2K problem *before* the Year 2000. However, once the actual date is past and we still come across systems that have crashed because of the Y2K problem, then solutions we tried before the millennium no longer provide the same advantages that they did in the "prevention" effort. Before the Year 2000, we were justifiably interested in fixing the date, which would permit uninterrupted running of the software systems and a corresponding smooth transition of the organization into the new millennium. The difference was that in attempting the fixes before the event we were dealing with *unknown* data from the future and the associated logic. We were trying and testing all possible permutations and combinations of the new millennium's data that was going to be input in the system. Once we reach the milestone, though, we are looking back at the historical data of the past. These are the known data that are already in the system. Thus, once we are over the January 1, 2000 hump the perspectives in dealing with the Y2K issue change (Figure 3.1). We are interested in only that part of the historical data which is still important to the organization. We have the luxury of dumping the irrelevant historical data during the resurrection process. For example,

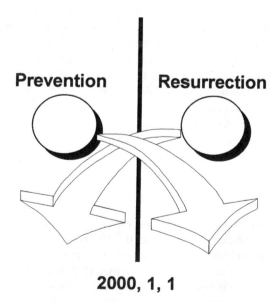

FIGURE 3.1   In resurrection, we are over the January 1, 2000 hump.

a bank that backs up its dormant and closed accounts in a large historical database will only be interested in the dormant accounts that can be revived in the new millennium. Data related to the closed accounts may still be backed up but need not be converted to the new databases.

In dealing with the Y2K issue *after the fireworks* (or over the hump), we also have the opportunity of saving on the testing of Y2K data and code. As mentioned before, the Y2K event will have conducted a real-life test of the system for us. Testing the system while it is in operation has *never* been considered as an option by the IT community because testing has everything to do with prevention *before* the event occurs and not during the operation of the system. Year 2000, though, provides a unique situation wherein the system will have been tested in real life. It is important to record all crashes of the system during its operation across the Y2K hump and utilize that information during the dissection activity. Detailed test planning and testing activities should be conducted on the resurrecting system and not on the system that has crashed. The results from the Y2K hits provide the starting point for the resurrection work.

Over the Y2K hump also means that the world has experienced the change to the new millennium and, therefore, it is in a mood for change. This is expected to be reflected in the functioning of the IT departments as well. This mood for change provides the necessary sociological and psychological support for changes in the areas of technology and methodology. This places the resurrection work in a different category to the prevention effort of the past, which seemed to carry a certain amount of "drudgery" in it — mainly because of minimal technological growth for the Y2K teams. Since the resurrection philosophy in the new millennium is on recreating the systems rather than fixing them and since that process will involve detailed use of new technology, it should lead to a more positive kind of work environment than the one that existed during the Y2K prevention effort.

Despite the differences in the resurrection work discussed above and the potential advantages of working on the Y2K problem in the new millennium, the work done in the past on the prevention of Y2K also has a contribution to make in the resurrection effort. We have discussed the various color codes that describe the level of preparedness of organizations for the Y2K problem. If some of the well-prepared organizations (green, blue, and gold) are hit in the Year 2000, they will have the experience of locating the date problems during their prevention effort. For these organizations, dissecting a Y2K-hit system will be easier compared with the yellow or red colored organizations. The tools used for testing Y2K applications can still play an important part in the dissection work that would be conducted after the Year 2000 hump. Furthermore, the intensity of the Y2K hit would be much less for well-prepared organizations. Therefore, in some situations where intensity of the hit is mild and where the systems need only a small patch in a module that is familiar, the work may turn out to be similar to the prevention effort. Prevention effort, although unsuccessful (since the system has been hit!), also may enable the organization to carry out its operations for a short while by bypassing or suspending the Y2K-affected modules or by switching over to manual mode.

Thus, we see that during resurrection the main area where the prevention effort of the past provide some advantage to the Y2K-hit organization is the dissection activity (described in detail in Chapter 5). Beyond that, it is not recommended that any effort be spent in testing the Y2K-hit system. Resurrecting the organization by reengineering its processes is the most beneficial way of handling the Y2K problem after the Year 2000 hump.

3.1.2 It's not all Maintenance

One of the main reasons why the business community took a long time to start the Y2K prevention effort was the fact that the entire effort seemed to be a maintenance activity. The focus of the prevention effort was to locate and fix the 2-digit date that neither increased the functionality of the product nor improved the speed of processing. These reasons appeared to be not much different from the reasons I used in *not* taking my car for regular servicing. Servicing a car apparently does not add anything to its functionality. It goes to the mechanic and comes back looking pretty much the same. So long as the car is able to transport me from one place to another, the urgency to take the car for its regular maintenance doesn't seem to impress me. Fixing the date problem in computer systems was essentially a maintenance problem, and a very large maintenance problem at that. From a pure business perspective, it was not an attractive investment — in fact, it was not an investment at all. It was a maintenance nightmare without the benefits. For most business people, it was just money down the drain.

On the technical side, the Y2K fixing did not seem to provide the challenge or the career path to the more energetic programmers and project managers of the industry. In fixing the problem, knowledge of the legacy systems was essential. Of the many young programmers fresh from courses in Java and C++, hardly anyone could be enticed to work on a COBOL system. However, in resurrection the tables are effectively turned. Technical understanding of the Y2K-hit system is still considered essential, but not to the extent that was required in *fixing* the Y2K bug. The aim of understanding the "old" technology is limited to extracting the salvageable data and functionality of the system. Resurrection effort will be undertaken by means of new technology. This proves to be an attractive option for people working on the project.

From the business angle, a new system that has the functionality of the old system *and* a lot more in terms of new products and services is a much better choice than fixing the date problem in the existing system. Use of technology (such as object-orientation and distribution) also facilitates easier maintenance of the new systems. Thus, changing business requirements can be easily and quickly reflected in the systems (as compared with the legacy systems, where the changes took longer time to implement). Speed of processing also may improve (for the same functionality) resulting in a spin-off business benefit. Finally, in many situations where the Y2K hit is a severe one and when the organization starts losing business and goes down the path described in Figure 2.4, all these arguments on advantages of resurrection may only be academic. There may not be much choice left for the business managers of the company but to resurrect. All available resources will be mustered and put in to the resurrection process.

3.1.3   DISCUSSING THE BENEFITS

When a Y2K resurrection process is undertaken, the organization has to subject itself to the process discipline described in detail in the next chapter. This process discipline enables the organization to perform the dissection of the Y2K-hit system and the resurrection of the new system by means of certain well-defined activities and their corresponding tasks. The resultant advantages to the resurrecting organization include direct benefits (like having a resurrected organization based on a technologically advanced software solution), spin-off benefits (like providing consulting to other organizations), and innumerable opportunities (like the potential for exploring new or niche market segments) that need to be converted into benefits. Also, some of these benefits are quantifiable and others are abstract. A list of strategic benefits to the resurrecting organization includes:

- Recognition and acceptance of information technology as a strategic tool for business.
- The advantage of reengineering the business, which would not be an easy task if the organization is continuing as is.
- A list of all applications that exist within the organization providing a detailed inventory of the software asset.
- A list of all databases, their types and usage, and the data that reside within them. This will provide an inventory of all the databases and the data contained within them.
- Opportunity to move away from the weight of the legacy systems.
- The resurrection process provides the organization an opportunity to introduce new technology within the organization's processes, which was not easy in the normal working of the enterprise.
- Changing the methodology or the way the organization works is not easy. Because of the "mood" of change that prevails in a resurrecting organization, this is made easier.
- As the new organization is redesigned, there is an opportunity to use the new technology and new approaches to development, resulting in a robust architecture that will last for a longer time period.
- A well-engineered organization that is based on processes is also a quality organization. This is one of the major benefits of resurrection — once the resurrection process is followed, the resultant systems have quality in them. The process also has the opportunity for certification.
- When the organization has resurrected itself, it may be required to provide help to its business partners should they need it. The organization also may start providing consulting work to other organizations, or "in sourcing" business engineering projects. This can result in a strategic advantage that far outweighs the original effort of resurrection.
- As the resurrection work proceeds, the project management becomes more streamlined. The resurrection exercise is like a major team-building exercise with a common goal and with a sense of urgency around it. This

benefits the project managers, in that it makes them concentrate on the essential tasks.
- In order to resurrect successfully, the resurrection team needs involvement from every member of the organization. This results in a total "buy-in" by the employees in the activities of the organization. The major advantage is heightened employee awareness that would otherwise take a long time to initiate.

These benefits are discussed in greater detail in the subsequent sections.

3.2 RECOGNITION OF INFORMATION TECHNOLOGY AS A STRATEGIC TOOL

3.2.1 IT in a Supporting Role

Until the advent of the process-based organizations (or at least serious thinking in that direction), information technology was usually considered only in its supporting role. The IT manager would usually report to the chief financial officer of the company, and his main purpose would be to provide support to the myriad management information systems in the company. The traditional support role of IT included maintaining payroll, personnel, accounts, general ledger, inventory, etc., with the aim of supporting the main business activity of the organization. Performance of the IT role could be judged by faster and cheaper ways of doing the same things again and again. Age-old hierarchical structures and redundant processes were still there, only they were done in a shorter time span with the help of computers.

Expertise in these processes provides the starting point for the formal requirements for the new processes. Although the new processes are radically different, the people who have been performing the old processes know the requirements from the user's viewpoint quite well. This knowledge of theirs from the supporting role can now be leveraged in formalizing the requirements.

The knowledge from the support role of IT also can be helpful when a Y2K-hit application is dissected. For example, technical knowledge of the data structures can be helpful in identifying currently hit fields, as well as fields that have the potential for further hits. Knowledge of the programming language being used permits understanding requirements that may not be formally documented.

This "local" knowledge of the data and applications can provide significant benefits in the overall resurrection process. Furthermore, the resurrection of the organization using a process-based approach puts IT in a more strategic role than the previous maintenance role.

3.2.2 IT in a Strategic Role

The Y2K resurrection process promises to provide the strategic role of information systems within business that has been recognized by many leading business thinkers (e.g., Porter, 1985[1]) a long time before the millennium bug came to be recognized as an issue. Porter was among the first to formally promote the strategic role of information technology in order to provide competitive advantage. In the case of resurrecting from a Y2K hit, technology will play a major role in the design of new processes. The new processes within the organization are not merely supported by IT; many of them come into existence *because of* IT. A simplistic example would be the cash withdrawal process from the automated teller machines (ATMs). This process came into being only because of the ATM. Thus, far from being a support function, IT plays a strategic and significant role in the overall business. When the date problem hurts business, the sensitive nature of IT and the dependence of business on IT, will become obvious. Resurrection within the given timeframe will not be successful or even possible unless all the technological advantages have been leveraged.

More specifically, the resurrection process highlights the strategic role of IT because:

- It takes the onus away from date-related maintenance.
- Instead, it provides for creation of new business processes.
- Many of these processes are there because of the technology — highlighting the role of technology in the new business.
- It enables reorganization of the data in line with the strategic direction of the business.

3.3 THE BUSINESS ENGINEERING ADVANTAGE

Business engineering, or reengineering the business based on processes, is the result of effective Y2K resurrection exercise. However, business engineering implies "burying the old ways of thinking and replacing them with a new approach."[2] This requires a radical change in the way an organization operates. Therefore, business engineering always had a major hurdle to cross, that of the existing processes. It was relatively easy to come up with new processes, but the challenge was to either integrate them with the existing business processes or use them to replace the existing ones. Both options were difficult because the existing processes were serving specific business needs on a regular basis. A Y2K hit and a subsequent resurrection promises to be a blessing in disguise for the business engineering attempts. If a Y2K problem hits processes that are redundant or are overheads to the organization, then the opportunity for the organization to replace them is obvious. However, the overall resurrection effort provides the impetus to replace major processes that would become cumbersome in time, and that could not have been replaced without shutting down some business functionality. A Y2K hit has effectively closed some functionality of the business. Since the Y2K resurrection effort concentrates on reengineering rather than fixing the existing processes, the organization derives the following advantages as a result of resurrection.

1. It will come to know and understand the existing processes in the business.
2. It will be able to identify and eliminate the redundant processes.
3. It will be able to reengineer its processes, including forward engineering new processes.

3.3.1 EXISTENCE OF PROCESSES

In order to resurrect, we will have to dissect. This dissection will lead to identification of many processes in the organization that the organization was not aware of. These can be automated processes that the software system was serving, or they can be manual processes that were unearthed as a result of the Y2K hit. For example, if an insurance claim process required a manual transfer of a form from one department to another (perhaps to get a signature), then a Y2K hit in the associated software process will not only highlight the software process, but the manual process also will be unearthed. This is what the reengineering team looks for.

3.3.2 REDUNDANCY OF PROCESSES

It is not always easy to identify redundancy in a process — especially if the process is satisfying the day-to-day requirements of the business. Thus, in the insurance claim example, it is possible that a software process may be running in parallel with a corresponding manual process. This can happen if an insurance claim form is not only transferred manually from one department to another, but also is electronically transferred through a software system or a software procedure. If this overall working is affected by Y2K and if the process of transferring the form stops due to the hit, then the investigation into its cause will inevitably lead to the discovery of the redundant processes.

3.3.3 REENGINEERING RELEVANT PROCESSES

Having identified "hidden" and redundant processes, the aim is now to reengineer these processes so that the end result is a process-based organization. One of the advantages in reengineering the new processes is that they are no longer faced with the Y2K problem. Although the new code still has to consider the date when it deals with branching and sorting logic for "behind the Y2K hump" data that is still relevant, still it is a new piece of code being written with full awareness of the date issue. Furthermore, in reengineering the relevant processes, we are not forced to improve upon them. The opportunity of discarding Y2K-hit processes is available and should be exercised. This is especially true of the redundant processes.

3.3.4 FORWARD ENGINEERING PROCESSES

As we resurrect the organization, we use more and more of the new technology. There can be many processes that are initiated *because of* the technology. Designing and implementing these new processes can be called forward engineering. We are able to engineer these processes as we have the opportunity of using new technology and methodology in the resurrection effort.

3.4 INVENTORY OF APPLICATIONS

A Y2K resurrection attempt makes the organization take stock of its applications — with an aim of dividing them into applications that are essential and useful and

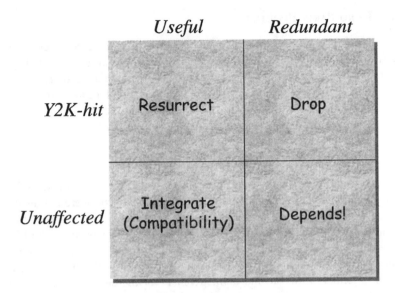

FIGURE 3.2 Taking inventory assists in the streamlining of applications and processes.

applications that are less useful or not useful at all (Figure 3.2). Indeed, organizations at yellow and above level of preparedness that have attempted Y2K prevention will have arrived at some sort of inventory of their applications. Just like the processes described in the previous section, the investigation of a Y2K hit provides opportunity to investigate and drop the applications.

3.4.1 IDENTIFICATION OF ALL APPLICATIONS

Identification of applications results in taking stock of their following attributes.

- *Number* — how many applications exist within the organization? This can be measured not only in terms of applications, but also in terms of some standard metrics (like LOC) that were used in the prevention attempt.
- *Value* — this can be judged based on the purpose the application serves within the organization. If the application is hit by Y2K, that still does not mean it has no value. This is because even a Y2K-hit application may be used as a valuable source for new requirements, providing salvageable options.
- *Versions* — what is the status of this application? How many previous versions it had and where are they all stored (e.g., have they been backed up? Are all users upgraded to new versions?)?
- *Licenses* — do we have enough licensed versions of the software? Since software is very easy to copy, it is usually difficult for even "honest" organizations to keep track of their licenses. A Y2K hit provides an opportunity to get a handle on the licenses for the products.

3.4.2   Third Party Products

In case of third party products that were under maintenance contracts, a Y2K hit will draw attention to these maintenance and support contracts for such products within the organization. There may be a need to upgrade these contracts or redraw them in light of the events in Year 2000. The Y2K problem also may provide an opportunity to move away from unfruitful contracts. New vendors can be investigated and new contracts can be signed in the wake of a Y2K shake up.

3.4.3   End-User Applications

With the availability of end-user programming tools like Visual Basic and Access, end-user applications have grown exponentially. People who were not aware of the date-related problems write many of these applications. When applications stop functioning on their desktops, they will be forced to seek help from the IT departments within the organization. This will result in a much better inventory of the existing applications within the organization. As a result of this awareness, applications can be either shifted to the mainstream IT or the end-users can be provided with more information of the new tools and techniques available so that they can build applications that serve a more useful purpose within the organization.

3.5   INVENTORY OF DATABASES

Along with applications and processes, the Y2K hit provides the opportunity to create a detailed inventory of the organization's data and the databases in which these data reside. Data of the organization reside in a large number of databases — some within the IT department, but many within the domain of the end-user. A Y2K hit even at a single database level can bring to surface all these databases.

3.5.1   Databases — by Usage

One way of taking an inventory of the databases is to find out their usage within the organization. There are a large number of databases being used for different purposes within the organization. These include:

- *Large production databases* — contain the live data for the company and they are the first to be hit in a Y2K disaster.
- *Development databases* — contain the newer and older versions of the data model but not the large amount of production data. They are likely to be affected by the semantics or the logic of the Y2K problem rather than the content.
- *Test databases* — contain a large amount of data for both positive (verifying correct data is accepted by programs) and negative (verifying incorrect data is rejected) types of testing. These test bases would have been the first line of defence for Y2K hits. However, considering the fact that

the organization has already been hit, these databases may not have served their purpose. They may be used for testing resurrection.

- *Historical databases that store past data* — affected only if the record has to be retrieved from them. Otherwise, historical databases would not be influenced by Y2K hits.
- *Backup databases* — primarily used for temporary backup of data. It was common in legacy applications to back up data on a separate database for sorting purposes.
- *End-user databases* — in addition to the databases mentioned above, these are used by users themselves for development and production purposes. Their importance derives from the business needs they serve for the organization.

Furthermore, each of these databases has versions — a development database may change its version every week as new data models are incorporated in the system, but the version of a production database may not change for months or years. These are the various types of databases that the organization will come to know in its resurrection attempt.

3.5.2   DATABASES — BY TYPES

Apart from the usage of the databases, it is also essential to consider the *type* of the database. These types can include the following:

- A traditional hierarchical database.
- A relational database (which is what most business organizations and personal PCs will have).
- A more sophisticated object-oriented database.
- An object-relational database.

A Y2K resurrection process will enable the organizations to gather information on all types of databases that they have and create an inventory of these databases.

3.5.3   IDENTIFYING EXISTING DATA

In addition to identifying and documenting the types of databases that the organization has, the Y2K hit also provides an opportunity to identify and document the type of data that exist within these databases. Identification of the existing data is different from identification of the databases in which these data reside. Some databases continue to grow as data gets added to them, and no maintenance ever takes place on them. This results in "dead data" being carried by the databases. Data also can be centralized, distributed, backed up, stored off-site, within test beds, and so on. A formal resurrection process will identify all of these data and it will enable the organization to "trim" its databases so that they do not continue to carry "dead" data.

3.5.4 DOCUMENTING DATA MODELS

Documentation of the data models is the logical result of the investigation of the extent of the data and the various types of databases described above. This can be considered as an advantage of the resurrection process since, without the hit, we would never have known the existence and proliferation of these databases within the organization.

A typical relational database (which is the main type that we concentrate on) grows in two directions: rows get added as more and more data are poured into the database, and columns can get added/removed as new data structures come into play. While adding and deletion of rows is a routine part of database activities, columns need to be added or removed only after considerable thinking. The columns represent the fields that are stored within the tables of a database. The columns within a table and way the tables are related to each other through keys and indexes, forms part of the data model. New date-related data would have to be reorganized within these tables. Where dates are part of the keys to join tables, particular importance will have to be paid to the documentation of the new tables. This important aspect of data model documentation will take place during the formal resurrection process.

3.5.5 DOCUMENTING STORED PROCEDURES

Stored procedures — or SQL scripts — perform operations like adding and removing data from the database. These operations are typically performed on a relational structure with well-defined rows and columns. They could be run on their own or they might be called from a program. Usually, the focus of documentation is on applications. Therefore, the only documentation available on the stored procedures is the procedures themselves. In resurrecting from a Y2K hit, it may be necessary to understand all the procedures that deal with dates. Stored procedures that sort data, especially the data based on date-key, will have to be formally documented during the resurrection attempt.

3.6 MOVING AWAY FROM LEGACY

3.6.1 THE LEGACY IMPORTANCE

Legacy applications comprise code written a long time ago in a procedural language like COBOL. These applications were produced in the days of business computing where a large amount of code was written without the benefit of a software engineering process. The complexity of the legacy applications arose from the fact that the languages used in writing these applications could not express the real-life business situation with which they were meant to deal. To add to the complexity, there was no efficient mechanism to store and retrieve data. Usually, the applications stored their own data through either a flat file structure or ISAM or, at best, relational data structures.

Despite being technologically primitive, these legacy systems continued to exist for a long time and have even grown over the years. The primary reason for this is that many legacy systems served the fundamental needs of the users (e.g., end of day totals for the branch of a bank). The dependence of the users on their ongoing service has resulted in their need without any downtime. Thus, although technologically not comparable with modern day applications, these systems could not be easily removed or replaced in a production environment.

3.6.2   THE LEGACY WEIGHT

In addition to the users not being able to afford any down time on them, there were additional problems when replacement of a legacy application was attempted. These included:

- The procedural code was not very easy to divide into modules, making it very difficult to replace the system module by module.
- The upgrade or replacement of such a system had to be usually a "big bang" effort, demanding greater risk which many were not prepared to take.
- The "big bang" conversions also were not convenient from the point of view of the users as they would prefer to have more time to switch over to the new system.
- There was almost always a need to run both systems in parallel for some time before effectuating a change over. This resulted in duplication of data and additional maintenance problems associated with such duplication.
- To compound the problem, these systems were not supported by enough technical and user documentation — making the task of documentation a challenge in itself, before anyone could think of upgrading the system.
- The people required to maintain these applications were no longer coming out of the university, requiring the organizations to hold on to the legacy programmers they had. The programmers, aware of their own dwindling market, were not interested in sharing their knowledge readily, leading to the sociological factors preventing moves away from the legacy applications.

Thus, although the maintenance of these systems was costing a lot, it was not easy or convenient for organizations to replace them. Furthermore, the more these applications stayed within the organization, the more they were modified and enhanced to serve the additional functionality of the users. Although this mushrooming of additional modules in these applications without the benefit of formal requirements resulted in a technical nightmare, the functionality served by these applications continued to remain critical to the business of the organization.

3.6.3   REDUNDANT AND INFLEXIBLE CODE

The needs served by the legacy systems and the mushrooming of their functionality continued to complement each other, resulting in a spiral of continuously growing code that was inflexible and also redundant to a large extent. Traditional COBOL programs had the same functional code repeated in various areas. Consider a standard customer information system within a banking application. This application would have functions such as retrieving an account's balance, determining the credit eligibility of a customer, computing an employee's salary, and applying cash to a general ledger appearing repeatedly in a system. If the method of determining a particular account balance changes and that function appears in the system many times, every single program that performs that function had to be located and modified. Programmers carried out these changes only in the areas of their own interests. Hardly, if ever, was a full impact analysis done before introducing the changes. Resurrection provides the opportunity for the organization to eliminate these unmanageable systems.

3.6.4 OPPORTUNITY TO SUNSET SYSTEMS

When one or more of these legacy systems are affected by the Y2K problem, they influence the routine functioning of the organization. All the arguments that prevented the legacy systems from being migrated to new technology and platforms can now be turned against them. Thus, a Y2K hit, especially a severe hit, is likely to shut down the system (however unwittingly for the organization). The users of the system and the clients that were served by the system are all affected by this Y2K affected shut down.

Thus, a Y2K-hit application is a "once in a 1000 years" opportunity to sunset the legacy applications and bring in new technology to serve the needs of the users. If properly managed, the Y2K fireworks provide a chance for the organization to move away from its legacy weight by resurrecting quickly and efficiently. The arguments that justify this move can include the fact that once the application is down due to the hit, it may not be cost and time justifiable to attempt to fix the date and continue with the application. "The size and cost of the task of converting software is horrendous, and no company will want to carry the cost of conversion if that particular area of the business is likely to be unprofitable in the next 5 years."[3] Thus, although a "down" application will hurt the organization, it is also an opportunity to sunset the old systems. This will open the way for the organization to bring in technology that can be used to model new application on processes rather than products (as was the case with legacy code).

Indeed, many of these arguments were true even before the Y2K hump. However, many organizations were hoping that at least *they* would somehow escape the date problem. When the Y2K bug appears and the applications are physically shut down, the arguments for moving away from legacy weight and recreating new applications and processes are very compelling.

3.7 INTRODUCTION OF OBJECT TECHNOLOGY

Many organizations in the late 1990s have been using the object-oriented approach to their information systems work, in some form or other. This usually includes using some object-oriented language and, hopefully, an associated methodology to develop the systems. We discuss here the various factors that affect the introduction and use of the object-oriented approach and how a Y2K-hit organization can convert its plight into advantage by systematic introduction of object-oriented approach to not only its Y2K resurrection effort, but to all other developments within the organization.

3.7.1 REDUCED RESISTANCE TO CHANGE

Use of the object-oriented approach requires a shift in mindset. Henderson-Sellers[4] describes this change of mindset as shifting from asking questions like: "what does the system do?" and "what is its purpose?" to asking "of what objects is the system comprised?" and "how can I model the system dynamically using objects and their behavior?" This change is not always easy, as there is a considerable difference between thinking in a structured way as compared with thinking in an object-oriented way about the system.

However, because of the Y2K hit, the entire IT department is expected to be in a flux with every aspect of the IT function changing. This atmosphere of change can be utilized in order to introduce new technology as one can expect reduced resistance to this change. The shift in mindset required for an object-oriented approach can be accomplished in an environment where everything else is changing.

3.7.2 NEW APPROACHES

The transition to object-orientation requires a transition of various aspects of software development — one is the methodology employed in object-oriented software development. Resurrection of a Y2K-hit system is facilitated by the object-oriented approach (discussed in greater detail in Chapters 8 and 9). Therefore, successful resurrection provides the advantage of applying new approaches to software development.

3.7.3 ACCEPTANCE OF TOOLS

Use of object-orientation in resurrection is facilitated by the use of tools that enable design and documentation of the various models within the process. However, people have their own preferences in using or not using tools. These preferences are not always dictated by logical reasoning. In this atmosphere of change leading to object orientation, one can expect ready acceptance of tools for modeling and design as it is too early for groups to align themselves to a particular tool or tool vendors. On the other hand, tool vendors are likely to find a "good" market for their products, resulting in their quick modifications and deployment in the market. These arguments on acceptance of tools also apply to other tools that automate functions such as testing and metrics.

3.7.4 NEW LANGUAGES

The new approaches to OO development are not only supported by their corresponding tools but also by OO languages. Languages such as C++, Smalltalk, Eiffel, and

Java are becoming extremely popular, as they are able to provide a relatively smoother transition from the object-oriented designs into code. These languages (like the tools) have their own patrons and champions. An OO-based resurrection attempt provides the organization with an opportunity to select and deploy an OO language. The experience of using this language can later be used in other development work.

3.7.5 OPPORTUNITY FOR TRAINING

If normal projects run into time and cost constraints, then training is one of the first items that suffer. However, in a Y2K resurrection attempt, the choice the organization faces is similar to "now or never." The attention of the entire organization is likely to be involved in the resurrection attempt. Therefore, normal budgetary constraints may not be so severe on this project since resources will all be concentrated on resurrection. This provides the IT shop with the opportunity to conduct formal training sessions — essential in the use of object technology. The atmosphere of formal training resulting from this exercise can be fostered for later developments.

3.7.6 HARDWARE AVAILABILITY

The arguments for training in the previous section also apply for hardware. One of the reasons for popularity of OO approaches has been the availability of cheaper and faster hardware. The Y2K hit provides the organization with the opportunity to bring in new machines and servers for the new applications.

3.8 FOUNDATIONS FOR A ROBUST ARCHITECTURE

The advantages of moving away from the legacy weight and using object technology to do so is coupled with the advantage of creating a robust architecture for the new system. This advantage of creating a sound architecture for the resurrecting system accrues from the fact that the IT industry now has considerable experience in creating software architecture. The opportunity to create a sound architecture exists also because all the building blocks of the resurrecting system are new. The architecture is not limited by the legacy past.

3.8.1 NEW BUILDING BLOCKS

When the resurrection exercise takes place, most of the modules used in creating the reengineered processes will be new. These modules or "building blocks" of the software solution also are developed at a time when the concepts of modularization and encapsulation have matured. Therefore, unlike the legacy code that they are replacing, the new designs can be made up of tightly encapsulated building blocks. This would result in a "pluggable" architecture, wherein building blocks can be put together in various ways to satisfy different user requirements, resulting in the foundation for a robust architecture.

3.8.2 ARCHITECTURAL EXPERIENCE

To enable us to produce the modularized building blocks for the new architecture, we now have a wealth of experience captured in architectural patterns.[5] With the advent of distribution, system architecture has taken a quantum leap. The architectural activities play a major role in the resurrection process (described in detail in Chapters 8 and 9). Furthermore, our experience in providing architecture for software systems has grown to an extent where we do not use technology for the sake of using it. For example, object orientation is no longer limited to a single class level. It is shifting its focus to the use of components as building blocks of the software solutions.

3.8.3 USER LITERACY AND PARTICIPATION

In contrast with the era where systems had no architecture, the new millennium will see major involvement from the users of the system at all levels of the system development life cycle. In addition to the obvious advantages during acceptance testing and deployment, user involvement is likely to provide significant benefits at the architectural level. Users can influence not only the inhouse development, but also procurement of third-party building blocks that can be directly reused in the current system.

3.9 CREATING QUALITY

The IT industry has approached quality from various angles including testing, documentation, metrics, measurements, etc. The major emphasis of quality, though, has been on improving the *process* of software development. We discuss here the "quality" advantages that an organization derives in resurrecting from a Y2K-hit.

3.9.1 CLIMBING UP THE CMM MODEL

One of the major contributions to the world of software quality process has been the Software Engineering Institute's (SEI) Capability Maturity Model (CMM).[6] The five levels of CMM are initial, repeatable, defined, managed, and optimized. A quick look at these CMM levels indicates that for an organization to position itself at any of these levels it should have processes that are properly defined and the ability to repeat these processes. Understandably, not many organizations were interested in a repeatable "Y2K conversion" process. When, for a long time, many of us could not see the advantage of going through the Y2K conversion process even once, obviously the need to repeat the process could not be justified.

However, when we resurrect, we are putting in place a process that the organization can use for its subsequent software development activities. Therefore, as compared with the Y2K prevention exercise, the resurrection exercise has applicability that goes beyond the date problem. While the Y2K-hit system provides the starting point for the resurrection exercise, this starting point can be the requirements for a new application that need not be a Y2K-hit application. Thus, the organization has an advantage in terms of making the resurrection process CMM compatible by making it repeatable. As well as providing quality within the organization, certification of the resurrection process also can provide advantages in dealing with other quality conscious organizations. The ability of the organization to deal with large-scale problems is proven when it successfully resurrects.

3.9.2 EASIER IN RESURRECTION

It is easier to incorporate quality within the processes during resurrection as compared with the work done during Y2K fixes. This is so because the resurrection effort results in new processes that can be quality conscious right from their design. Thus, a resurrection process provides all the advantages of implementing a new process and quality through the new processes.

3.9.3 IMPORTANCE OF DOCUMENTATION ACCEPTED

Documentation is the curse of the programming community, and programming without documentation is the curse of the project management community. Resurrecting from the Y2K hit provides the opportunity for a culture change from cursing documentation to following a well-documented process. This effort is supported by the availability and ease of use of HTML-type tools, resulting in easier documentation and cross-referencing of a process. This, obviously, results in a higher quality within a process.

3.9.4 MEASUREMENTS AND METRICS

One can't control and improve that which one can't measure. This is true of all work related to Y2K. The focus of measurement during the "fixing" effort was to estimate time and budgets that had to be dedicated to the conversion. Although these measurements are still important, what is more helpful to the quality effort is quality metrics. For example, metrics like coupling and cohesion which describe the quality of a design, did not play a significant role in Y2K conversions. During resurrection when we attempt to rebuild the system using object-oriented techniques, metrics (like coupling and cohesion metrics) provide a valuable insight into the quality of the newer designs. The mapping between the existing legacy code and the new object-oriented code also can provide metrics that highlight the productivity of an organization in resurrection. This may find applicability in other non-Y2K reengineering exercises.

3.10 INSOURCING BUSINESS ENGINEERING PROJECTS

Having gained the experience of bringing a Y2K-hit organization back to life, the resurrection team can look forward to more opportunities to capitalize on its success. One would expect a successful resurrection team to have the character of a "war veteran." Only a highly disciplined approach from this team can help the organization. Promoting a successful resurrection work can provide recognition of the success achieved — and a lot more.

3.10.1 RECOGNITION OF SUCCESS

Before the resurrection work begins, we expect the plight of the organization to be fairly well known to the rest of the world. The effect on employee morale as well as the company's listings has been already discussed. When the organization resurrects, it will still have the attention of the parties that were affected by its woes. The recognition of its success is likely to be instantaneous — especially if it is one of the earlier organizations to resurrect. This will provide personal satisfaction to the people who work on the resurrection project. It also will restore the dwindling stocks of a company, if the resurrection is timely.

3.10.2 PROVIDING CONSULTING SERVICES

If an organization resurrects quickly and effectively, not only is it able to put its systems back in place, but it is also able to help and guide other Y2K-hit organizations in getting back on their feet. This provides opportunities for the organization to use its resurrection skills in generating new business for itself. This new work includes the consulting and training opportunities that will arise as a result of the resurrection. This was the main business of the gold-level organization. If the business direction of the resurrecting organization is different from consulting, the experience gained in resurrection can still be effectively used in consulting to business partners.

3.10.3 PROVIDING METHODOLOGY AND TOOLS

Resurrection will require the organization to develop expertise in the use of methodologies and tools. These methodologies will contain a lot more than the methodologies (if any) used during the Y2K prevention effort. Details of object-oriented methodologies and tools that form part of the resurrection process are discussed in Chapter 8. As a part of the use of methodologies, the Y2K resurrection process also will accumulate "real life" data on the process, the legacy to object-oriented mapping, data models, and so on. Future working, based on this data, is likely to be more substantial than working without the metrics. These metrics provide advantage if the organization decides that in-sourcing external resurrection is a part of its business.

3.11 REENGINEERING PROJECT MANAGEMENT

Taking the reengineering discussion further, Champy[7] in *Reengineering Management* mentions the need to reengineer not just the work the organization does but also the management of the work. "Its about us, about changing our managerial work, the way we think about, organize, inspire, deploy, enable, measure, and reward the value-adding operational work," he states. Resurrection exercise provides management to streamline its activities and reengineer itself.

3.11.1 CONCENTRATES ON ESSENTIAL TASKS

Project management changes as a result of the Y2K resurrection process. All routine project management tasks are put on hold as the enterprise attempts to resurrect itself. Therefore, project managers start concentrating only on the essential tasks. All mundane tasks, that were occupying considerable time earlier on are done in a short time.

Along with the recognition and acceptance of the strategic role of IT comes the need of the information systems (IS) management to accept it as an activity worthy of their efforts. If the IS executives continue to remain burdened with traditional IS management issues such as systems' uptime and program maintenance, they will have little or no time to spend on exploiting the strategic opportunities possible through modern-day information systems.

3.11.2 OPPORTUNITY FOR CREATIVE SOLUTIONS

Project management during the Y2K resurrection work will be anything but routine. The activities that investigate the Y2K-hit system will have to be aware of the "salvageable options" from the affected system. The resurrection process will include the three dimensions of the process discipline. Managing an iterative and incremental development project that starts with a Y2K problem but ends up as a reengineered organization is going to be an extremely creative process providing considerable satisfaction to the management team. The resurrection project will need, as well as provide, ample creative opportunities in project management that are not readily available in routine management of projects. These creative solutions will be supported by a dedicated team that will be personally interested in resurrecting the Y2K-affected system.

3.11.3 USING PROJECT MANAGEMENT TOOLS

Project managers occasionally tend to manage by the seat of their pants. Such management starts with the use of mental models and progresses, at the most, to tools like spreadsheets and project. Although these tools have an important role to play in resurrection and we do use them as a starting point for the project, it is the dynamic aspect of resurrection that provides opportunities to the project manager to use corresponding "dynamic" project management tools. During Y2K resurrection, the organization has the opportunity to reengineer its project management based on dynamic project management tools (discussed in further detail in Chapter 5, Sections 5.11 and 5.12).

3.11.4 FLATTER STRUCTURE

Project management during a Y2K resurrection effort (and the management structure as a result of the resurrection) will be a "flatter" structure compared to the original hierarchical management structure. This is an advantage to the resurrecting organization as it can use the technology and the people it has in order to produce a reengineered management — in addition to a reengineered project. This has been described in greater detail in the sociological dimension of the resurrection process (Chapter 10).

3.12 HEIGHTENED EMPLOYEE AWARENESS

Resurrection will see the organization undergoing phenomenal technological changes. However, these changes will be based on the stability of the team. We do not expect the people to change. In fact, the resurrection process should see more and more involvement of people from all levels of the business in the day-to-day activities of the business. It is a subtle yet important advantage of resurrection.

3.12.1 AWARENESS OF PROBLEMS

A Y2K hit will not be a localized problem that exists in a small corner of the enterprise. If the Y2K hit has reached a level where the organization has to resurrect, then the problem will have reached a level where every employee of the company will be aware of the criticality of the situation. This focus of the employees will result in the employees becoming aware of many other problems that the organization could be facing. Consider the situation where the supply chain to the organization is broken because of a Y2K hit. The employees involved in the resurrection process will come to know not only the software system that use to provide the support, but also associated problems of the supply chain like the inventories and the pricing.

3.12.2 BUY-IN: THE SOLUTION

Resurrection will not be possible without the involvement or buy-in of almost all employees within the organization. This is so because, as against a Y2K fix which could be achieved by a small team of IT professionals, resurrection involves changes to both software and business processes. A much wider awareness of the problems of the IT department and an equally wider acceptability of the solutions provided is the opportunity provided by resurrection.

3.13 MEASURING THE STRATEGIC BENEFITS

Having discussed the various strategic benefits in resurrection from a Y2K hit, we now summarize these benefits by viewing them through an informal metrics. It is not recommended that this metric be applied to measure the strategic benefits of an industrial-strength resurrection exercise. The measurement process would be very complex and time consuming and may not be worth the effort. The idea behind presenting this metric is to simply highlight the advantages discussed in the earlier sections by using a simple formula, and also to highlight the additional or strategic advantages compared to the normal advantages one may gain for a short time if one simply fixes the Y2K problem.

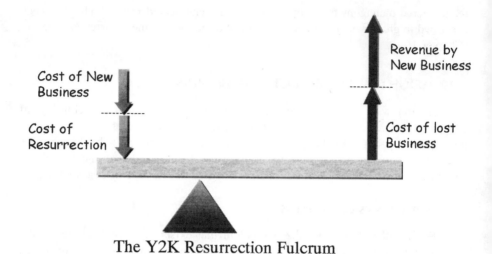

The Y2K Resurrection Fulcrum

FIGURE 3.3   Working out the advantage factor.

3.13.1 STRATEGIC ADVANTAGE FACTOR

A simple metric that would highlight the advantage of resurrection is called the *advantage factor*. This advantage factor can be understood by looking at Figure 3.3. For the sake of this "theoretical" understanding, we assume that the business still has a few clients which it stands to lose without the resurrection effort. We have discussed the steps and the likely timings of the effect of the Y2K hit as the systems of the organization are affected by the bug. If the organization is still breathing (i.e., if it still has the financial strength left to do something about its plight), then we expect the senior management of the organization to make the choice of resurrection. The process of resurrection will cost the business, but it also will help reduce the cost of loosing clients. This would be the immediate advantage by conducting the resurrection process. This advantage is expressed by the simple formula.

$$\text{Advantage factor} = \text{cost of lost business/cost of resurrection} \qquad (3.1)$$

For example, if the company is likely to loose $500K (K = 1000) due to the Y2K hit, and if the cost of resurrecting the company is $200K, then the advantage factor will be

$$\text{Advantage factor} = \$500K/\$200K = 2.5 \qquad (3.2)$$

This looks like a scenario easily justifiable by those in charge of making business decisions. However, this advantage is still *not* a growth in business, but simply targets reducing the losses. By strategic advantage, we mean the advantages that are derived *over and above* the normal advantage of resurrection. Although business found it initially uninteresting to invest in Y2K prevention, when it comes to resurrection the chances of acceptance of the process is high. For some businesses that are losing clients so rapidly that they are about to collapse, the choice may already have been made. However, it would still appear more attractive to the directors of the company, if the expenditure of resurrection provides additional advantages that make the whole exercise attractive.

If the business undergoing resurrection is able to derive *additional* advantage of new business or is able to derive benefits that position it ahead of its competitors, then those benefits can be called the *strategic advantage factor*. This advantage is in addition to the reduction in the cost of lost business. Furthermore, because of the resurrection experience, the additional costs to the organization in generating new business would be less (in absolute terms) than the revenue resulting from such business.

Formula (3.1) would now be rewritten as

$$
\begin{aligned}
&\text{Strategic advantage factor} = \\
&(\text{cost of lost business} + \text{revenue by new business})/ \qquad (3.3) \\
&(\text{cost of resurrection} + \text{cost of new business})
\end{aligned}
$$

For example, if the revenue from providing consulting services on resurrection work can be calculated and if the figure is, say, $250K and if the additional cost of providing for such consulting work is $50K, then putting those figures in Formula 3.3 (along with the figures from Formula 3.2) gives:

$$
\text{Strategic advantage factor} = (\$500K + \$250K)/(\$200k + \$50K) \qquad (3.4)
$$

This gives a strategic advantage factor of 3.0, which is an improvement over the advantage factor of 2.5. These figures are only there to discuss the idea of strategic advantage as compared with the normal advantage in resurrecting an enterprise. There is no simple means of arriving at these figures in real life.

In this chapter we have argued that there are a number of normal advantages as well as many strategic advantages in the resurrection process that go way beyond the simple understanding that it is the date problem that we are fixing. While the resurrection process aims to get the business back on track, the additional benefits make the exercise all the more worthwhile.

3.13.2 STRATEGIC BENEFITS ACCRUE IN TIME

Once the organization is hit, it has a short time window in which to decide whether it wants to resurrect or not. A formal process of evaluating alternatives can be employed in order to achieve this. However, in most cases, either the organization is still breathing, in which case it has to attempt resurrection or it has already collapsed and no decision needs to be made.

When the organization proceeds with resurrection, it results in many direct benefits to the organization, as well as spin-off benefits. The internal technical and organizational advantages as well as external business and consulting advantages have been discussed in this chapter. However, these advantages take some time to accrue. As shown in Figure 3.4, the first and immediate effect of a Y2K hit is the

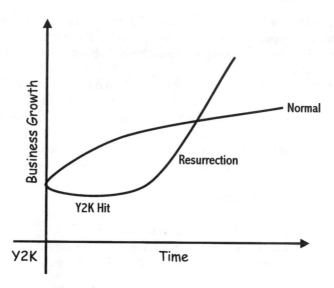

FIGURE 3.4   Strategic benefits from Y2K resurrection.

drop in business. This is not much different from what happens when an organization decides to reengineer itself. During a reengineering exercise, old processes are given up and new ones are introduced. The result is an initial drop in productivity until the new processes mature as employees get trained in them and they start serving the customers of the company.

It will be reasonable to assume that, when the resurrection process starts, the business will have already registered losses. The resurrection process itself will not provide immediate relief from this situation. This is because, when we resurrect a company, we do not attempt to fix the date and leave the rest of the processes as they are. Date-fixing has been attempted for the past few years. The same tools and techniques can be applied to handle the date problems of the organization. What we attempt here is to leverage the Y2K hit by reengineering the organization.

The formal resurrection results in the organization giving up its old hierarchical approach and reinventing itself. It also comes to "know itself" better by getting hold of the detailed inventory it carries of its IT assets. The redundant processes also are understood and eliminated. These benefits will eventually provide more value for money from the resurrection process to the company than just the restructuring of the date field. Furthermore, once the company has undergone the resurrection process and is functioning in its "re-engineered" mode, it can leverage its knowledge and expertise in helping other organizations that may be hit by the Y2K bug. This will result in a higher value for the strategic advantage factor, discussed in the previous section.

3.14 KEY POINTS

1. In Y2K prevention effort, the event is yet to happen. It is in the future. In the resurrection work in the new millennium, the dates of concern are in the past.

2. The Y2K hit is an opportunity to resurrect rather than simply fix the date problem. This resurrection effort has more advantages than those of simply building a new system.
3. These benefits include recognition of IT as a strategic tool, inventory of the organization's IT assets, opportunity to introduce new technology, and creating a quality conscious and robust system architecture.
4. Having gained the experience of resurrecting from a Y2K hit, the organization is in a position to help other organizations and business partners who may find themselves in a similar situation.
5. A Y2K hit and the subsequent resurrection are likely to be a single problem that is faced by everyone in the organization. This is likely to heighten awareness of the employees to the problems faced by the organization. It is a single project in which every employee of the organization is likely to be involved, resulting in a positive culture.

3.15 NOTES

The thinking on strategic advantage discussed in this chapter is based on the understanding that whenever we take a strategic view, it implies major up front expenses (or even possible losses in the present) for the sake of potential profits in the future. Strategic decisions usually imply nonlinear relationship between the inputs and the returns and there is a long time factor involved before the returns climb above the input. That is the reason why strategic decisions are difficult to make as compared with short-term tactical decisions. A Y2K hit can be viewed as a direct loss to the organization. Alternatively, the organization can view the loss in a more strategic way and accomplish everything it can that required closing down the existing system (which it could not afford to do in its day-to-day operations).

3.16 REFERENCES

1. Porter, M. E., *Competitive Advantage,* Collier Macmillan Publishers, London, 1985, 33–39, 326–329.
2. Jacobson, I., Ericsson, M., and Jacobson, A., *The Object Advantage: Business Process Engineering with Object Technology,* 1995, 2.
3. John Davidson reporting Mrs. Judith Merryweather from Institute of Chartered Accountants in Australia, in the *Australian Financial Review,* August 1997, 24.
4. Henderson-Sellers, B., *A Book of Object-Oriented Knowledge: An Introduction to Object-Oriented Software Engineering,* 2nd ed., Prentice Hall, Upper Saddle River, NJ, 33, 1977.
5. Buschmann, F., et al., *A System of Patterns: Pattern-Oriented Software Architecture,* John Wiley & Sons, New York, 1996.
6. Humprey, W. S., *Managing the Software Process,* Addison-Wesley, Reading, MA, 1989.
7. Champy, J., *Reengineering Management: Managing the Change to the Reengineered Corporation,* Harper Collins Publishers, Glasgow, U.K., 1995, 3.

4 The Process Discipline for Y2K Resurrection

A white cloud is a mystery — the coming, the going, the very being of it. A white cloud exists without any roots … but still it exists, and exists abundantly … All dimensions belong to it, all directions belong to it. Nothing is rejected. Everything is, exists, in a total acceptability.

Osho, 1978[1]

Abstract   The multiple schizophrenic personality of an enterprise hit by Y2K is likely to show up in myriad noncohesive ways. We need to understand the organizational structure and behavior of such an enterprise in order to make sense of it before we can work on resurrecting it. One good way of understanding an enterprise is by creating its "process model." The same process model can be used in development of software systems that form the backbone of the enterprise. We start the discussion in this chapter with the need for modeling, its advantages and limitations, and a look at white clouds as a model for the process model for resurrecting and/or rebuilding Y2K-hit organizations. The process model is introduced by way of comparison with an insurance claim process. The formal definition of a process is provided next. A simple cooking example is used to describe a process and its three orthogonal dimensions. These dimensions detail the *what, how,* and *who* of a process and are made up of process elements — the actors, activities, tasks, and deliverables. These process elements are described along with their notations and flow of activities. While the discussion on a process remains theoretical, when a process is "instantiated" it results in a flow of control called a *process thread.* Discussion on the concept of process threads, iterations in a development process, and measurement of processes follow. Before a process can be applied to any area of work (such as Y2K resurrection), it needs to be scoped so that the process threads can be measured and controlled. This process scope is discussed followed by the mapping of the software development process to a business process. This chapter should prepare our theoretical understanding of a detailed process model so that we can apply it in recreating a resurrection process, which will be described in the next chapter.

4.1   A CHAT ON MODELING

Before we can start modeling the enterprises in the new millennium, we need to understand what modeling entails, its need in the resurrection exercise, and its advantages and limitations. The aim of resurrection is to build an enterprise on the basis of a model that is flexible and fine granular and one that permits the enterprise to absorb large disturbances in the environment in which it exists. This requirement of the model comes from the fact that the next millennium promises to be a world of rapidly changing technology that is going to affect the enterprise in various ways that we cannot fully comprehend at this stage. Furthermore, as described in Chapter 2 (Figure 2.2), because of the significant sociological role that the enterprise has to play in the new millennium, it is important to create a model that reflects this sociological dimension of the organization's functioning. The discussion on modeling builds the background for the process discipline. This process discipline is used in resurrecting an enterprise from the ashes of its Y2K hit. Herein are considered the needs for modeling in a process discipline and its advantages and limitations.

4.1.1 THE NEED FOR MODELING

Modeling serves many purposes in the real world. While a model is necessarily incomplete, as it cannot incorporate every possible real-life situation, it still serves many valuable purposes. The primary goal of modeling is to help us understand the reality around us. Thus, one purpose of modeling an enterprise is to give us a good idea of what the real enterprise is. For example, the model of an enterprise relevant to an accountant contains the profit and loss accounts and the balance sheets, whereas that of the personnel department is contained in the organizational chart and the hierarchy. A flow chart that describes the flow of control in a structured program also is a model of the real program.

In order to give us a good idea of what the reality is, it is important for the model to have different views depending on the need of the user. Thus, a model enables viewing of the same reality from different angles and from different levels. When modeling an enterprise, it is particularly important that the models that are created serve the specific purpose of users who are placed at different levels within the organization. There is a need for the model to take the same input and show it in different ways. For example, the accountant's view of an accounting process is different from that of the general manager. Therefore, modeling is required to provide a representation of the process *from the viewer's perspective.*

An enterprise — especially a Y2K hit enterprise — depends heavily on its software systems. In order to model such an enterprise, it will be essential to model its software systems. Thus, modeling will enable the teams that are entrusted with rebuilding the enterprise after a Y2K hit to make sense out of the organization's processes. Modeling also helps in making sense out of the large amount of data and the databases in which the data resides. Modeling enables analyses of the data and converts it into information. Although a Y2K hit is considered as a problem of information systems, many thinkers still do not believe that we live in an information age. "Today's computerized enterprises are drowning in data, a fate made possible by the chip ... we are not living in the information age. Information implies meaning. We are living in the data age."[2] One of the main purposes of modeling is to take us from a data age towards an information age. The tools and techniques of semantic modeling would then become useful by providing meaning to the data that are stored in the organization's databases. Thus, we see that modeling is a tool that allows us to understand the reality and also view it in many different ways. With reference to the current problem at hand, modeling is a tool that will enable us to understand the state of a Y2K-hit organization. The complexity of the organization's behavior will be simpler to understand by creating its model.

4.1.2 MODELING AS A CREATIVE CAUSE

The initial attempt at modeling an enterprise is to represent its data in a way that is meaningful to the person who wants to understand the organization. Thus, for a Y2K hit, we will create the model of the organization and its systems as they exist now, and then try and understand the modules that are hit by the date problem. However, that is not the only purpose of modeling the enterprise and its systems. When we attempt to model an enterprise, we are aiming beyond data and meaning. Not only are we content with extracting meaning from the data, our aim also is to ensure that this meaning or information is a true and creative cause for new and reengineered business processes of the Y2K enterprise. If modeling has to play a role in the development of a new enterprise, then not only should it provide meaning to the reality that exists, but it should also be a *creative cause* for a new and, as yet, nonexistent reality. This will assist us in resurrecting the Y2K-hit enterprises quickly and efficiently. It also will enable us to adopt the new and rapidly emerging technology of the new millennium in the best possible way. For example, it is not enough for a model of a branch reconciliation process to show us where the Y2K problem has occurred. A model should also help us create a new process that would satisfy the user (in this example the teller and the branch manager) in a way that takes advantages of new technology and reduces the hierarchy in performing the job.

When we talk of creativity using models, we are not limiting our discussion to simply modeling the routine payroll and accounting applications. Although we would like to understand the modules in these routine applications that are hit by the date problem, the aim is not to merely automate them and make them faster. The purpose of the modeling exercise is to provide reengineered solutions to even routine applications so that the result is a user-focused solution. Furthermore, although the prime output of the business systems is their information, modeling helps in many systems that primarily do not deal with data processing. Typical examples are process control systems for power plants or patient monitoring systems in hospitals. The primary purpose of these systems is not the *information* they impart, but the *process* they perform.[3] Modeling can be extremely creative and economical in these systems. The technology used in these process-control systems is a means rather than the end in itself. Thus, the models continue to be a creative cause of new developments in both business and process-control systems.

4.1.3 ADVANTAGES OF A MODEL

As shown in Figure 4.1, we have established that enterprise modeling serves two clear purposes:

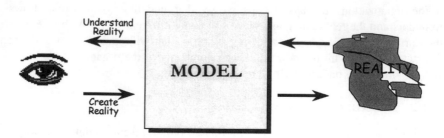

FIGURE 4.1   Advantages of modeling.

1. To understand the complex reality.
2. To be a creative cause for a new reality.

Thus, modeling will help us understand the reality of Y2K hits and it also will help us resurrect the new organization. Specific reasons why modeling is able to serve the purpose of understanding and creating the reality are as follows:

- Eliminates all the irrelevant things from the view. A model is an abstract representation of the reality and, therefore, the modeler has a choice of removing things that are not relevant for the purpose for which the model is built. For example, a hospital administration system that provides information to the administrative staff need not present the detailed diagnosis of a patient.
- Enables the modeler to concentrate on the essentials by representing the parts of a system or company that are relevant for the purpose for which the model is being created. For example, when the discussion is on date, the modeler can create multiple ways of understanding date only. The model may not worry about other parts of the system that do not deal with the date.
- A cheap way of understanding potential new creations. For example, it is cheaper to build the model of a house and explore its limitations or make changes to it, rather than building a new house and then making the changes. This is equally true of software systems where changes at later stages to an implemented system can cost many times that of a change early in the software's life.
- A safe way of understanding the reality. It is better to sit in a simulator and land a 747 jumbo jet, than to attempt a real landing without enough experience. Use of a model will be helpful in understanding the year 2000 reality, especially if the IT community does not have enough experience in resurrecting from a Y2K hit.
- While a model helps where we don't have previous experience in handling the situations, it also enables use of previous experience if we have one. For example, the model of a house is created from the knowledge and understanding of generations of builders. This helps the new architects and builders in reusing the available knowledge, and creates new and

improved understanding that enhances the overall knowledge of the community.
- Provides the end-user with a means of giving input before the final product is ready. A model is a means of involving the end-user or the sponsor of the product in its creation at an early stage of its life cycle.

4.1.4 CAVEATS AND LIMITATIONS

Despite its advantages, use of a model in order to create a new entity has its own limitations. It is essential to be aware of these limitations to enable us to make the best use of the modeling tool. Some of the specific limitations of modeling are

- A model is an abstraction of the reality. Therefore, it does not provide the complete picture of the real situation. A model is, thus, subject to the interpretation of the observer.
- Unless a model is dynamic, it does not provide the feel for timings. Since the reality itself is changing, if the model does not change accordingly, it will not be able to convey the right meaning to the user.
- The user of the model should be aware of the notations and language used to express the model. For example, when the design of a house is expressed using a paper model, it is necessary for the user to know what each of the symbols means. Nonstandardized notations and processes can render a model less useful.
- A model may be created for a specific situation. Once the situation has changed, the model may no longer be relevant

With the purpose of modeling and its advantages and limitations clear in our mind, we look at an element from real life to see if it can provide us with a model that represents the process of rebuilding a Year 2000 enterprise.

4.1.5 SOFTWARE DEVELOPMENT LIFECYCLE MODELS

Models can be of various types. A flow chart is a visual model (perhaps paper-based) of a software program. A house may be modeled using wooden blocks. Many models can be simply created in the minds of the users in order to describe reality. In the case of software development processes, information technology professionals have gone beyond the boundaries of the traditional IT entities in order to describe what happens when software is developed. Most notable of these models is the "waterfall model" representing the software development lifecycle as a process that starts with analysis, goes to design, and finally to implementation — just as water falls from a higher level to a lower level — without going back to the previous step.[4] However, when the IT community started discussing the iterative and incremental nature of object-oriented development, the waterfall was not sufficient to represent what happens during the development process. The "fountain model" better represents the iterative nature of object-oriented software development lifecycle.[5] In a fountain model development can climb up from the requirements pool to analysis, and from analysis to design before falling back in the pool of requirements. The iterations can be repeated at analysis, design, and development levels.

These models (and many other models, as the spiral and the pinball models) have been popular because they are able to describe the process of software development in an understandable way.

4.1.6 THE MODEL WE NEED

What would represent the process of resurrection from a Y2K hit? Which model can represent an enterprise that is free from the rigidity and inflexibility of the original organization that was hit by the date problem? During resurrection, we aim to create a process-based organization. Therefore, we search for a model that would represent the behavior of an organization that is based on processes. Thus, the model we are searching for is not only meant to help us understand the existing organization, but also the creative aspect of what to incorporate in the new organization. Furthermore, a careful observation of the organization and the processes within the organization indicates that the processes have three dimensions and that those three dimensions are orthogonal to each other. For example, within a hospital organization, we find activities that are related directly to curing the patient (investigations, operations), activities that deal with the administration (accounting and invoicing of patients), and activities related to human relations (motivation and morale) of the hospital staff itself. Thus, we need a representation that does justice to the three-dimensional behavior of an enterprise. The dimensions of a process and the internal behavior of an organization we are trying to create are represented aptly by looking at white clouds.

4.1.7 A LOOK AT WHITE CLOUDS

White clouds have interesting characteristics. They are carefree and relaxed and appear to be completely oblivious to competition — as if they are already beyond competition. They belong to all three dimensions and all the dimensions belong to them. I always find it funny that an entire jetliner with its 350 tons of cargo, fuel, human bodies, and all, can go through these white clouds, and yet they remain serene and unperturbed, as if nothing has happened. I think the secret lies in the fact that a fluffy white cloud is essentially "fuzzy." There are no rigid internal structures within the white clouds. Therefore, they don't resist, but instead absorb everything around them. It also is very difficult to discern a hierarchy within the clouds. Although some may appear big and others small, there is no clear hierarchy because the external boundary is very fuzzy. This hazy boundary allows the white cloud to move in an imperceptible way in any direction that it wants to go and absorb (or get absorbed by) other clouds. The flexibility, lack of rigid internal hierarchy, innate ability to absorb, and finer granularity of its composition are some of the characteristics of a process that can be derived from the white clouds. These also are the characteristics we want our resurrected organization to have in the next millennium. Thus, we consider the white cloud model as a representative model of a process-based organization, as well as a representation of the resurrection process itself.

4.2 A PROCESS MODEL

We discussed the purpose and the ideal characteristics of a model. We also stated how the white clouds are able to represent a process and, therefore, they are also an ideal representation of a process-based organization. We now proceed with the discussion of an organization that is modeled by using these processes.

So, what is a process model? And how can one model an enterprise based on processes?* And how would this modeling be different from the traditional hierarchical model? The answers to these questions are in the domain of business process reengineering (BPR). The reengineering of business processes is quite relevant to the resurrection of dynamic enterprises in the next millennium. We consider how our process model can represent a process-based business transaction as against a hierarchical business transaction.

4.2.1 A HIERARCHICAL VIEWPOINT

Figure 4.2 shows a traditional organization of an insurance company. The company has a variety of products and services, one of which deals with receipt and settlement of claims for car insurance. This includes claims for damages to and theft of private and company-owned motor vehicles. In a traditional organization, the work would be organized in four separate departments, each dealing with one aspect of the claim. These departments are the claims, verification, administration, and accounts departments. The claims department would receive all claims for insurance payment for car thefts, the verification department will deal with investigations, and the accounts department will deal with the final payments. In between, there will be an administrative department that may deal with the job of informing the claimants whether their claim is successful or not. In the case where a claim is rejected, the administrative department sends out a letter of rejection. If the claim is accepted, it informs the beneficiary that the "claim is now with the accounts department and the payment will follow in due course." Finally, the accounts department draws out the check, and mails it to the claimant.

FIGURE 4.2 A hierarchical insurance claim organization.

---

* For that matter, how can one model "baking a cake" based on processes?

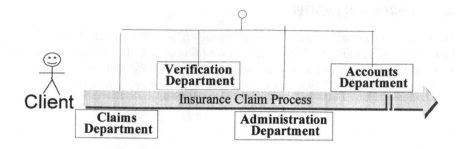

An Insurance Process cuts across Departments

FIGURE 4.3 A process-based insurance claim organization.

Not only is the settlement of claim fraught with limitations, but these are the limitations that are exacerbated by a Y2K hit. For example, if the claimant rings to find out the status of her claim, the phone call would have to be directed to as many as three other departments before the status could be ascertained. Each of the departments has a specific job to do and has its own specific agenda and a budget to support that agenda. Occasionally, the agenda of the four separate hierarchically organized departments may clash, and so would the career aspirations of those who head the departments. The job of the chief of all departments is restricted to managing the coordination between all four departments. The organizational structure is not satisfactory from the customer's viewpoint, as well as from that of the employees of the company. From the Y2K angle, this is the organization that has to consider all four departments in the investigation of the Y2K hit. Being a coarse granular and centralized organization it has less opportunity to maneuver in response to external crises. For instance, when hit by Y2K, the four departments provide a rigid hierarchical framework that prevents options like shifting to a manual system and, thereby, get a breathing space.

4.2.2 A Reengineered Process-Based View

The essential nature of a process model is that it cuts across the hierarchy of a traditional organization and gets directly involved with serving the customer of the company. It is a collection of activities that takes one or more kinds of input and creates an output that is of value to the customer.[6] Thus, a process model deals with the basic purpose of the organization — to serve the customer. This is achieved by modeling the organization around the customer rather than around the hierarchy of the departments and its people.

Figure 4.3 shows how the insurance claim organization (described earlier in Figure 4.2) can be based on a process. The basic process of such an organization is to accept claims and settle them. Thus, the work that this organization has to do is handle the claims right from their application through to their settlement. Thus, instead of organizing the departments in a hierarchy, they are organized around the basic process of "claims: from application to settlement." The software systems and the people within the departments support this basic process. Thus, even if the departments exist, these departments and all the people within the departments are organized around the processes that supports the business. When a customer makes a claim, she is not concerned with the hierarchies and the particular responsibilities of each department. What concerns the customer are the claim and its status. In a process-based organization, when the customer rings to inquire about the claim, the enquiry is handled by one single person who owns the process. Thus, answers to all questions related to the claim, as well as its status, are known through a single process rather than through four departments.

4.2.3 Reasoning for a Process Model for the Y2K Enterprise

A process model is extremely relevant to what we are trying to do with an organization that is hit by the Y2K problem. Not only do we want to fix the date problem, but we also want to leverage the opportunity to reengineer the business in a way that will be relevant to the next millennium. When we try to understand the Y2K-hit organization, we do so based on the process model. When we fix the date and recreate the organization, we do that based on a process model as well.

So what do we want from the process model that will be relevant to our resurrection exercise? The initial requirement of the model is to allow the enterprise to shed all characteristics that made it explode in the first place. Furthermore, it should enable us to create the new enterprise which is able to handle the changing nature of the business in the new millennium. Specifically, the new enterprise we want to build should have at least the following characteristics:

- The new enterprise should be as flexible as possible. This would mean that the enterprise should be able to handle different types of businesses within its domain comfortably.
- It should not be hierarchically structured. This will enable the business to remain flexible and to perform the process-based activities that will result from resurrection.
- The boundaries between the organization and the society, as well as between the organization and technology, should not be rigidly defined. This will enable the organization to influence, and be influenced by, society in a positive way.
- It should be able to absorb rapid changes in the external environment. With the "shrinking world" resulting from technological advances, the effect of far-off changes are felt quickly. We want the organization to be able to understand and absorb the changes as fast as they occur.
- Its movements with relation to the external environment should appear soft and non-threatening. The response to changes in the external environment needs to be strategic. Instead of large-scale movement of personnel and inventories and large changes to production schedules, the responses should be in small parts and focused.
- It should be able to adapt to the changes coming from within the organization. These would usually be the changing technology and its

application within the organization. However, the changes also can relate to the method of working of the organization or individuals who work within the organization.

- It should be finer granular — which means its systems and modules should be smaller in size. This will enable the organization to manage itself in a much better way as it can change its internal processes quickly if the external processes change, based on its finer granularity.

The characteristics of a process-based enterprise also are the characteristics of the model that we have used to represent the new enterprise — the white clouds. A process-based enterprise has an internal structure that, in many ways, resembles the white clouds. These enterprises do not have a rigid hierarchical structure within them. Instead, they are made up of processes which are flexible enough to absorb large changes from both inside and outside the organization. Furthermore, dynamic and distributed processes also have the characteristics of fuzziness which renders the movement of an organization imperceptible from outside. Thus, when we are resurrecting an organization from a Y2K hit, we are trying to build an organization that is represented by the white clouds. The process of building such an enterprise also is based on white clouds. We, thus, are using the process of resurrection in order to reengineer an enterprise that is process-based. What follows is a detailed and formal definition of a process. This definition will be used in describing and measuring the resurrection process and its various dimensions.

4.3   FORMALLY DESCRIBING A PROCESS

We examined the advantages and limitations of a model. We also considered the three-dimensional white clouds as an appropriate representation of a process. Our aim is to represent the organization based on a process model. It is now necessary to describe a formal framework for the representation of the process model. This is achieved by means of a formal definition and a corresponding example of the cooking process.

4.3.1   A PROCESS DEFINITION

The formal definition of a process is not much different from what we commonly understand a process to be. *Process* is defined in the *Oxford Dictionary* as:

1. A course of action or proceeding, especially a series of stages in manufacture or some other operation.
2. The progress or course of something (*in the process of construction*).

From this definition we infer that a process involves a course of action that is performed by a series of steps. The definition also indicates *movement* — it indicates that a process represents a dynamic behavior rather than a static or hierarchical organization of work. A process, by this definition, is essentially a set of activities that are performed in a given sequence. However, this sequence is dynamic and it can be created based on the given situation in which the process is performed.

When we consider the multidimensional nature of a process, each of the dimensions can be treated as processes in themselves. Therefore, each of these dimensions contains a set of activities that follow the process model. Activities from each of the three dimensions are executed in different sequences when a process is actually performed. Therefore, it is important to remember that as long as the progress or course of action of a process is maintained, activities from the three dimension of a process may intermingle with each other. Occasionally, activities from different dimensions may happen simultaneously.

Other characteristics of these activities or set of actions are that they are performed on a *thing* or an *object*. Furthermore, in order to perform these actions, a certain set of tools or equipment might be required. It is also reasonable to extend the understanding of a process by assuming that the actions within the process will have to follow a certain discipline. It is also necessary to have *someone* performing this set of actions. The output or the end result of these activities is one or more deliverables.

This explanation of a process can be better understood by using an example.

4.3.2 A SIMPLE COOKING PROCESS

Consider the process of preparing a meal. It starts with the raw material for cooking the meal, as well as the tools needed to carry out the tasks. In the case of baking a cake, it would include the flour, butter, eggs, and other raw materials, as well as the pots and pans, the oven, and other associated tools. These are the technological aspects of the process of cooking a meal.

However, the cake will not get baked unless the raw materials are mixed in a certain proportion and in a specific sequence. This information may be available in a book or a video that describes the mix and the sequence in baking the cake. This would be the detailed recipe or "method" to be followed in baking. This is the methodological aspect of the process of baking a cake.

Finally, the cook may be influenced by the motivational factors (e.g., whether it is a professional cook who is getting paid for the work he is doing, or whether it is the mother who is baking cake for the family). The general condition of the kitchen, including whether it has enough ventilation and light, whether it is air-conditioned, and the distance of the oven from the work bench, all would play a significant role in the final output from the process of baking. Thus, the skills of the cook, his previous experience at baking the cake, and the environmental conditions in which the process is taking place, constitute the sociological dimension of the process of baking a cake.

4.3.3 PICTURING THE PROCESS

Figure 4.4 graphically shows (by using the notations described in detail in Section 4.5) the simple cooking process. There are two formal actors who are involved in the production of the final deliverable or meal. These are the chef and the sponsor.

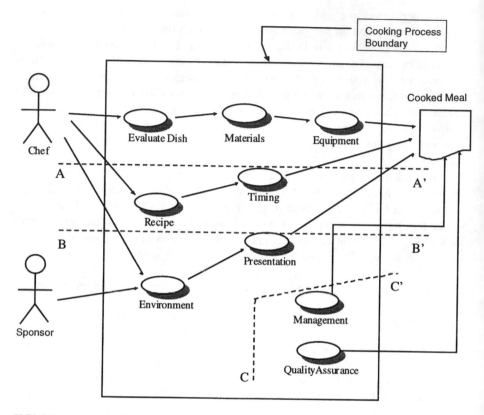

FIGURE 4.4   A cooking process.

The process is made up of a series of activities that are called: evaluate dish, materials, equipment, recipe, timing, environment, presentation, management, and quality assurance. Once the notations are described and understood by the participants in the process, the representation of the process using this picture plays a significant role in conveying the activities, their sequence, and the final deliverable they are producing, to the actors in the process.

4.4   THE THREE DIMENSIONS OF A PROCESS

4.4.1   DESCRIBING THE DIMENSIONS

The three distinct dimensions of the cooking process became evident as we described the process. After representing the process in picture form, it is now easier to understand these dimensions and the activities that go on within them.

The first dimension of the process develops an understanding of the materials on which the actions are performed, as well as the tools that help in performing those actions. This forms the technological dimension of a process. In the cooking example (Figure 4.4), the activities related to this dimension of the process are above the line A–A': evaluate dish, materials, and equipment.

The second dimension of the process is the step-by-step guide as to "how" a particular process is to be conducted. The discipline of conducting a process comprises a sequence of well-defined tasks that are organized in a specific order. This discipline or *method* of working constitutes the methodological dimension of a process. In Figure 4.4, these are the activities between lines A–A' and B–B': recipe, timing.

The third dimension of the process deals with the people who are going to take responsibility for the actions and carry them out by following the prescribed methodology. An understanding of the dimension of the process that deals with the people who carry out the tasks and the environment or the organizational context in which those tasks are carried out, results in the sociology of the process. It is the sociological dimension of a process. The relevant activities in Figure 4.4 are between B–B' and C–C': environment, presentation.

The overall management of the entire process continues to be a part of all three dimensions. Furthermore, the activity of quality assurance is going to continuously influence the deliverable. Therefore, quality along with management forms part of all dimensions of the process.

4.4.2 THE ORTHOGONAL PROCESS RELATIONSHIP

It was mentioned that the three dimensions of a process are processes in themselves. They are made up of a subset of the overall set of activities within a process. However, these activities from the three dimensions may not be sequential. Some activities from one dimension of a process may be carried out first, followed by activities from the other dimension of a process. Taking the cooking example further, we may first get the recipe book and go through the recipes (Activity: recipe — from the methodological dimension of the cooking process) and then decide what we want to cook (Activity: evaluate dish — from the technological dimension of the cooking process). Thus, the three dimensions of a process are not sequential. Occasionally, they may be carried out in parallel. For example, the cleaning and setting up of the kitchen (sociological dimension of the process) may go on, along with the study of the recipe (methodological dimension of the process). However, sequential or parallel processes are more theoretical. In a real situation of cooking, the three dimensions of the process will be executed depending on the management of the overall process discipline. We can say that the dimensions of a process are *orthogonal* to each other — each influencing the other aspects of the dimension. This is very well represented by the white cloud model, that was described earlier on. The dimensions of a process as they exist in a cloud and their orthogonal relationship, are shown in Figure 4.5.

Some of the observations we make about a process and the dimensions within the process are

- A process is essentially made up of three dimensions.
- Each dimension of the process is a process in itself.
- Each of the three process dimensions can have dimensions within.

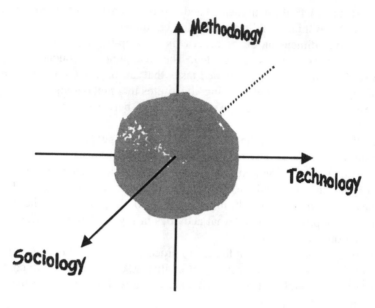

FIGURE 4.5 The orthogonal relationship of the process dimensions.

- Processes are conducted by a set of activities.
- Activities within the processes have a flow.
- Activities from all three dimensions may be conducted at the same time.
- The relationship between the three dimensions of a process is orthogonal.

We have developed an understanding of the dimensions of a process in order to appreciate how the overall process is conducted. The three dimensions essentially answer the questions of "what, how, and who" in a process. These dimensions are now described in detail.

4.4.3 "What" in a Process

The "what" in a process is the dimension of the process that answers everything related to the raw material with which the process will be conducted. It is concerned with the technology of the process. Many factors from the technological dimension influence the overall output of a process. These factors include the quality of material that is being used, the availability of the material, and the appropriateness of the tools that are used in the process. Thus, everything that deals with the "what" in a process plays a part in influencing its deliverable. In our cooking example, the influence of the raw material and the tools on the process can be summarized as in Table 4.1.

4.4.4 "How" of a Process

The "how" or the methodological aspect of the process deals with the steps to be followed in producing the deliverable. It is essentially a glossary of the distilled

TABLE 4.1
Influence of Technological Factors on the Final Deliverable

	Material	Tools
Availability	Without flour, butter, and egg, cake can't be baked	Pan and the oven are necessary to bake a cake
Quality	The grain in the flour, the quality of the butter, etc., will influence the final outcome — taste of the cake	Is the oven able to provide the correct temperature? Is the pan leaking? These will all influence the quality of cake.
Appropriateness	Will maize flour do instead of wheat flour? Should I use margarine in place of butter?	My friend has not returned the pan she borrowed. Should I bake the cake in a normal plate instead?

experience of a number of people over a period of time. The "how" of a process is instrumental in conserving effort when the process is conducted. Taking the cooking example further, the "how" of the process is the recipe book for the baking process. The activities within the methodological dimension of the process will deal with how the process is to be conducted. The approach presented in the recipe book must be standard and should be easily understood by the person who is following the process. Therefore, use of suitable notations and language to express the "how" of a process and relevant training and experience for the person who is following the instructions are some of the essential factors in the final outcome of the process (Table 4.2).

4.4.5 "WHO" IN A PROCESS

Following a method, as described in the recipe book, is still not going to produce the desired deliverable. Application of the methodology is the purview of the person who is applying it. It depends on the skills and experience of the person, as well as the environment in which he is working. Thus, skills, experience, and environment form the basic sociological factors. These also are called *soft* factors, as they deal with the softer or human relations issues in a process. The other reason why they are called soft factors is that they are not easily quantifiable.

TABLE 4.2
Influence of Methodological Factors on the Final Deliverable

	Recipe (Methodology)
Notations	Are the notations in the recipe understood? Does a pan mean a pan, and is the picture of mixing flour and eggs clear?
Language (description)	How is the process described?
Documentation	Is the recipe book covered with plastic? How many copies of the book are available?

TABLE 4.3
Influence of Sociological Factors on the Final Deliverable

Cook

Skills	What is the skill level of the cook? Is he trained to bake the cake? Is he in a position to understand the notations and language expressed in the recipe book to help him bake the cake?
Experience	What is the previous experience of this cook? For how many months/years has he been baking cake? Has he baked only one cake at a time? Or has he handled large orders before?
Environment	Is the kitchen well ventilated? Are there any assistants to help this cook in baking the cake? Is it a friendly place? Is he relaxed in the cooking environment or is he under pressure to produce a cake?

Skills, one of the factors influencing the final outcome of a process, requires regular training, especially when new ways of doing things and new equipment become available on a daily basis. Experience comes from practising the skills developed in a real environment. In addition to the skills and experience, it is also important to consider the motivational factors and their influence on the process. Is the person baking the cake doing it for a living or for the joy of cooking? Finally, the manner in which the deliverable is presented and the timing of the presentation is also important. These are some of the sociological factors that go on to influence the final outcome of the process, and they are shown in Table 4.3.

4.5   PROCESS ELEMENTS

Having formally described the process and its three dimensions, we now describe the "elements" in a process, the role they play in the outcome of the process, and the notations that are used to represent them.

4.5.1   NOTATIONS FOR PROCESS ELEMENTS

Figure 4.6 shows the notations that are used in describing a process. The notations are mostly self-explanatory. They also are simple and can be easily drawn by hand on chalkboards, facilitating process-based discussion. A brief description of the notation follows:

Actor: This is the person responsible for carrying out the process.
Activity: The activity is what happens as a result of the actor performing his tasks. The activity has a starting and an ending point and it may be performed in a sequence or in parallel.
Task: This is what the actor actually performs; a sequence of events that together constitute an activity.
Flow: This designates the sequence in which activities may be performed. It shows the general direction of the process and is not binding on the process.

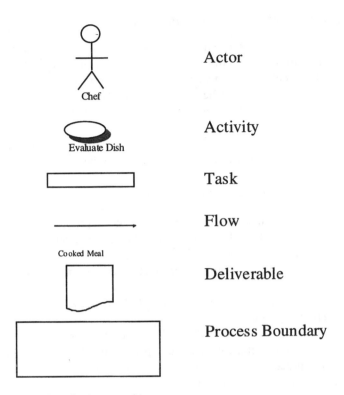

FIGURE 4.6 Notations for process elements.

This is because in an iterative and incremental development, the flow is likely to return back to the initial activities.

Deliverable: This is the end result of the process. It can be a physical deliverable (such as a document) or it can be a nonphysical deliverable (such as a motivated team).

Process: This is the overall set of activities and tasks that are carried out by the actors in order to produce the deliverable. The process is shown by the process boundary that surrounds the activities that are carried out as a part of the process.

Process-threads: A process-thread is effectively an instance of a process. We have discussed how a process is made up of three dimensions and that these three dimensions are orthogonal to each other. A process-thread effectively links activities from different dimensions of a process. Although not shown separately in the Figure 4.6, it provides a major understanding to the project manager on the "real" process flow, which cuts across the three dimensions.

Out of the elements of a process described above, there are four elements that are of major interest to us. These are the basic elements or the building blocks of a process. They are actor, activity, task, and deliverable. These elements and their characteristics are described in greater detail below.

4.5.2 THE "ACTOR" ELEMENT IN A PROCESS

The actor is an element of the process that is essentially concerned with its socio-logical aspect. Actor is the one that interacts with the outer boundaries of the process and deals with the deliverable. An actor is the one who carries out the process, but she also can be the recipient of the process. For example, in a cooking process, the cook is the primary actor. The cook will follow the activities by carrying out the tasks specified within these activities and achieve the deliverable — the meal. However, the sponsor also is an actor who is involved in providing the finance for the project. The resultant deliverable (the meal) from the cooking process might be consumed by the sponsor of the project.

Some of the characteristics of an actor are

- It is usually a human being who deals with the process.
- An actor should be able to understand the activities that concern her and that form part of the process.
- The actor should be able to appreciate the flow of activities within a process.
- The actor should have the necessary skills to carry out the tasks within the activities of interest.
- It is desirable for the actor to be motivated to perform the tasks.
- Occasionally, an actor can be another process that may be required to deal with the process being designed. In such a situation, the characteristics of a human actor do not apply.
- Depending on the scope of the process, the actor element can have multiple instances. For example, a large development process may have 20 pro-grammers, as opposed to a small scoped process with only 2 programmers.

4.5.3 THE "ACTIVITY" ELEMENT IN A PROCESS

The activity element in a process is the controlling element for a set of tasks within the process. Therefore, the activity element on its own doesn't have the same concrete existence as the tasks. Actors carry out activities by performing a sequence of tasks within the activities. Occasionally, an activity element may have pre- and/or post-conditions. However, some activities may begin before the previous activity is completed, and at times activities may be carried out in parallel. In these situations an activity may not have very well defined pre- and post-conditions. Some of the characteristics of an activity element are

- Activity is the overall controlling element for a set of tasks.
- It is helpful in understanding the flow of events.
- Some activities may begin before others end. Thus, activities may be carried out in parallel.
- Activities are accomplished by completing the set of tasks that they encompass.
- It is not essential for all tasks within an activity to be accomplished in one iteration.

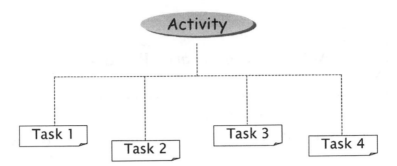

FIGURE 4.7 Activity and tasks.

Activities are comprised of tasks. Therefore, when the controlling activity is described, it is also essential to describe the underlying tasks and the sequence in which these tasks are accomplished. The relationship between activities and tasks is shown in Figure 4.7.

4.5.4 THE "TASK" ELEMENT IN A PROCESS

The task element in a process discipline is the atomic element in the working of a process. As shown in Figure 4.7, tasks are carried out under the umbrella of the encompassing activity. Thus, the purpose of the well-defined tasks is to complete the activity under which they fall. Some of the characteristics of the task element are

- The smallest unit of the elements in a process, i.e., they need not be further subdivided before they are performed.
- A set of tasks carried out in a specific sequence. The designer of the process usually specifies this sequence. Sometimes a task from another activity might be happening at the same time as this particular task.
- The result of execution of tasks in a sequence is the completion of an activity.
- Have a concrete existence of their own. This implies that when a task is completed, it is effectively an incremental completion of the activity under which this task is performed.
- Can be put in a project plan. Thus, they can be assigned a time for completion and resources to complete them.

4.5.5 THE "DELIVERABLE" ELEMENT IN A PROCESS

The deliverable is the final output or result of the process. The actors are involved in various activities that are performed by executing a set of well-defined tasks. These tasks result in the final output from the process — the deliverables. Deliverables can be concrete, as in a set of documents, or they can be abstract, as in a "motivated work force." In the cooking example we have been discussing, the final deliverable is a baked cake. Deliverables may result at the end of iteration or they may be produced incrementally — at the end of each iteration of a process.

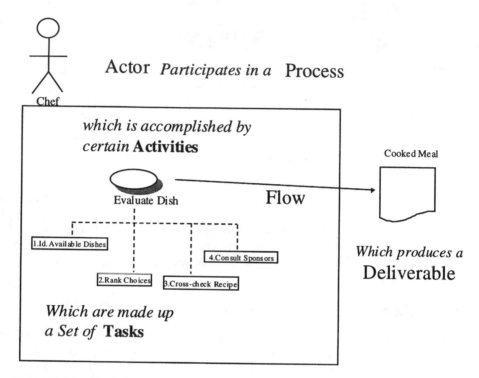

FIGURE 4.8 Semantics of the notation.

4.5.6 SEMANTICS OF THE NOTATION

Figure 4.8 shows the semantics of the notations as they are used in describing a process. The actor participates in a process which is accomplished by certain activities. These activities have a certain flow. However, some activities may be carried out in parallel because activities within a process can begin before other activities have ended. Activity (such as *evaluate dish* in the cooking example) is made up of a set of tasks. These tasks are numbered and are carried out in a sequence. In the *evaluate dish* example, the tasks are

Task 1: Identify available dishes — This would produce a list of all dishes that can be cooked. A number of factors (such as availability of raw materials, etc.) will influence the ability of the cook to produce a dish for himself or make it available to the sponsor.

Task 2: Rank the available choices — This task places the list of possible dishes that can be prepared in a priority order. This list is influenced by the availability of the dishes. Obviously, if a dish is not available, it cannot be ranked in this list. The ranking enables the sponsor to choose the alternatives to the first choice. For example, if the methodology for the first choice (indicated by Task 3) is too complicated, the second choice may be produced.

Task 3: Crosscheck recipe — Once the choices are put in a sequence we need to ensure that the recipe (the book of methodology) is available and that it contains enough details to enable the cook to produce the deliverable. This task can iterate with the previous task. If a crosscheck with the methodology indicates that the first ranked choice cannot be produced, the second choice within the previous task becomes the first choice of production.

Task 4: Consult sponsor — Finally, we need to consult with the sponsor. Cooking the pasta may be on top of the list because of ease of cooking or the personal choice of the cook, followed by baking the cake. However, consultation with the sponsor may result in the cake being the final deliverable.

These tasks carried out under the umbrella of the activity, *evaluate dish,* are followed by other tasks from subsequent activities within the cooking process. The end result of the process is the deliverable — the cooked meal (in this instance, a baked cake).

4.6 THREADS OF A PROCESS

4.6.1 DEFINING A PROCESS-THREAD

An instance of a process is a process-thread. Therefore, a process-thread is a real life representation of the flow of activities within a process. In the formal description of process dimensions, each dimension is made up of a set of activities and these activities are accomplished by means of tasks. However, when an actual process is executed, activities from all dimensions take place — some in parallel and others in a sequence not necessarily described by the neat flow of the activities within the dimensions. These intermingling of activities and tasks within the activities results from the practical implementation of a process. When we follow the sequence of activities in the practical execution of a process, we are following a process-thread. Thus, a process-thread cuts across the three dimensions of the process and result in the production of the deliverable.

4.6.2 IDENTIFYING A PROCESS-THREAD

Each process, as described using the process discipline, can be executed in a number of ways. For example, the cooking process can be accomplished by study-ing the recipe book first and following that with collecting the raw materials, or the other way around. When we want to identify a process-thread, we have to follow it with a "real life" situation. We can step through a process by means of a "sample" and discover the activities and tasks that need to be performed. The "subset" of activities and tasks resulting from this particular instance of the process identifies the process-threads.

4.6.3 NEED FOR A PROCESS-THREAD

Hammer and Champy[7] have argued for the need for multiple versions of the same process. When we were dealing with the mass production market, it was enough to have a standardized process which would result in large numbers of the same product. However, when we deal with specific markets, and more importantly, specific cus-tomers within the markets, it is not enough to have just one standardized process. We need multiple versions of the same process doing different things, depending on who the actor is. Thus, the process-threads satisfy the need to represent different execution sequence of a process depending on the situation in which the process is being executed.

4.6.4 BROKEN PROCESS-THREADS

When a process does not produce the deliverable it is supposed to produce, it is said to be broken. However, when we talk of processes we are actually talking about an implementation perspective. Therefore, when a process does not produce output, it is essential to look at the actual process-thread that has been broken. In case of Y2K hits, the date problem is going to affect a significant number of process-threads, so that they are unable to produce the required deliverables. Even if an organization is not based on the reengineered processes, it is still important to view the organization through the window of processes, and identify process-threads that exists and that are broken as a result of Y2K (or any other problems). These are the threads that will be reengineered first or replaced by process-threads that make use of other "unbroken" threads.

4.7 ITERATIONS IN A DEVELOPMENT PROCESS

4.7.1 NEED FOR ITERATIONS

A development process starts with the first activity and finishes with the final activity at the end of which a deliverable is produced. However, not all activities are performed in one go, and neither are all tasks within the activities completed in the first attempt. The development process proceeds in iterations. This approach also is well supported by the object-oriented approach to software development (see detailed discussion in Chapter 8). Usually there are three iterations to the process: the initial, major, and final iteration (Figure 4.9). A simple development process may not need all three iterations since all activities and tasks may be completed in the first attempt. However, for large and complex development, all three iterations may well be needed. Furthermore, when a process goes through the iterations, it is not necessary for the three dimensions of the process to be in balance. Sometimes the technological

	Initial	Major	Final
Technological	50%	30% (80%)	20% (100%)
Methodological	30%	40% (70%)	30% (100%)
Sociological	20%	30% (50%)	50% (100%)

FIGURE 4.9 Dimensions completed during typical iterations in a process.

dimension may drive the process, at other times the methodological or sociological dimensions. We discuss the value of iterations in a process-based resurrection and how the various activities and tasks within the three dimensions of a process are undertaken during the iterative development process.

4.7.2　INITIAL

The initial iteration would usually involve half or even more than half of the activities of one dimension. If it is a technically driven development, then it is reasonable to expect 50% of the technological activities to be complete at the end of the initial iteration. At this stage the activities of the methodological dimension might be 20% complete and those of the third dimension just starting or about 5% complete. However, it is not essential for a project to be driven by technology. Sociological or "soft" factors also are being accepted as important drivers of a development process. Management patterns,[8] which would enable a project manager to reuse the abstracted knowledge of previous projects, are one of the outputs of this "soft" thinking. If a project is driven by these sociological factors, then it is the sociological activities that will be half complete.

4.7.3　MAJOR

The major iteration comprises completion of at least 80% of the activities of the driving dimension of the process. Thus, for a project that is being driven by the technological dimension, most of the technological activities that deal with the material and tools for the project will be completed at the end of the major iteration. At this stage, many of the methodological activities also will be completed. However, activities from the third dimension (in this example, the sociological dimension) will only be about 30% complete. If on the other hand, the sociological dimension drove the process, then the 80% completion of activities would apply to the sociological set of activities.

4.7.4　FINAL

During the final iteration in a development process, all of the remaining activities are completed. This implies that all tasks within the activities will have been completed and the end result would be the deliverable. The quality assurance and project management activities that continue through all dimensions of a process, also will be completed during the final iteration. Thus, irrespective of the dimension that has driven the project, all activities come to fruition at the end of this iteration and the project enters the maintenance phase (not discussed here).

4.8　MEASUREMENT OF PROCESSES

Description of the process discipline would not be complete unless we discuss a way of measuring and quantifying a process. A metrics for measuring processes as a single unit is presented here, together with the justifications for such a metric.

4.8.1   WHY MEASURE PROCESSES?

Any measurement or metric is essential in providing us a benchmark that can be used by us to make estimates and conduct comparisons. In other words, we use the metric essentially as a means of communicating the quantity of work. A metric is a much better way for comparing and understanding scientific entities than by plain English descriptions that are subject to various interpretations. These are the reasons why it is essential to measure a process as well. Although interpretation and use of the data are still subject to the skill and experience of the person who is using the data, measuring and documenting a process serves many purposes. Some of these include:

- Helping us understand the process better by providing a benchmark.
- Helping others understand the process by enabling easier communication of the process.
- Providing a set of historical data for future estimations of time and cost.
- Providing a set of historical data for refining the efficiency of the process.
- Enabling us to make comparisons between processes or compare the same process executed at two different points in time.

We have already discussed that a process is a model of the reality and not the reality itself. Therefore, a process is necessarily incomplete. Measurement of such a process also will be insufficient in order to describe the complete reality. However, because of the aforementioned uses of metrics, we will attempt to create a metric for the process model.

4.8.2   ARRIVING AT A SINGLE UNIT

These metrics will convert the various elements of the process into a single unit to facilitate estimations and comparisons. Rather than providing conclusive numbers, the metric is meant to provide indicative numbers that can be used in budgeting and project planning activities. They also can be used in refining the processes when applied to different situations. The metrics presented in Table 4.4 is made up of the four elements (actors, deliverables, activities, and tasks) for the cooking process described earlier on.

TABLE 4.4
Arriving at the Measure of the Cooking Process (Total Units)

Description of the Element	Number of Elements in the Process	Weighting per Element	Total Strength: Units for the Element
Actors	2	100	200
Deliverables	1	100	100
Activities	9	10	90
Tasks	40	20	800
Total Units	**52**		**1090**

This measurement of the cooking process is a figure that represents the entire process. However, it also can be used to measure just a dimension of the process. Measuring one dimension and comparing that answer with the other dimensions of a process can provide valuable insight into the manner in which these dimensions influence each other.

4.9 PROCESS SCOPE

A process scope determines the extent of applicability of the process. For example, not every actor described in a process will come into play in a resurrection attempt. A small hit will not require the elaborate preliminary preparations, nor will it require a detailed management of the resurrection. On the other hand, a severe hit for a red organization will require a detailed resurrection work.

A process-thread is an attempt to create an "actual process" from the process discipline. The scope of the process determines the number of process-threads and the types of activities and tasks that will be included in such a process-thread. Process scope can be determined together by the person who has the "dollar" responsibility for the process and the person with the technical know-how (usually the project manager).

4.9.1 DEFINING THE SCOPE

At the beginning of a process, as in case of the cooking example, it is essential to define the scope of the process. This definition includes the following:

- The general size of the process.
- The specific size of the process (as, perhaps, determined by the process metrics).
- The number of process elements required in the process (i.e., the actors, activities, tasks, and deliverables).
- The results expected at the end of each iteration. For example, some projects may have a significant deliverable at the end of the initial iteration, whereas others at the end of the major iteration.

The scope indicates whether the effort required in a process is *small, medium,* or *large.* This understanding is important in creating the process-threads for the implementation of a particular process.

Astute project management requires the project manager to carry the scope of project in his sleep. The scope of the project should be a continuous and dynamic entity that forms a continuous understanding of the project in the mind of the project manager. Re-scoping and de-scoping of the project need to be accepted as part of the project management alternatives to be exercised if the need arises.

4.9.2 INFLUENCING THE PROCESS-THREADS

The alternatives available in determining the scope of the project can be supported by (but not driven by) the process-threads. Given the cooking process, a typical

TABLE 4.5
A Process-Thread Based on Small Scoped Cooking

Description of the Element	Number of Elements in the Process	Weighting per Element	Total Strength: Units for the Element
Actors	1	100	100
Deliverables	1	100	100
Activities	5	10	50
Tasks	25	20	500
Total Units	**32**		**750**

process-thread for a restricted scope of resurrection would be as shown in Table 4.5. The table shows a different number of elements within the process (although note that the "weighting per element" still remains the same). This is so because if, for example, we are baking the cake for ourselves we may drop some activities and some tasks within the activities that might be necessary for a formal baking. This will determine the new metrics and the effort required in cooking. A situation different to this one would be where the cake is baked for a marriage reception. This would require two or three chefs and more weighting on the activities and tasks performed during the baking. The situation of a "take away" cake would be different still. Creation and measurement of the process-thread will depend on the perspective of the user (i.e., whether you are the cook or the customer).

4.10 PROCESS MAPPINGS

What we have discussed so far is a detailed process model. This model has applicability in many development projects, including the resurrection project for a Y2K-hit enterprise. The two main areas of interest to us in applying the process model are the software development process and the business process. We have described the three dimensions of the process model. Each of these three dimensions of the process applies to any process-based work such as software and business. What is presented here is the applicability of the process model to software and business processes and their mapping.

4.10.1 A SOFTWARE PROCESS

A software process is the process that deals with the development of software. Yourdon[9] describes a software process as a "system for building systems." Therefore, he further argues that it makes good sense to use familiar modeling tools such as data flow diagrams, entity-relationship diagrams, object-oriented diagrams, etc., as the basis for modeling a software process. Thus, analysis, design, and programming would form a major part of the software process. Being a process, it is easy to model the software process on the process discipline described in this chapter. Thus, a software process will be made up of the three dimensions of a process. There will be the technological, the methodological, and the sociological dimensions to a software process. For example, the development of object-oriented software programs for a banking application would be made up of the following:

- The intricacies of the software language used.
- The methodology used in development of the system.
- The morale and motivation of the programmers, testers, and project managers.

4.10.2 A BUSINESS PROCESS

Similar to the software process described above is the business process. The business process deals with the process-threads related to the three dimensions in conducting the business. Consider the three dimensions of a process model that apply to the business process of opening a bank account. These dimensions include:

- The technical know-how of opening a bank account (e.g., the rules and regulations of account opening).
- The method of opening an account (e.g., should the ATM card be issued first or the minimum cash required to open an account accepted first).
- The transaction between the teller and the customer forms the third dimension of the process model, vis-à-vis the sociological dimension.

4.10.3 SOFTWARE–BUSINESS RELATIONSHIP

The software and the business processes described in the previous section have specific domains from where they are derived. The business processes essentially come from the problem domain. They deal with the boundary between the organization and society. These business processes are supported in their functioning by the software systems that are delivered by using the software processes. Thus, the software processes derive from the solution domain. This is because the software processes are meant to provide solutions to the business processes.

Needless to say, the distinction is not as clear-cut as described here when we deal with real life business and software processes. Many software processes form an integral part of the business of the organization. This is true especially if you are a consulting firm whose business processes deal with the sales of the software processes that are used by its consultants and developers. However, in the businesses that are described here as Y2K hits, we are considering the software processes as providing the solutions that support the business processes dealing with the customer.

4.10.4 MAPPING WITH THE PROCESS DISCIPLINE

The business processes as well as the software processes are made up of the three dimensions of the process discipline. These processes, however, are not executed independent of each other. They continue to exist together and, occasionally, a software process that is supposed to be a part of the solution domain may actually be a part of the problem domain. For example, the entire discussion of Y2K, which

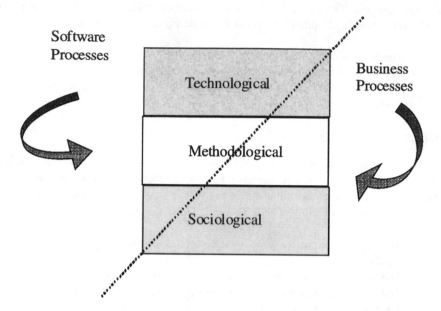

FIGURE 4.10   Mapping the software and business processes with the process discipline.

is now accepted as a business problem, has its origins in software. Therefore, it is the software process that has to be understood and refined as much as the business process when we discuss the survival and resurrection of the organization after a Y2K hit.

The difference between the software and the business processes is that the software process tends to have a larger technological dimensions *compared with* the business process. It is important to note that, as independent processes, the business or software process may have the three dimensions in balance. It is only when the software process is compared with the business process that the technological dimension seems to play a bigger role in the software development. For example, the choice of programming language may be more important to a programmer, whereas the choice of *natural* language (words spoken) is perhaps more important to the teller. This mapping is shown in Figure 4.10.

4.11 KEY POINTS

1. Modeling serves two important functions, (1) understanding the reality that exists out there and (2) creating a new reality.
2. White clouds provide a model for a process. This model can be applied in creating process-based enterprises in the new millennium.
3. A process model is different from a traditional hierarchical model because it cuts across the boundaries of the hierarchy within the organization, and serves its real purpose — that of providing service to its customers.

4. A process has three dimensions — technological (deals with "what"), methodological (deals with "how"), and sociological (deals with "who"). These dimensions are processes themselves.
5. Processes are made up of process elements. The four major elements of a process are the actors, activities, tasks, and deliverables.
6. An instance of a process is a process-thread. This is the real-life invocation of a process.
7. The scope of a process determines whether the work performed within a process will be small, medium, or large. This scope of the process provides an good understanding of the process elements that will be required for the process-threads.
8. Processes are driven by iterations (initial, major, final) and activities and tasks within the process dimensions may be repeated within these iterations.

4.12 NOTES

The model of the white clouds, as applicable to the resurrection process, occurred to me when I was returning from the OOPSLA (Object-Oriented Programming Systems Languages and Applications) Conference in 1996, as I flew from San Francisco to the Olympic 2000 city of Sydney. The journey is entirely over the Pacific Ocean and there is hardly any land in sight. Formed by the unhindered marriage of the sunrays with the water, these white clouds stretch in abundance for thousands of miles, as far as the eye can see or the plane can fly. They represent a process whose growth is relaxed yet certain, providing an ideal model for the process-based work that I was doing. The other interesting aspect of this journey was that you pass over the International Date Line. It is a funny experience of growing a day younger or a day older (depending on the direction of your flight) literally within seconds.

The cooking example is further developed from a simple yet helpful example in describing a process by Younessi and Henderson-Sellers.[10]

4.13 REFERENCES

1. Osho, *My Way: The Way of the White Clouds,* 1978, Element — Dorset, Massachusetts, Queensland, from the Introduction.
2. Shelton, R., Enterprise object modelling: knowing what we know, *Hotline on Object-Oriented Technology,* 3: 3, 1, 3, 1992.
3. Odell, J., 1996, Object-oriented methodologies, *Report on Object Analysis and Design,* 2: 5, 5–8, 53, Jan–Feb 1996.
4. Sommerville, I., *Software Engineering,* Addison-Wesley, Reading, MA, 1989.
5. Henderson-Sellers, B. and Edwards, J. M., The fountain model for object-oriented system development, *Obj. Mag.,* 3: 2, 71–79, 1993.
6. Hammer, M. and Champy, J., *Reengineering the Corporation,* Allen and Unwin, St. Leonards NSW, Australia, 1994.
7. Ibid., 55.
8. Coplien, J., *Technology of Object-Oriented Languages and Systems,* Keynote address, TOOLS25, Melbourne, Australia, November 1997, IEEE.
9. Yourdon, E., *Rise and Resurrection of the American Programmer,* Yourdon Press, Upper Saddle River, NJ, 1998, 94.
10. Younessi, H. and Henderson-Sellers, B., *Obj. Mag.,* 7: 8, 38–42, 1997.

5 The Y2K Resurrection Process

It is particularly striking how processes that occur on a microscopic scale — say, in nuclear physics — seem to be fine-tuned to produce interesting and varied effects on a much larger scale — for example, in astrophysics.

Prof. Paul Davies in *The Mind of God*[1]

Abstract   This chapter starts with a discussion of the core concept of the resurrection philosophy. There are a number of ways in which companies can be resurrected. We present an argument for the resurrection process to be driven by the technological dimension, since that was the dimension that caused the problem in the first place. The likely steps in the resurrection process and their probable timing of events follow these arguments. These timings of resurrection have a rough correlation with the degree of Y2K preparedness of the enterprise. The "process discipline" developed in the previous chapter is used to describe the resurrection process for a Y2K-hit enterprise — through the preliminary activities and the three core dimensions of technology, methodology, and sociology. These dimensions are processes in themselves and they form a major part of the discussion in the remaining chapters of this book. In this chapter, we discuss in greater detail the preliminary activities of the resurrection process which include budgeting, nominating a "resurrection champion," scoping the resurrection process, highlighting the strategic advantages of the resurrection attempt, and mustering political will to go through the process. Finally, how the resurrection process will proceed through the initial, major, and final iterations is discussed along with a "sample" resurrection project plan.

5.1 THE Y2K RESURRECTION PHILOSOPHY

We start this chapter with the philosophical background of resurrection. How can we describe resurrection in a nutshell? What is the role of the various dimensions of a process discipline in resurrection? How are the activities and tasks within the process discipline implemented in the resurrection process? These topics together with the broader applicability of the resurrection process are discussed in this section.

5.1.1 CORE CONCEPT BEHIND RESURRECTION

Figure 5.1 shows a simplistic structure of the software systems of a Y2K-hit organization. Typically, these are legacy systems written in a procedural language and

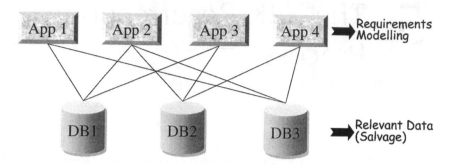

FIGURE 5.1   Core concept behind resurrection.

accessing a hierarchical or an earlier version of a relational database. DB1 and DB2 have been converted during an earlier "prevention" effort (an orange or a yellow level of preparedness). Application App3, which accesses database DB1 and DB2 (which might be a file or a set of tables) is affected by Y2K. Perhaps there is a problem with the sorting logic within App3, wherein data are not appearing in the right sequence. The issues worth noting in this scenario and its repercussions are as follows:

- The sorting logic within App3 is noncompliant. Therefore, it fails to consider the 4-digit year supplied by the databases DB1 and DB2. Instead, it takes the first 2 digits and converts them into year for the purpose of sorting.
- And/or, it stores the sort from DB1 into DB2, thus corrupting DB2 in the process.
- Or any other combination of events that leads to App3, DB1, and DB2, being hit by Y2K.

In Figure 5.1 the application App3 and the database DB1 and DB2 are initially affected. The reason why, say, App4 may not be initially affected is that it may be a monthly or a quarterly accounting run that hasn't been executed yet. When App4 accesses DB2, it has the potential of crashing, as it will start dealing with the Y2K-affected data in DB2. If the application App4 doesn't physically stop, then it is likely to use that data for its quarterly totals and store those totals in DB3. This leads to DB3 being corrupt. App2 can be a reporting program that uses data from all three databases, leading to total Y2K-hit fireworks within the system. App1 can join in the "painful fireworks" depending on its logic and the data it accesses for its processing.

The standard response for this problem will be to fix the logic in App3 and the data in DB1 and DB2. Our assumption is that when this organization was hit it was at an orange or yellow level, wherein it has already started with some investigations and/or fixes for the Y2K problem. Therefore, the approach it is likely to take is to continue with the fixes of DB2 and App3.

The arguments throughout this text are based on the presumption that there are many advantages to be gained by *not* rushing in and providing a quick fix to the date problem when it occurs in the new millennium. Instead, the suggested aim is to resurrect from the Y2K hit and produce a process-based system that will provide many of the strategic benefits discussed in Chapter 3 to the resurrecting organization. Thus, the resurrection process for the Y2K-hit system shown in Figure 5.1 would be

- Following a process-based approach to resurrection.
- Dissecting the applications (starting with App3 and proceeding with the rest of the Apps) to determine their existing and "hit" functionality.
- Salvaging the functionality that is relevant — although we accept that retrieving requirements for the new system from COBOL logic is very difficult (discussed in detail in Chapter 7, Section 7.5).
- Writing the Requirements Model for the new systems by bringing together (1) the salvaged options from the Y2K-hit applications and (2) business processes for the new organization.
- Considering the architectural issues in resurrecting the Y2K-hit system.
- Dissecting the databases (starting with DB2) of the Y2K-hit system in order to identify data that are still relevant to the new millennium.
- Salvaging only the data that are relevant and the data that are needed by the new applications.
- Validating and verifying the entire exercise by means of quality assurance activities including those of thorough testing.

The result is a process-based organization that has derived the advantage of the new functionality, as well as sleek data. Thus, the basic philosophy is to dissect the "hit" system, identify the salvageable entities, produce new requirements and new architecture, and complete the resurrection.

5.1.2   THE DRIVING DIMENSION OF RESURRECTION

The core concept behind the resurrection effort suggests that there is a significant amount of technical work involved in dissection and salvaging activities, followed by the reengineering of processes. In this resurrection effort, all three dimensions of the process are involved. However, the types of activities that take place within these dimensions are different. How do they differ?

The Y2K problem started off as a technical issue with the 2-digit date field within the company's systems starting to cause the problem. As the problem percolates throughout the systems, each of the three dimensions of the organization are affected* as the business comes to a halt. This is shown in Figure 5.2, wherein the movement of the pendulum within each of the three layers indicates the extent of activities taking place within the dimensions during the Y2K problem.

---

* Albeit unknowingly at this stage because the affected business may not be based on process discipline.

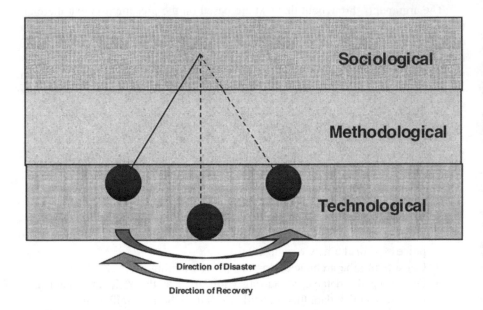

FIGURE 5.2   Movement in the three dimensions during disaster and recovery.

The movement was the maximum within the technological dimension. The major events in the Y2K crash happened in the technical areas of the company. For example, the systems could not handle the input or the output of the date-related data. Perhaps the systems were unable to store the data correctly. The logic based on the date field within the software systems suffered. All these aspects of the date problem are technical and they mostly occurred within the computer languages or databases of the legacy systems.

The manner in which an organization worked (its methodology) had lesser responsibility in causing the problem. And in most likelihood the systems that are hit are so old that the method used in their development was mostly home grown. These methods were so specific to the software shop that built the product that the nuances of a particular method could not be blamed for the Y2K crash. The changes in the methodological dimensions will relate to the way in which the organization develops its systems while it resurrects. However, that modification is not the same as the radical change we envisage in the technological dimension of the organization. Therefore, the methodological dimension in the middle of the pendulum in Figure 5.2 indicates lesser movement in this dimension of the Y2K resurrection process.

The sociological dimension of an organization's process certainly cannot be blamed for the Y2K problem. Although sociological factors contribute to the success or failure of a project, in the case of a Y2K disaster they were not the cause of the organization's troubles. Sociological factors had the least influence, if any, on the Y2K disaster. It is more appropriate to say that the "sociology" of the organization bears the effect of the Y2K problem rather than being its cause. The top end of the pendulum, which has the minimum movement, is a representative of this minimal sociological cause for the Y2K problem. When the resurrection process commences, it is essential to "hold on" to the sociological dimension. Sociology does play an important role in the resurrection of an organization, but it is the one that provides the stability — like the hinge of a pendulum — while the technology is changed and the methodology is modified.

Thus, the dimensions of the resurrection process are influenced in the same proportion in which the dimensions themselves have caused the Y2K problem. The philosophy of resurrection, therefore, is driven by the "swing of the pendulum" in the three dimensions. The movement of the pendulum in the sociological dimension is the minimum, indicating that sociology is not undergoing radical change. The activities within the sociological dimension of the resurrection process are carried out by (and for) the people that are already there in the organization. The sociological dimension provides the crucial hook or stability on which the resurrection process can hang. Methodologies for development of systems, as well as for serving the business needs of the organization, will undergo some modifications indicated by the greater movement of the pendulum (compared to that in the sociological dimension) in both the disaster and the recovery direction. The technological dimension, as shown by the maximum swing of the pendulum, will require a large amount of work and it will be the driving dimension of the Y2K resurrection process.

5.1.3 APPLICABILITY OF THE RESURRECTION PROCESS

Although it is the Y2K problem that has initiated this discussion, we argue that the resurrection process has a more universal applicability than that of surviving a Y2K hit. When we talk of resurrection, we are discussing the rebuilding of the organization. This rebuilding can take place when its systems are affected by Y2K. It also may take place when the organization decides it has had enough of the old technology it has used for so long and that it needs to do something about the mounting competition from the market. There can be a variety of reasons that go beyond the Y2K hit when an organization decides to resurrect. Many of the ideas and concepts expressed in this discussion would apply to any resurrection exercise irrespective of what has caused the resurrection to occur. Figure 5.3 shows how the resurrection process forms a curative wrapper around the Y2K disaster. The wrapper would remain the same if, say, the problem were a broken process-thread due to age-old technology. This is possible because in resurrection we don't just fix the date. We have a process map for many other types of development work. However, if the cause was not Y2K, then the driving dimension of resurrection may be different to the technological dimension. This will change the extent of activities that take place within each of the dimensions that were shown in Figure 5.2, but the overall wrapper of the resurrection process around the cause will still remain valid as shown in Figure 5.3.

5.2 STEPS IN Y2K RESURRECTION

Having discussed the philosophical background of resurrection, we now consider the sequence and timings of events in the resurrection process at a higher level.

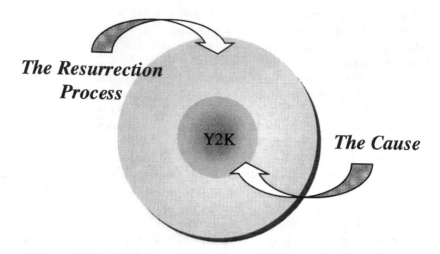

A large amount of the "Resurrection Process" would
still apply even if the "Cause" were other than Y2K.

FIGURE 5.3   Applicability of the resurrection process.

These events would later be converted into concrete project plans for the resurrection
process.

5.2.1   SEQUENCE OF EVENTS IN RESURRECTION

Theoretically, a resurrection process can start as soon as an organization discovers
it is having a date problem. This discovery can happen over a wide range of time.
Many organizations are already experiencing the Y2K problems much before the D-
day of 1/1/2000 (some example firecrackers in Chapter 1 describe this). Others may
experience the problems after a few months or even years after the arrival of the
new millennium. The resurrection process will depend on many factors including
the timing of the discovery of the Y2K problem. Therefore, the discussion on
sequence and timing of events in the resurrection process cannot be very precise as
far as the actual dates are concerned for many organizations. We consider the
sequence and timings as an example that would provide us with an idea of what is
likely to happen as we proceed with resurrection.

The sequence of events in the resurrection process (Figure 5.4) begins with the
same primary question that was asked towards the end of the Y2K explosion: "Are
we still breathing?" If the answer to this basic question is in the negative, the entire
discussion on resurrection becomes purely academic. In order to resurrect, it is
essential that the organization is at least at a stage where it has enough financial
strength left to do something about its problems (which are now more than just
fixing the date). Even if the management does not go through a rigorous process in
ascertaining the financial state of the company, it is a question whether the company
is in a position to resurrect or not (i.e., whether it has the money for the resurrection

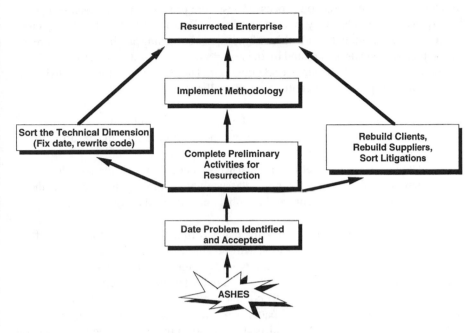

FIGURE 5.4   Sequence of events in Y2K resurrection.

process). This question derives from the fact that the other alternative is that the company is already in the hands of the receiver, or taken over, or insolvent.

Once the organization becomes aware of its financial ability to resurrect, it begins the process of resurrection by identifying and accepting the date problem. This is not the technical testing and locating of date, but a very general higher level acceptance of the problem. Therefore, this acceptance of the date problem is not specified as a separate activity within this process. If the organization had problems other than the Y2K date problem, then those problems need to be recognized and accepted by the senior management of the company.

Having realized that it is still breathing and that it has a high-level idea of the Y2K problem, the organization starts putting the resurrection work within the process discipline. In order to draft its resurrection plans, though, the organization needs to know the timings and resources available for resurrection. This is partly determined and influenced by the intensity of the hit. In Section 2.6 (Figure 2.5) we have described the intensity of hit as a function of the level of preparedness of the organization. Figure 2.3 described the color codes indicating the level of preparedness for the Y2K problem. This intensity of hit influences the extent of resurrection work or scope of resurrection.

Having had this brief understanding of its position, the organization proceeds with the "preliminary" activities. These preliminary and core activities of the resurrection process are described later on. These preliminary activities "kick start" the resurrection process followed by the three dimensions of the core resurrection process. These are the technological, the methodological, and the sociological dimensions of the resurrection process. These core processes are not necessarily run in sequence. They also may not be run in parallel. They follow the white cloud model and are executed in all three dimensions according to the process-threads. These process-threads are created by the resurrecting organization and they are based on the needs of specific resurrection situations. The three respective dimensions of the resurrection process concentrate on the following:

- The technological activities handle the core date problem.
- The methodological activities bring the discipline into the resurrection process.
- The technical and methodological work is coupled with the sociological activities that handle the people issues within the organization and the confidence of the clients and suppliers outside of the organization.

As a result of the activities taking place within the three dimensions of the resurrection process, the organization will be able to re-establish contacts with its lost clients and bring them back within its folds. If the chain of suppliers was broken due to the date disaster, then it will be restored after the core activities within the resurrection process come closer to completion. The Y2K-hit enterprise also may find itself in the middle of a legal battle. Creation of the resurrected enterprise also will involve sorting out all the legal issues related to the date problem. Finally, the end result of the overall resurrection process is an organization that is process-oriented, flexible, and customer-oriented; essentially a reengineered organization that offers more and gains more than what it was doing when the date problem struck.

5.2.2 PROBABLE TIMING OF EVENTS IN RESURRECTION

A probable set of timings for the occurrence of the sequence of events described in the previous section is provided in Table 5.1. These timings indicate the resurrection timings of a "typical" medium-to-large organization. The timings shown in the table indicate that the Y2K resurrection process for a typical organization is likely to take around 1 year to complete. This 1-year resurrection process will be affected by the intensity of the Y2K hit, resulting in a skewing factor similar to the one described in the sequence and timings of Y2K explosions (Section 2.4). The difference is that when the organization was being hit, better Y2K preparedness was delaying the effect of the hit, whereas in resurrection, that same level of preparedness helps in hastening the steps in resurrection. Thus, the skewing factor is a function of the intensity of the Y2K hit, which is itself a function of the level of preparedness of the organization for Y2K. In case of explosion, the higher intensity hastens the effect of the Y2K hit, whereas in resurrection the higher the intensity the slower is the resurrection.

5.3 ADVANTAGE OF PREPAREDNESS IN Y2K RESURRECTION

We had described the six stages of the level of preparedness of the organization in Figure 2.3. Out of those six stages the last two stages of Blue and Gold are the

TABLE 5.1
Sequence and Timings of Resurrection

Sequence of Events	Probable Timings
1. Date-related problem identified and accepted (customers affected)	April–May 2000
2. Complete the preliminaries to resurrection	May–June 2000
3. Timeline based on level of preparedness	July 2000
4. Sort the technical dimension (including dissection and salvage options)	July–August 2000
5. Implement the methodology	August–October 2000
6. Rebuild client confidence	November–December 2000
7. Rebuild supplier confidence	November–December 2000
8. Sort litigation	January–February 2001
9. Complete resurrection	March 2001

ones that are least likely to be hit by Y2K. However, if they are hit then the chances of them getting back on their feet quickly are very high. The remaining four colors of Green, Yellow, Orange, and Red are the likely stages where organizations will be when they are hit. The amount of time and effort that will be required for organizations at each of these stages (or levels of preparedness) to resurrect from the Y2K hits is shown in Figure 5.5. It would be worthwhile considering the advantages that these organizations derive in terms of their levels of preparedness when they are hit and, as a result, when they attempt resurrection. Furthermore, it is important for organizations to start realizing their levels of preparedness *even*

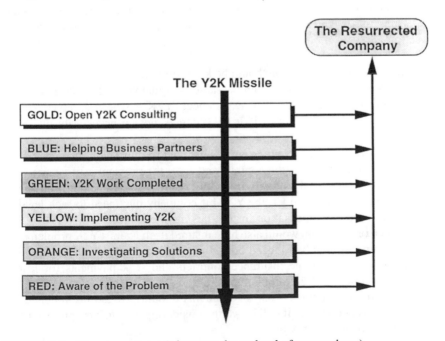

FIGURE 5.5   Time to resurrect (advantage due to level of preparedness).

before they are actually hit. Understanding their level of preparedness provides these organizations with an opportunity to start improving on their preparedness for the Y2K problem — in other words climbing the color codes and going from red to orange to yellow to green. For each of this level of preparedness, we consider the specific advantages we derive when we resurrect and how this level of preparedness can be improved.

5.3.1 GREEN

The green organization is the one that has completed its work on the Y2K project. If the Y2K fixing work has been carried out in a methodical and meticulous way, then the likelihood of the organization being affected is very low. However, it is still possible that the organization is hit by Y2K (see Section 2.3). Not only is the possibility of a Y2K hit very low for a green organization but it is hoped that the resurrection time and effort would also be minimal. This is so because:

- The relevant areas of code and data that are affected are likely to be known.
- The organization already has a Y2K-aware culture.
- It has experience in fixing the date problem.
- Knows the people who have worked on fixing the problem.

Overall, one would expect a green level organization to resurrect from a Y2K hit very quickly and restore its business back to normal. The scope of resurrection for a green organization should be kept minimal. Thus, the scope would not include all the detailed activities and tasks as described in the resurrection process. Some of the issues that a green level organization should consider to ensure a quick resurrection are

- The scope of resurrection should be kept minimal.
- If reasonably competent, retain the same staff that worked on the Y2K fix in order to capitalize on their experience. (Y2K has been accepted as a "big" problem. Thus, even if it fails, it may not be necessarily due to incompetence.)
- If the work was done by an external consultant (or third party) then ensure that the vendor honors the contract and fixes the problem as it occurs.
- Investigate the legal obligations of the third party. Depending on the provisions of the contract, the Y2K-hit company may need to seek legal help to secure compensation for lost business, etc.
- A green organization would also have insured itself against Y2K problems. If the organization had indeed bought an insurance policy, this would be the time to revisit the insurance contracts and seek payments for lost business due to a Y2K problem.
- The current thinking is that governments should provide tax relief for Y2K prevention work. It will be worth considering any such tax provisions for Y2K resurrection work.

5.3.2 YELLOW

Since the yellow level organization is the one that is still in the process of implementing Y2K, some of its systems might already be converted whereas others might not be. Thus, there is likely to be a mismatch between applications within the organization — some converted and others not. This mismatch also is possible between the data and the application. Thus, if the data of the organization have been ported from 2 digits to 4 digits but the applications are not, then that is likely to lead to a Y2K crash. It is also possible that the data and the applications were converted but were not tested, resulting in a Y2K crash. Some of the issues that a yellow organization should consider (and derive benefits from) when it works on the Y2K resurrection are

- Identify and log the details of the Y2K crash. The crash that has occurred will be a "real life" crash and its investigation should form part of the dissection activity as described in Chapter 7, Section 7.5.
- Do not continue with the attempts at prevention; they are no longer relevant in the new millennium.
- Commit the resources that were used in prevention work into the resurrection work.
- The scope of the resurrection should be detailed enough to enable the organization to derive the strategic benefits of resurrection.
- Include all the major activities and tasks from the three dimensions of resurrection.
- Take care of the internal and external sociological factors; inform employees internally of the situation and appeal for support. Inform business partners externally and, if relevant, seek their support.

5.3.3 ORANGE

The chances of an orange organization being hit by Y2K are very high. We had categorized an organization as orange if it was still in the process of investigating the Y2K solution. Since the organization was at investigation stage there is very little to salvage from the Y2K prevention effort. Some of the issues that need to be considered by an orange organization in order to derive whatever benefits it can from its level of preparedness (!) are

- Since the orange level organization will have considered the ways in which it would be affected by the date problem, its dissection activity should start with the information gathered previously on the ways in which the date problem will crop up within the organization.
- No more effort should be spend in planning for prevention (note that this organization was still at a planning stage and was trying to work out how to fix the date problem when the disaster struck).
- Scope of resurrection should be major — including all preliminary and core activities.

- All resources, including time, budgets, and people who were being drafted for the Y2K prevention work, should now be dedicated to resurrection.
- Seeking internal support as well as informing business partners of the situation with the duel aims of soliciting their support and maintaining their trust should be done at the earliest.
- Legal council and help should be sought as a matter of priority — especially if the lack of compliance by the organization appears to be a likely cause for legal liability.

5.3.4   RED

An organization at the red level of preparedness is just aware of the possibilities of Y2K hits. Therefore, there is very little difference between such an organization and the one that is effectively not aware of the problem at all. Apart from the small differences in the organizational structures (e.g., rigidity, bulkiness, hierarchical), there is no major difference between a red level organization and an organization that is starting its Y2K prevention activities from scratch. Therefore, all aspects of resurrection apply to an organization at this level of preparedness. In terms of level of preparedness, following are the issues that should be considered during resurrection:

- The major asset this organization has is its clients and its suppliers. Therefore, the first and immediate consideration for this organization should be to make a sincere attempt to hold on to its business partners.
- The organization should commit itself to resurrection. This commitment also should be made public by providing the business partners with the resurrection project plan.
- Another major asset of this organization is its sociological aspect — its employees, its people. There will be an urgent need to seek the confidence and trust of the employees.
- This is an organization that will go through a complete technological revolution as we described in the resurrection process. All the strategic advantages should be exploited by this organization in its resurrection process.

If the organization identifies itself as a red-level organization, then it will have taken one important step towards its preparedness for Y2K. Just being able to identify itself at a particular level of preparedness for Y2K would require the organization to go through the internal "self examination" process as discussed in Section 2.3. Having identified its preparedness level (as red), the organization can make serious attempts to move to a higher level of preparedness, if the disaster has not already struck.

5.4   DESCRIBING THE Y2K RESURRECTION PROCESS

We have discussed the core philosophy behind resurrection, the sequence and timings of resurrection, and the advantages an organization can derive because of its level of preparedness when it resurrects. We now describe the process of resurrection including its preliminary and core activities.

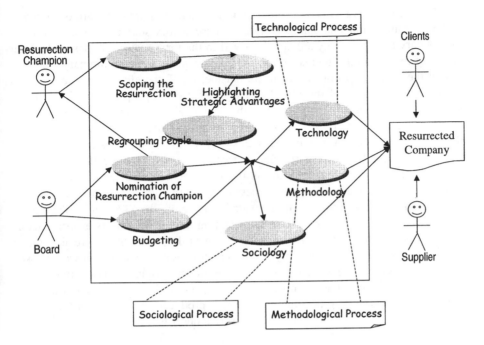

FIGURE 5.6 The resurrection process based on process discipline.

5.4.1 THE RESURRECTION PROCESS

Figure 5.6 depicts the resurrection process within the framework of the process discipline. This resurrection process translates the resurrection philosophy into concrete actionable items. Essentially, the resurrection process is made up of two groups of activities:

1. The preliminary activities that need to be completed before the resurrection work can begin.
2. The three core activities of resurrection — the technology, methodology, and sociology of resurrection.

It is worth noting the following with regards to the activities within the resurrection process:

- At a micro level, the activities themselves are processes. Therefore, the three formal activities are eventually expanded into full blown processes of their own.
- In practice, the transition from preliminary to core activities is not watertight. Thus, if some of the preliminary activities overlap the core activities, it still does not amount to violation of the process discipline.
- In a smaller scoped resurrection process, the preliminary activities may appear to verge on the sociological dimension.

The main actors involved in the preliminary activities are the board of directors and the resurrection champion. Although these actors start their work with the preliminary activities, they are also involved in the three main activities in the later stages of resurrection. The reason for their involvement in the preliminary activities is that they are the people who run the business and, therefore, they are the ones who are hurt because of the Y2K hit. They are also the people who will have the power within the organization to make the decisions on the time and amount to be spent on resurrection. Therefore, the people who run the business are involved in the preliminary decision-making activities of a resurrection process.

The end result of the resurrection process is the deliverable called *resurrected company*. The resurrected company is the reengineered organization for the new millennium. Thus, the resurrection process provides the strategic advantage that goes way beyond the date-fixing attempts made by us before the Y2K hump. This resurrection process delivers a new look organization that deals with its external actors (the clients and the suppliers) by keeping them in the center of the process, rather than at the end. This will inevitably result in restoration of contacts that were broken earlier on when the organization was hit. The process discipline-based approach to Y2K resurrection will have a more positive impact on the external actors involved with the organization's process than the effect produced by the uncoordinated and frantic activities of the schizophrenic enterprise described in Chapter 2.

5.4.2 PRELIMINARY AND CORE ACTIVITIES IN RESURRECTION

As their name suggests, preliminary activities are responsible for preparing the organization for the core processes within resurrection. This preparation may start as soon as it is identified that the organization has been hit by Y2K. However, the organization need not wait for an explosion before it starts resurrection.

Revisiting the sequence and timings of the Y2K explosion described in Section 2.4 indicates that the explosions start off as a technical problem (in the given example in Table 2.1, it is in January 2000). For a typical medium intensity hit, the problem will influence the ability of the organization to serve its customers within a month or two. This inability of the organization to serve its customers starts getting reflected in the business that is being lost to the competitors.

As soon as any of the above events indicate that the organization is going to go through a detailed hit and that it will result in a medium-to-severe hit, it will be advisable to start with the preliminary activities of the resurrection process. Awareness of the possibility of a Y2K hit and the recognition and acceptance of the initial events within the sequence of explosion as the date problem starts to unfold within the organization, are extremely important in getting the preliminary activities going. Once the preliminary activities have commenced, the time and effort required in resurrecting and the overall losses that the business will suffer in the mean time will depend on the level of preparedness of the organization.

As a part of the preliminary activities, the main actor (the board of director) nominates the resurrection champion, who is then responsible for coordinating the overall resurrection effort. Note that these preliminary activities do not include detailed technical work at this stage. This is because, unless the organization has the financial strength and the socio-political will to resurrect, it is meaningless to start working on the technology.

The preliminary activities that will initiate the resurrection process are as follows:

- Budgeting — involves the initial decision of availability of funds for the resurrection process to proceed.
- Nomination of a Resurrection Champion — the board nominates a senior person to oversee the resurrection attempt.
- Ascertaining the scope of the resurrection — the extent of work required in the process. The scope influences the process-threads for resurrection and the number of activities and tasks involved in resurrection.
- Highlighting the Strategic Advantages — essentially "selling" the advantages of the resurrection process to the senior management of the company. This also will sociologically prepare the technical team for the resurrection process.
- Regrouping Employees — employees concentrate their efforts in getting the organization back on its feet in the shortest possible time. Herein, we also work on creating an atmosphere that is politically conducive to the resurrection process.

Once the preliminary activities of resurrection are completed, the core activities of resurrection can start. These are the activities within the technological, methodological, and sociological dimensions of the resurrection processes. These three dimensions, which are processes themselves, form the backbone of the resurrection attempt. They are described in detail in the next six chapters. In this chapter we only discuss the preliminary activities. This is followed by a discussion of the iterative nature of the resurrection process and how the activities from the three dimensions of the process can be put in an iterative project plan.

5.5 BUDGETING

Although the resurrection process starts with the question, "Are we still breathing?," it is in this preliminary activity of budgeting that the figures for the resurrection process are put together. The people involved in this decision making would primarily be the board of directors including the chief executive office (CEO) and the chief financial officer (CFO). This is because the entire decisionmaking at this stage is related to the business aspect of the resurrection process.

5.5.1 Ensure Ability to Spend

We mentioned earlier on that in order to contemplate resurrection, one of the important characteristics of the "hit" organization is that it still exists. If it has already "crossed the red" by completely exploding so that it is financially no longer solvent, then it will not be in a position to make any decision regarding its future. The share prices of the company are likely to have reached the panic levels and the company is most probably in the hands of the receivers. Therefore, the surviving executives of the company may not be in a legal position to make any decisions. However, we assume at this stage that the company is still breathing and that the board of the company still has the ability to use the remaining resources of the company in order to attempt resurrection.

5.5.2 ALLOCATE BUDGETS

Once the company understands its solvency, it has to decide on the amount that it intends to spend, or the amount it *can* spend, on the resurrection effort and allocate the budgets accordingly. Arriving at and allocating the resurrection budget has a different goal than the Y2K prevention budget. The goal of the Y2K resurrection effort is to rebuild the systems. Therefore, the budgets have to cater to the software development effort including the initial effort at dissecting a Y2K-hit system as well.

Even if the preliminary activities have started early enough, there will still be a need to provide for further losses in the business before the resurrection exercise will start producing the positive results. Therefore, the budgets for resurrection not only include the amount needed to rebuild the system, but also include the potential business losses.

The positive aspect of resurrection is that it is not simply fixing the date problem. The resurrection process attempts to recreate an organization that is "process-based." Thus, unlike the budgeting exercise for prevention, wherein the organization spends only to stay in business, the resurrection budget also is a budget to win new business for the organization. Furthermore, because the system is rebuilt, it may not be necessary to budget for the type of testing demanded of a Y2K prevention project. Judicious use of the dissection and salvage activity (described in Section 7.5) leads to considerable reduction in the time and amount needed for performing the date-specific tests. The savings can be used to thoroughly test all aspects of the resurrecting system.

The budgeting activity also will be influenced by the fact that the resurrection process is not accomplished in one go. It will be an iterative process and the budget will have to be divided into each of the possible iterations during resurrection. Overall, the resurrection budget is supported by the strategic advantages discussed in Chapter 3.

5.5.3 ASSIGNING BUDGETARY RESPONSIBILITY

The budgets are decided in consultation with the person who has the financial experience of working with the company. The person who is made responsible for the resurrection budget should have the following skills:

- The ability to successfully use the budget.
- Able to report on the progress of the process to the board.
- Able to monitor the resurrection process based on its iterative nature.

The person who ultimately takes the budgetary responsibility for resurrection is the resurrection champion. Thus, along with the budgetary activity, another activity that takes place as a part of the preparation for resurrection is the nomination of the resurrection champion.

5.6 NOMINATION OF THE "RESURRECTION CHAMPION"

Figure 5.6 shows the activity of Nomination of the Resurrection Champion as flowing from the board. Along with assigning the budgets, the board also is involved in the nomination of the resurrection champion. Modeled on the white clouds, the resurrection process has no difficulty in continuing with the two activities in parallel. This activity produces the resurrection champion. Therefore, the flow of the process is pointing from this activity to the resurrection champion in the Figure 5.6. Once the resurrection champion is nominated, she takes over the responsibility of the overall resurrection process.

5.6.1 IDENTIFY POTENTIAL CANDIDATES

An ideal resurrection champion is the person who is responsible for the business aspect of the company. Although technology is the cause of the date problem, the effect is felt by the business. Furthermore, the solution we are discussing also is having an effect on the business (as it is not just fixing the date, but producing a system based on reengineered processes). Therefore, the person in charge of resurrection has to have sufficient business interest in the resurrection work.

It is also a person with sufficient financial interest in the company. For example, the CEO of the company who also has shares in the company would be the ideal person to handle the job of resurrection. In some situations, where the CEO is not in a position to look after the resurrection effort, the person who has financial responsibilities of the company, e.g., the chief financial officer performs this role. Where the company itself is an information system company, the chief information officer, CIO, can perform this role. In any case, it is advisable to have an internal person performing this role. External or consulting help, if required, should be advisory only.

5.6.2 PUBLICIZING THE APPOINTMENT

After a potential candidate is nominated for the job, it is important to make the appointment formal and publicize it. This will make the intention of the company very clear to the internal and external parties involved. Internally the employees, especially the ones working in the technological dimension of the resurrection process, will find great support in a role that is dedicated to bringing the company back on its feet. Externally, the advantage of publicizing such appointment can result in support to the possibly sagging share prices as well as the overall image of the company in the market.

5.6.3 DECIDE REPORTING GUIDELINES

Once the resurrection champion is nominated it is important to provide her with a set of guidelines on how and when she will report the progress. It is essential not to have a rigid hierarchy in the resurrection process because it is precisely the hierarchy the process is trying to get rid off. If the responsibility for resurrection is shared by two individuals (for example, a CFO and a CIO are together made responsible for most of the effort), it will be necessary to delineate the reporting responsibilities of each of them. Reporting guidelines need also to consider the fact that the resurrection process is iterative. For example, the resurrection champion would provide a report to the board of directors at the end of each iteration or at the end of some predetermined activity within iteration.

5.7 SCOPING THE RESURRECTION

Providing a scope for the Y2K resurrection work at an early stage is important because it helps in setting the tone for the rest of the activities that ensue. Some of the factors that influences the scope of the Y2K resurrection process are as follows:

- Level of preparedness of the organization.
- Severity of the hit.
- Choice of Resurrection — inhouse or third party.

During this activity, the resurrection champion (with input from the board) tries to answer the question of how extensive the resurrection process should be. Depending on the scope of resurrection, process-threads can be created from the process. The number of activities and tasks performed during the process does not necessarily determine this extensiveness of the resurrection process. The process-threads resulting from the scope of the resurrection process will be a function of the following:

- The number of times an activity gets repeated.
- The number of actors performing a particular activity.
- The amount of work involved in testing and deploying the resurrecting system.

Since the intensity of the Y2K hit also influences these factors, it would be appropriate to say that the scope of the resurrection process is influenced by whether the organization suffered a mild, medium, or severe hit. A brief description of categorizing the scope of resurrection follows.

5.7.1 SMALL SCOPE

The scope of resurrection is small when the organization is in a position to get back on its feet quickly, without going through the rigors of all activities and tasks described in the resurrection process. This would happen if the impact of the Y2K hit on the customers of the organization was minimal. Although a Y2K problem internal to the company is also important, its effect on the company's revenues will not be as drastic as an external problem. Therefore, for mild hits with limited influence on internal (e.g., administrative) systems, the scope of the resurrection should be small.

5.7.2 MEDIUM SCOPE

When the Y2K hit is severe enough to start causing immediate revenue loses, the scope of resurrection will be at least medium. In case of the medium resurrection, it would be essential to continuously balance the loss of revenue with the cost of resurrection. If a critical business function of the organization is affected (as would be the case when a Y2K hit is categorized as medium or severe), it will be essential to have manual backup procedures before a medium scoped resurrection can be started.

5.7.3 LARGE SCOPE

The large scoped resurrection process would include every aspect of resurrection discussed in this book. It is important to note that the process metrics for the large-scoped resurrection would be higher than the medium-scoped resurrection *even if* the number of activities and tasks were the same in both scopes. This is because of the number of times the same activities and tasks get executed in a large-scoped resurrection will be higher than the number of times they are executed in the medium-scoped resurrection. The number of actors performing the activities also will be higher in the large-scoped resurrection process.

Finally, the legal issues in Y2K will have an influence on the scope of resurrection. If the organization is likely to be embroiled in legal proceedings, because of its own noncompliance with Y2K or because it is taking legal action against a noncompliant business partner who caused the crash, then the scope of resurrection would be large. This large-scoped resurrection would have to budget for not only the normal resurrection activities but also the work that will have to be done in the legal domain.

5.8 HIGHLIGHTING STRATEGIC ADVANTAGES

The strategic advantages of the Y2K resurrection process were discussed in detail in Chapter 3. This activity ensures that the strategic advantages are highlighted to various actors within the resurrection process.

5.8.1 SHORTLIST STRATEGIC ADVANTAGES

Not all advantages discussed in Chapter 3 will apply to all organizations. Before we can highlight the advantages, it might be worthwhile shortlisting the possible advantages of resurrection in the context of the company that has been hit. For example, the advantage of moving away from the legacy systems may not mean much for a small PC-based software development shop that is hit by Y2K. For such a small shop, the advantage of resurrection may lie in terms of usage of newer "object" technology, or even a "soft factor" such as heightened employee awareness. It is essential to shortlist the business and technical advantages of resurrection that are relevant to the organization and then highlight them to the employees — especially the employees who will work on the resurrection process. These advantages also may be used by the resurrection champion in justifying the resurrection process to the board and obtaining the budget for the same.

5.8.2 HIGHLIGHT ADVANTAGES TO THE SENIOR MANAGERS

It is the responsibility of the resurrection champion to highlight the advantages and the strategic advantages of the resurrection process to senior managers. These senior managers, including the project manager and the quality assurance manager, will play a significant role in the overall resurrection process. Therefore, it is essential to enlist the support of these managers during the resurrection. Advantages like reengineering of management and insourcing of business engineering and Y2K resurrection work are likely to be of high interest to the senior management.

5.8.3 HIGHLIGHT ADVANTAGES TO THE TECHNICAL TEAM

It is also important to highlight the strategic advantages to the technical people who will work on the programs and the methodologies in resurrection. It is important to inform them that the work, which they will put in, is not restricted to simply date conversion. There is a lot more to working in resurrecting from a Y2K hit than just fixing the date. The technical team will be interested in advantages that place the technical team members in a personal and professional growth situation (like the business engineering advantage). Inventory of systems and databases, as well as opportunity to provide a robust architecture and using object technology are the kind of professional advantages that need to be highlighted to the technical team members.

5.9 REGROUPING THE PEOPLEWARE

Regrouping the peopleware is essentially getting the resurrection team ready for the Y2K resurrection work. This activity also ensures that the rest of the organization is aware of the resurrection plans. If employees perceive the organization as a "hit" organization and if the resurrection effort is not sufficiently publicized, then they are likely to lose interest and their morale can go down. One of the results of the Y2K explosion is the potential exodus of the talent from the organization. This activity attempts to mitigate the negative sociological influence of the Y2K hit and, instead, brings the people together before the formal resurrection starts. The attempt is to iron out as many political issues as possible before the technical challenges are handled. Finally, this activity meets with the budgeting activity, as shown in Figure 5.6, and leads to the commencement of the core activities.

5.9.1 SETTING UP THE TRANSITION ATMOSPHERE

Regrouping the people is basically managing the transition of the organization from a Y2K-hit organization to a resurrecting organization. This requires the resurrection champion to manage all aspects of change, including the technical and cultural aspects. This task also manages the transition from the preliminary set of activities to the core activities from the three dimensions of resurrection. The primary way this can be achieved is by communicating to everyone concerned the status and the plans for resurrection.

5.9.2 COMMUNICATING THE RESURRECTION

As a result of the Y2K hit and the effect it will be having on the long-term stability of jobs, etc., employee morale is likely to be low. Therefore, the resurrection champion will have the task of regrouping the people who are going to participate in the resurrection process. This effort of regrouping will be effectuated by communicating to the employees how the resurrection will not only fix the date problem but also will reengineer the company without loss of jobs.

5.9.3 IDENTIFY POLITICAL HOTSPOTS

All development activities are fraught with politics. Since the resurrection exercise also is an exercise in reengineering, one would expect many people to have vested interest in the success (or otherwise) of the resurrection effort. In her effort to regroup the peopleware of the organization, the resurrection champion will have to identify the political hotspots, the internal conflicts, and the vested interest of people who are involved in the resurrection exercise. Because of the visible nature of the problem that the company is facing, it will be difficult to hide the various "interested" groups and their personal and political agenda. It will be essential to monitor the political will of the senior management and to create an atmosphere where the organizational objectives and those of the individual are brought together.*

5.9.4 IRON OUT ISSUES

Once the hot spots within the resurrecting organization are identified, it will be essential to sort these political issues as quickly and effectively as possible. There arc various ways in which political issues could be sorted out. Although these issues form part of the sociological aspect of a process, they are important in a technologically driven exercise. The people and the issues that are likely to create friction within the organization and the resurrection team will have to be sorted out. This would involve highlighting the strategic advantages of resurrection — again. It also would involve retraining of personnel and stressing the fact that the organization has no choice and that the people within will *have* to get together and resurrect.

5.10 BALANCING THE DIMENSIONS OF THE Y2K RESURRECTION PROCESS

We described how the driving dimension of resurrection is the technology. However, sociology will play a significant role in the resurrection process. It is important to strike the right balance between these two seemingly opposing dimensions of the resurrection. In this section we consider the issues related to this balancing of dimensions within the process of resurrection.

---

* A detailed discussion of the individual and corporate (team) objectives and the result of their alignment (or misalignment) is provided in the sociological discussion of the resurrection process in Chapter 10, Section 10.7, and Figures 10.4, 10.5, and 10.6.

5.10.1 FOLLOWING THE WHITE CLOUD ROLE MODEL

In our discussion on the process discipline in the previous chapter, white clouds were described as an ideal model for the processes within the resurrecting company. In addition to providing the model for the company, we also discussed how the white clouds provide the process model for the resurrection process. The white cloud model is important because it provides us with a three-dimensional understanding of the process.

In balancing the three dimensions of the resurrection process, it is important to notice that the dimensions of a process and the activities within the dimensions are orthogonal to each other. The resurrection process is fuzzy, therefore the metrics used in the process are only indicative. However, they still serve a useful purpose in understanding the weighting of each of the three dimensions within the process. The resurrection process metrics can be used in balancing the three dimensions.

Furthermore the boundaries of the resurrection process are not rigid. Therefore, there is always provision for external actors to influence the process. Similarly, the organization is able to influence the external actors and their quality of life. The effect of the resurrection process on the business and through the business on the society is similar to the effect of technology on business and society, as was shown in Figure 2.1.

5.10.2 BALANCING TECHNOLOGY WITH SOCIOLOGY

Being a process, the resurrection process can be potentially driven by any of the three dimensions of the process. However, as argued earlier on, we are driving the resurrection process through technology. In other situations where people issues are overbearing, a process can be driven entirely by its sociology. In case of a Y2K resurrection effort, it is essential to balance the technology with sociology. Figure 5.7 shows the importance of technology as the driving dimension of Y2K resurrection. The resurrection process is positioned such that there is more weighing on the technological aspects as compared with the sociological aspect on the resurrection. This weighing is not so much in terms of the importance of the process, but of the weighing resulting from the process-threads that will be created in each of these dimensions. Given a certain amount of resources, it will be essential to spread them out as described by the Figure 5.7, by positioning the Y2K resurrection process more closely to the technological axis. A sociologically driven process will position the process more closely to the sociological axis. Finally, if more resources are available, note that the axis itself can be shifted further out, representing more resources for both dimensions of the process. In such a situation, positioning of the resurrection process might be towards the center of the figure.

5.11 ITERATING THE Y2K RESURRECTION

The Y2K resurrection process is iterative. It is made up of three main iterations of the process discipline: initial, major, and final. Depending on the driving dimension of the resurrection process, a set of activities and tasks are completed within each of the three iterations. Detailed descriptions of the core activities and tasks form

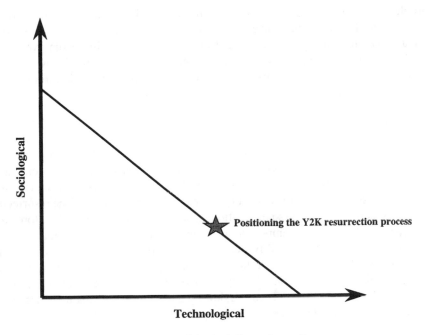

FIGURE 5.7 The technological vs. sociological dimensions of a process.

part of their respective chapters. Here, we only consider how the resurrection can iterate within the three dimensions.

5.11.1 INITIAL

The initial iteration of the core processes will start when most of the preliminary activities have been completed. The core activities during this iteration of the resurrection process may start with the activity of dissection (TA01 – Chapter 7) within the technological dimension coupled with the activity of alternative evaluation (MA01 – Chapter 9) from the methodological dimension. Some activities from the sociological dimension also may appear during the initial iteration, depending on how well the resurrection process is funded and the timing and urgency of producing a resurrected system. The end of the initial iteration can be a checkpoint, when the progress of the project gets reported and when the original estimates on the project are revisited and revised. This can result in revising the scope of the project and, possibly, re-scoping the activities in the remaining part of the project. The project plan is updated accordingly.

5.11.2 MAJOR

During the major iteration of the resurrection process a large number of technological activities will be completed. The methodological activities and tasks are completed by more than 50%, and the sociological activities would be 30% completed. Note that these percentage completions imply the completion of the process-threads and not necessarily the activities as described in the process dimensions. For example, if three actors perform a methodological activity, at least two of them will have completed the tasks assigned to them within that activity. Furthermore, reporting according to the checkpoints takes place during this iteration. Scope of the project is again revisited during this iteration. During this time, it will become very clear whether the resurrection process has succeeded or not. Efforts put in by the resurrection team need to be recognized during this iteration. This recognition need not wait till the end of the entire process.

5.11.3 FINAL

During the final iteration all the remaining activities from all dimensions are completed. The technological activities will be in their final phases and the sociological activities will have been completed. During this iteration, the project management and quality assurance activities further ensure that the final output of the resurrection process is according to the specifications provided by the users. Therefore, user acceptance testing will be completed during this iteration. The project manager also will have the added responsibility of "closing the project." Legal issues within the organization — especially those related to noncompliance of Y2K — will be sorted out during this final iteration. Finally, post deployment reviews of the software systems will be carried out. These reviews will enable easier maintenance of the system in its production phase.

5.12 AN ITERATIVE Y2K PROJECT PLAN

Integrating the three iterations described above in a project plan necessitates the use of dynamic project management tools and techniques. Creation of this high-level project plan forms part of the core methodological activity of project management. However, the iterative project plan is discussed here because creation of a sketchy plan at this preliminary stage of the resurrection project can provide valuable input into the preliminary budgeting activity. Thus, in a way, creation of the project plan here amounts to putting the scope of the resurrection project on paper or in a tool. The purpose of many activities and tasks described in this plan will become clear as we proceed through the respective chapters on the three processes of technology, methodology, and sociology. The aim of the plan is not only to indicate how the activities and tasks from the three dimensions are sequenced, but also to show how they will be performed in an iterative way.

5.12.1 THE PROJECT PLAN

Figure 5.8 shows the resurrection project plan for a medium hit. The scope of the resurrection process also is medium. This enables us to discuss the example plan without going into the extreme situations of large-scoped resurrection. As mentioned earlier, the major difference between the medium and large scopes is that in a large-scoped project, the number of actors involved will increase, and so will the overall weighing of the activities and tasks. Thus, the resurrection process metrics for each of the dimensions within the resurrection process (described in the discussions on the respective dimensions) plays a significant role in the project plan estimations.

ID	Task Name	Duration	Start	Finish	January 16							Ja	
					M	T	W	T	F	S	S	M	T
1	Scoping the Resurrection	2d	January 17, 2000	January 18, 2000									
2	Budgeting	2d	January 19, 2000	January 20, 2000									
3	*Iteration: Initial*	42d	January 21, 2000	March 20, 2000									
4	MA01: Alternative Evaluation	2d	January 21, 2000	January 24, 2000									
5	MA02: Project Planning	4d	January 25, 2000	January 28, 2000									
6	TA01: Dissection	10d	January 31, 2000	February 11, 2000									
7	TA02: Create Technical Environment	5d	February 14, 2000	February 18, 2000									
8	SA01: Staffing	4d	February 21, 2000	February 24, 2000									
9	SA02: Team Formation	4d	February 25, 2000	March 1, 2000									
10	TA07: Hardware	3d	March 2, 2000	March 6, 2000									
11	MA07: Quality Planning	4d	March 7, 2000	March 10, 2000									
12	Project Management	3d	March 13, 2000	March 15, 2000									
13	Quality Assurance	3d	March 16, 2000	March 20, 2000									
14	*Iteration: Major*	83d	March 21, 2000	July 13, 2000									
15	MA04: Requirements Modelling	10d	March 21, 2000	April 3, 2000									
16	MA06: Solution Design	8d	April 4, 2000	April 13, 2000									
17	TA03: Rewrite-Modify-Customise	20d	April 14, 2000	May 11, 2000									
18	TA05: Data Creation	5d	May 12, 2000	May 18, 2000									
19	TA06: DataBase	10d	May 19, 2000	June 1, 2000									
20	TA04: Software Integration	10d	June 2, 2000	June 15, 2000									
21	SA04: Environment (E) Factor	3d	June 16, 2000	June 20, 2000									
22	SA05: Motivation	3d	June 21, 2000	June 23, 2000									
23	SA09: Advertising	4d	June 26, 2000	June 29, 2000									
24	Project Management	5d	June 30, 2000	July 6, 2000									
25	Quality Assurance	5d	July 7, 2000	July 13, 2000									
26	*Iteration: Final*	28d	July 14, 2000	August 22, 2000									
27	MA09: Testing	8d	July 14, 2000	July 25, 2000									
28	MA10: Metrics	5d	July 26, 2000	August 1, 2000									
29	SA11: Litigation	4d	August 2, 2000	August 7, 2000									
30	SA06: Process Refinement	5d	August 8, 2000	August 14, 2000									
31	Project Management	3d	August 15, 2000	August 17, 2000									
32	Quality Assurance	3d	August 18, 2000	August 22, 2000									

Project: Figure58ProjectPlan.MPP
Date: February 6, 1999

Task	Rolled Up Task
Progress	Rolled Up Milestone ◇
Milestone ◆	Rolled Up Progress
Summary	

FIGURE 5.8 The Y2K resurrection project plan.

Here, the resurrection project plan only deals with typically a red to yellow organization with a medium-to-severe hit.

5.12.2 ITERATIVE PROJECT MANAGEMENT TOOLS

The project plan in Figure 5.8 is created using Microsoft Project. While placed under the three iterations, this project plan does not exhibit sufficiently the iterative nature of the resurrection process. Tools that consider iteration are able to take the activities and tasks of the resurrection process and place them within the context of an iterative

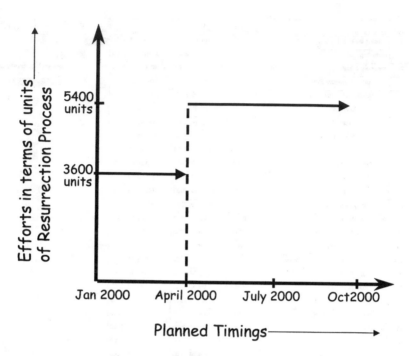

FIGURE 5.9   Refining the resurrection plan.

framework. Thus, the project management within the resurrection process will have to consider both types of tools — the linear project planning tools like Microsoft Project as well as the tools that consider iterations within the resurrection process.

Detailed examples of how the resurrection process can be placed within an iterative tool are provided in the Appendices. Appendix C describes a tool called MeNtOR Assistant — MAT™. This appendix contains details of how the resurrection activities and tasks can be entered within the MAT tool and how they can be iterated as the resurrection process iterates. Appendix B contains the WhiteClouds™ tool, which is based on the process model described in this book. This tool also is iterative in nature and helps in providing not only detailed cross-referencing on all activities and tasks within the three dimensions of resurrection but also excellent tracking mechanisms for the activities and tasks.

5.12.3 REFINING THE PLAN AT THE END OF EACH ITERATION

The resurrection plan is not a static document. It is essential to continue to update the plan at the end of a milestone. The end of each iteration of the resurrection process is the time to update the project plan. This is also the time when the budgets of the resurrection process can be "check pointed." This is the time when the re-scoping of the project plan may take place, if deemed necessary.

Effect of such refinement can be shown using Figure 5.9. We assume that the iterations in this plan follow the rule of thumb of 3 to 4 months per iteration. In the graphic representation of the project plan, the resurrection effort starts with 3600 units of a process* for the initial 3 months. If the resurrection starts in the month of April 2000, then the first iteration is supposed to complete in July 2000. After the end of the first iteration, the effort will be increased from 3600 units to 5400 units. This could be because the sociological dimension of the resurrection process is now coming into play. The increased effort is planned to last for the next two iterations (major and final) resulting in a resurrected company at the end of 9 months (January 2001). Now if the first iteration ends in 4 months time instead of 3 months (in May 2000 instead of April 2000), the planned vs. the actual productivity of the resurrection team can be arrived at as follows:

$$\text{Planned Productivity} = 3600 \text{ units of process/3 months}$$

$$= 1200 \text{ units per month}$$

$$(5.1)$$

$$\text{Actual Productivity (ascertained at the end of first iteration)}$$

$$= 3600 \text{ units of process/4 months} \qquad (5.2)$$

$$= 900 \text{ units per month}$$

With normal productivity, the resurrection project was supposed to be completed by October 2000. However, at the end of first iteration, we have arrived at the revised productivity figure of 900 units per month. The adjustment factor for the rest of the effort is given by:

$$\text{Adjustment factor} = \text{Actual Productivity/Planned productivity}$$

$$900/1200 = 0.75$$

$$(5.3)$$

Equation 5.3 indicates that the effort of 5400 units of process for the 6 months will have to be updated to one of the following options:

1. The effort of 5400 units for 6 months will have to be refined to 5400/.75 = 5860 (approximately 5900).
2. The time of 6 months will have to be refined to 6/0.75 = 8 months.

In both cases though, we have already lost a month in the initial iteration which should be accounted for in all further calculations. Note once again that this example highlights the importance of revisiting the project plan and re-scoping the resurrection process should the need arise. The actual dates and timings will vary depending on the severity of the hit and the skewing factor described earlier on.

---

* These measurements of number of units in a process are based on the metrics discussed in the chapter on process discipline. The actors, activities, tasks, and deliverables are calculated based on their importance to the project and the past history of their performance within the organization (if such a history exists). This total would be used in estimating the effort to be put in, in the resurrection process. In this hypothetical example, the number of units arrived at is 3600.

5.13 LAUNCHING THE CORE PROCESSES

As we come closer to completion of the preliminary activities, the activities within the core processes are just starting. The preliminary activities produce a sketchy project plan as well as budgets for the resurrection work. During the actual resurrection, these budgets are spent and the project plans finalized and updated. The next six chapters deal with the discussion of the three dimensions of resurrection and place them in their corresponding process discipline. Since the area between the completion of the preliminary activities and start of the core activities is not watertight, launching the core activities may not be a specific event. The entire resurrection will gradually slide from preliminary to core activities, as the white clouds do from one area of the sky to another. The understanding of this transition can help in reporting the resurrection to the board of directors, as well as promoting the resurrection within and outside the company.

5.14 KEY POINTS

1. The core concept of resurrection is to extract the functionality from the existing system and salvaging the relevant data.
2. Technology is the driving dimension of resurrection. Methodology needs modifications. Sociological dimension provides the stability in the resurrection process.
3. The resurrection process has a wider applicability than just recovering from the Y2K hit. It can be used in order to reengineer an organization and its processes. In that case the activities and tasks relevant to the Y2K work can be ignored.
4. The level of preparedness of the organization affects the timings in Y2K resurrection. The higher the level of preparedness, the swifter is the resurrection.
5. The preliminary activities of resurrection (budgeting, nomination of resurrection champion, scoping the resurrection process, highlighting the strategic advantages, and regrouping of employees) are important in setting up the "mood" for resurrection.
6. The core activities within the technological, methodological, and sociological dimensions of resurrection were mentioned here, but will be discussed in great detail in their respective chapters.
7. Transition from preliminary to core activities is a grey area and the shift is akin to the movement of white clouds in the sky.
8. An iterative project plan for the initial, major, and final iterations of the resurrection process was presented and iterative project management tools referred to in the Appendices.

5.15 NOTES

Thanks to John Warner of Object-Oriented Pty Ltd. for providing detailed input on the MAT™ tool for iterative process management. Thanks also to Rajesh Pradhan of CASE Digital Inc. for his input on the WhiteClouds™ for iterative management of the resurrection process.

5.16 REFERENCES

1. Davies, P., *The Mind of God: Science and the Search for Ultimate Meaning,* 1992, Penguin, 196.

6 Technology in Year 2000

The selection of which programming language to use in a given project is typically a binary issue, meaning that it is either a moot point or it is a hotly contested and almost a religious one.

Grady Booch[1]

Abstract   The essence of the technological challenge in resurrecting from a Y2K hit revolves around understanding the technology in which the problem has occurred, the technology that can and has been used in investigating the problem, and the technology that would be used to rebuild the new organization. Thus, although technology has been the major cause of this "anti-festival" in Year 2000, it also is the means to resurrection. The discussion in this chapter includes languages, databases, middleware, networking, hardware, and so on. These topics are discussed from the technological angle of "what" — what is the problem and what can solve it? In solving the problem, we take advantage of the opportunity of bringing in new technology and removing the old technology. The activities and tasks required to bring about this new technology are discussed within the format of the process discipline in the next chapter.

6.1 ESSENCE OF TECHNOLOGICAL CHALLENGE IN RESURRECTION

6.1.1 "WHAT" OF RESURRECTION

Technology is generally accepted as the major cause of the Y2K problem. It also can provide the solution to the problem. When the technological dimension of Y2K resurrection is discussed, it essentially deals with "what" caused the problem, and "what" can be used to solve it. Thus, the technological discussion of the Y2K problem involves the following:

- Technology in which the problem exists.
- Technology used in dissecting the problem.
- Technology used in resurrection.

Each aspect of the technology is considered as an ingredient or the "raw material" that can be put to use in resurrecting the Y2K-hit organization. This technological dimension has to be appropriately coupled with the methodological and sociological dimensions of the resurrection process in order for the organization to get back on its feet. The discussion in this chapter builds the technological background of the problem and the solution. The formal activities and tasks of the technological dimension are described in the next chapter.

When we discuss the technology in which the problem exists, we are essentially discussing the existing legacy code containing 2-digit dates in its data and logic that is likely to have caused the systems to crash and the organization to "explode" in the first place. The aim in understanding the existing technology in resurrection is different from that in a prevention effort. During the prevention effort of the past, the Y2K work started and ended with the old technology. However, in resurrection, understanding of the old technology is developed only to an extent to permit us to conduct successful investigation of the affected system and identify any salvageable options.

Thus, dissection in the Y2K resurrection process helps identify the modules affected by Y2K and the specific areas within the modules such as the data, their definition, the logic, and the presentation that are facing problems. I prefer to call this investigative activity *dissection* because the system that is being investigated has already crashed. The aim is not to test the system in detail to find out how to fix it, but to provide a means to see if there are any areas of the system that are still salvageable. We may expect a sizeable amount of data within the affected system to be still valuable. This data will have to be salvaged by means of appropriate conversion mechanisms. The technology of conversion has already been used in the Y2K prevention effort of the past. A part of the same technology can be used in salvaging the valuable parts of the Y2K affected system.

First we understand the technology in which the problem exists and the technology that will help us in dissecting and salvaging valuable parts of the current system; then we discuss the technology that is used in rebuilding the new system. The resurrecting software system will provide the basis for the new business processes of the resurrecting organization. Therefore, when we consider the rebuilding of the new system we are essentially considering the ways in which the new organization will be functioning. Thus, the concepts of business process reengineering play a significant role in the technological dimension of the resurrection process. We consider the technological aspect of reengineering, with the Y2K-hit system as the starting point for the resurrection exercise. The raw materials that play a significant role in dissection and resurrection are

- Programming languages used in the existing code and the new applications.
- Databases in which the existing data was stored and the new data models in the new databases.
- Middleware and the opportunities it presents in the resurrection effort.
- Opportunities to warehouse the data using the concept of data mining, especially in applications that depend on a large amount of historical data for analytical purposes.
- Role of hardware in the new organization.
- Role of networks in the new organization.

TABLE 6.1
Summary of Role of Technology in Y2K Hits and Resurrection

Technology	Role in Y2K Hit	Role in Y2K Resurrection
Languages	Logic errors	New logic
Databases	Date errors	Salvaged data; temporary storage
Data mining	Scant	Sophisticated queries for processing
Middleware	Scant	Distributed architecture; assist in transition
Networks	Bottlenecks	Assist in distribution
Packages	Scant	ERP solutions resulting in integrated business
Hardware	BIOS, slow speed, less memory	Faster development, deployment

The influence of technology in causing the Y2K problem and its role in resurrection after the Y2K hit, is summarized in Table 6.1.

6.1.2 OLD WAS GOLD

Prudent adoption of new technologies, such as the ones presented in Table 6.1, always carry the potential of providing competitive advantage. This advantage becomes all the more important in the new millennium, as technology becomes easily and cheaply available, and is adopted by a large number of competing organizations. Old technology does not hold up to the "old is gold" adage. The technological factors of languages, hardware, databases, and networks have progressed phenomenally in the past few years. In the new millennium these advances present a totally different face of computing than what it was when the Y2K bug was inserted within the computing code. Therefore, in each of the technological factors that we discuss here, it is essential to accept the "power of the new," and utilize that power in resurrecting the organization. Implicit in the discussion of these factors is the fact that the current knowledge and understanding of these factors will become old pretty soon. Therefore, when the resurrection process adopts new technology, it will have to be aware of the fact that the technology can change during the adoption process itself, and plan accordingly. For example, for a COBOL software shop, adopting C++ as a programming language brings in new technology. However, within C++ itself, there have been considerable advances in the way classes were designed and developed. These advances need to be incorporated in the resurrection process.

Thus, the essence of technological challenge in the resurrection process is to correctly identify the new technology and then adopt it in the development process. Some compelling arguments in pursuing this challenge of using newer technologies in resurrection are

- Languages are easier and cheaper to use; compare the use of a Visual C++ or an Eiffel workbench with that of a COBOL compiler on a mainframe.

- Languages and databases are faster to use. This has a significant impact not only on the performance but also on the development life cycle of the system.
- New technologies encompass sophisticated development tools, for example, CASE tools that help create designs and convert them to code and back (reverse engineering); creation and management of data models.
- Excellent hardware support. Newer hardware platforms are able to support development using new languages and databases, resulting in a much faster development environment (than, for example, a Y2K conversion environment which has to deal with the traditional hardware technologies).
- Newer technologies are well supported by the other two dimensions of a process: methodology and sociology. For example, it is easier to find programming skills in Visual Basic than in COBOL (one of the reasons for skyrocketing costs of conversion); or there are good methodological tools to support the methodological approach to, say, object-oriented development.
- It is well supported by its respective vendors. For example, new versions of language compilers (e.g., 32-bit VC++ compiler) are supported by their corresponding operating systems (e.g., 32-bit NT).

While the use of new technology provides significant benefits to the organization, it has not always been easy to bring in new technology. As discussed in Chapter 3, it is the Y2K hit and the subsequent crash that, if managed properly, provides opportunities for the organizations to bring in new technology that can be used in resurrection of the system. If indeed the systems have crashed due to Y2K, the hit organization must not waste any more time and effort in trying to fix the system. The chance to move away from the "legacy" legacy and adopting the new technology should be taken. A discussion on how this is done follows.

6.1.3 SAMPLE FROM A FIRECRACKER

We considered the HIGH-LOW-Value firecracker as an example describing Y2K hits (Chapter 1, Figure 1.4). We extend that example further and consider it in the context of the various technologies that will be used in the resurrection process.

6.1.3.1 Data

Table 6.2 provides a sample data from a typical student registration database of a university that registers students for various courses and keeps track of their fees paid, etc. Three students with identifications (IDs) 10101, 10200, and 11010 are shown in the database, together with the courses they attended (or want to attend), date, and amount of fees paid.

Most of the firecrackers discussed in Chapter 1 have the potential of affecting this data. We consider the data definition and the "sample" logic that deals with the data in Table 6.2 and the ways in which it is affected by the Y2K problem. The

TABLE 6.2
A Y2K Hit Set of Data

| Student ID | Student Course | Fees Paid Date | | | Amount ($) |
		Day	Month	Year	
10101	AA1	10	02	00	400
10101	AB1	10	02	00	500
10101	BC2	15	09	00	400
10101	BC3	15	09	00	400
10101	AC1	15	09	00	400
10200	AA1	11	02	00	400
10200	AB1	11	02	00	500
10200	BC1	28	09	00	400
10200	BC2	28	09	00	400
11010	AA1	12	02	00	400
11010	BC1	20	09	00	400
11010	BC2	20	09	00	400
11010	BC3	20	09	00	400

same data and logic is used in discussing the role of languages and databases in resurrection.

6.1.3.2 Data Model

Following is the data definition (in COBOL) for the data described in Table 6.2.

```
01  STUDENT-RECORD
     05  STUDENT-ID              PIC  9(5).
     05  STUDENT-COURSE          PIC  X(3).
     05  FEES-PAID-DATE.
          10  FEES-PAID-DATE-DAY     PIC  99.
          10  FEES-PAID-DATE-MONTH   PIC  99.
          10  FEES-PAID-DATE-YEAR    PIC  99.
     05  FEES-AMOUNT             PIC  9(4)v99.
```

Currently, this data definition in the DATA DIVISION of COBOL is representing the data described in Table 6.2. However, the same data can be stored in different ways, including hierarchical, relational, and object-relational data storage. When different mechanisms to store the data are used, the data definition that represents the data also changes accordingly.

In all cases though, the important point in this data representation is the 2-digit year field. In handling the data model, the Y2K work had to consider the issues of mapping this model with a newer representation of 4-digit date. Changes to the data model would occur because of data compression, adding an extra flag to indicate the year, and so on.

6.1.3.3 Logic

A sample algorithm (also discussed in Section 1.4) that updates the data is as follows:

```
MOVE LOW-VALUES TO FEES-PAID-DATE.
IF <fees paid> THEN
    MOVE TODAYS-DATE TO FEES-PAID-DATE.
```

Later on, during the processing of the student details before the results of the semester are sent out, the following logic comes into play:

```
IF FEES-PAID-YY = 00 THEN
    <skip record>
```

If TODAYS-DATE (containing 00 in the last two digits in Year 2000) is moved to FEES-PAID-DATE field, the logic incorrectly assumes that the students have not paid their fees and skips their record. We consider the languages and databases in the context of this "sample" error — from the point of view of investigating the error and the ways in which newer technologies help in resurrecting from this situation.

6.2   LANGUAGES IN RESURRECTION

Within the technological dimension of the resurrection process, understanding of computer languages is developed for the following reasons:

- Most of the legacy applications that are affected by Y2K had the software language as the primary means of expression. Thus, languages were not supported by the sophisticated data manipulation tools of today. Languages also did not need the middleware tools that we need today. Large applications were written entirely in the language of choice — like COBOL, C, and PASCAL. These languages are the major candidates for logic-related Y2K hits.
- Languages like C++, Smalltalk, and Java are the major candidates to be used in the rebuilding effort. Their understanding — especially in how they help in rewriting the date-related logic — can be very helpful in the resurrection process.

Based on the core philosophy of resurrection (Figure 5.1) and resulting from the activity of dissection and salvaging (considered in detail in the technological activity TA01, described in the next chapter) the major salvageable entity is likely to be data. The resurrection process accepts the importance of relevant data from the existing organization. Therefore, the data models represented by the affected language (in this discussion it is COBOL) will be of interest in enabling extraction of salvageable options from the hit system.

Because of the importance of salvaging the data, though, the computer languages likely to be popular during the resurrection effort are the ones that are data-centric. These data-centric languages happen to be the object-oriented languages that enable encapsulation of data and functions — features that provide significant advantages during resurrection and, therefore, used extensively. There are many languages that boast object-oriented features. The languages mentioned briefly in this chapter are C++, Java, and Smalltalk. The aim is not to study the features of the languages in great detail (not because it is not important, but because there is already enough discussion in the OO literature on languages). Our attempt is to develop an understanding of how the Y2K-affected code can be reengineered by use of an object-oriented language.

Furthermore, the focus of development in the new millennium will be shifting from writing a class (at the finest granularity) or writing a system (at the coarsest granularity) to writing components (optimum granularity). This will provide substantial reuse within the development environment.* Mapping of the affected system in COBOL to the components in the OO language of resurrection is considered here. Although the DATE component is used as an example, other components also can be developed using the same approach. This should permit the technical teams who know the language in greater detail to take the hints provided here and develop solutions based on the object-oriented designs (resulting from the activities within the methodological dimension of the resurrection process).

6.2.1 COBOL

Understanding of languages like COBOL provide an ability to localize the Y2K problems and conduct further dissection in the relevant areas. The sample firecracker in Section 6.1 uses the COBOL syntax to describe the data and the logic. Software systems that are written in COBOL language need to understand the two areas of the Y2K problem as follows:

1. The DATA DIVISION of a COBOL program describes the layout of the data. An example of this data layout is the *data model* that describes the data shown in Table 6.2. The *data model* within the COBOL program is the primary originator of the Y2K problem.
2. The PROCEDURE DIVISION of a COBOL program contains the logic of the system. This logic uses the data representation in the DATA DIVISION in order to store and retrieve data. Thus, logic that deals with storage and retrieval of data cooperates with the DATA DIVISION in order to create the Y2K hit. Furthermore, there is a large amount of logic in the PROCEDURE DIVISION that deals with the data *after* it has been retrieved from the corresponding data storage mechanism. Examples of this logic are the comparison and branching logic, sorting logic, and so on.

---

* Concept of granularity has been discussed in greater detail in the methodological dimension (Chapter 8, Section 8.5), as it has more to do with "how" of a process rather than the "what."

Although a Y2K hit is not easily discerned as occurring within the DATA DIVISION or the PROCEDURE DIVISION, it is still worthwhile for the resurrection team to attempt to note separately the Y2K errors occurring within each of these divisions of a COBOL program. This can influence the approach taken in resurrecting the affected system. For example, an error in the data representation implies the salvageable data will need additional logic in order to correctly expand it to 4-digits for use in the resurrecting system. However, if the data was correctly converted during an earlier effort at prevention and it is only the branching or sorting logic that is having a problem, the Y2K hit itself may get categorized into a "small" hit and, therefore, may not require a full-scale resurrection.

There are a number of tools that assist in searching the data and the logic to locate the date occurrences within the programs. This has been a part of the standard Y2K prevention effort and, therefore, not described in detail here. Some of the prevention effort will find useful application during the dissection work.

6.2.2 C++

C++, a superset of the C language, is likely to find good use in the resurrection process because of its proximity to C. C++ came late on the market (as compared with COBOL), hence the chances of finding logical Y2K bugs in C++ itself are less. If C++ systems are affected by Y2K, there is a high chance that the problem is related to data representation (usually within a relational or hierarchical database) rather than the logic of the program itself. Thus, our focus in studying C++ is in using it for the rebuilding process.

By using the object-oriented capabilities of the C++ language, the developers can provide a wrapper around the data that contains the date problem. This wrapper will provide the logic that will interpret the date implicitly. This can be achieved by designing the resurrection around the data that is salvageable.

However, should the Y2K problem occur in the logic of the hit system, a simple wrapper around the data will not solve the problem. The logic within the existing system will have to be rewritten, forming the essential activity of Rewrite-Modify-Customize (Activity TA03: described in next chapter). The approach of concentrating on the rewrite of functional algorithms for date routines will be helpful where a large number of mathematical functions are affected by the Y2K problem. In the case of mathematical function libraries, the data types are few, but the logic including operations and methods is large. Those are the ideal situations for use of the functional capabilities of C++.

In either a rewriting or a wrapping exercise, the object-oriented nature of C++ can be used to create a DATE component. This date component can be designed in such a way that it can handle both the 2-digit and the 4-digit dates. This is because the data that are salvaged from the Y2K hit will need either (1) a flag to indicate whether fees have been paid or (2) an expanded 4-digit representation of the date that can still be used as a flag to indicate whether fees have been paid. A sample use of C++ to represent such a date component in resurrection is shown below. This design encapsulate the data and the behavior so that the complexities of date

manipulation are hidden from the users (i.e., other systems and programmers) of
the date component. Detailed design for a DATE component is shown in Figure
9.6. It is carried out in Task MT06-2.

```cpp
class Fee
{
public:
    Fee()
    {
        m_dAmount = 0;
        m_pFeesPaidDate = new Y2KDate2D;       //(or
    Y2Kdate4D)
    }
    virtual ~Fee()
    {
        delete m_pFeesPaidDate;
    }
    bool FeePaid()
    {
        if (m_pFeesPaidDate->Y2KResurrected())
            return (m_pFeesPaidDate->GetYear() !=
    0);
        else
            return ((m_pFeesPaidDate->GetYear() !=
    0) &&
                    (m_pFeesPaidDate->GetMonth() != 0)
    &&
                    (m_pFeesPaidDate->GetDay() != 0));
    }
    void SetPaidDate()
    {
        m_pFeesPaidDate->Today();
    }

protected:
    Y2KDate*    m_pFeesPaidDate;
    double      m_dAmount;
};

class Course
{
protected:
    std::string    m_strStudentCourse;
    double    m_dFee;
};
```

6.2.3 SMALLTALK

Smalltalk, as a stricter object-oriented programming language, has been tried and tested successfully in developing solutions for simple and complex problems in simulation, expert systems, and integrated programming environments. Because of the fact that small code segments of the program can be edited and installed avoiding lengthy compile and link sessions, the language makes an ideal choice in resurrection when the application has to be released in an incremental fashion. When the new application requirements can be satisfied by part conversion of data but requires new logic, Smalltalk can provide that incremental logic much more easily than C++. Furthermore, because of the complexity of the existing legacy applications, this language also may prove useful in modeling the existing application during its dissection phase after a Y2K hit.

A sample "Fee" subclass from a Smalltalk (Visualwave) code that would resurrect the *data model* and the *logic* affected by the Y2K problem (as shown in Table 6.2) is described below. As in case of the C++ code, this logic reflects the data component designed during the methodological process (Task MT06-2).

```
Object subclass: #Fee
    instanceVariableNames: 'feesPaidDate amount '
    classVariableNames: ''
    poolDictionaries: ''
    category: 'Bhuvan'!

!Fee methodsFor: 'methods'!

feePaid
    feesPaidDate y2KResurrected
        ifTrue: [^(feesPaidDate year ~= 0)]
        ifFalse: [^(feesPaidDate year ~= 0 & fee-
    sPaidDate month ~= 0 & feesPaidDate day ~= 0)].!

initialize
    feesPaidDate := Y2KDate2D new. " or could be
    Y2KDate4D new. "
    amount := 0.!

setPaidDate
    feesPaidDate today.! !

Object subclass: #Y2KDate
    instanceVariableNames: ''
    classVariableNames: ''
    poolDictionaries: ''
    category: 'Bhuvan'!
    "-- -- -- -- -- -- -- -- -- -- -- -- -- -- -- -- -- --"!
```

```
Y2KDate class
    instanceVariableNames:  ''!

!Y2KDate class methodsFor:  'methods'!
new
    ^super new initialize.! !

Y2KDate subclass: #Y2KDate4D
    instanceVariableNames: 'feesPaidDateDay fee-
    sPaidDateMonth feesPaidDateYear '
    classVariableNames: ''
    poolDictionaries: ''
    category: 'Bhuvan'!
```

6.2.4 JAVA

Java is a cross-platform programming language that is based on the idea that the same software should run on many different kinds of computers. In addition to its applicability on business computing hardware, it is also able to run on various consumer gadgets. Java developers claim that the Java platform will be used in building the next generation telephones, TV sets, and smart cards.

This can provide many options during resurrection, especially when we are dealing with devices other than computers that have failed during the Y2K fireworks. Furthermore, because of its relative ease in interfacing with legacy systems and relational databases, Java provides a popular mechanism to build front-ends to existing applications whose back-end data is not affected by Y2K.

Since Java is able to run on any kind of machine, it is possible to integrate the resurrection work that involves a PC, a Macintosh, a network of computers, or a main frame machine. Also, the tools that are developed and used in salvaging data can be easily transported and run on different platforms. Finally, the Java software in resurrection can be used to tie together the data from the mainframe with the newer applications.

In addition to the direct benefits of using Java in resurrection work, the language also has application in enabling the organizations in the new millennium with internal and external communication channels through their Web sites. This would help streamline and satisfy the needs for communication during and after resurrection by improving and enhancing the flow of information between departments, suppliers, and customers. Many large organizations are already using the Java technology on the Internet as well as on their own intranet to integrate their existing computing systems and to extend their business to customers partners and vendors on the network. The same approach can be used during resurrection as well.

The example we used in presenting C++ and Smalltalk is now repeated for Java.[2] The classes shown in this example can be used from a Java application or applet, as required. (Note that in Java each class is in a separate file, so this code will need to be split into multiple source code files containing one class each.)

```
import java.lang.*;
public class Fee
{
     protected Y2KDate    m_pFeesPaidDate;
     protected Double    m_dAmount;
     public Fee()
     {
         m_dAmount = 0;
         m_pFeesPaidDate = new Y2KDate2D;    //(or
Y2Kdate4D)
     }
     public Boolean FeePaid()
     {
         if (m_pFeesPaidDate.Y2KResurrected())
             return (m_pFeesPaidDate.GetYear() != 0);
         else
             return ((m_pFeesPaidDate.GetYear() != 0)
     &&
                             (m_pFeesPaidDate.GetMonth()
!= 0) &&
                             (m_pFeesPaidDate.GetDay() !=
0));
     }
     public void SetPaidDate()
     {
         m_pFeesPaidDate.Today();
     }
}

public class Course
{
     protected String    m_strStudentCourse;
     protected Double    m_dFee;
}
```

6.3   DATABASES IN RESURRECTION

Study of databases is extremely important in the Y2K resurrection process for the same reasons that we studied the languages — in understanding where the problem lies and in developing newer solutions for the resurrecting system. We discussed in Chapter 2, Section 2.10 how the effect of Y2K on the data eventually leads to the schizophrenic behavior of the enterprise. Understanding of databases in the resurrection process provides for efficient dissection of the schizophrenic data. This, in turn, facilitates conversion of salvageable data that can be used by the resurrecting application.

In addition to understanding the problem, the role of databases in the resurrection process also expands to provide data models that will represent the new process-based designs. Thus, we consider the relational and object-oriented databases as places where the salvageable data from the Y2K-hit system and new data of the process-based system will be stored. Salvageable data from the existing database will be ported across to the new databases by making use of the standard conversion mechanisms that were also used in the Y2K prevention effort. The difference being that in the prevention effort, data conversions were more or less expansion of date fields. In resurrection, we expect to not only convert the data, but also reformat and add more data that could be used in the new systems. This results in practical considerations in using combination of object-oriented and relational databases (called object-relational databases) as well. We consider the important types of databases from dissection and rebuilding viewpoint.

6.3.1 HIERARCHICAL

The hierarchical databases were the first generation database systems that were popular because of the database management functions they offered including a data definition and manipulation language for collection of records (e.g., CODASYL, IMS). These also are the databases likely to carry the Y2K bugs in them. The best approach to handling the Y2K problems in these databases is to "re-create" their data models into a newer and more easily manageable database system and port the "salvageable" data into the new database. In addition to solving the Y2K-related problem faced by the system, this resurrection also will remove many restrictions of these traditional databases (e.g., being able to store only textual data). For example, consider an insurance application that processes claims. This application requires traditional data elements such as the name and coverage of each person insured. The hierarchical databases could only store the name and coverage in a textual format in a hierarchical fashion. Resurrection of the hierarchical database in, say, an object-relational structure not only improves access to the information, but also provides opportunity of storing images like the photographs and facsimile of the event and linking it to the name or identity of the person who was making the claim.

The major technical challenge in resurrecting a hierarchical database will be identifying the salvageable contents of the database. As compared with a relational database, where the data definition in terms of tables and rows is easily understandable, a hierarchical structure could be quite complex. For example, the data shown in Table 6.2 could be stored in two ways in the hierarchical database:

1. Exactly as shown in the table with each occurrence of course–date combination per row.
2. Course–date occurrences indexed and spread horizontally.

Each type of storage had its own advantages and limitations. These advantages and limitations also apply when it comes to dissecting and salvaging the data. For example, if stored as one occurrence per row, the logic of converting the data would be easy (no indexes), but the amount of data to be converted would be more (as the student-IDs would get repeated for all course–fee combination). However, if all the semester-related data for a student are stored in one row, the data storage would get defined as follows:

```
01  STUDENT-RECORD
     05  STUDENT-ID                    PIC 9(5).
     05  STUDENT-COURSE-DETAILS    OCCURS 4 TIMES.
         10  STUDENT-COURSE-CODE PIC X(3).
         10  FEES-PAID-DATE.
             15  FEES-PAID-DATE-DAY      PIC 99.
             15  FEES-PAID-DATE-MONTH    PIC 99.
             15  FEES-PAID-DATE-YEAR     PIC 99.
         10  FEES-AMOUNT                 PIC 9(4)v99.
```

This data definition assumes that the student can have a maximum of four courses per semester. Thus, if the student goes for less number of courses, data space gets wasted. The advantage, in terms of storage and retrieval of data, is that only one access of the database provides all details of the courses, fees paid, and the amount for the student. In dissecting this data structure, if *any one* occurrence of the date field is identified as having date problem, it may become necessary to salvage all the data including the date fields to the new database.

6.3.2 RELATIONAL

The second generation relational database systems provide a substantial step forward for many applications over their precursors. Not only do they simplify the way in which data can be stored and retrieved, but they also make it easy to model the new database. Thus, the role played by relational databases in Y2K resurrection includes:

- Providing ease of modeling the data storage — this is primarily derived from the sound mathematical background of the relational theory.
- Ability of the databases to access and manipulate the data by using the nonprocedural query language.
- Delineation of the data storage from the applications that use the data — this feature will have significant influence in Y2K dissection as it will be easy to separate the date problem occurring in the data from that in the application logic.

Some of the currently popular relational databases include Sybase, SQLServer, Access, and Oracle. These and many such relational databases coming from different vendors and released in a number of versions, provide not only the data storage and retrieval capabilities but are also accompanied by a wide variety of tools to help create and manage data models. These tools include the sophisticated administrative tools which permit easier maintenance (e.g., modifying the SQL — structured query language, queries) and administration (e.g., periodic backups, retrievals) — tools that were not easily available in their hierarchical counterparts.

Although the relational databases appeared much later than the hierarchical databases, they were still used extensively in applications that were *not* Y2K conscious. Therefore, as far as the Y2K problem is concerned, these databases have the well-known problem of using 2 digits to store the year field for the dates. Thus, a significant number of relational databases are likely to be affected by the Y2K problem. The "prevention" effort in these databases was the standard expansion of the 2-digit date field to the 4-digit one, and modifying the SQL and the application logic to handle the expanded 4-digits. However, the date field forms the key to many SQL queries that use the date in comparisons, branching, and sorting logic. Dissection and resurrection within relational databases will have to consider the logic as well as the data structure within the relational environment in the resurrection process. Resurrection will not only require the expansion of the data representation from 2-digit to 4-digit, but it will involve considerable rewrite of SQL queries to handle the requirements of the new system.

Furthermore, new SQL statements also will have to be written in order to conduct an intelligent conversion of the salvageable data from the existing data model into the new resurrected model. As discussed through the formal activities in the next chapter, conversions will be based on the result of the dissection activity. We need to know the data that is still relevant as against the data that is redundant or irrelevant in the new system. Data conversion during the resurrection process is likely to be from hierarchical to relational, or from relational to relational structures.

6.3.3 OBJECT-ORIENTED

We discussed the role of object-oriented programming languages in the resurrection process. OO languages provide the major advantage of handling complex data manipulation within a program. However, in order to deal with persistent objects, the programmer must tediously convert objects into their corresponding relational structures and use the SQL tools to store and retrieve the data. This tedious mapping from the objects within the application to the tables within the relational database is avoided by the use of an object-oriented database. Object-oriented databases allow the programmer to continue to use object abstractions right out of and to the disk level by providing the ability to directly save to disk the complex data types that have been created in the memory. Similarly, retrieval of objects need not be in two phases (retrieval from the tables and then mapping to the objects), but as one single process in which objects stored on the disk are retrieved as objects rather than as tables. Thus, Object Database Management Systems (ODBMSs) extend the benefits of the OO programming languages by providing persistence to complex objects, which may be made up of not just plain text and numeric data, but also pictures, audio, video, and so on.

Object-oriented databases still have not found commercial popularity because business applications find the neat rows and columns of a relational database extremely attractive compared with the ability of ODBMSs to handle complex designs. Business data in applications like banking and finance are more organized than the data in maths intensive scientific, engineering, or navigational systems. Therefore, there will be fewer business applications using object-oriented databases affected by the Y2K problem than corresponding users of RDBMSs. ODBMSs are likely to be used in resurrection when there is a need to provide persistence to the objects designed as a part of the new application.

6.3.4   OBJECT RELATIONAL

There has been some ongoing effort to incorporate the benefits of object orientation into the existing relational database management systems. This would enable the designs to combine the complex data types of the objects with the ease of storage and retrieval of a relational database. These efforts are also attractive for organizations trying to protect their investment in relational technology while they try to leverage the advantages of object technology. Technically, the relational technology is extended towards object orientation by adding support for BLOBS (binary large objects) and abstract data types with their appropriate operators. The end result of this bringing together of the two technologies is the Object-Relational Database Management Systems (ORDBMS) that enables the developers to build complex data structures as part of real-world business solutions and then reuse these building blocks in providing the applications used by the end-users.

Two of the major advantages of object-relational databases are:[3]

1. New data types leverage traditional relational database management system (RDBMS) services.
2. Developers are provided with reusable, baseline object capabilities for integration into a broad range of end user solutions.

These also are the advantages of the ORDBMS that can be put to use in Y2K resurrection effort. Because the data management system is able to handle complex objects, it provides opportunities to combine the salvageable part of a relational database together with the newly resurrecting data models. Combining the two types of data by using an ORDBMS structure and wrapping it with the middleware tools discussed later on might provide one of the best technological options during the Y2K resurrection work. We presume though that the application has a need to store complex and sophisticated data such as arrays, lists, directed graph structures, hierarchies, trees, and large-structured objects such as sound and images. In the absence of such complex data types and in the absence of the need to combine salvageable data with new data, pursing the object-relational databases will not provide greater advantage over relational databases in resurrection.

6.3.5   THOUGHTS ON DATABASE CONVERSION

Solution to a Y2K problem in any of the aforementioned databases would require dissecting the data content and the data model and then converting the data content into a newly designed data model. Therefore, work related to databases in a Y2K resurrection effort deals with conversion from hierarchical to relational, relational to relational, hierarchical to object-oriented, relational to object-oriented, and, occasionally, from relational and object-oriented to an object-relational database. Dissecting the database would result in an understanding of the salvageable options. These salvageable options provide the starting point for the organization of the new data model by providing an understanding of how the data is organized in the current database. It is important to remember that when we resurrect, we do not just convert. The requirements for the new system would be modeled based on the activity of requirements modeling (Activity MA04: Requirements Modeling, described in Chapter 9, Section 9.7). These requirements would also influence the manner in which data is stored. Therefore, the new data models are likely to be significantly different from the existing ones — not only in the technological aspect of storage and retrieval but also the manner in which they are organized.

6.4 DATA MINING AND RESURRECTION

While we considered databases in resurrection in the previous section, the data content within those databases in the new millennium is not going to be the same. With quantum jump in hardware capabilities and supporting database technologies, resurrecting organizations in the new millennium will have to brace for a deluge of data that is stored within their databases. A discussion on data mining is considered relevant within that context.

6.4.1 DATA EXPLOSION AFTER Y2K RESURRECTION

When we consider the technology in Y2K resurrection, we have to consider the fact that our technology will have to come to grips with not just gigabytes but terabytes (and beyond) of data in the new millennium. While the quantity of data continues to almost double every year, the amount of meaningful information that can be derived form this data is decreasing rapidly. This is due to the fact that large amount of data makes finding and sorting, and hence deriving meaningful knowledge, difficult. Post-resurrection organizations will have to consider not only the amount of data that is stored within their databases after the resurrection is over, but also the complexity and frequency of update of large-scale databases and the problem of loosing valuable information in the depth of the data storage.

Furthermore, the resurrection process also has to consider the fact that the time available to make business decisions is reducing drastically. For example, home loan applications that could take 6 to 8 weeks for processing using a legacy system could be processed within a couple of days due to new technology and a reengineered business process. This means the information that the decisionmaker uses has to be dug out and correlated very quickly. The technology that facilitates this digging of information and making sense out of it is called *data mining*. We consider data mining in order to ensure that the resurrecting system is not merely a Y2K-compliant system, but also has the ability to provide business value in the new millennium.

6.4.2 UNDERSTANDING DATA MINING

A simple query like "requesting a list of all customers whose balance is above $1000" is satisfied by standard database query mechanisms as mentioned in the discussion on databases. However, business has a need to view the data based on various conditions. These conditions are likely to change dynamically. For example, if the query is to request a list of all customers whose balances are *likely to reach* beyond $5,000 in this quarter, then satisfying that query will need some background computation by the software application. The application will have to create *trends* and then extrapolate those trends for the customers in order to ascertain whether they should be selected. Although extrapolations and multiple queries were used in some form in the older applications, they were not supported by the corresponding data storage mechanisms. With the availability of data warehouses and data mining techniques, the resurrecting organizations are likely to reap business benefits in terms of "trend" information on its customers and products, cross-selling of products and services and so on.

6.4.3 RELEVANCE OF DATA MINING IN Y2K

As mentioned before, data mining is relevant to the Y2K resurrection process because it is able to provide the three-dimensional drill-down functionality for queries that sift large amount of data with relative ease and intelligence. Furthermore, the multiple entry points in a data warehouse also permit different starting points for users who have requirements quite removed from each other. For example, the entry point for a query by a bank teller on a customer's profile will be different from the entry point of the manager of a bank who is trying to offer a high-end loan to the customer. The relevance of data mining in the next millennium includes the following:

- Assisting business decisionmaking, especially the decisions that rely on a large amount of historical data.
- Converting vast amounts of salvageable data into meaningful information. Data mining considerations will provide strategic advantage to the resurrecting organization that a plain vanilla conversion of salvageable data will not provide.
- Since the sophistication of the customers also is improving, it will be essential to use the three-dimensional drill-down structure provided by data mining techniques in order to understand and deal with the customer at an appropriate level.
- Discovery of unsuspecting relationships between chunks of data that would have been overlooked by traditional data querying techniques.
- Speed of analysis from data mining will assist in speedier responses to changing business situation, as well as supporting process-based business.
- Reduction in the large number of reports that were produced in the legacy systems in order to satisfy the multidimensional needs of the user. In the Y2K-hit system, one would expect collaboration and analysis of a number of reports in order for the information to be meaningful. Data mining

avoids this need to print multiple reports, as it provides a single consistent view from any desired angle.

6.5 MIDDLEWARE IN RESURRECTION

We considered the advantages of newer languages in providing faster and cheaper ways of writing code for a resurrecting system. We also considered the issues related to storing and retrieving data from their storage mechanisms within a resurrecting application. We now consider the important issue of integrating the application logic and the underlying database. This was not a major issue on the mainframe systems as the data and the programs that processed the data were usually kept together and were available on the same machine. However, as we progress towards the new millennium the issues of distribution and, therefore, of bringing together the various distributed elements will be of prime importance. For example, if a solution requires Visual Basic for the front-end and C++ for the backend, SQLServer for the data storage and Active pages to make it Internet aware, the question is "how can the solution be glued together?" The answer is provided by what is popularly known as *middleware*. Middleware is the glue that brings together various components of a system and is an indispensable technology in a Y2K resurrecting system.

Furthermore, as the technology of distribution (or of bringing distributed objects together) is pretty new, the chances of the middleware components themselves being hit by the Y2K problem is pretty slim. Thus, the focus in studying middlware is in understanding how it can help in the solution, rather than in investigating it for the problem. The exceptions to this situation can be the actual elements that are brought together by the middleware that may include traditional databases and applications that are hit by Y2K. Middleware will once again be a part of the solution rather than the problem as it will enable identification and isolation of Y2K-hit parts and also help in replacing them during the resurrection process.

Because of the enormous importance of distribution in resurrection, it is discussed in great detail in Chapter 12. Herein, we briefly mention the two important candidates of this new technology in distribution and the role they can play in the Y2K resurrection.

6.5.1 CORBA

CORBA, or Common Object Request Broker Architecture, is an Object Request Broker that was defined by the OMG (Object Management Group) to provide an open standard that enables gluing together of objects irrespective of their language of development and the platform on which they operate. This led to CORBA's popularity in a heterogeneous environment — precisely what we expect during a Y2K resurrection. During resurrection effort, we are likely to be dealing with the environment and platform of the application that is hit and the development environment of the new application.

Through the Interface Definition Language (IDL) of CORBA, which has standard interfaces to languages like C++ and Smalltalk, it is possible to integrate the new development environment with the tools for resurrection as well as the Y2K-hit application. Thus, CORBA tends to provide an good heterogeneous distributed OO environment for resurrection.

OMG's effort has further resulted in the Internet Inter-ORB Protocol (IIOP) that provides a mechanism for resurrection effort through the Internet. There are many vendors who offer tools and techniques that are CORBA compliant. These tools can play a valuable part in the resurrection process.

6.5.2   DCOM

Distributed Component Object Model (DCOM) is a Microsoft product and is the distributed version of the Component Object Model (COM), which was designed and developed to provide for message passing between various Microsoft applications. DCOM is based on the interface model of COM. DCOM allows the tools to be used without having to worry about the semantics differences of the underlying languages, but within the Microsoft development environment (e.g., Windows NT).

If the Y2K resurrection effort is conducted entirely within the Microsoft development environment, then DCOM will have a much larger role to play than CORBA. However, this decision of using DCOM vs. CORBA will depend on the type and extent of the technology used in the dissection as well as resurrection effort.

6.6   ENTERPRISE BUSINESS SOLUTIONS AND RESURRECTION

The core resurrection philosophy, discussed in the previous chapter (Figure 5.1), describes how the data can be salvaged and the functionality can be remodeled along the lines of Business Process Reengineering (BPR). The activity of customizing a solution package (TA03: Rewrite–Modify–Customize, Chapter 7) is one of the possible ways the resurrection process can satisfy the required functionality of the organization. This option is technically attractive as the customization focus reduces the possible pressure of full-scale rewrite on the resurrection team. Customizable packages for business solutions can play a significant role in resurrection and are discussed here.

6.6.1   ENTERPRISE RESOURCE PLANNING (ERP)

The enterprise-wide business solutions have become popular under the banner of ERP (Enterprise Resource Planning). An ERP solution claims to seamlessly integrate and consolidate mission critical operations of a business such as financials, administration, and human resources in a single computing environment. Therefore, ERP solutions based on customizable packages can provide an excellent alternative (to a complete rewrite of the applications) in the resurrection process. Sharing of single data repository will result in consistency and accuracy. Usage of technologies such as workflow and online analytical processing will help in streamlining the work within the new organizations — providing advantages way beyond those of merely solving the Y2K problem. ERP solutions will ensure that the staff in the resurrecting organizations spends less time on administrative tasks than they used to do before resurrection. The saving in time can be used to focus on the organization's core business.

More specifically, the advantages of ERP solutions in the Y2K resurrection process are

- Shared data repository means data conversion effort need not be duplicated.
- Data consistency also implies date conversions or date modifications need not be repeated — they can be the same set of data for various applications.
- Pre-formatted reporting facilities that are Y2K compliant (this needs to be confirmed, however most ERP solution providers, such as the ones discussed next, claim to be compliant).
- Potential for increased productivity as many of the administrative functions of the organization (e.g., staff in a bank wanting to check their own balances or their payslips) can be downloaded to the employees themselves.
- Facilitation of integration with desktop applications; email; fax; and interactive voice response, workflow, and electronic forms.
- Step-wise integration with other systems within the organization that may *not* have been affected by the Y2K problem and, hence, fully salvageable.

ERP has become popular with the arrival of packages like SAP™, PeopleSoft™ and Oracle Financials™. The only (and substantial) effort that needs to be done in these packages is their customization. Thus, in situations where the only salvageable entity is the data, it might be worthwhile planning the Y2K resurrection effort around these enterprise business solutions. A brief discussion of these packages follows.

6.6.2 SAP™

SAP (Systems, Applications, and Products) is claimed to be an open multi-tier client server software system application designed to manage business information needs of an enterprise. The SAP layers are made up of a network of database servers, presentation servers, and the middle layer of business applications that control the logic of the business transactions.

Solution applications within SAP span a wide range including banking, hospital, publishing, insurance, money and foreign exchange markets, telecommunications, production planning, and process industries. The R/3 reference model within SAP can be used to simulate processes within the resurrecting organization — especially how the organization will look after data conversion and other salvage operations. Thus, the reference model also should be able to provide help in the dissection and salvage activities of the resurrection process, eliminating functions that are redundant and irrelevant.

SAP R/3 also claims Y2K compliance, with all date fields stored as 4-byte fields, and also retrieved, displayed, and printed in 4-digits. The package has been tested by many independent consultants for a wide range of data both before and after the

Y2K hump. The third party interfaces of SAP convert a 2-digit data of business partners to a 4-digit one as it is processed and stored. Depending on the level of preparedness of the organization for its Y2K preparedness, this feature will be important in helping business partners reach Y2K compliance — and if they are hit, resurrect.

6.6.3 PeopleSoft™

PeopleSoft also claims to be an integrated enterprise wide solution that would encompass applications from all areas of the business. Because of its ability to integrate with other applications within the organization, the PeopleSoft solution is also attractive when the organization is facing a piecemeal Y2K resurrection. PeopleSoft claims to be able to customize their applications to the specific needs of their clients, integrate with other software vendors, or extend and build their own solutions, all of which can prove to be valuable in the Y2K resurrection process.

6.6.4 Oracle Applications™

Oracle, as a database vendor, has a long association with storing and retrieval of date-related data. That being the case, Oracle's ERP solutions provide an attractive alternative in the resurrection process. The Oracle Applications suite of products is made up of modules including Oracle Financials, Oracle HR, Oracle Manufacturing, etc. Depending on the type of Y2K hit an organization has suffered and the needs of the organization to resurrect (either one module or the entire enterprise-wide software systems), these Oracle modules can be introduced within the organization during the resurrection process.

6.7 NETWORKS AND COMMUNICATIONS IN RESURRECTION

Compared with the business applications and the databases, networks and communication protocols have lesser possibility of being directly affected by the Y2K problem. However, they will play a significant role in the resurrecting system. Appropriate use of existing protocols as well as shifting to newer and more sophisticated networks and protocols will have to be considered during the resurrection process. These issues are briefly discussed below.

6.7.1 Communication Protocols

Communication protocols provide the means by which data can be exchanged over a network. These protocols also provide ability to exchange information like mails and messages as well as provide the infrastructure for client-server architecture. For example, the TCP/IP network protocol provides the ability to transfer data and information across various platforms. The "routable" nature of this protocol means that with TCP/IP the resurrection team can seriously consider the web as a part of its solution. On the other hand, protocols like NetBEUI may provide quick and easy solutions for applications running on local networks and on similar platforms.

6.7.2 ACCESS MECHANISMS

Consideration to access mechanisms is an important part of the network in providing overall resurrection solution. These considerations include the various ways in which data may be accessed remotely and the issues associated with such access. For example, access mechanisms will have to consider the provision of dedicated lines, automated or manual dialing, speed of access (and the associated bandwidth issues), security and confidentiality of data, and so on. Remote backups and download of data on local machines will have to consider issues of network traffic during peak and off-peak times. For example, large backups and download of data may be done at night instead of daytime when other kinds of traffic (like mail) is high. Finally, access mechanisms also will consider releasing newer versions of the applications remotely (e.g., via the company's intranet or similar remote access facilities).

6.7.3 REALTIME DATA

Realtime data is a special case of overall access considerations in which the application using the data needs to do so instantaneously. Processing of data in these applications is ongoing. In resurrecting these applications, it is not sufficient to resurrect the data and the behavior alone. In addition to the data and logic resurrection, it is also important to maintain the response time or the speed with which the ongoing data is being processed. Networks and communication mechanisms will play an important role in applications that use realtime data. For example, realtime update of financial market data is crucial for the applications that analyze and predict market trends. These applications would require a dedicated network with sufficient bandwidth to be able to carry the data load in terms of volume and time, and form part of network considerations during the resurrection process.

6.8 HARDWARE AND RESURRECTION

The need for hardware during the resurrection effort can be summarised as follows:

- Hardware used in design and development of the resurrecting system.
- Hardware used in deployment of the resurrecting system.
- Hardware used in testing the new system.
- Hardware itself having Y2K problems.

Dealing with these hardware-related issues in Y2K resurrection is expected to be one of the easier activities in resurrection. Although it would be impractical to consider replacing large mainframes within a day or two, the same cannot be said of problems occurring in PCs and desktop machines. Within the time and budgets allocated for hardware within resurrection, it should be convenient to replace the hardware that exhibits Y2K problem. The cost of locating BIOS errors in smaller machines and the cost of replacing the errant motherboards with new hardware are minuscule compared with the expenses in locating and fixing software problem.

Reduced hardware costs at all levels of hardware have made it possible to procure and install new hardware relatively easily in developing and deploying system. This advantage will be used to its maximum in resurrecting Y2K-hit systems wherever hardware is involved. Furthermore, falling hardware prices also are supported by their easy and ready availability. Short delivery time, a wide range of vendors, and international availability of hardware has made it strategically convenient to replace end-user hardware. This is also true in the development environment as much as it is true of the deployment environment. Newer and cheaper hardware for the development environment should have a significant impact in reducing the development life cycle.

6.9 KEY POINTS

1. When we discuss technology in Y2K, it includes discussion of the technology in which the problem exists, the technology used in dissecting the problem, and the technology used in resurrecting the new system — this was presented by extending an example from the firecrackers discussed in Chapter 1.
2. COBOL was discussed as a language that is likely to suffer the maximum Y2K hits, whereas C++, Smalltalk, and Java were discussed with respect to their potential as languages to be used in resurrection.
3. Hierarchical databases were discussed as prime candidates for Y2K hits and so also the relational databases. However, relational, object-oriented and object-relational databases were also discussed in the way they can assist resurrection.
4. The importance of databases in Y2K resurrection goes beyond the traditional needs of storing and retrieving data. The phenomenal growth in data storage capacities, likely to be part of any resurrecting system, imply that search for "meaning" from "relevant" data will be important in large databases. This was discussed under the topic of data mining.
5. The importance of middleware in resurrection was underscored — and left for further discussion in Chapter 12.
6. The role of ERP packages also was discussed and some solution packages for a new millennium business were mentioned.
7. Network technology and the role it plays in Y2K resurrection was discussed.
8. The role of hardware in Y2K hits and resurrection was mentioned.

6.10 NOTES

Thanks to Michael Riley for his valuable discussions on C++, Oskar Schlegl and Gina Sugay for their comments on the Smalltalk example, and Rajeev Arora for input on the Java language. Sagar Agashe's experience on networks and communication was very helpful and so was a study by Kennith Trinh on data mining. Practical experiences of Subodh Deshpande for information on SAP, Vivienne Counter for PeopleSoft, and Vidyanand Karandikar for Oracle came in handy in the discussion on use of packages in resurrection.

6.11 REFERENCES

1. Grady, B., *Best of Booch: Designing Strategies for Object Technology,* Ed Eykholt, Ed., SIGS New York, SIGS Reference Library, 1996.
2. Example based on work done by Rajeev Arora in Schneider, J. and Arora, R., *Special Edition using Enterprise Java,* Que Publications, Indianapolis, IN, 1997.
3. Ranen, M. and Bayliss, D., New application architectures: extended data types offer fresh content capability, *Obj. Mag.,* 7:6, 55–60, August 1997.

7 A Technological Process

Ours is an industry constantly faced with new tools, programming languages, hardware, operating systems, and concepts. It's only natural that we're prepared to abandon old technologies that are no longer relevant and take advantage of exciting new technologies.

Edward Yourdon
from *Rise and Resurrection of the American Programmer*[1]

Abstract Having discussed the various aspect of technology in the previous chapter, we now place that understanding within the framework of the technological process. We start by describing the technological process and the associated actors, activities, and deliverables. This is followed by an in-depth discussion of the tasks related to the technological activities. Activities and tasks are numbered in order to provide a better cross-referencing facility when this description is referred to in the rebuilding process. This technological process, dealing with the "what" of the overall rebuilding process encompasses the activities of dissecting the existing system, rewriting software systems, preserving and re-entering data, relevant databases, customizing third-party software, hardware, configuration, network, and data delivery. The aspects of quality assurance and project management that deal with the technology of resurrection are also described within the technological process framework. Finally, an indicative metrics that measures the size of the technological process is described.

7.1 DESCRIBING A TECHNOLOGICAL PROCESS

The technological process has a major role to play during the resurrection exercise, as it is the driving dimension of resurrection. The technological process deals with the raw material or the "cement and concrete" of rebuilding the enterprise. This includes all technical aspects of resurrection like the languages, the corresponding databases, the networks, and the delivery mechanism. The conceptual aspect of these raw materials was discussed in the previous chapter. Here, we concentrate on placing these raw materials in the process discipline, so that they can be systematically and effectively applied in the resurrection process.

We have discussed that the 2-digit formatting of the date in the organization's software systems was a technological problem. Therefore, when we investigate the Y2K problem, we will need to have some appreciation of the existing technology in which the problem had occurred. This investigation, as discussed in Section 7.5, is called the activity of dissection (TA01). Our arguments on resurrection stress the

169

fact that when we resurrect, we do a lot more than simply fixing the 2-digit problem. Therefore, the focus of the dissection activity is restricted only to identifying the salvageable areas of the data and the programs of the "hit" enterprise. This should be achieved in minimal time if the focus has to be on resurrection. After that is achieved, the process of resurrection would be common for any attempt at resurrecting, irrespective of what caused the problem.

We also note that the technological dimension, although the driving force behind resurrection, does not work independent of the other two dimensions of the resurrection process. The activities within this dimension are orthogonal to the activities from the methodological and sociological dimensions. Therefore, the technological activities discussed here are not necessarily carried out in the exact sequence in which they are mentioned here. A process-thread, which is an instance of a process and which would cut across all dimensions of resurrection, would dictate the sequence of activities. This process-thread is the implementation of the resurrection process described in this book, and it depends, in addition to a number of practical factors, on the severity of the Y2K hit, the size of the organization, the rigidity and bulkiness of the organization, and its level of preparedness for Y2K problem. Thus, the discussion of the technological process in this chapter can be termed as the *vanilla* technological process.

7.1.1 THE PROCESS FIGURE

The technological dimension of the resurrection process is made up of the technological actors, activities, tasks, and deliverables. These are shown in Figure 7.1. There are a total of 11 activities within the technological process, and they are made up of a total of 55 tasks. The tasks provide the steps for completion of the activities. The basic deliverable is a software system that forms the basis for the resurrected company.

7.1.2 A HIGH-LEVEL PROCESS FLOW

The flow of the technological process starts with a short and sharp attempt at dissecting the Y2K-hit system. The explicit aim of the dissection activity is to find as many salvageable options as possible. Almost parallel with the activity of dissection is the activity of creating technical environment. The technical environment is primarily the development environment of the resurrection team and where the compile–link–build of the system will take place. This is followed by the detailed technical work on rewriting–modifying–customizing of software. The programmer and the variations of the programmer actor are involved in most of these technical activities.

The database manager deals with the activities related to the database and the data entry. The database manager is a variation of both the programmer and the project manager. The database manager creates and maintains the data model and administers the database. Furthermore, if the resurrection team decided to re-enter the data, the database manager organizes and manages the activity of data entry. Data entry is a likely activity in case of small- to medium-sized organizations, wherein the amount of data is limited and, therefore, it is cost effective to re-enter rather than write conversion programs.

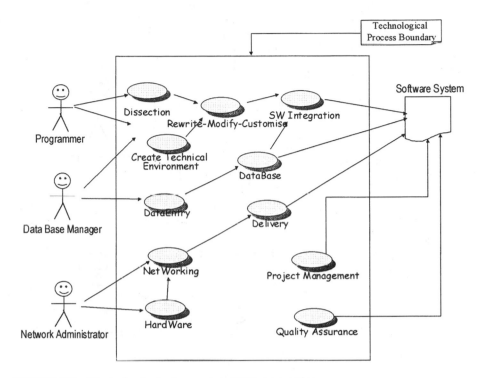

FIGURE 7.1 The technological process in Y2K resurrection.

Another activity of importance is that of networking. This activity deals with the evaluation of the existing network, as well as upgrading it for further development. This activity also is involved in upgrading the network in the production environment, should that be the case. The activity of networking leads into the activity of delivery. The delivery mechanism is important when the resurrected enterprise is designed based on a distributed architecture resulting in a need to deliver the data in a distributed fashion.

The activities of project management and quality assurance span across all three dimensions of the resurrection process. However, within these activities, there are some tasks that are specific to the technological dimension and others that relate to the other two dimensions of the resurrection process. The process flow in Figure 7.1 shows the activities of project management and quality assurance with respect to their technical aspects. These activities of project management and quality assurance help in producing a quality resurrected system that is delivered on time and within budget.

7.2 TECHNOLOGICAL ACTORS

The technological actors derive from the basic actor called *programmer* (Figure 7.2). Most activities within the technological process deal with the language, database, hardware, and tools used in resurrection. Therefore, the technological actors

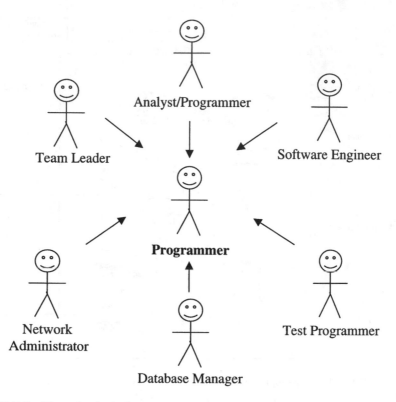

FIGURE 7.2 The technological actors.

comprise people involved in the roles of writing software, managing network, and modeling database. Specifically, we have the analyst/programmer who will analyze the requirement at unit level and will be writing and modifying the system. The software engineers are involved in both analysis and design activities. Test programmers examine the designs from testing viewpoint and produce test designs and test cases accordingly. They may also write test harness for testing the system at program or class level. The team leader is an actor managing a small team of developers and their corresponding technical environment (e.g., configurations, build environments). The database manager handles the database issues, and the network administrator the network issues. Project management and quality assurance continue to play an important role in the background. Therefore, the actors related to these activities are not mentioned as primary actors. Their description appears in greater detail in the methodological dimension of the resurrection process. Below is a description of the three primary technological actors.

7.2.1 Actor: Programmer

The programmer is the prime actor for the technological process. She should be competent in the use of the language and the environment used in the resurrection process. In addition to competence in the language of choice (e.g., C++ or Java), this actor also should be proficient in the associated technologies (e.g., DCOM, CORBA). It will be essential to provide continuous training to this actor in the use of languages and corresponding databases. The training aspect of this actor is discussed in the sociological dimensions of the resurrection process.

Another important activity that will involve this actor is that of dissection. The expected quick dissection of the Y2K-hit system will need some technical skills in reading and understanding the existing code and data. If the Y2K-hit system is a large system then it will be essential to use the tools that help in analyzing the existing system. Usage of Y2K-related tools were a part of the prevention effort. Therefore, organizations at yellow or green level of preparedness will have a few people (variations of this actor) who can use the tools for dissection. Skills in prevention will only be useful during the dissection activity, beyond which they will not be of much value during Y2K resurrection.

7.2.2 ACTOR: DATABASE MANAGER

The database manager plays the duel role of being a technical programmer as well as a manager during the resurrection. Therefore, this actor is a derivation of the programmer (when dealing with the technological aspect of resurrection) as well as the derivative of the project manager (when dealing with the methodologies and management of the database).

This actor is expected to be familiar with the existing data models, especially the ones that are affected by the date problem. This knowledge of the database manager will lead to her involvement in the dissection effort from the database viewpoint. She will be involved in the modification of current designs and, finally, design of the new data model. The familiarity with the existing database means that this actor continues to be involved in the day-to-day management of the current database. Because of the varying demands on this actor, it is likely that there will be more than one person playing the role of the actor (database manager).

Should the salvage options resulting from the dissection indicate that there is a large amount of data within the existing database that needs to be converted then the database manager will be involved in the exercise to ensure correctness and relevance of the conversion. Should there be a need to enter new data, this actor will be involved in coordination of that data entry effort.

Furthermore, use of stored procedures within the database in order to populate the database tables with new data and usage of facilities like triggers in order to initiate automatic procedures, are all part of the database manager's job. This actor, along with the analyst/programmer and the software engineer actors, also is involved in the software integration activity wherein the newly created and/or modified database and the newly written code are put together to provide the complete solution.

Finally, the database manager is involved in the evaluation activity (in the methodological dimension) if the organization is going for a new database to satisfy its data needs.

7.2.3   ACTOR: NETWORK ADMINISTRATOR

The network administrator is an actor responsible for the evaluation and upgrading of the network for both development and production environment. Once again, depending on the size of the organization and the extent of development and production activities taking place, the role of this actor would be performed by one or more people.

The network administrator is involved in managing the current network, participating in the evaluation of new network (including the hardware to be used, e.g., the space and speed of the server), and ensuring that the data and software delivery takes place correctly. Some upgrades (e.g., from 16-bit to 32-bit NT programming environment) may happen only after suitable upgrade to the hardware. Therefore, this actor also may be involved in the activity: hardware during the initial iteration.

7.3   TECHNOLOGICAL DELIVERABLES

7.3.1   APPLICATION

The resurrected organization is based on the processes served by the software application (Figure 7.3). Therefore, the application (or the software system) coming out of the technological process is one of the main deliverables of the process. This application (or a set of applications) may result from:

- Rewriting the previous application that was affected by the Y2K problem (rewrite).
- Modification of the Y2K-hit application (modify).

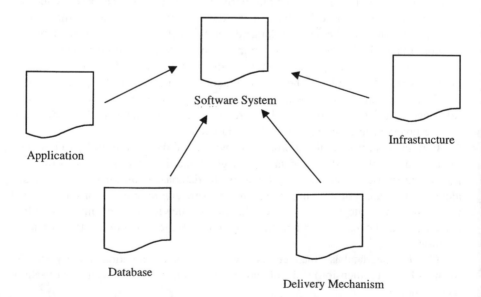

FIGURE 7.3   Variations of the technological deliverables.

- Customization of a third party application in order to deliver the set of new functionality.

Thus, this deliverable is an application or a set of applications resulting from any of the above three choices or a combination of them. Note that the database, delivery, and other support mechanism are a part of the overall software solution. However, they are considered as separate deliverables mainly because the activities required in order to produce these other deliverables are different from the ones used in producing the application.

7.3.2 DATABASE

The database is another major deliverable of the technological process. This deliverable will contain the following types of data:

- Converted data (if there is a substantial amount of salvageable data in the "hit" database).
- New data that, in addition to the re-entered data from the "hit" database, will be the new data that the organization may already be generating.
- Merged data, made up of new, converted, and re-entered data.

The database deliverable results from all the activities that are performed in evaluating the type of database, the data that will go into it, the corresponding data models, and the procedures that are used in accessing and storing data. The database deliverable has to eventually work with the application deliverable in order to provide the final solution to the organization.

7.3.3 DELIVERY MECHANISM

The delivery mechanism is important in situations where the data is stored across the network and is remotely accessed by the application. The importance of the delivery mechanism can be appreciated in applications that store, retrieve, and process large amount of historical data, especially when the applications are dealing with trends and predictions. These applications rely on a large amount of data to be delivered to the application and processed in order to arrive at the trend figures. The mode of accessing the data (e.g., dial up, direct, through the Internet) is a part of this delivery mechanism.

7.3.4 INFRASTRUCTURE

The infrastructure involves everything that is outside of the other deliverables discussed in the technological process. Thus, this deliverable includes the platform on which the database is stored and the application is executed. For example, the network and the common services used by the application would form part of the infrastructure deliverable. If the solution were a Web-based application, this deliverable would include the Web elements of the solution (e.g., the browser and the way it is used by the application, speed of data delivery).

7.4 TECHNOLOGICAL ACTIVITIES AND TASKS —
WITH ITERATIONS

The activities and tasks are the two "action elements" of the technological process. The actors perform the activities by following a set of well-defined tasks. Table 7.1 provides a bird's-eye view of the activities and their corresponding tasks. As mentioned earlier, not all activities would follow one another in the sequence provided in the process diagram. The process-threads or the instance of the process will dictate the final sequence. Furthermore, not all tasks within the activities are performed in one attempt. The entire resurrection process is iterative and incremental. Therefore, during each iteration, only some of the activities will be performed. Also, only the relevant tasks for the iteration within the activities are performed in each iteration. Suggested iterations during which the activities will take place are provided in the Table 7.1. Depending on the scope of the resurrection project, these activities may get performed in iterations other than the suggested iterations.

7.5 TA01: DISSECTION

The activity of dissection identifies as many aspects of the Y2K-hit system as possible that are of business and strategic relevance to the user. Thus, the activity of dissection makes use of some of the experience we gained when we were trying to prevent a Y2K hit. The prevention work predominantly concentrated on testing the system for Y2K bugs. During dissection we will be testing the system for areas affected by the date. However, there are a few differences between the Y2K prevention exercise and the dissection carried out during the resurrection effort.

The main philosophical difference between dissection and Y2K testing is that in dissection the aim is not to find date errors and fix them. Instead, we look for everything that can be 'salvaged' from the existing system that will provide some value to the new system. Therefore, we do not try to understand fully all the technical aspects of the system. Dissection is scoped in such a way that the activity takes a very short time to complete. This is so because during dissection (as against testing before the Y2K hump), the system is assumed "dead" — i.e., not functional. Thus, the restrictions of the "live" system should not be there, ensuring that the dissection activity is not distracted by the demands of the real system. This ensures that time and effort are not wasted in maintenance or in searching endlessly for bugs in the system. Two possible exceptions to these situations are

1. When the system is serving a vital function within the organization (despite the Y2K hit). It might then be essential to take it off-line or create a backup before the dissection is carried out.
2. It is a mild hit, which requires a very simple fix for the date problem in a known and small area of the system.

During dissection, we examine the system from its logic, database, and front-end aspect, to see what are the areas that can be resurrected, and how they should be sequenced. In addition, we consider many other parts of a hit solution that can

TABLE 7.1
Technological Activities and Tasks with Probable Iterations

Technological Activities	Technological Tasks
TA01: Dissection Iteration: initial	TT01-1: Scope the dissection TT01-2: Dissect data TT01-3: Dissect logic TT01-4: Dissect presentation TT01-5: Shortlist salvageable options
TA02: Create technical environment Iteration: initial	TT02-1: Setup language TT02-2: Deal with the operating system TT02-3: Install database TT02-4: Install network TT02-5: Relate to hardware
TA03: Rewrite–modify–customize Iteration: major	TT03-1: Environment familiarization TT03-2: Estimate effort TT03-3: Review date errors TT03-4: Prototype TT03-5: Code TT03-6: Unit test code TT03-7: Incident solving
TA04: Software integration Iteration: major	TT04-1: Bring the software together TT04-2: Ensure consistency with database TT04-3: Verify against requirements TT04-4: Verify performance TT04-5: Incident solving TT04-6: Regression testing
TA05: Data creation Iteration: major	TT05-1: Review date errors TT05-2: Scope the data creation TT05-3: Automate data conversion TT05-4: Manual data entry TT05-5: Verification of data TT05-6: Backup and history of data
TA06: Database Iteration: initial–major	TT06-1: Evaluate database TT06-2: Distribution in database TT06-3: Create data model TT06-4: Create stored procedures TT06-5: Administration of database
TA07: Hardware Iteration: initial	TT07-1: Evaluate current hardware TT07-2: Upgrade to new hardware TT07-3: Maintenance of hardware TT07-4: Security of hardware
TA08: Network Iteration: initial	TT08-1: Evaluate current network TT08-2: Upgrade network TT08-3: Network maintenance
TA09: Delivery Iteration: major	TT09-1: Evaluate existing delivery mechanisms TT09-2: Upgrade delivery mechanism TT09-3: Ensure data delivery TT09-4: Ensure software delivery

---

TABLE 7.1 *(continued)*
Technological Activities and Tasks with Probable Iterations

Technological Activities	Technological Tasks
TA10: Quality assurance	TT10-1: Test plan
Iteration: Initial–major–final	TT10-2: Test design
	TT10-3: Test cases
	TT10-4: Code walkthrough
	TT10-5: Documentation
TA11: Project management	TT11-1: Manage build environment
Iteration: initial–major–final	TT11-2: Take charge of working version
	TT11-3: Manage configurations/versions
	TT11-4: Organize database and network
	TT11-5: Update project plan

---

provide value to the resurrection effort. For example, the user guides or the help system of the hit application can provide a very good starting point for requirements modeling.

7.5.1　TT01-1: Scope the Dissection

This task involves quantifying the extent to which we want to dissect the Y2K-hit system. It is likely that a date problem deep inside the data structure or the logic of the system may bring the system to a halt. This may be a small problem to fix, but not so easy to detect. If the results of the fault are catastrophic (which is what we expect in a few cases), that does not mean the resurrection has to be lengthy and complicated. We need to put the dissection work in perspective. This task will consider the following factors in arriving at the scope for dissection:

- Nature and type of the Y2K problem that has caused the system to crash — if the nature of the Y2K bug is known, then the scope of the dissection can be small.
- Technology of the system — if the affected system has old technology, the scope of dissection should be as small as possible. Such a system will not provide many salvageable options.
- Budgets — low budgets mean the organization cannot afford to conduct detailed dissection activity. This would further reduce the scope of dissection and may not provide many salvageable options.
- Availability of tools and people — if there is not enough expertise in dissecting the existing system, it may not be worth training new people in "how to test a system for Y2K."
- Areas for investigation — data, logic, or presentation. It is highly unlikely that only one area of the system is affected. However, the affected area can dictate the scope of resurrection by deciding on the extent of testing needed in order to identify salvageable options.

Note that this is an iterative task and that the results from the subsequent tasks of dissection of data, logic, and presentation may influence the scope of dissection.

7.5.2   TT01-2: Dissect Data

The task of dissecting the data deals with the data content of the hit system. It also may include investigation of the data model. The aim of the task is to re-test the database for the data that are affected by the Y2K hit. However, testing the affected data is the starting point for identifying and testing the remaining data for possible salvageable options. What can be salvaged in terms of data is more than just the Y2K-hit data. Therefore, dissection of data needs to keep in mind the other data within the system that are relevant to the organization.

Data dissection is expected to be easier to detect in comparison with logic dissection. This is because once an error is detected in one field, the rest of the fields are likely to have a similar date error. Therefore, during dissection of the data care should be taken to avoid unnecessary dissection. Once a decision to salvage a table is taken, it serves no purpose to test the remaining fields of the table or the data within the table.

The data dissection activity can be supported by the testing concepts of equivalence partitioning and boundary values (see Chapter 14). Tools for testing and data conversion also can be useful during this task.

7.5.3   TT01-3: Dissect Logic

Dissection of logic within the applications is carried out with the aim of salvaging the requirements for the new system. As discussed in the core philosophy of resurrection (Chapter 5, Section 5.1), it is not easy to create requirements models out of COBOL logic. However, an attempt is made to put together any existing requirement and the logic within the application programs in order to arrive at salvageable options from the Y2K-hit system. Some examples of the result of logic dissection are branching of control based on dates, sorting logic based on date as the key fields, and so on.

Depending on the scope of dissection, this task also ensures that we go as deep within the code as is necessary to salvage the requirements, and no further. By keeping in mind the fact that during resurrection we are going to rewrite a large amount of the code, we ensure that the scope of dissection does not expand unreasonably.

Furthermore, we also ensure that the logic dissection concentrates only on the applications that are still relevant to the organization. This may happen in two iterations. For example, initial dissection of a Y2K-hit banking system may reveal that the areas of customer information are still intact (because the birth dates entered were in 4 digits), but the interest calculation has gone wrong. This will lead to only the areas of interest calculation being investigated in greater detail during this task. This is also the area or subsystem within the application that has high priority when it comes to specifying requirements for the resurrecting system. Thus, this task can provide a valuable starting point for further discussions with the users, who may then be encouraged to participate in the writing of the formal requirements for the resurrecting system.

7.5.4 TT01-4: DISSECT PRESENTATION

Presentation includes all means of communication with the user. In a Y2K-hit system, we expect the presentation to include a substantial number of printed reports. Thus, printed reports from the mainframe, user interfaces as well as user guides, and other support material form part of the presentation.

In the absence of formal requirements (or even in conjunction with them), the dissection of the existing requirements can be carried out by investigating the user interfaces of the existing system. It is important to note that if the system has crashed because of Y2K, its functionality will *not* necessarily be wrong. Therefore, functionally, the screen shots of the existing system (albeit not date compliant or even not functioning) are still able to provide the basis for formal requirements. Help files, training material, and any other documentation related to the system that is presented to the end user of the system provides invaluable input in the dissection of the presentation.

7.5.5 TT01-5: SHORTLIST SALVAGEABLE OPTIONS

Based on the three previous tasks within this dissection activity we have a list of salvageable options that are arrived at from the data, the logic and the presentation. During this task, we make a list of all entities within the Y2K-hit system that are still relevant to the organization. This task is also iterative and the list of salvageable options will continue to be influenced by the results of the dissection tasks. In turn, the list should assist in revisiting the scope of the dissection exercise. Thus, if at the end of the initial iteration, there is a large amount of data and presentation that can be salvaged, then it indicates that the Y2K-hit system has a lot of entities that are of value to the organization. Therefore, this will imply that we should carry out further detailed dissection work to identify more salvageable options. These salvageable options are related to the rest of the activities within the resurrection process. Therefore, they are described within the activities where they are relevant. The salvageable options contain the data content, data model, program logic, user interface, printing, user guides, and so on.

7.6 TA02: CREATE TECHNICAL ENVIRONMENT

The activity of creating the technical environment can run in parallel with the dissection activity (TA01). However, it would usually form part of a process-thread that starts from the methodological activity of alternative evaluation (MA01), wherein the alternatives to various approaches for resurrection are discussed. Thus, this activity of creating technical environment would create the technical environment for the resurrection process, based on the decisions taken during the alternative evaluations.

The actor programmer is involved in creating the technical environment for development purpose. The actor project manager, through the activities of project management, will be providing support in the creation of technical environment. The activity of creating technical environment is accomplished by means of tasks that handle languages, operating system, database, network, and the hardware. Most of these tasks are carried out during the initial iteration of the resurrection process.

7.6.1   TT02-1: Setup Language

This task deals with the software language used in resurrection. The choice of language can be from (but not restricted to) the languages discussed in the previous chapter: C++, Smalltalk, and Java. During this task, the language of choice is made available to the development staff. The language compilers may be made available on individual machines or on the server. Local standards on use of the language (e.g., variable names, global vs. local attributes) are also decided during this task. An attempt is made in this task to ensure that the usage of the language is made consistent across the development environment.

Salvage Options — A mapping between the Y2K-hit language and the language used in resurrection can provide a good idea on the development metrics. Knowledge and understanding of the hit language also helps in dissection work. Therefore, setting up and understanding the hit language may be occasionally required.

7.6.2   TT02-2: Deal with the Operating System

This task deals with the installation of the operating system on the development machines. The choice of the operating system may iterate with the previous task of choosing the language of resurrection. When a choice of language and operating system is available, then that choice would be dictated usually by the non-functional issues within the system. Thus, issues like development costs, programmer preference, performance, etc. would have an influence on the choice and installation of the operating system.

7.6.3   TT02-3: Install Database

This task deals with installation of the database for the resurrection effort. Like the language and the operating system, the development (and deployment) database will be decided during the alternative evaluation. If the resurrection is based on a relational database, this task will install and manage databases like Oracle or SQLServer. Fine tuning of the database and setting up of routine administrative functions will follow.

Salvage Options — If there is an existing database, then the procedures used in managing and administrating the database can be used for the new database as well.

7.6.4   TT02-4: Install Network

The configuration of the network, its access to the development team, and the management of the network falls under this task. The network administrator would typically get involved with the programmer in installing and/or upgrading the network. After installation, the development network may have to be fine-tuned. It would also need on going administration in terms of setting up users of the system, assigning privileges to the users, and ensuring security of the network.

Salvage Options — If the Y2K problems were in the existing network then a change or upgrade would be inevitable. Otherwise, the existing network should be fully salvageable. The security procedures also are salvageable.

7.6.5   TT02-5: RELATE TO HARDWARE

The task of hardware is related to creating the hardware environment for resurrection. It involves procurement, installation, and testing of the machines that will be used for development. This task would usually be conducted after estimations for the speed and memory size of the development machines have been made. Further consideration needs to be given to the language, operating system, and database that will be supported by this hardware. Capacity of the machines for the individual developers, for the overall development server, and off-site backups will have to be considered.

Salvage Options — It is advisable to upgrade the hardware from the one that was used when the organization was hit by Y2K. However, the salvage option is to use the existing hardware for additional testing, backups, and other support type work.

7.7   TA03: REWRITE–MODIFY–CUSTOMIZE

This activity of rewrite–modify–customize is made up of three sub-activities:

1. Rewriting new software to satisfy existing functionality and provide some more functionality.
2. Modify the current software through a small scoped dissection and fixing.
3. Customize a third-party package that provides the current functionality and provide some more functionality.

Thus, if the decision is made to rewrite the entire application, then this activity will concentrate on analyzing, designing, and coding of the new system. Modifications to the existing system may be driven by the list of salvageable options. If the dissection of the Y2K-hit application leads to some parts of the application that are still valid, then we may have to work at modifying and integrating them in the new solution. If the resurrection team chooses packaged software developed by a third-party software in order to satisfy the functional requirements, then this activity will concentrate on customizing such software. In practice, one would expect all three aspects of this activity to take place during resurrection.

Being a core technical activity, the primary actor for this activity of rewrite–modify–customize is the programmer. Variations of the actor programmer (like the test programmer) would be involved during the execution of this activity. This activity takes place during the major iteration of the resurrection process.

7.7.1 TT03-1: Environment Familiarization

The task of environment familiarization deals with trying out the technical environment created in the previous activity. It would require the programmer to familiarize herself with the environment in which the build of the application will take place. Therefore, this task deals with everything created during the creation of the technical environment. However, actors will concentrate more on the areas of the technical environment that are relevant to their work (e.g., the programmer concentrates on the languages, the database manager on the database). Relevant initial training and mentoring for the development environment can be associated with this task.

Salvage Options — One does not expect the Y2K-hit to have a future in the organization (especially when the resurrection process has been launched). Therefore, it is reasonable to expect that technical people will be eager to transit from the 'old' technical environment to the 'new' environment in which the resurrecting system is being built. Their technical experience serves the useful purpose of dissection — but not much beyond that.

7.7.2 TT03-2: Estimate Effort

Once the programmer and her variations have familiarized themselves with the technical environment it will be essential for them to start estimating effort required at unit level for the programmers. It is not the detailed estimation process that a project manager goes through, in order to arrive at her project plan. This task is more at the programmer level, when each class has to be coded from the specifications provided. Therefore, the result of this task may not be a formal estimate. Having familiarized herself with the technical environment, the programmer can make a rough estimate on the effort that will be required in understanding the specifications and coding the classes.

Salvage Options — An understanding of the complexity of the Y2K-hit system will be extremely helpful in this task. A metrics that map the "old" code to the "new" one also will be a salvageable entity, providing valuable input into this "rough" estimation effort. For customization, the class level estimation may not be required, instead an estimate on integrating the new package within the solution may be required.

7.7.3 TT03-3: Review Date Errors

The dissection activity will have identified all relevant areas of the system that are affected by the date problem. This task reviews all the date errors to ensure that the solution does not suffer from the same problem that caused the crash. If this activity has a large percentage of modification (as against a large rewrite), then reviewing the date errors is all the more important. Modifications can include placing of wrapper classes around the Y2K-hit date data or code. This task of reviewing the date errors will ensure that all new coding work is aware of the cause of the problem.

7.7.4   TT03-4: PROTOTYPE

Prototyping is an essential element of any major programming work. In this activity of re-write, modify, customize prototyping provides two valuable aids to the technical team:

1. Technical — it ensures that the proposed solutions will work at technical level. The technical prototype ensures that the languages and databases will scale up to the requirements of the new system.
2. Functional — it ensures that the users of the system understand and relate to the proposed solutions. The prototypes also assist in further eliciting correct and detailed requirements for the new enterprise.

At programming level, prototyping can be done using tools such as Visual Basic and Delphi. Tasks within the methodological process (Chapter 9, MT04-4) are supported by this task at technical level. Therefore, this is an implementation of the methodological task of prototyping. This task also relates to the sociological tasks dealing with usability and quality of the user interfaces.

Salvage Options — Existing user interfaces and printouts provide a valuable input into the prototyping task. Although the existing user interfaces are not expected to provide "user-centered" designs, they can be used in ensuring that all existing requirements are covered in the new development. Existing user guides also can provide input into prototyping the user interfaces.

7.7.5   TT03-5: CODE

Coding is involved in all three types of resurrection activity in rewriting, modifying, and customizing. This is the largest and most complex of task in resurrection. A number of programmer actors will be involved in this task. The task of coding follows from that of prototyping. Predominantly a part of the major iteration, this task will nevertheless be performed more than once in different iterations.

A large-scale implementation of the designs produced during the methodological activities of requirements modeling (MA04), architecture (MA05), and solution design (MA06) takes place during this task. Rewriting and modification activities will require coding the date components designed during MT06-2, and reuse of existing or third party components specified by reuse designs (MT06-3).

When third party interfaces are customized, this task will deal with understanding their APIs (application programming interfaces) and integrate the code.

Salvage Options — Depending on the result of the dissection activity, we may have application logic as a salvageable option. However, we do not expect to salvage a large amount of code from the "hit" application. Therefore, it will be mostly the functionality of the application that will be salvageable and used in modeling the requirements of the new application. If during our dissection we discover that the existing "hit" code needs major modifications, then we know that we have to salvage the functionality represented by that code, but the logic itself will not be salvageable.

7.7.6   TT03-6: Unit Test Code

After the coding task is completed the task of unit testing is undertaken. Testing is an activity that is conducted throughout the resurrection process. However in this task, the testing work is limited to only testing out the unit or the class or the program that has been coded. The technological activity of quality assurance (TA10) predominantly deals with the writing of test cases for testing the system at technical level. Use cases written in the TA10 activity may be used in conducting this task.

The detailed "how to" of testing is described in the methodological activity of testing (MA09). Thus, the activities of MA09 (how to) and TA10 (what to write) together deal with the design and writing of test cases. During this task of unit test code these test cases may be used at a single unit/class level by the individual programmer in order to test out his or her code. However, using formally written test cases is not mandatory during this task. The testing can be informal and is conducted by the author of the code herself.

Salvage Options — Existing test cases from the hit system can provide valuable checkpoints for the new test cases. Relevant test data also can be salvaged and used in unit testing the new classes.

7.7.7   TT03-7: Incident Solving

Once the software is coded or customized and unit tested, it is expected that some errors will be found. These errors could be in programming or enhancement to the functionality or they could be simply incidences reported by the test team. These are called *software incident reports* (SIR). (See Chapter 14.) They could be stored in a simple system and their progress monitored. In this task these incidents are solved at unit level and the task of unit testing is performed once again. Therefore, the incidences at this stage may not be a part of formal regression testing. Re-testing of the corrected code takes place after it is fixed and this task is performed by the same programmer who is writing and testing the code in the previous tasks.

7.8   TA04: SOFTWARE INTEGRATION

A quick look at Figure 7.1 shows that this activity of software integration (TA04) plays a vital role in bringing together the various *technical* aspects of resurrection that might have been conducted in isolation until now. The previous activity (TA03) includes rewriting, modifying, and customizing of the code. The activities of data creation (TA05) and database (TA06) deal with creating new database, incorporating new data model, and populating the database with salvaged data. These data-related activities might be conducted in parallel (and separately from) the code-related activity. The activity of software integration brings together the output of the activities related to code (TA03) and data (TA05, TA06), tests the system, and places the software system in the context of the final solution to be delivered.

7.8.1 TT04-1: Bring the Software Together

The coding and testing work that takes place during the previous activity of rewrite–modify–customize (TA03) is still at an individual class or module level. Therefore, the output of the TA03 activity still would not be the final application as the modules may not be cohesive. The task of bringing the software together is aimed at integrating the relevant components together by treating them as one complete system rather than a bunch of isolated components. This task views the software as a single solution and integrates the modules related to logic, data, and presentation.

7.8.2 TT04-2: Ensure Consistency with Database

Supporting the previous task of bringing the software together is the task that ensures consistency of the application with the underlying database. Thus, the previous task, although aware of the database, is focused on placing the various components of the application together. This task ensures that the front-end application is consistent with the data model as well as the data content within the database. The salvage options within a typical Y2K resurrection effort would mean that a part of the data is converted and that the data model is redefined. If the resurrection effort chooses a relational or an object-relational database (which it most certainly would, if the "hit" database is a traditional hierarchical structure — see Chapter 3, Section 3.5), then this task will ensure that the new data model is consistent with the application software. Therefore, this activity of software integration would iterate with the activities related to the database. This task also assumes more importance if the database solution is a distributed solution.

7.8.3 TT04-3: Verify Against Requirements

Integrated components (classes and the corresponding database together) need verification from the users before they can be termed as a fully integrated software solution. This task ensures that the components that are brought together at technical level are relevant to the requirements. This task is greatly assisted by the activity of requirement modeling (MA04, Chapter 9). The use-case description within that activity provides the process-threads for the business flow of the system. This business flow can be used to verify that the technical solution being put together is indeed satisfying the business need. In an object-oriented solution, because of its advantages of seamlessness and small semantic gap (shown in Chapter 8, Figures 8.2 and 8.3 and discussed in Section 8.3), it will be possible to identify in the solution the objects that satisfy the business requirements.

7.8.4 TT04-4: Verify Performance

Once the application and database is put together and we have ensured that it satisfied the functional requirements, it is essential to verify the speed and performance of the solution. This is particularly important for real-time applications that depend on instantaneous responses for their business functions. Although response times in a business application may not be as critical as a complex process-control application or life saving applications in a hospital, all solutions need to be verified against their performance requirements. The prevention effort of fixing the date was not overly concerned about performance of the system that was being fixed. Since the system was still the same, there was little opportunity to improve on the performance. Those resurrecting applications have the opportunity, as well as the responsibility, to enhance response times — made possible by use of the technology discussed in the previous chapter. Performance related to the application (i.e., the speed of computing), performance related to database (i.e., the speed of storage and retrieval of data), and performance related to the network (i.e., transmission of data), will all play important roles in the overall performance of the resurrecting software.

7.8.5 TT04-5: INCIDENT SOLVING

While we discussed incident-solving at programming level (TT03-7), here we solve incidents related to the previous four tasks of software integration. These incidences also can be bugs within the system, performance related issues, or problems with integration of data with the applications. Just as we solve incidences in unit testing, we also solve incidences in the overall software solution. Furthermore, the incidences within this task (TA04-5) also are recorded in the formal way by means of a software reporting system (see Chapter 14).

Salvage Options — A number of salvage options from the hit system should be available for this task. Not all incidences are bugs within the system. Many incidences can be explained with the help of users of the system. If a record of similar errors (and their corresponding explanations) is available from the previous system, then it will provide immense value to this resurrection task.

7.8.6 TT04-6: REGRESSION TESTING

Once individual incidences are solved and the application or the database is corrected, it becomes important to test the entire system together. It is important that every time a major incidence is solved or a new functionality is added that this task of regression testing is performed. This task can benefit by the use of automated testing tools.

7.9 TA05: DATA CREATION

The Y2K problem has been a date-related problem that affects both the application and the database. This particular activity of data creation is related to recreating new data, should that be required in order to populate a new database.

7.9.1 TT05-1: REVIEW DATE ERRORS

This is the first task within the activity of recreating the data. The date errors that have caused the system to crash are reviewed during this task (note that we are not testing the system for date errors; that has already been achieved by the activity of dissection). The date errors can provide indication of the data content that will have to be recreated. Many errors will be the types of firecrackers we described in Chapter 1. These are direct date errors. There are other errors in data that are not direct errors. They are the errors in data that are derived from the existing data by means of some calculations. For example, if the difference between two dates provides the number of days required for interest calculations, then the date error exists in not only the two date fields, but also in the number of days calculated. A review of the date and associated data will provide indication of the extent of recreation.

Salvage Options — The operations related to date entry in the hit system are the most likely candidates to appear in the shortlist of salvageable options. Functionally, the date entry operations (e.g., entering FEES-PAID in Chapter 6, Table 6.2) are not going to be different. These date entry fields lead to other salvageable options in terms of data.

7.9.2   TT05-2: SCOPE THE DATA CREATION

We start with the date-related data and review the rest of the data in order to determine the areas that need to be recreated as a part of the resurrection process. The decision revolves around the need as well as the technical advantage in recreating the data. Scope of the data creation is determined by the amount and complexity of additional coding required in order to convert the relevant data. The more complex the logic to convert the data, the bigger will be the scope of data creation.

The scope of the data creation also includes the following considerations:

- Structure and depth of the data that has to be converted.
- Structure of the new database where the data will be entered.
- Dependency of the data to be created on other data.
- People available to re-enter the data.
- Tools/programs needed to re-enter the data (these can be one-off programs written to help the data entry effort).

Salvage Options — Following is a list of possible entities that can be salvaged during (and that can benefit by) data creation:

- Reference tables — all the reference data within the existing system should be considered in the scope of data creation (e.g., type data — student types, account types, etc. — would form part of reference tables). These reference data are likely to be smaller in size as compared with the rest of the data within the system and may be easily re-entered.
- Flags — flags are used extensively to determine the state of the data. Stand-alone flags should be physically re-entered rather than programmatically converted.
- Interim data — all interim data and tables should be scoped *out*. Tables and files that are used temporarily in order to manipulate data should not be converted. However, their data models might still be relevant.

7.9.3   TT05-3: AUTOMATE DATA CONVERSION

Once we have identified the date data that have to be recreated, we have to decide whether to use tools to automate the job of doing the re-creation of data or whether to do it manually. If tools are used in data conversion, then this task is not much different from the work done during Y2K prevention. The reason why the data is being converted is different, but the techniques used in the conversion need not be.

During a tool-based conversion, all issues related to date and data conversion will have to be considered. For example, it will be essential to consider the right moves for the date data, otherwise we are likely to end up with the problem shown in Figure 1.5. It is also important to consider technical issues like 16- to 32-bit moves. When going from 16 to 32 bits as in case of NT operating systems, there is a chance that the data that are converted may not be correctly converted in the resultant application.

Salvage Options — For organizations at yellow and green level of preparedness, there will be a lot of salvageable options that are derived from the Y2K work that has already taken place in the organization. Automated tools used in conversion attempt can be reused during this salvage operation. Metrics for conversion also can be used during this task.

7.9.4   TT05-4: MANUAL DATA ENTRY

In situations where converting the data automatically is not feasible, consideration should be given to manual data entry. Situations where the data conversion is very complex and requires significant coding, manual data entry will provide an excellent alternative. This option may not apply to systems with a large amount of data, but for small- to medium-sized businesses especially using PC based systems, it may be worthwhile re-entering data manually. Manual data entry of up to a few thousand records is a much better choice than the corresponding programming effort. However, manual data entry may still need some screens for data entry and control totals for verification of the effort.

Salvage Options — Existing screens from the affected application may need some modifications, but they can still be used in providing a front-end to the manual data entry effort. Data that has been recorded manually because of the crash of the software system would also form part of the salvage operation.

7.9.5   TT05-5: VERIFICATION OF DATA

This task is essential in providing confidence to the resurrection team that the newly created data is accurate and sufficient. The task can be performed by programmatically cross checking the results of the conversion and also by spot-checking converted data. In case of manual date entry it is possible to use the age-old techniques of checking the parity or the totals at the end of a batch. Data creation has to ensure that the new date is correctly converted and the new records within the database integrate well with the new applications. Verification of data ensures that that is happening.

7.9.6 TT05-6: BACKUP AND HISTORY OF DATA

This task is concerned with the regular backup of data that accumulates every day. Data creation will have to be followed up with this task of backup of the data that has been created. Applications that depend on historical data in order to arrive at trends or applications that have audit requirements that need a large amount of audit data are the ones that will be considered through this task. This task also ensures that the database administrator is in a position to recreate a historical snapshot of the database. Data creation has to consider the implicit conversion and the fact that there is a possibility of "mixed" data (i.e., some that is converted and other that is not) before the entire resurrection exercise is completed. Backing up of the database on a regular basis will enable tracing of mixed data should that occur during re-creation of data.

7.10 TA06: DATABASE

The activity of the database is related to the previous activity of data creation (TA05) and is performed predominantly by the actor database manager. This activity is related to the methodological activity of alternative evaluation (MA01) that provides us with the "how to" of evaluation. This activity of database is related to the evaluating and finalizing of database, creating a new data model, conversion of salvageable and loading new data, as well as managing and administrating the database for the newly resurrected enterprise. This activity deals with creation and maintenance of the stored procedures to access and store relational data.

7.10.1 TT06-1: EVALUATE DATABASE

The technological team during the initial iteration of the process carries out the task of evaluating database. By prototyping the database for its speed and capacity as well as scalability for large application, it is possible to ascertain the database that will be used in the new enterprise. The choice between modifying the current database vs. going for a new database will have to be decided during this task (assisted by the tasks within the alternative evaluation activity MA01). Evaluation of databases can be made by considering the various types of database (relational database, object oriented, object relational, and so on) and their applicability to the new applications.

Salvage Options — Existing performance figures of the Y2K-hit database provide an excellent source of information on the kind of performance that will be expected of the new database. All limitations of the existing database should be listed and used in evaluating the new database.

7.10.2 TT06-2: DISTRIBUTION IN DATABASE

This task ensures that the distributed aspect of database is considered within this activity. Being an aspect of distributed computing, a distributed database enables operations to be distributed across machines. Therefore, it is essential that we consider the distributed databases in relation to the hardware and network on which the database will operate — over and above the basic need for distributing the data in relation to the applications that will use the data. However, this task does *not* dictate the need for a distributed database. The decision to go distributed will depend on the overall architecture of the system. This task will depend on the architectural decisions made for the system. If the system architecture is distributed, then this task will play an important role in the database activity.

Salvage Options — Distribution for the sake of distribution will not provide the advantages of distributing the database. Distribution in a database should depend on the need to distribute business functionality. This need for distributing the business functionality should be derived from the existing functionality of the Y2K-hit system and its specific limitations due to lack of distribution.

7.10.3 TT06-3: Create Data Model

This task deals with creating the new data model for the recreated and converted data. A data-centric approach to object-oriented design is a part of this task. This task is greatly assisted by CASE tools like Rational Rose that are able to produce an entity-relationship diagram from an object-oriented model. While this task can iterate with the design tasks described in the methodological activity (MA06), it is advisable to produce a data model as early in the iteration as possible. The initial class diagrams can be converted into a logical model that can provide a good understanding to the database designer as to the number of tables, their sizes, and their access mechanisms that will be required in the final model. This initial model can be followed up with the physical model of the database which is implemented. Identifying the most efficient mechanism for storing and retrieving data will depend on the indexes created by the database designer. Therefore, access requirements as well as the estimated size of the production database play an important part in creation of the data model.

Salvage Options — The data division of the COBOL application provides an excellent starting point for the new data model. This is not to suggest that the new data model should be based on the old one, for that will prevent us from using many of features that the new technology provides. Instead, the old data model should provide only a starting point and also as a crosscheck once the new model has been created. The size of the data within the existing database will be very helpful in estimating the size of the new database. This information (as well as the data models created in this task) will be helpful in the conversion and storage of data.

7.10.4 TT06-4: Create Stored Procedures

Access to the data within a relational database is through the stored procedures. This task ensures that the access to the database is through a consistent interface provided by the stored procedures. Members of the resurrection team who are not writing the application programs should write these procedures. This is so because the design and implementation of procedures is a specialized task that requires a good understanding of the underlying data model, as well as the technology of the resurrecting database.

Salvage Options — In a resurrection process, one expects to find a large number of stored procedures doing the tedious tasks done by the procedural programs of the hit system. It would be reasonable to find a large number of date-based queries to the database which will be executed by the stored procedures. The procedural programs that dealt with accessing the hit database can provide valuable functional requirements for the stored procedures. Keys and indexes in the old database can also provide information for data mining operations in the new database.

7.10.5 TT06-5: ADMINISTRATION OF DATABASE

Administration of the resurrecting database includes similar tasks to the administration in any database system. This includes monitoring and managing the performance of the database, assigning users and providing them with access to the database, maintaining database versions, providing for rollback of database in case of corruption, and enabling backups and offsite backups of databases on a regular basis. Depending on the type of database being used in resurrection, additional issues like physical distribution of database, security mechanism for data access, data mirroring, and so on, will come into play.

Salvage Options — All administrative procedures of the existing database can be salvaged and modified to suit the procedural requirements of the new database. These include the number of backups taken per week/month, offsite storage procedures, and so on.

7.11 TA07: HARDWARE

The activity of hardware is carried out during the initial iteration of the technological process. The actor network administrator would be involved in this activity. Input from the preliminary activities like budgeting also is possible. The evaluation, upgrade, and maintenance of hardware essentially remain technological activities.

7.11.1 TT07-1: EVALUATE CURRENT HARDWARE

This task is involved with evaluating the existing hardware for the resurrected enterprise, and handling the BIOS-related problems if they occur in the organizations systems. The hardware is evaluated for the speed, its storage capacity, and its ability to integrate well with other hardware in the organization. Evaluation of hardware should be considered in the cost of procurement because during the resurrection exercise the demand on hardware is likely to be more than what is expected within a normal development exercise. These extra requirements come from the need to provide conversion environment for the dissection and salvaging of the data. Thus, the current hardware should be evaluated to ascertain whether it could satisfy the need for development testing as well as deployment of the new system.

Salvage Options — The age of the current machines and the accounting mechanism (whether the hardware is leased or purchased) would be one of the many good sources of information that can be used in evaluating the current hardware.

7.11.2 TT07-2: Upgrade to New Hardware

Based on the results of the previous task of evaluating the current hardware, a decision can be made regarding upgrading the hardware. The hardware upgrade may be specific to the development team wherein the need for larger and faster machines can be justified. Changes to the production hardware would require careful planning and should be done only when the resurrecting application will need the upgrade. Upgrading the server, network, and individual machines is a special task that should be handled by the operations or the networking group.

7.11.3 TT07-3: Maintenance of Hardware

The task of maintaining the hardware deals with physical location and inventory of the machines, routine changes to the disk drives, memory chips and network cards, and maintaining of peripheral devices such as drives for backing up data (e.g., CD writers, tape backup) on the network and the server. This routine maintenance can either be done in-house if there is enough staff or it can be outsourced if the company does not want to spend time and money in hardware maintenance.

7.11.4 TT07-4: Security of Hardware

Since hardware is a valuable physical entity within the development environment, it is essential to secure the hardware by means of procedures, electronic and physical keys, and by maintaining regular inventory of the location and owners of the machines. The hardware inside a machine, such as the memory chips and the network cards, needs careful monitoring by the network administrator.

7.12 TA08: NETWORK

Although recreating the logic and salvaging the data are the vital aspects of the resurrection process, they need the support of the networks and delivery mechanisms. There is less chance of the network itself being directly affected by the Y2K problem, but it needs to be considered to ensure successful resurrection. The actor network administrator, through this activity of networking, ensures that the network is evaluated, upgraded, and maintained throughout (and beyond) the resurrection process.

7.12.1 TT08-1: Evaluate Current Network

This task evaluates the current network from a number of angles. These include:

- The type of network (token ring, star, etc.) and its influence on the hit system.
- The load on the network (number of file servers, printers, print servers, internet servers, and so on).
- The number of total users as well as the number of users likely to be logged in at a particular time with projections of future user numbers (especially important for the production network).

- Type of users or clients — DOS, Windows, NT, Unix.
- Security of the current network — protection by passwords, firewalls, physical disconnection using timeouts, etc.

These and factors like these will determine the quality of the current network. These factors also will influence the network used in the resurrecting system. Traffic on the network (depending on the number of users and the type of activities carried out by the users) will be measured and evaluated against current and future needs.

Salvage Options — Details of current network usage including the number of users and their types will provide valuable information in evaluating the current network. Security requirements of the users (e.g., number of log-on attempts allowed on a bank's network) also can be salvaged from the existing system.

7.12.2 TT08-2: UPGRADE NETWORK

Upgrades to networks include the upgrades to the software (e.g., newer versions of the networking software like Novell or NT) or upgrades to the physical network itself. An organization would seldom change its physical network unless it has the need and the opportunity of doing so. Y2K resurrection brings about an atmosphere of change and the upgrade of the physical network is also possible as a part of this change.

Some of the advantages of upgrading the network during resurrection are

- Ability to handle high-speed traffic (e.g., going from 10BT to 100BT, fast Ethernet).
- High-speed printing (together with correct physical location of printers).
- More security to the network by providing additional firewalls, etc.

7.12.3 TT08-3: NETWORK MAINTENANCE

The network needs continuous monitoring during development and production. The maintenance work performed by the network administrator includes:

- Availability of the network to all relevant users at all appropriate times.
- Ideal configurations as well as physical locations of printers and backup devices.
- Creation and maintenance of appropriate user groups.
- Availability of secure remote access using remote access services, dialing in, etc.

Salvage Options — Existing user groups, access procedures (e.g., password timeout after no log-in for a set number of days), etc. will provide many salvageable entities during the maintenance of the upgraded network.

7.13 TA09: DELIVERY

The activity of delivery is closely associated with the previous activity of networking. While a network ensures that the organization's infrastructure has the *capability* of delivering, the activity of delivery (TA09) ensures that the data (and even the software) is actually delivered in a timely and orderly fashion wherever it is required. Delivery of data becomes more important when the architecture of the resurrecting system is distributed.

7.13.1 TT09-1: EVALUATE EXISTING DELIVERY MECHANISMS

Data delivery within the existing system would take place when the mainframe provides results from the processing performed at a central location. The results of the calculation are delivered to the user who is most likely to be connected to the mainframe by means of a "dumb" terminal. Just as delivery of data from a central server is important, it is also important to evaluate the existing data collection mechanisms, if relevant. For example, data from the financial market trading may be collected on a regular basis and fed into a central database. The mechanism for transferring the data in real time is important to the resurrecting system.

7.13.2 TT09-2: UPGRADE DELIVERY MECHANISM

Once the delivery mechanism is evaluated for the purpose it serves as well as the speed with which it delivers data/information, it may be essential to upgrade it. This upgrade may be a higher speed delivery mechanism or location of data/information delivery at a point where it makes more sense to the business.

7.13.3 TT09-3: ENSURE DATA DELIVERY

Once the delivery mechanism is upgraded, it will have to be tested to ensure that the data is getting delivered to its destination. In case of a new distributed architecture, the client machine also may be performing some processing. It is essential to know whether sufficient data are being made available by the data delivery mechanism for the client to perform meaningful processing.

7.13.4 TT09-4: ENSURE SOFTWARE DELIVERY

In addition to delivering data, the delivery mechanism should be able to handle the delivery of software. Indeed, if the resurrecting system is a Web-based application, it will practically need no delivery. However, in case of other solutions, the developed application will have to be delivered to the clients before they can start using it. A network-based delivery mechanism will ensure that the software need not go through the physical mode of delivery but, instead, is delivered through the same mechanism that delivers the data.

7.14 TA10: QUALITY ASSURANCE

This activity continues throughout the life of the resurrection process. It starts with the methodological process, wherein the quality plan and associated quality resources are put in place. Within the technological dimension, the quality assurance activity includes tasks that are related to lower level program testing. The tasks associated with testing so far are TT03-6 (unit test code), TT04-4 (verify performance), TT04-5 (incident solving), TT04-6 (regression testing), and TT05-5 (verification of data). All these tasks are related to the technical program level testing. The activity of quality assurance (TA10) forms a wrapper around all the testing-related tasks within the technical dimension of the resurrection process. The activity also relates to the methodological activity of quality planning (MA07), testing (MA09), and quality management (MA11). However, the focus is more on testing the programs and converted data at a unit level.

7.14.1 TT10-1: TEST PLAN

The task of test plan is related to providing detailed input into the test planning activity that would be carried out in the methodological activity of testing (MA09). Test planning is again a continuous process that will involve planning for the resources in terms of hardware and people and the machines where testing will take place. It will be impossible to produce an accurate test plan in the methodological dimension without technical input on the testing process. This task (TT10-1) aims to provide that input. Detailed discussion on testing (Chapter 14) describes the actual test plan that will be produced as a result of this (and associated) task.

Salvage Options — The extent of testing already conducted within the organization for its Y2K preparedness will be an important salvageable option. The resources used during previous testing, the time taken for the testing, and the quality of testing itself, all provide input into the task of test plan.

7.14.2 TT10-2: TEST DESIGNS

Since the object-oriented approach to development will result in production of components, this task will concentrate on producing test designs for each of those components. Thus, test designs are themselves testing components corresponding to the components being developed by the development team. Once again, the focus is on the lower level technical aspect of test designs.

7.14.3 TT10-3: TEST CASES

The test cases written during this task are the ones that will be used to conduct the unit testing of classes and data mentioned in the previous activities. The format of test cases and how they should be written is discussed in the corresponding methodological tasks.

7.14.4 TT10-4: CODE WALKTHROUGH

The task of code walkthrough, performed as a quality assurance activity, is a white-box testing technique. The classes can be examined by following the logic step by step. Thus, apart from physically testing the code by means of test cases, the code walkthrough ensures that the syntax and semantics of the code are high. Only the important and/or complex part of the code needs to be subjected to a code walkthrough. It would be impractical to conduct this task for the entire resurrected code. However, code walkthrough may be used as a part of the dissection activity if the complexity is high or if the salvageable value is high.

7.14.5 TT10-5: DOCUMENTATION

Documentation is both implicit and explicit in many methodological activities of the resurrection process. For example, a solution design or creating a set of standards assumes that it will be documented. However, the focus of TT10-5, this documentation task, is on the documentation at the class or program level. It is vital that the code is properly documented by means of appropriate comments, as well as with reference to the corresponding designs from where it is derived. Cross-referencing the data models within the underlying database is also important, especially for data-related classes.

7.15 TA11: PROJECT MANAGEMENT

Like the quality assurance activity, the activity of project management continues throughout all three dimensions of this iterative and incremental life cycle of the resurrection process. However, again as with the previous activity, the focus of the tasks within this (TA11) activity is more on the technical issues within the project. The activities of project planning (MA02) and project management (MA03) from the methodological dimension relate to this activity.

7.15.1 TT11-1: MANAGE BUILD ENVIRONMENT

One of the important tasks of the project manager (at a technical level) is to ensure that the technical environment where the system is being built is monitored continuously. Many productive hours are lost as a result of mismatch of compilers (e.g., 16 bit vs. 32 bit) between two machines, mismatch of databases, and so on. Any factor that prevents the creation of the executable of the new system on a regular basis should be handled in this task.

7.15.2 TT11-2: TAKE CHARGE OF WORKING VERSION

The resurrecting system should be incrementally developed as a working prototype. Therefore, the project management activity should ensure that a working version of the product is almost always available. This task ensures that a technical demo of the product can be conducted at any point in time during the resurrection work.

7.15.3 TT11-3: MANAGE CONFIGURATIONS AND VERSIONS

Using configuration management tools is an essential task of project management at the technical level. This task ensures that not only all the programs developed are under version control, but so are all the designs and associated documentation for the resurrection work.

7.15.4 TT11-4: ORGANIZE DATABASE AND NETWORK

This task deals with coordinating the database and the network to ensure that the build of the application is possible on a regular basis. This task deals with the management of installation, backups, and population of the database during development.

7.15.5 TT11-5: UPDATE PROJECT PLAN

This task provides input into the process of updating the overall project plan. Thus, this task may not necessarily be conducted here. It is more of a reminder that the technical input to the project plan would be essential at those designated checkpoints (ideally, the iterations).

7.16 SIZE OF THE TECHNOLOGICAL PROCESS

Measuring the size of the technological process provides an indication of the effort required within this dimension. The scope of the resurrection process will have an influence on these metrics. The number of process-threads resulting from the scope of resurrection will increase or decrease the value of the process metrics arrived at here. The methodological dimension has the formal responsibility (in terms of the metrics activity MA10) of measuring the size of the process. The following Table 7.2 provides an indication of how the technological process can be measured. This will have to be translated into measurement of a set of process-threads within this dimension.

7.16.1 CAVEATS

- This assumes a typical team of five programmers.
- The database and network actors are considered as a single unit.

TABLE 7.2
Size of the Technological Process

Description of the Element	Number of Elements in the Process	Weighting per Element	Total Strength: Units for the Element
Actors	7	100	700
Deliverables	4	100	400
Activities	11	10	110
Tasks	55	20	1100
Total Units	**77**		**2310**

- As mentioned before, the implementation of the technological process will contain multiple process-threads.
- The weighing can change depending on the number of roles played by a person.
- The weighing also will change depending on the driving dimension of the resurrection process. Since the technological dimension is the driving dimension, the weighing in the example process metrics will change to a higher value than the value assigned in the corresponding methodological and sociological dimensions.
- The activities and tasks may be repeated more than once in each iteration; this also may be reflected in the weighing of the process metrics.
- The level of preparedness of the organization will have an overall effect on measurement of all resurrection processes. The better the preparedness for Y2K, the less effort will be required in resurrection. Therefore, the process metrics multipliers discussed in Chapter 8 (Table 8.2) will have to be considered in the measurement effort here.
- An update of this metric or creating variation of this metric per process-thread may be required in practice.

7.17 KEY POINTS

1. The technological dimension of the resurrection process deals with the "what" of resurrection.
2. This "what" of the resurrection process includes the technical activities (like coding, database, and so on) and deliverables (like the application, database, delivery mechanism, and the technical infrastructure).
3. Technical actors like the programmer, database manager, and network administrator perform these activities. However, variations of these actors also join in the work.
4. The activity of dissection deals with the existing "hit" system. It investigates the Y2K-hit system to identify the starting point for the resurrection work. A list of salvageable options is produced by the dissection work. Data is expected to be one of the main salvageable entities.
5. The salvageable options resulting from the dissection activity would selectively apply to the remaining technological activities.
6. The process metrics indicates the way in which the technological dimension within the resurrection process can be measured. The final figures of the process metrics will depend on the process-threads.

7.18 NOTES

Sagar Agashe has worked on the local area networks as well as the wide area networks for a long time. His input in the activities of networking (TA08) and Delivery (TA09) was very valuable. Anant Chitale, whose expertise is in the area of telecommunication networks, also supported the need to consider networking activity.

7.19 REFERENCES

1. Yourdon, E., *Rise and Resurrection of the American Programmer,* Yourdon Press, Upper Saddle River, NJ, 1998, 155.

8 Methodology in Year 2000

A map is most valuable to the foreigner in the territory but of less use to the seasoned traveller in that part of the world.

Brian Henderson-Sellers,
on the road map analogy for OO methodologies[1]

Abstract There are several aspects of "how" we do things and especially so in a complex process of rebuilding an enterprise that is hit by the Y2K bug. These "ways of doing things" have undergone considerable scientific study resulting in the field of methodologies. Technology drives the resurrection process. Methodology guides the process by enabling creation of correct architecture, relevant and reusable designs, optimum utilization of available hardware and network resources, and so on. Thus, methodology is different from the actual technology. This chapter starts with the essence of the methodological challenge in the Y2K resurrection process. A detailed justification for why methodologies should be used and a suggested "road map" approach to their use is provided. One of the approaches to handling the date issues in the new organization is by wrapping the dates with a "date class." This is the beginning of an object-oriented approach to software development and forms one of the major discussion topics in this chapter. Arguments for the use of object-oriented approach to resurrection follow. Two well-known unified approaches to object-oriented methodologies are mentioned with an aim of using them in the methodological process in Chapter 9. This is followed by a discussion on formal requirements, reuse in object orientation, and the role of patterns in reuse. The other major advantage of object orientation is quality. This is discussed in the context of Y2K resurrection. Quality needs metrics. Documentation also enhances quality. These are discussed next. Finally, some relevant CASE tools for object-oriented development are mentioned.

8.1 ESSENCE OF THE Y2K METHODOLOGICAL CHALLENGE

8.1.1 "How" of Resurrection

Methodology is a dimension of the process discipline that deals with the "how to" of the process. Within the resurrection process, methodologies play the important role of specifying how an organization hit by Y2K can be brought back on its feet. This would include how the requirements for the resurrected organization are specified, how the solution is designed, how the "ashes" from the existing organization (including data and application) are salvaged, and how the entire process of resurrection is planned and executed. The "how" of resurrection also deals with the quality management activities that ensure that the resurrection process has followed quality standards and that the resultant deliverable satisfies the requirements specified.

Methodologies have played a limited role in the development of the systems that have crashed due to the Y2K problem. Thus, the Y2K crash cannot be attributed to methodology. It is more of a technological problem. Therefore, the methodological dimension (especially of the business processes) of the organization need not be subjected to the same radical changes that the technological dimension undergoes (see Figure 5.2 in Chapter 5). The technological dimension undergoes a revamp as the organization gives up its old technology and adopts the new one. However, when the methodological aspect of a business process is considered, the change is supportive rather than radical. The change is limited to ensuring that the new technology is put to best use during resurrection. This includes the ways in which the process is specified, measured, and used in integration of the technology in the overall solution. It also includes changes enforced by technology to the way in which the business processes were conducted. For example, the method by which an account balance inquiry was made within a banking system would change with the advent of an Internet application.

In addition to guiding the development work, methodologies in resurrection may be used in supporting the investigation of the existing data and applications. As mentioned in the technical aspect of dissection of the Y2K-hit system (activity TA01 in the previous chapter), the aim of dissection is not so much to find out what went wrong, but to determine what is still right and, therefore, of value to the resurrecting system. Methods and tools in the Y2K prevention work have been extensively used by the IT community. However, within this methodological dimension, we may consider using parts of the object-oriented methodologies (like the architecture diagrams or the use cases) in order to understand the "hit" system and what can be salvaged from it.

Thus, the methodological dimension of the resurrection process includes the "how to" of:

- Supporting the investigation of the existing applications and databases with an aim of shortlisting salvageable entities.
- Supporting the conversions (if essential) of the "hit" data and applications.
- Justifying and deciding on a formal methodology (an object-oriented methodology) for the development work.
- Producing architectures and designs for the new enterprise.
- Maximizing the quality and reuse that would result from the use of object-oriented development techniques.
- Measuring and standardizing the resurrection effort.

Although some of these methodological factors have been attempted during the prevention exercises of Y2K, here we discuss them in the context of resurrection. Indeed, if the organization has already attempted a disciplined approach to prevention, it will be at a higher level of preparedness represented by the yellow or green color codes (Chapter 2, Section 2.3). This preparedness is likely to help the organization to adopt to the object-oriented approach to resurrection quickly and effectively. More importantly though, if the organization did not follow a methodological approach in the first place, then it will benefit by the introduction of an organized approach to development through this methodological dimension of resurrection.

8.1.2 WHAT COMPRISES METHODOLOGY

A methodology is a set of instructions, guidelines, and heuristics that is *implementable* within a commercial environment addressing technical and managerial issues.[2] Methodologies in resurrection discuss and provide these guidelines and heuristics that are essential in recreating the software system that would support the processes in the new organization. Salvaging whatever we can from the existing applications and the existing data may be helpful. However, it is more important to come up with a design that will enable the organization to meet the challenges of the new millennium. The methodological approach to such a design and development would enable the organization not only to leverage from whatever asset it had, but also to convert the Y2K loss into a strategic advantage by undergoing a disciplined approach to resurrection.

When we discuss the methodological dimension of resurrection especially in the context of software development, it includes many factors that influence the overall software output of the development process. These factors that make up a methodology are broadly divided into two groups:

1. The factors that deal with the actual development process, such as modeling of requirements and designing of solutions.
2. The factors that support the development, such as quality and metrics.

As has been mentioned before (and also discussed in greater detail in this chapter), the software development aspect of the methodological dimension of resurrection is based on the use of object-oriented methodologies. Therefore, when we consider what comprises the methodologies, object-oriented methodologies will be at the back of our minds. This will include the architecture, the requirement models, and the designs that reflect the object-oriented approaches to development. Before we consider the details of object orientation though, let us have a look at the needs and justifications for a methodology within the software development process.

8.2 JUSTIFYING METHODOLOGIES IN A PROCESS

The software development world is not always convinced that it needs a methodology. One of the reasons for this lack of conviction is that at times projects do succeed without any systematic approach. These are usually small projects with short-term goals. These projects do not seem to have strategic value to the organization. In this section, we discuss the need for a methodological approach in resurrection and the application of methodologies as a road map to resurrection with an aim of deriving strategic benefits from the entire exercise of resurrection. The resurrection project manager can follow a methodology and at the same time facilitate creativity within the resurrection team. This can be achieved by looking out for the unknowns or the road factors in driving the resurrection project. A discussion on the need for methodologies, relating them to project size, and using them as a road map in resurrection follows.

8.2.1 NEED FOR METHODOLOGIES

Software development has become a team activity because the required software systems are so large and complex that one person in a reasonable amount of time cannot produce them. This is true of the development effort during resurrection as well. However, software development is also an individualistically creative task, comparable in some ways with composing music, designing buildings, and writing books.[3] If this creativity is taken to the extreme, it occasionally results in a bunch of brilliant individuals pulling the project in separate directions. Therefore, it is essential to use the methodologies in order to guide the development effort. Even the critics agree on "the need for methodologies that are flexible, cost effective, and responsive to our users needs; methodologies which allow human creativity to flourish."[4]

Thus, we see that methodologies have a responsibility to facilitate creativity and at the same time provide for management of large and complex software projects such as the resurrection project. For mild Y2K hit and a small scoped resurrection attempt (e.g., a local PC-based system that requires only a small code change or data fix), a methodology may not be mandatory. However, as correctly pointed out by Henderson-Sellers,[5] advice on how to undertake the technical construction of an object model is *inadequate* for a real project larger than a few person-weeks. In case of a resurrection attempt, the development team also may have to balance between the time and resources available for resurrection and the benefits it aims to accrue in the future as a result of resurrection. Developing and documenting the resurrection using methodologies will provide the essential background for the resurrection teams which they can utilize in future developments by reusing the product of resurrection (the technical application), as well as the approach to resurrection (the methodological discipline). Finally, the quality of the resurrected company will reflect the methodological approach that was used in its resurrection, making use of methodologies essential for a "good" resurrection.

8.2.2 RELATING METHODOLOGIES TO PROJECT SIZE

As mentioned earlier, there can be some resurrection effort that may not need methodologies. The resurrection work that may succeed without a formal methodological approach may have one of the following characteristics:

- It could be a small-sized system/project usually not exceeding 1 to 3 people.
- Its scope of resurrection is small, therefore, it is dealing with small data or code fixes and/or conversions.

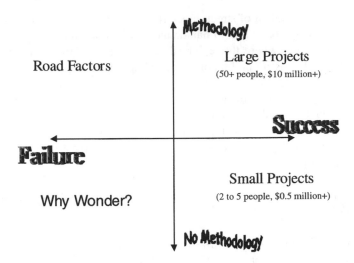

Road Factors

Methodology

Large Projects
(50+ people, $10 million+)

Success

Failure

Why Wonder?

Small Projects
(2 to 5 people, $0.5 million+)

No Methodology

FIGURE 8.1   Relevance of methodologies to project size.

- The organization has already reached a high level of maturity in its preparedness for the Y2K problem (silver, gold).

However, in general, the resurrection effort would need the support of a formal methodological approach in order to succeed. These aspects of the success or failure of a project with respect to methodologies are summarized in Figure 8.1. The figure also depicts the situation where the project might fail even with the use of methodologies. These are the projects that have used the methodologies without due considerations to the "road factors" or the sociological factors in a project. A discussion on the road map approach to the use of methodologies follows.

8.2.3   THE ROAD MAP APPROACH

Methodologies need to be flexible rather than rigid in order to cater for the practical realities of software development. This is true especially of the Y2K resurrection, as the practical aspect of resurrection is likely to include many factors that are outside the technology and tools used in the resurrection process.

This practical way of using a methodology has been discussed and presented by Unhelkar and Mamdapur.[6] According to them, the use of a methodology in software development is similar to the use of a street directory in planning a trip. A street directory helps in deciding which roads to follow to reach the destination using the shortest route and in the quickest time. A good street directory can even tell about traffic signals, roundabouts (circles), and one-way streets. However, the directory is not blamed if the road is closed due to maintenance, if the journey is not completed due to an accident, or if the car breaks down by hitting a pothole on the road. As far as using directories are concerned, they are used without complaining about the dynamic aspect of a particular road and address. However, the methodologies and tools that are the equivalent of street directories of software development sometimes bear heavy criticisms for failing to handle the driving conditions.

Some of the areas where the technical development (of the resurrection work) is directly supported by a good methodological approach are

- Modeling the requirements.
- Good analysis and design techniques.
- Scheduling and iterating the project.
- Applying quality assurance standards and metrics to estimate and control the development.

Some other areas where the resurrection work may not find direct support from the methodology are

- Human relation issues within the department.
- Financial stability or instability of the company.
- Vacillating user requirements.
- Technical competence (or incompetence) of the staff.

These factors, which can be generally classified as sociological factors, can and do contribute to the success or failure of a software project. A perfunctory examination of some of the well-known object-oriented methodologies will reveal that they do not deal with many such factors. They were not meant to deal with the sociological aspect of software development.*

In case of Y2K resurrection (especially using object-oriented techniques), it will be essential to use a methodology, but only as one would use a road map. Thus, just as determining a good route from available choices is made easier by using a road map, similarly methodologies are able to help projects determine how to adopt new technologies and tools in an easier way. However, just as road maps do not tell us anything about the driving conditions, similarly methodologies tell us nothing about what will happen when the actual resurrection project is underway. At that time it will be essential to start looking outside the methodologies — at the driving conditions of the project. It is important to look consciously for factors *outside* the methodology that can and do influence the project. Used in this fashion, a methodology will provide sufficient guidance and direction to the resurrection effort, without subduing the creativity of the individuals within the development teams.

8.2.4   Ups and Downs of Methodologies

During the resurrection, sometimes the methodology will appear to be doing more than expected by providing a perfect road map that can be followed. At other times, though, the road factors may take over and it may become necessary to temporarily suspend strict adherence to the methodology while these factors are handled.

---

* Sufficient guidance on the road factors is provided within the resurrection process through the sociological dimension of the process, as discussed in Chapters 10 and 11.

However, because of the overall direction provided by the methodological dimension of the resurrection process, we expect the project to remain on track.

Finally, despite the importance of methodologies, and the fact that using it as a road map is the ideal way to incorporate it in the overall elements of a project, we mentioned some situations in the previous section (Figure 8.1) wherein following a methodology may not be essential. One would indeed scoff at a person if he were to open a street directory every day in the evening while driving home from work. In spite of rain and closed roads, he is still able to reach home without touching the street directory lying in the glove compartment. Similarly, good developers who have gone through a certain development more than once may be chagrined if forced to follow a methodology to do their development. These are the situations where the sociological dimensions of the resurrection process come into play. However, one does not expect the resurrection project to be simple. Certainly we do not have sufficient "resurrection experience" (we haven't crashed sufficiently for the resurrections to begin) to attempt resurrection without a methodology.

8.3 USING OBJECT-ORIENTATION IN THE RESURRECTION

Having justified the use of methodologies in a process, we now specifically consider the use of object orientation and the OO methodologies within the resurrection process. Object-oriented design has evolved to help developers exploit the expressive power of object-based and object-oriented programming languages by using the class and object as basic building blocks of the system. Its corollary is the structured design (usually the designs of the Y2K-hit systems) that evolved to guide developers who were trying to build systems using algorithms as their fundamental building blocks. While the structured methodological approach was perhaps suited for the available technology at that time, it would be less advantageous to consider a similar design approach when we are trying to resurrect a Y2K-hit system. The resurrecting systems being built for the new millennium need to take advantage of the object-oriented approach with an aim of building (and using) components that will leverage the new technology and its corresponding advantages discussed in the previous two chapters. The advantages of object-oriented methods are directly translated into not only fixing the date problem, but also in reengineering the organization's processes. The specific advantage of object orientation in the Y2K resurrection effort is discussed next.

8.3.1 ADVANTAGE THROUGH OBJECTS

Since object orientation provides advantages in the reengineering effort and since we have already mentioned that our effort at resurrecting the Y2K-hit business is directed at business engineering, object orientation has a vital role to play in the resurrection effort.

Earlier thinking on object orientation concentrated on deriving the benefits of reuse. By one estimate, productivity gains demanded from object technology were not a mere 100%, but 10 to 20 times over the conventional tools and technology.[7] Reuse is still one of the major benefits of using object orientation, but the focus of reuse has shifted more from unit-level reuse to component-level reuse (see Section 8.5).

Another major benefit of object orientation is the profound effect it has on the way we construct software (i.e., in an incremental and iterative way), resulting in regular deliverables at the end of each iteration. This results in visibility of software and business modules throughout the development life cycle of the system. The users are able to see the results of the development effort. Their participation in the process increases and so does their buy-in in the product.

Our aim in the resurrection exercise is to derive the benefits of object orientation in reengineering processes that are affected by Y2K, and also in reengineering other processes that may be inefficient or redundant. Specifically, these benefits are

- Object model maps well with reality. The semantic gap between objects in business domain and that in the solution domain is less compared with that in the structured solutions. This will enable smooth translation of the requirements of the resurrecting system into the corresponding designs.
- In the object-oriented approach, object models grow from analysis to design to implementation and, therefore, there is no need for a "seam" to stitch these business and solution domain models together.
- Due to the seamlessness of the object-oriented models, it is possible for the designs to grow in the reverse order (bottom-up) as against the traditional top-down approach. Thus, it will be possible to design and implement a comprehensive date component and incorporate it in the later higher level designs.
- Use-cases and scenarios provide the necessary tools for requirements modeling that can be used to create business models of a new usable company. This will enable user participation in the resurrection process.
- Reusability facilitates "what-if" scenarios for a resurrecting company with patterns and frameworks providing higher level reuse. Thus, reusing and, therefore, without spending any effort in designing the date component can produce a couple of alternative designs.

8.3.2 SMALL SEMANTIC GAP

Most of the large systems hit by the Y2K bug were developed using the structured development approach (e.g., entity-relationship, modeling). During the development of such systems, considerable effort was required to translate the user requirements to system requirements. In a traditional system design the focus was the functions rather than the "real" objects within the system. Therefore, as the system development progressed, data would become separated from the procedures that were used to manipulate the data. As a result, the business model gets transformed into an impenetrable procedural representation. The large semantic gap between the requirements of the user and the solution provided by the system meant that there were essentially two media of communications, first, what the user was requesting, and second, what the developer wanted to know. What the user specified

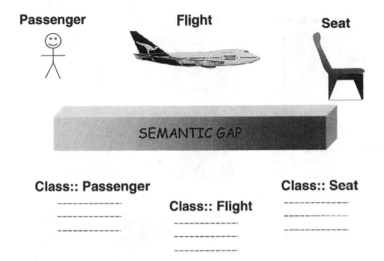

FIGURE 8.2   Small semantic gap in object orientation.

could not be directly identified in the software system solution provided by the developer.

Object orientation plays a decisive role in modeling enterprises to enable them to re-engineer as well as to forward-engineer processes. A good argument for using object orientation to model companies is that it models the company in a way that is very close to the real thing.[8] What the user is requesting need not undergo a major translation before the developer understands the requests. In other words, there is a very small semantic gap between the external reality and the object-oriented model (Figure 8.2).

The small semantic gap happens because the object that is identified at the analysis phase is likely to continue to exist during design and implementation phases. Having started with an object at the analysis stage, it is possible to keep adding attributes and functions to that object in order to satisfy new behavioral requirements. Further addition of the attributes and behavior do not change the identity of the object — that identity continues to remain the same from analysis to design and to implementation. This will greatly facilitate the participation of the user in the resurrection process, wherein he can relate to the semantics of the objects in the requirement stage (use case view) as well as in the designs (class models).

8.3.3   SEAMLESSNESS

Seamlessness is due to the small semantic gap discussed in the previous section. It means there is no major translation from the analysis to the design to the implementation stages in an object-oriented development. Objects discovered in the analysis stage remain as an entity through to implementation. For example, consider Figure 8.3, which represents the classes for the user representation of the system in the previous Figure 8.2. An object *passenger* at analysis stage would remain a *passenger* object even in implementation. Thus, if an object continues to exist from

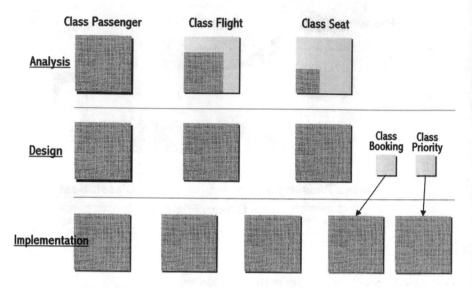

FIGURE 8.3 Seamless transition in OO.

analysis to implementation, it remains the same entity and does not change from the user's perspective. Therefore, in object-oriented development, the transition from analysis to design to implementation is seamless.[9,10] Objects identified at the analysis stage grow into objects at design, and are finally implemented.* There is no "seam" between these various stages of development. This ability of the object-oriented model to map well with the reality has major advantages during the resurrection effort. It is possible to identify objects within the Y2K hit system that can be easily translated by the seamless growth into the solution system.

During OO development, there are two ways in which classes grow:

1. The application classes exist in all stages of development — analysis, design, implementation, and maintenance — and as one proceeds through the development stages, these classes get filled up or augmented with additional functionality. Thus, the development is iterative with no apparent "seam" between the various stages of development.
2. Newer classes get "added" to the existing set of classes either through inheritance or association. Thus, the overall solution domain grows through the development stages. As shown in Figure 8.3, the *passenger, flight,* and *seat* objects, identified at analysis stage continue to grow as they are filled up in design, but at the same time newer classes *matching* (of seats to passengers), and *persistence* classes have been added to the overall system. These newer classes have significance only at the

---

* As against the traditional approach wherein the entity during analysis is *transformed* into design and then finally into implementation entities. The transformation from analysis to design to implementation of a structured approach is not present in an object-oriented one.

implementation phase and not at the analysis phase. This makes the solution seamless.

This ability to provide seamless solutions is important for good designers who tend to work at multiple level of details and abstractions simultaneously. This will especially be true during the resurrection exercise wherein designers will be working on significantly wide abstractions, for example, from dissection to OO testing or from date component to major subsystems. The object-oriented approach enables work at multiple levels of abstraction (one cluster at analysis level, the other at design level, and the third at implementation level) without any major translation from one model to another, making it an ideal approach to resurrect a Y2K-hit enterprise.

8.3.4 CHOOSING TOP DOWN VS. BOTTOM UP

The ability of the object-oriented approach to enable multiple levels of abstractions means that it is possible to work with OO down at the class level or higher up at the major subsystems and component level (Figure 8.4). When the system design starts from the highest abstraction (system) to the subsystems and then the classes, it is called the top-down approach to object-oriented development. The bottom-up approach is also important and it happens when the lower level objects are identified first and then a wrapper is put around them in order to form cohesive reusable components. Because of its ability to provide bottom-up approach, it is possible to produce the lower-level classes first and then wrapping them up with the higher-level designs. In his discussion on migrating to object technology, Graham[11] interestingly declares, "This tested time-box philosophy means that it is quite permissible and safe to write the code before the design is done ..." This bottom-up approach to object-oriented development comes in handy when we attempt to redesign and produce the date-class for the date routines that are affected by Y2K, before designing the rest of the application.

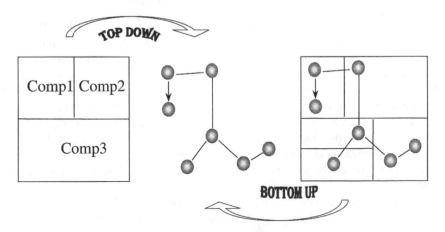

FIGURE 8.4   Top-down vs. bottom-up approach in OO designs.

A pure top-down or bottom-up approach to object-oriented development is theoretical. In practice both top-down and bottom-up approaches to object-oriented designs are taking place simultaneously. We may call this the "middle-out" approach.

The Y2K resurrection process aims to derive advantage from both top-down and bottom-up approaches to object-oriented development. As mentioned, by identifying the date that has been hit, it is possible to wrap it in a date class and use in the system using the bottom-up approach. More importantly, using the top-down approach, requirements specified for the reengineered Y2K processes can be directly mapped to solution-level objects.

8.3.5   OBJECT-ORIENTED METHODOLOGIES

Object-oriented methodologies enable the resurrection team to derive maximum benefit out of using the object-oriented approach to resurrection. We discussed the need and justification of methodologies and the advantages of object orientation. OO methodologies enhance the advantages of object orientation by providing a disciplined approach to OO development. However, the initial problem with OO methodologies was that there were a plethora of methods to choose from. The Object Management Group's (OMG) special interest group on analysis and design described 27 different object-oriented methods.[12] Hutt[13,14] in his two books has surveyed between 16 and 21 methods including Booch, Coad et al., Demeter, Fresco, Fusion, SOMA, Objectory, Rumbaugh, Shlaer/Mellor, SSADM, and Wirfs-Brock et al., to name but a few. Apart from this large number of *recognized* methodologies, there are a number of "second generation" methodologies[15] (e.g., MOSES, BON, Syntropy, OOram) and probably many others that were never published or were home-made concoctions derived from one or more of these recognized object-oriented methodologies. The effect of this is confusion in the software development community followed by debates between programmers and designers[16] with most end users preferring to sit on the sidelines rather than betting on the wrong horse.

8.3.6   BRINGING OBJECT-ORIENTED METHODS TOGETHER

In his tutorial at OOPSLA'96 in San Jose, Fowler[17] laments, "With a plethora of notational differences, many of which are entirely arbitrary, the simple modeler such as myself feels like banging the gurus' heads together until they pick a common cardinality symbol." This plea is true of almost all practitioners utilizing methodologies. In the context of resurrection, it will not be easy to choose from the range of diverse object-oriented methods and use them in designing new processes. Luckily, for the resurrection work likely to take place in the new millennium, the OO world also has recognized the need to unify the existing methodologies. Unification of methodologies in the OO world is accomplished by bringing the methods together based on meta-models, thereby facilitating consistency at both research and industrial level.

In addition to the benefits of a sensible number of methodological approaches to choose from, unification of methodologies bring in other benefits. For example, we need case tool support in order to successfully implement methodologies. New ideas, new thought processes, and new methodologies, however good, would find it difficult to get industrial acceptance and usage without the support of such tools. On the other hand, industry would like to accept methodologies and tools that support their approach and which have been tried elsewhere. This sets the ground for unifying the commonality in various approaches to software development. A common core meta-model for the object-oriented approach, with various methods derived from it based on different requirements and situations, would find ready acceptance in the industry. The tool vendors would be able to produce their CASE tool base model based on this meta-model. This base model can then be augmented depending on new methodological approaches that are variations of the basic approach, such as the one we are trying to apply to the Y2K resurrection process.

Such attempts have been made by the OMG in considering the Unified Modeling Language (UML, which brings together elements from OMT, Booch, and OOSE) and Object-Oriented Process, Environment, and Notation (OPEN, merger of MOSES, SOMA, Firesmith, and Synthesis). These can be called the *third generation* methodologies and are of use to us in the resurrection attempt. The aim is to use them in designing and implementing the Y2K resurrection process. The potential roles that a unified methodology can play in a Y2K resurrection effort include:

- Use of its semantics and notations to address the need to model existing processes as well as specifying new processes.
- Providing the semantics that would address the modeling issues in the new millennium. These issues specifically relate to component technology and distributed computing.
- Provide extensibility mechanisms that would enable enhancement of the meta-model itself.
- Make it conducive for CASE tool vendors to produce corresponding tools for the methodologies using the meta-model.
- Provide common semantics that would facilitate interchangeability of the models amongst different tools.
- Enable sharing and storage models by providing interface to repositories.

8.3.7 Unified Modeling Language (UML)

The Unified Modeling Language (UML) is a result of unification of three popular approaches to object-oriented designs:[18] Booch, Object Modeling Technique, and Object-Oriented Software Engineering (whose commercial version is Objectory). UML is accepted as a standard modeling language by the OMG and is used for specifying, constructing, visualizing, and documenting the artifacts of an object-oriented software system. The UML focuses on a standard modeling language for object-oriented (and component-based) development. However, this unification is limited to the notation and language of modeling and it does not extend to the OO development process. The UML also targets the modeling of concurrent and distributed systems which is of interest to the resurrection effort. UML is supported by Rose, the popular OO tool from Rational Software.

8.3.8 OBJECT-ORIENTED PROCESS, ENVIRONMENT, AND NOTATION (OPEN)

OPEN is a third generation, fully object-oriented methodology that encapsulates business issues, quality issues, modeling issues, and reuse issues, within its life cycle using the object-oriented paradigm. OPEN leverages off existing methodological modeling techniques as found in MOSES, SOMA, Firesmith, to name a few. OPEN's heart is a pair of two-dimensional metrics that provides probabilistic links between Activities of the life cycle and Tasks, which are the smallest unit of work within OPEN. A second two-dimensional matrix then links the task to the techniques. A meta-model and notation, called OML (OPEN Modeling Language), supports OPEN. The metamodel is based on the COMMA meta-model. The notation has been designed for usability. Various CASE tools, such as ObjectMaker, SimplyObjects, and MetaEdit support it.

The main difference between the two attempts at standardization is that while UML is initially concentrating on meta-model and notation, OPEN considers the full life cycle of OO development and pays due attention to the process. As Yourdon[19] puts it

> And one of the things that's most interesting about OPEN vs. UML in the short term is that while both have a very rich and comprehensive diagramming notation, only OPEN provides the thorough, comprehensive emphasis on process.

8.4 REQUIREMENTS MODELING FOR Y2K RESURRECTION

Formal requirements modeling for the Y2K resurrection is derived from the OO approaches discussed in UML and OPEN. Although there might be differences in the two methodologies, both agree that formal requirements modeling is essential for a well-designed object-oriented system. The essential elements of a requirement model for Y2K resurrection would include:

- Creating new scenarios for the resurrected enterprise — these would be based on the process-based business engineering principles.
- Modeling the business domain in an object-oriented way — based on the business scenarios described above.
- Scenarios showing the functionality of the existing system and areas in the system that are hit by Y2K (this would be of help during the dissection activity TA01).
- Specifying the dynamicity of the business models using tools like the interaction and sequence diagrams.
- Specifying the initial user interface for the system that later can be refined through a detailed user-centric user interface modeling (this forming part of the sociological aspect of the resurrection process).

8.4.1 USE CASES AND SCENARIOS

A number of authors have considered ways to express new requirements which can be process-based. The most popular of them has been Jacobson et al.'s use case approach.[20] It is common to put the requirements for a new system in plain English text that is usually provided by the user. However, the same informal descriptions were made formal (and popular) by Jacobson et al. and formed the basis of their approach to reengineering. The use case approach concentrates on taking the objective specification and using it to build a use case model. A use case model has been defined as an "outside" view of the company. The use cases assist in capturing processes of the new business. This use case model is then converted to build an ideal and a real model iteratively.

Scenarios are instances of use cases. Thus, while a use case describes the flow of actions for how a user will withdraw cash from a bank account, scenarios talk specifically about how John or Mary would withdraw $100 from his or her account. For the existing system that is hit by Y2K, they can be derived from various sources such as:

- Executing the current applications.
- Reading the user-guides.
- Understanding the online help.
- Chatting with the users of the system.
- Investigating any training material that was available for the system.

Unless the Y2K hit has caused the application to "physically" crash in the sense that it is not executable any more, it should be able to provide a good starting point for business scenarios for the new system. Discussion sessions with the users of the affected system can provide additional information on the use cases being developed. Users may write the textual part of the scenarios themselves. However, we need to take care in this exercise not to be constrained by the existing system. Therefore, limitations of the current system can be put aside for the time being as new business scenarios are created. An example of a use case diagram for withdrawal of cash from a bank account is shown in Figure 8.5.* The elipses represent the use cases and the "stick men" are the actors, who interact with the system by the use cases. The accounting system is an external system (also shown as actors).

8.4.2 CLASS DIAGRAMS IN OO DESIGNS

Business object designs derive from the business scenarios and use cases. Following on from the seamlessness existing in object-oriented development, the objects apparent in the use case view of the business will appear as classes in the solution domain. Figure 8.6 shows a sample class diagram related to the cash withdrawal use case diagram shown in the previous section. This class model encapsulates the relevant dates within their respective classes. This design will not only take care of the Y2K problems associated with the hit system, but also will provide a reusable and extendible design to be used in the future development work within the organization.

---

* In UML Notations. For more details, see Jacobson et al. OOSE.[20]

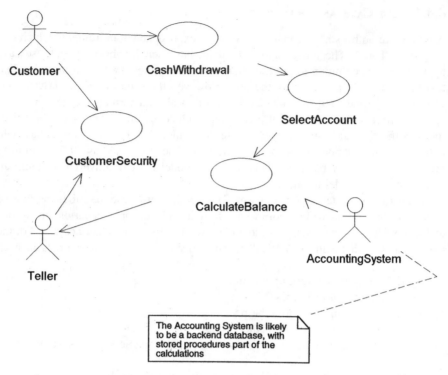

FIGURE 8.5 Use case diagram for cash withdrawal from a bank account.

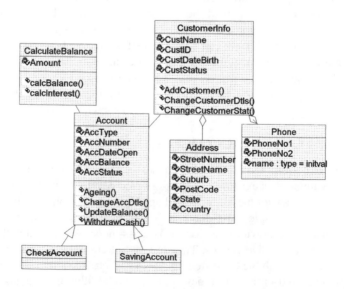

FIGURE 8.6 Class diagram for banking module.

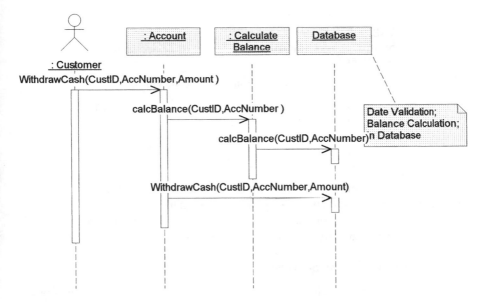

FIGURE 8.7   A sequence diagram for cash withdrawal from a bank account.

8.4.3   Dynamicity in OO Designs

The class model described in the previous section is the static view of the resurrecting system. In addition to this static view, it is also important to show the dynamic view of the system. This is a representation of the messages that are passed between the objects in the system. Figure 8.7 depicts this interaction between objects. The message "WithdrawCash" is received by the Account object which then sends a relevant message to calculate the balance after withdrawal. Results are stored in the database. Many sequence diagrams are required to show the interaction between a set of classes.

8.5   REUSABILITY IN Y2K RESURRECTION

Using OO approach to resurrection provides us with the opportunity to reuse software in various ways including:

- Reusing the code and designs produced during a development cycle (initial iteration) of the resurrection process during the later cycles of the same, or another, development.
- Reusing the code from third party library vendors for both routine tasks as well as domain specific tasks; these can be the date components mentioned earlier on.
- Reusing part of the existing code (not related to the date problem) by wrapping it and enabling access to it based on a well-defined interface.
- Reusing part of the documentation and help routines that fit well with the resurrected processes.

TABLE 8.1
Summary of Dimensions of Reuse in OO-Based Resurrection

Dimensions of Reuse in the Resurrection Process

Targeted level	Dissection, analysis, design, coding, documentation
Scale	Unit, components, patterns
Type	With, for
Granularity	Coarse, fine

The various dimensions of reuse in object-orientation and the ways in which they get applied to resurrection are summarized in Table 8.1.

We discuss some of the advantages of reuse in OO resurrection next. This discussion is in the backdrop of the dimensions of reuse.

8.5.1 REUSE AS OLD AS SOFTWARE

While our aim is to take advantage of the reusability made easier by object orientation, reuse itself is not new to the software development community. "The notion of reusing software is one that developed at a very early stage in the history of computing, and the main motivation of the development of subroutine libraries was software reuse."[21] In fact, even before subroutines were written for reuse, the programming community used to employ a still simpler way of reuse: cut and paste a piece of code. Perhaps that is one of the reasons why the date problem, instead of being localized in one place, is found across all programs of a large legacy system. It was not possible to localize the date code to one area (or component, as one would do with object orientation). Date routines were "cut and pasted" across the various subsystems in a large solution.

Today, though, many organizations want to achieve systematic reuse which is domain focused and based on a repeatable process and concerned primarily with the reuse of higher level life-cycle artifacts such as requirements, designs, and subsystems.[22] We are able to take advantage of reuse starting right from reusing individual lines of code and individual classes (by inheritance) through to whole groups of classes organized into a framework, and their repeatable behavior encapsulated in a pattern. No longer do we think of reuse at a single line of code or even at a class level. The entire thinking on object-oriented reuse (and, in fact, object orientation itself) is shifting towards the component-based approach to development and reuse. Reuse at the component level has potential to provide higher benefits in terms of productivity. Component designs as well as "pattern-level" reuse is the one that provides major productivity benefits of reuse in object-orientation. Thus, the granularity at which reuse can operate in a project ranges across classes, frameworks, and subsystems.[23]

8.5.2 WITH AND FOR REUSE

Another dimension of reusability in object orientation that needs to be considered during the resurrection process is the type of reuse. In the previous section we discussed reusability of classes at various stages (analysis, design, and so on) of software development. Reusability is not only applicable when some existing class or component is being reused. It also applies when a class or component is being refined for future reuse. The former reuse is called "with" reuse, whereas the activity of generalizing classes for future reuse is called "for" reuse. For example, "with" reuse occurs when an off-the-shelf library is being incorporated in the new design, and "for" reuse occurs when a date component, already produced, is further *generalized*. This generalization will enable the date component to be reused in subsequent subsystems in addition to the one for which it was produced.

While discussing reusability, the advantages of "with" reuse are immediately apparent. When a system reuses a large amount of design and code from a previously designed system, it has less work to perform during the current iteration. However, the organization that wishes to derive advantages from reuse also has to produce designs that could be stored in a library for future reuse. These designs have to be as generalized as possible. Effort is required in generalizing these designs and their corresponding code. The extra effort that the team has to put in, in order to generalize the component for reuse, is not visible, as it is the productivity of the "with" reuse team that goes up by the effort of the former. Organization of teams and their corresponding reward structures becomes important in these situations. This leads to the sociological discussion on reuse, which is discussed in detail in Chapter 10, Section 10.5 (team model within OO).

8.5.3 Granularity in OO Reuse

One of the important points to note in this discrimination is that reusability applies to different sized systems in different ways.[24] Benefits derivable from reuse depend on the way those systems are designed at the outset. For example, a 20-story building requires a totally different base than a 2-story townhouse. The *foundations* of a system whose classes are to be reused in 20 projects need to be necessarily *different* from that of a system with only a couple of projects to follow.

Card and Comer[25] suggest that project requirements should be aligned by establishing a feed-forward mechanism in which you consider the requirements of future (or concurrent) projects *explicitly* as you develop software to satisfy the current project's requirement. In resurrection, we are trying to do precisely that. Instead of merely fixing the date problem, we are working out the future needs of the organization by putting the requirements in formal scenarios and then building the object models based on these scenarios. By ascertaining the various solution domains as well as the number of likely projects in which the reusable components produced by the resurrection teams will be used, it is possible to make an educated guess on the granularity required for such a design.

There are a number of theoretical arguments[26] also supported by the practical experience of object-oriented programmers[27] that small objects are usually more usable than large ones. A date component that has to satisfy 20 scenarios (or to be used in 20 projects) will have to have a different (much finer) granularity than a component that is to satisfy only two scenarios (which would have a coarser granularity). Thus, we observe that granularity is an important dimension of reuse during resurrection.

8.5.4 LOCATING CLASSES FOR REUSE

An important issue in reusing components developed for "for" reuse is the cost of finding components that meet a particular development need. The most profoundly elegant framework will never be reused, unless the cost of understanding it and then using its abstractions are lower than the programmer's perceived cost of writing them from scratch.[28]

During Y2K resurrection, classes written in the date-related modules or classes written during the initial iteration of the resurrection process will be reused during the later iterations only after they have been successfully located. Without some efficient and effective method of locating previously written classes, ease of reprogramming a class will discourage spending time in locating existing code. The retrieval tools that are supposed to assist the users in locating a particular component need to contain more sophistication than simply query matching. It is not enough for the retrieval tool to assume that retrieval is a simple matter of matching well-formed queries to a repository.[29] If the potential users of a reusable component believe that a component that solves their problem may exist, but that they are unable to define the problem or the solution adequately then they will not achieve much reuse in their work. Tools to assist in locating components for reuse, as well as proper and complete documentation of components developed for reuse, is a major step towards large-scale reuse in the resurrection process.

8.6 PATTERNS IN Y2K RESURRECTION

When we talk of reusing design, we are talking of reusing a thought process. One of the most popular approaches to reusing software and designs has been the use of patterns on the object-oriented scene. Patterns result from capturing the thought processes of numerous experts and abstracting them to a higher level of generalization. These higher level abstraction can then be applied to newer situations without undergoing the same rigors of thinking, as would be required if we were to start from scratch.

8.6.1 PATTERNS AND Y2K

In this context of the above description of a pattern, one may argue that there is no place for patterns in any Y2K-related work. There is no technical challenge to the work and neither are we going to face another Y2K bug for (hopefully) another 1000 years. These arguments, although partially true for the Y2K prevention work, are not necessarily true for the Y2K resurrection effort. In a preventative situation, our horizon for the entire date-related work was the Year 2000 itself. In case of the resurrection work, we are beyond the Year 2000 hump (Figure 3.1). There is no immediate event horizon (like the actual arrival of the Year 2000 in the prevention work) where the development work can be called complete. Instead, the development is expected to last us for years and decades to come in the new millennium — followed by enhancements to the existing work and undertaking new development. Patterns are likely to play a significant role in reengineering an organization that is for the future. Although they may provide abstractions for the repetitive searches (especially for the date) during the dissection activity (TA01), they are more important in the modeling of requirements and development of object-oriented designs by fostering component level reuse. Patterns related to recognizing a problem (in case of TA01, it is the date problem), the way in which the problem is isolated, redesigned, and then integrated in the new system, can all play a valuable part in the Y2K resurrection effort. Since we expect a significant percentage of Y2K resurrection effort to include distribution, patterns for distributed designs and managing distributed processes can play a vital role in increasing reuse and improving quality of the overall solution.

8.6.2 DESCRIBING PATTERNS

The idea of patterns capturing design expertise originated with the architect Christopher Alexander. His book, *The Timeless Way of Building*,[30] remains an essential reading for the idea of patterns, which has been developed into design patterns as elements of reusable object-oriented software by Gamma et al.[31]

According to Alexander, "Each pattern describes a problem which occurs over and over again in our environment, and then describes the core of the solution to that problem, in such a way that you can use this solution a million times over, without ever doing it the same way twice." Even though Alexander was talking about patterns in buildings and towns, it is also true about object-oriented design patterns. Coplien[32] further defines a pattern as both a description of the thing being built and a process for building it; *a solution to a problem in a context* and that which resolves the forces at play for a given design decision. This definition provides the guidance in discovering and applying date related patterns to the resurrected designs. This is so because patterns can be found in Y2K hits, dissection, and the process of resurrection.

In addition to providing the guidance abstracted from the experts, patterns provide the constraints necessary to any art. Patterns define constraints and those constraints are helpful in encouraging novice designers to challenge their intuitive conclusions. Patterns enforce designers to think more deeply about the problem they are solving. Patterns capture emerging experience in a young domain — such as the object paradigm — so those nonexpert practitioners can avoid re-inventing the wheel. When novices find that their preconceived solutions do not fit any pattern, they are forced to think about the problem again. This introspection leads them to explore more alternatives than they would otherwise have considered and develop them so that they learn the expert's way of thinking.

For veteran designers with years of experience, patterns remind us of what we already know. Patterns provide help when the design life cycle reaches a situation where it gets stuck. The domain experts find in the pattern languages a rich foundation on which to build. New patterns emerge from holes in existing pattern languages; patterns from one language may provide analogies for a pattern language in another domain. For example, many of the patterns being used for object-oriented programming also apply to the structure of organizations. Similarly, patterns in Y2K resurrection may find application to other date-related problems within the organization that were not necessarily hit by the Y2K problem.

The recurring patterns of classes and communicating objects in many object-oriented systems, which can be identified by experienced designers, help solve specific design problems as well as make object-oriented designs more flexible and reusable. They capture the relationships between the modules within a system and thereby enable creation of a system architecture that is broader than any object or class hierarchy. Thus, the concept of patterns has direct applicability within the methodological activities of architecture (MA05) and solution designs (MA06) within the Y2K resurrection process. Finally, by addressing the issue of object size and number, patterns continue to support the concept of granularity in large-scale reuse.

Thus, it is seen that by capturing and documenting the recurrent behavior that is apparent to the experts, patterns play a significant role in all dimensions of reusability in Y2K resurrection.

8.6.3 Structure of a Pattern

For some of us, the patterns in Gamma et al.'s book are not new ideas.[33] We have been using techniques like them for years. What is new, however, is the notion of giving them names and standard forms and putting them in a catalogue. Formally, a pattern can be described by the following four essential elements of a pattern:[34]

The pattern name describes the design problem, its solutions, and consequences in a word or two.
The problem describes when to apply the pattern.
The solution describes the elements that make up the design, their relationships, responsibilities, and collaborations.
The consequences are the results and trade-offs of applying the pattern.

8.6.4 A Y2K Resurrection Pattern

One of the most common patterns in resurrection work that can be reused by organizations in the new millennium is the pattern of the resurrection process itself. Many of the activities and tasks performed during the resurrection process are abstracted at a sufficiently higher level to enable their application in many other development projects. What is happening during the resurrection work is the translation of the resurrection pattern into implementable process-threads. Within the resurrection pattern though, we may describe any of the process dimensions as separate patterns. Thus, a methodological pattern would encompass the methodological activities and tasks described in the methodological dimension of the resurrection process.

The pattern name — Implementing methodology in a Y2K resurrection process.
The problem — Choosing alternatives from available methodological approaches and implementing those approaches in the development work.
The solution — Perform Alternative Evaluation (MA01) based on the following tasks: background thinking, prioritizing high-level requirements, technological feedback, budgetary feedback, selecting alternative, and methodology decision.

The consequences — Selection and implementation of methodological approach is facilitated by the evaluation activity. However, some of the tasks within the alternative evaluation will not apply if the problem is not a Y2K-specific problem.

8.7 QUALITY IN Y2K RESURRECTION

8.7.1 REPEATABLE PROCESS

As discussed in Section 3.9, quality in Y2K resurrection is a definite advantage to the software development processes within an organization. Because a large portion of the resurrection process is applicable to many situations within the organization, a properly defined and repeatable process during the resurrection effort will find applicability in development effort after the resurrection has been completed. The activities and tasks within the resurrection process are well defined and are repeatable. Therefore, it should be possible to refine these activities and tasks as they are applied in the development work. As a result of this refinement of the process, the organization should be able to climb up the CMM levels as described in Chapter 3.

8.7.2 QUALITY FROM OO

Apart from the repeatability of the process, a key issue in discussing quality in resurrection is the use of object-oriented techniques. This is mainly because of the ability of OO classes to encapsulate data and functions together. The encapsulated classes can be made responsible for the date-related functions, removing that responsibility from all other areas of the system. Similarly, many other common functions can be put together in properly encapsulated components, which can be thoroughly tested and accepted in a library of component. Since the same component is reused throughout the system, it remains consistent in all modules where the component is reused. This has a positive effect on the quality of the system being developed. Furthermore, testing, measuring, and documenting the requirements and design, and then performing reviews on the deliverables from the resurrection process will increase the quality of the resurrected system.

8.8 METRICS AND MEASUREMENTS IN Y2K

8.8.1 PURPOSE OF METRICS

Metrics are tools for discerning different degrees of probabilities. Within software development, these probabilities can be estimated by measuring one or more of the following factors:

- Size of the system in terms of a predetermined measure.
- Person-months required for development.
- Correlation between reuse and productivity.
- Correlation between reuse and quality.
- Faults found per module, and so on.

In a Y2K resurrection, the job of metrics is to ascertain the amount of effort required for resurrection. This can be done by investigating the areas of the affected system and quantifying the results in an understandable form of measure.

As a part of the overall quality assurance work, the metric function relates to collecting the data related to the date errors, time taken to specify sufficient and correct new requirements, and overall effort in testing and fixing incidences in the resurrecting application. After collecting sufficient data (e.g., for one iteration of the resurrection process) and analyzing the results, we should have enough information to make educated guesses or discerning probabilities of similar factors affecting the timelines or quality in projects undertaken by the organization after the resurrection project is closed. "The objective must not only be to quantify product and process quality attributes, such as reliability, productivity, and time to market, but also to increase the predictability of these important attributes."[35]

Since estimations require due consideration to sociological factors, and since the IT community hasn't been considering these factors except of late, the IT literature is replete with stories of missed deadlines and budget overruns with or without the use of metrics.[36] Creation and use of metrics requires experience and judgement, as the influence of sociological factors is not easily quantifiable.

8.8.2 Metrics in Y2K Resurrection Process

In a Y2K prevention effort, metrics used to provide the scope for the work in prevention. In case of resurrection, the focus is on using the metrics that were available from the prevention effort (as would be the case with a yellow and above level organization) as well as using development metrics that are relevant to the new development during resurrection. Therefore, the focus of measuring systems and system-related attributes is now on the re-engineering processes rather than on the bug-fixing processes. Some typical metrics and their corresponding purpose in a Y2K resurrection effort is as follows:

Lines of Code (LOC) — This is a traditional software metrics used to estimate the scope of work in Y2K prevention. However, KLOC (Kilo or thousand Lines of Code) is not a good measure of object-oriented code. In resurrection, we will try and estimate the scope of the work by a metrics described in the next section. Therefore, LOC may not serve the same purpose in resurrection estimation that it served in the prevention effort.

Date occurrences per KLOC — Within the Y2K prevention effort, measurement of KLOC was followed by date occurrences per KLOC. In resurrection, it would again be helpful in getting the scope of the date problem as it exists in the current system. However, if requirements can be directly interpreted and rewritten for the new system without going through the logic of the existing code, then this metrics will not serve an estimation purpose in the resurrecting system. It will provide some academic understanding in correlating the resurrection work with the date occurrences in the "hit" system.

Date per 1000 rows in the database — This metric will be helpful in identifying the salvaging effort in a database, should relevant data be available in the "hit" database. However, the weighting given to this metrics should be different from that given to the date occurrence in the logic of the affecting system. This is so because even if there is a single type of date error in a database, it will be repeated 1000 times for 1000 rows. However, if there are more than one date columns in a row, then more date-related conversion will take place. Also, in resurrection, we may decide to dump the dead data and take only the relevant rows from the database. More relevant to the database measurement will be the number of date columns or fields in a row.

Cost of date conversion per LOC — This is a historical metrics as far as resurrection work is concerned. The resurrection work would *not* attempt to collect this metrics. However, if it is available due to earlier prevention effort, it may be used to provide some correlation between the resurrection and prevention work. It may also provide some help in budgeting the dissection activity within the resurrection effort. However, even in the budgeting process it should be remembered that we do not investigate the legacy technology in order to fix it — it is only investigated to an extent where we can salvage sufficient requirements from it.

Cost per date occurrence — Based on the date occurrences existing in the system, an estimate can be made of the cost per date occurrence in the resurrected system.

There are two other metrics that relate prevention to resurrection.

Data division to attributes — These metrics would map the number of fields in the data division of a COBOL program to the number of attributes in the corresponding classes in the new system. This mapping can indicate the efficiency in salvaging and representing data from the old system in the new system.

Procedure division to methods — Similar to the previous metric that relates data, this metric would relate the sections within the procedure division to the number of methods within the corresponding classes.

8.8.3 THE OBJECT-ORIENTED METRICS

Although lines of code is a popular way of collecting data related to fixing the Y2K problem, it will not be very helpful in collecting and analyzing data related to the resurrection work. Lorenz and Kidd[37] discuss a number of drawbacks of the LOC measure including inconsistency across languages and applications, inability to reflect complexity, and its inappropriateness as a measure of quality and progress. These limitations are further compounded in object-oriented systems due to reusability through inheritance and aggregation/association. Furthermore, with the focus of reuse in the resurrection effort, LOC is not a good measure of productivity in object-oriented systems since the smaller the number of LOC written, the greater the likelihood that significant reuse has occurred.

To circumvent these difficulties in measuring object-oriented designs, Thomas and Jacobson[38] have proposed a metric to measure the size of an object-oriented system, which has been further developed by Henderson-Sellers.[39,40] This is a much better way to measure an object-oriented system than the LOC, especially in an object-oriented development environment like the one within the resurrection process.

This metric states that, for a system with N object classes, each of size s_i, the size of an OO system is provided by

$$S = \sum_{i=1}^{N} s_i = \sum_{i=1}^{N} (AW_A + MW_M)_i \tag{8.1}$$

where A is the number of attributes in a class (weighting, W_A, less than WM) and M is the number of methods in a class (weighting, W_M language dependent)

Since the weighting factors are language dependent, the resultant size will be different for projects using different languages. Although more work is required to evaluate appropriate weights, W_A and W_M, if the *same* weighting factors were to be used *across* various projects which use the *same* language and have the *same* development environment, then we will be able to use the resultant figures to arrive at our productivity measure and, thereby, make estimations for the next project irrespective of the language. The argument is similar to the one used for the *last in, first out* (LIFO) or *first in, first out* (FIFO) accounting practice. Either of these practices is right, so long as they are used consistently across the organization during and beyond the Y2K resurrection effort. Furthermore, this metrics can be used to measure system size even during the design phase as the attributes and methods can be specified in a design tool much before the actual implementation of the resurrecting system starts.

8.8.4 RESURRECTION PROCESS METRIC

The resurrection process metrics provides an understanding of the resurrection effort. It comprises the four elements of a process as described in Chapter 4. There is a need to convert these four elements in to a single understandable unit which can be used for revising the project plans, etc. Since the actual resurrection metrics with its elements and weightings has already been discussed in Chapter 5, we do not go through the details of that metrics. What we mention here is the need for and application of the weighting factor to the resurrection process metrics.

Consider the resurrection metrics used in measuring the effort required in the technological dimension of the resurrection process, described in Section 7.16, Table 7.2. Since the level of preparedness of an organization affects the resurrection attempt for Y2K (e.g., the time and effort required to carry out dissection activity within the technological dimension), the resurrection metric needs a weighting factor to reflect this level of preparedness. For example, an organization at red level would have a multiplier of 1, whereas one at the yellow level would have a multiplier of 0.9. The suggested multipliers for the process metrics values depend on the levels of preparedness of an organization for Y2K (color codes described in Section 2.3). These multipliers are as shown in Table 8.2.

TABLE 8.2
Y2K Resurrection Process Metrics Multipliers

Red	Orange	Yellow	Green	Blue	Gold
1.0	0.95	0.9	0.85	0.7	0.7

8.9 DOCUMENTATION AND SUPPORT IN Y2K

A resurrection project will have to be supported by sufficient and quality documentation in order for it to succeed. This would encompass technical documentation as well as documentation for the users of the system.

8.9.1 TECHNICAL DOCUMENTATION

The technical documentation in a process includes the requirement documentation, the designs for the system, and the documentation for standards and measurement. While the technical personnel involved in the resurrection process can prepare some of these documents, it is advisable to have a technical writer on board to provide sufficient documentation. The documentation provides the following advantages in the resurrection process:

- It provides a repository of requirements and designs that are recorded during the resurrection process.
- It provides a link between two developers. This link is not merely between two developers working together. This link is provided even after a person leaves the organization, as the work remains captured in a document form. This can be referenced by the newcomer to the project.
- It is essential for implementation of a repeatable process. All technical documents provide the necessary knowledge that can be used again and again for subsequent development.
- It provides background for refining a process. In order for a methodological approach to be refined, it is essential to document it first.
- A technical document provides the starting point for quality reviews, like design walkthroughs.

8.9.2 USER GUIDES

The importance of user guides cannot be underestimated in any project. In case of a Y2K resurrection effort, user guides serve two major purposes:

- During the dissection activity, the user guide provides an excellent starting point for the new requirements. Due to the extreme importance of user-centered systems, many development approaches start with a prototype followed by a user guide. The user guide is "frozen" for an iteration of the development cycle to enable development to proceed in accordance with the needs of the user.
- At the end of resurrection, what we are producing in terms of user documentation is a comprehensive user guide to support the new system. This user documentation should be comprehensive, supported by detailed examples, and easily accessible. Thus, users should be able to navigate comfortably through the user guide in order to access what they want.

Although the user guides may be printed, it is becoming a norm to provide the guides in an electronic form. Both forms of presentation are important. Accessibility of the user documentation, the company standard for documentation, and updating of its versions as newer development effort takes place, is all important from the quality viewpoint. This should all be considered during the resurrection effort.

8.9.3 ONLINE HELP

Providing comprehensive help to the user is an important element of successfully resurrected software. This help should be available at the point where the user needs it the most — when she is stuck at a particular point in the application. The best way to provide this help is through online documentation and an example that is accessible along with the application. Some of the desirable features of online help are

- The help should be available at the point where it is needed the most, where the user is stuck. Therefore, the help should be context sensitive.
- It should be associated with suitable examples.
- Help relevant to the error that has occurred should come up automatically, so that a novice user is supported without much effort.
- The online help should be downloadable and printable — to provide further referencing.

In addition to the help available from the system, the user also may want support from the help desk. There are quite a few help desk packages available and they should be considered in recording and providing help. Analysis of the help calls can be correlated to the quality of the system. This information indicates the direction for possible future modifications and enhancements to particular modules of the system.

8.9.4 WIZARDS

Wizards are step-by-step directions provided by the system to set up the user with a supporting file or document that can be used in executing the system. A resurrected system should take the user through the required steps to enable him to set up the necessary views that would be used by him to perform his task. For example, a system dealing with bank tellers should be able to provide a series of steps for the teller to set up his own profile, as well as to create a set of views pertinent to the day's work. Such a view would provide the teller with all the details of the day's transaction in *the way he wants to see them*. This is especially important if the resurrecting system is using data mining techniques, wherein different users can view the same set of data in different ways. Wizards provided within the software system can help the user create and set up the views on the data warehouse that are most relevant to their work. Control totals and corresponding reconciliation transactions can also be set up using wizards. Thus, wizards play an important role in helping users in the use of the system by leading the users, one step at a time, through the process of setting up the system for use. They form an important part of a fully documented system.

8.9.5 AUTO DEMOS

Computer Based Training (CBT) is a type of documentation that is a software teaching tool embedded within the solution software. A CBT tool associated with software would enable the user to learn the intricacies of the software from the software itself. A comprehensive CBT package, although desirable, would require considerable effort and would be dictated by the budget for resurrection. However, an automated demo of the application supported by example would be an ideal documentation accompanying the application.

8.10 CASE TOOLS FOR OO METHODOLOGIES

Tools for development are the equivalent of the pots and pans for baking a cake, as discussed in the cooking example (Chapter 4). However, a large number of popular tools in the development of object-oriented solutions have come under the umbrella of object-oriented methodologies. The shortlisting and selection of tools, though, is a part of the evaluation activity within the methodological process. We discuss some of the popular methodological tools that can be used in the designs of resurrected systems. These tools enable the use of a particular methodological approach. They also influence the ease of designing and documenting the new system and, as a result, influence the quality of the resurrection process.

8.10.1 RATIONAL ROSE™

Rational Rose has become one of the most popular tools for designing software solutions using the UML methodology. It integrates the use case and logical view of the objectory process. It also enables conversion of class models to ER models, providing a first cut of the underlying relational structure that would support the new design of the resurrecting system.

8.10.2 OBJECT ANALYST™

Object Analyst is a tool developed by Tata Technologies India, Ltd. (TTIL, Pune, India) for the purpose of supporting development in client-server technology, networked and distributed systems, Internet solutions, procedural extensions to RDBMSs, and object languages and libraries. In addition to its code generation, reverse engineering, prototyping and documentation modules, Object Analyst's extension to RDBMS is an attractive feature in Y2K resurrection situations that deal with date problems in their relational databases.

8.10.3 METAEDIT™

Meta Edit is a tool that supports the OPEN methodological approach to object-oriented development. Because of its earlier association with MOSES methodology (one of the precursors of OPEN), MetaEdit was one of the first tools to support OPEN.

8.10.4 Visio™

Visio is essentially a software system drawing tool. However, it has become quite popular especially in describing distributed systems. Because of the importance we attach to distribution, Visio can play a good supporting role in documenting the resurrection process.

8.11 KEY POINTS

1. The essence of the methodological challenge in the resurrection process is to provide a detailed "how to" of resurrecting a new system.
2. This "how to" also includes the details of dissection and salvage activity within the methodological dimension of the resurrection process.
3. The need and justification for the use of a methodology within the resurrection process was described. The road map approach to use of methodology within software development ensures that the creativity of the individuals is not stifled and at the same time the project manager is able to look out for "driving conditions" within the project.
4. Advantages of object orientation within the resurrection process were described. This includes the advantages of seamlessness and small semantic gap within OO development.
5. Unification of OO methods, their advantages, and their examples (UML, OPEN) were described.
6. Essence of the requirements modeling activity within the resurrection process was described with the help of a use case model, a class model, and a sequence diagram.
7. Significance of reusability within OO and the various dimensions of reuse within the resurrection process were described in detail.
8. Because of the potential of repeating the resurrection process for causes other than the Y2K problem, patterns in resurrection were introduced.
9. Quality in resurrection implies defining and refining the process. This was discussed in the context of OO development.
10. Although lines of code is a popular metrics, the data from such metrics and collecting during prevention effort is of informative interest only. Alternative metrics for OO development were discussed.
11. Weighting factors for resurrection metrics are important because the timings and effort of the resurrection process are skewed depending on the level of preparedness of the organization. A suggested weighting scale for such level of preparedness was presented.
12. Importance of documentation is accepted within the resurrection process. Various forms of documentation and help for the resurrecting system were presented.

13. CASE tools that support OO development methodologies were mentioned briefly.

8.12 NOTES

The major difference between the overall resurrection process and the OO methodologies is that the OO methodologies form part of only one dimension of the three dimensions of the resurrection process. Although a full life cycle methodology talks a lot more about project management and quality assurance than a highly focused design method, still no OO method has taken into consideration the sociological dimension of a development process in detail, as in this resurrection process.

The extensive referencing of arguments within this chapter indicates that these topics are of both professional and academic interest to me. Many of the discussions presented in this chapter derive from the research I conducted as a part of my doctorate studies.

8.13 REFERENCES

1. Henderson-Sellers, B., Who needs a methodology anyway?, *J. OO Progr.,* 8:6, 1995.
2. Henderson-Sellers, B. and Edwards, J. M., *BOOKTWO of Object-Oriented Knowledge: The Working Object,* Prentice-Hall, Upper Saddle River, NJ, 1994, 22.
3. Sommerville, I., *Software Engineering,* Addison-Wesley, Reading, MA, 1989.
4. Szudrich, M., Opinion: methodologies for mediocrity, *Informatics,* (Publication of Australian Computer Society), 1:5, July 1993.
5. Henderson-Sellers, B., Who needs a methodology anyway?, *J. OO Prog.,* 8:6, 6–8, 1995.
6. Unhelkar, B. and Mamdapur, G., Practical aspects of using a methodology: a road map approach, *Report Obj. Anal. Design (ROAD),* 2:2, 34–36, 54, July–August 1995.
7. Wirfs-Brock, R., When will object technology meet its potential?, *J. OO Prog.,* 5:5, 6–8, Sept. 1992.
8. Jacobson, I., Ericsson, M., and Jacobson, A., *The Object Advantage: Business Process Engineering with Object Technology,* Addison-Wesley, Reading, MA, 1995.
9. Meyer, B., Object-oriented technology: a management perspective, Tutorial Notes, *TOOLS 9,* Sydney, 1992.
10. Henderson-Sellers, B. and Edwards, J. M., *BOOKTWO of Object-Oriented Knowledge: The Working Object,* Prentice-Hall, Upper Saddle River, NJ, 1994.
11. Graham, I., *Migrating to Object Technology,* Addison-Wesley, Reading, MA, 1994, 357.
12. Jacobson, I., Time for a cease fire in the methods war, *J. OO Prog.,* July–August 1993.
13. Hutt, A., *Object Analysis and Design, Description of Methods,* OMB/Wiley, 202, 1994.
14. Hutt, A., *Object Analysis and Design, Comparison of Methods,* OMG/Wiley, 212, 1994.
15. Henderson-Sellers, B. and Edwards, J. M., A second generation OO methodology: MOSES, *Obj. Mag.,* 1994.
16. Dodani, M., Archaeological Designers, *J. OO Prog.,* May 1994.
17. Fowler, M., A Survey of Object-Oriented Analysis and Design Methods, OOPSLA '96 Tutorial No. 45, San Jose, CA, 1996.
18. Booch, G., Rumbaugh, J., and Jacobson, I., The Unified Modelling Language Tutorial, OOPSLA '96 Conference, San Jose, Oct. 1996.

19. Graham, I., Henderson-Sellers, B., and Younessi, H., The OPEN Process Specification, Addison-Wesley, London, 1997.

20. Jacobson, I., Christerson, M., Jonsson, P., and Overgaard, G., *Object-Oriented Software Engineering: A Use Case Driven Approach*, Addison-Wesley, Reading, MA, 1992.

21. Sommerville, I., *Software Engineering*, Addison-Wesley, Reading, MA, 1989, 352.

22. Frakes, W. B. and Isoda, S., Success factors of systematic reuse, *IEEE Software*, 11:5, 15–19, Sept. 1994.

23. Henderson-Sellers, B. and Edwards, J. M., *BOOKTWO of Object-Oriented Knowledge: The Working Object*, Prentice-Hall, 1994, 419, 428.

24. Unhelkar, B. and Henderson-Sellers, B., The Role of Granularity in the Reuse of Object-oriented Systems, Proc. ACOSM '93 First Australian Conference on Software Metrics, Verner, J., Ed., Australian Software Metrics Association, Sydney, Nov. 1993, 51–66.

25. Card, D. and Comer, E., Why do so many reuse programs fail, *IEEE Software*, 11:5, 114–115, Sept. 1994.

26. Unhelkar, B., Effect of Granularity of Object-oriented Design on Modelling an Enterprise and its Application to Financial Risk Management, Ph.D. thesis, University of Technology, Sydney, 1998.

27. Unhelkar, B., Developing a financial market analysis product: a MOSES case study, *Developing Business Objects*, chap. 6, Carmichael, A., Ed., SIGS, 1997, 113–140.

28. Booch, G., Designing an application framework, *Dr. Dobb's J.*, 19:2, 24–32, Feb. 1994.

29. Henninger, S., Using iterative refinement to find reusable software, *IEEE Software*, 11:5, 48–49, Sept. 1994.

30. Alexander, C. et al., *A Pattern Language*, Oxford University Press, New York, 1977.

31. Gamma, E., Helm, R., Johnson, R., and Vlissides, J., *Design Patterns: Elements of Reusable Object-Oriented Software*, Addison-Wesley, Reading, MA, 1995.

32. Coplien, J. O., Generative pattern languages, *C++ Report*, 6:6, 18–22, 66–67, July–Aug. 1994.

33. Martin, R., Patterns: PloP, PLoP, fizz, fizz, *J. OO Prog.*, 7:8, 7–12, Jan. 1995.

34. Gamma, E., Helm, R., Johnson, R., and Vlissides, J., *Design Patterns: Elements of Reusable Object-Oriented Software*, Addison-Wesley, Reading, MA, 1995.

35. Wohlin, C. and Ahlgren, M., Soft factors and their impact on time to market, *Softw. Quality J.*, 4:3, 189–205, Sept. 1995.

36. Unhelkar, B. and Mamdapur, G., Role of OO metrics in managing the development of a financial markets analytical product: a case study, Jeffery, R., Ed., Proc. of ACOSM '95 Second Austrlian Conference of Software Metrics, Australian Software Metrics Association, Sydney, 1995, 168–177.

37. Lorenz, M. and Kidd, J., *Object-Oriented Software Metrics*, Prentice-Hall, Upper Saddle River, NJ, 1994, 4–5.

38. Thomas, D. and Jacogson, I., Managing object-oriented software engineering tutorial, *TOOLS '89*, Paris, 1989, 52.

39. Henderson-Sellers, B., The economics of reusing library classes, *J. OO Prog.*, 6:4, 43–50.

40. Henderson-Sellers, B., *Object-Oriented Metrics: Measures of Complexity*, Prentice Hall, Upper Saddle River, NJ, 1996.

9 A Methodological Process

Technology is only a tool which becomes useful when used by the Mind.

Rajiv Gandhi[1]

Abstract   The methodological process is a mental discipline that makes use of the tools of technology to achieve certain goals. The detailed understanding of object-oriented methodologies developed in the previous chapter is placed in the format of the resurrection "process discipline" in this chapter. This will enable us to follow the methodological approach to software development within the resurrection process. The methodological process includes the activities of project management, requirements modeling, analysis and design, implementation, quality assurance, reuse and standards, to name but a few. These activities and their associated tasks are described in detail in this chapter. A process metrics is provided at the end as an "indicator" of the effort required in the methodological dimension of the resurrection process. This metrics will change depending on the process-threads used during the actual implementation of the process.

9.1   DESCRIBING THE METHODOLOGICAL PROCESS

The aim of the methodological process is to formalize the "how to" of the resurrection exercise discussed in the previous chapter. Unlike the technological process, wherein radical changes in hardware, software, and networking could be taking place, the methodological process undergoes changes only to the extent that it can support the technological changes. The object-oriented methodologies discussed in the previous chapter and their requirements modeling, designing, reusability, and metrics approaches are all part of the methodological activities described here.

If the Y2K-hit organization had followed a structured method for designing its systems, then the technical teams will have to undergo a shift in mindset in order to adopt the object-oriented approach to development. Although this is a challenge, it is not as difficult as a situation wherein the Y2K-hit organization had not followed *any* methodological approach at all in its development. In that situation, the challenge starts from inculcating the methodological discipline in the development teams.

However, compared to the technological changes expected in a resurrecting organization, the methodological changes are fine tuning the "how to" of the organization. There are two aspects to this fine-tuning of the methodological processes:

- The way the organization works, which is the business methodology of the organization.
- The way the software development takes place.

This second aspect of methodology has a bearing on the way the organization works. The quality of business processes that depend on the software cannot be independent of the software processes. Thus, when we re-engineer, it is the software development methodology that will have influence on the business methodology of the organization.

In the previous chapter, we discussed in detail all aspects of the object-oriented approach to software development and its influence in a Y2K resurrection effort. In this chapter we try and put the object-oriented methodological approach within the resurrection process discipline. As is true with the other two dimensions, the methodological dimension does not work alone. Therefore, in reality, when we try to create a process-thread, it will pass through activities from any of the three dimensions of the resurrection process. For example, the activity of "alternative evaluation" (MA01) within the methodological dimensions may start off the overall resurrection process, followed by the "dissection" activity (TA01) from the technological dimension and so on. The methodological process continues to provide techniques to work with the technology, quality and standards, measurements and documentation, and an overall control of the resurrection process that would otherwise be missing. This methodological process is supported by the use of CASE tools for object-oriented methodologies.

9.1.1 THE PROCESS FIGURE

Figure 9.1 describes the methodological process in the Y2K resurrection exercise. The actors, activities, task, and deliverables that comprise the process elements come together to produce the software. There are three main actors (supported by one user actor), 11 activities made up of 60 tasks and five major deliverables.

9.1.2 A HIGH-LEVEL PROCESS FLOW

The methodological process commences when the actors' project manager and the architect get together to evaluate various aspects of the resurrection development process. This includes the technology and the budgets, as well as the tools to be used during the resurrection. Activities of requirements modeling, production of the architecture of the new system, and the low-level system designs then takes place. Management of the team also includes activities of project planning as well as the day-to-day management of the project. The activities of quality assurance include quality planning which leads to the activities of testing, metrics, and standards. Management of all these quality-related activities comprise quality management. Thus, like project management, quality management is the routine activity of managing quality and quality plans on a day-to-day basis.

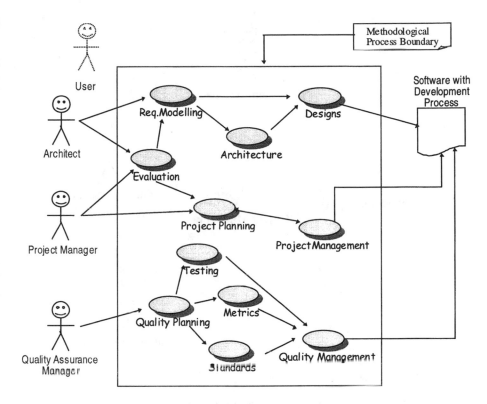

FIGURE 9.1 The methodological process in Y2K resurrection.

9.2 METHODOLOGICAL ACTORS

Figure 9.2 shows the prime methodological actor — project manager — and her variations. Variations of the actor include the architect who is involved in putting together the overall architecture of the system, the quality assurance manager dealing with the quality aspect, the database manager, who appears here as well as in the technological process dealing with the data issues, the methodologist, and the process consultants. The last two roles and, in fact, many of the other roles within the methodological process can be combined depending on the size of the organization and the scope of the resurrection attempt. The actor user also is an important part of the methodological process.

9.2.1 ACTOR: PROJECT MANAGER

The project manager is the primary actor for the methodological process wherein she is involved with the overall management of how the resurrection team goes about redesigning and developing the new processes for the resurrecting organization. The responsibilities of the project manager include planning the activities and tasks within the resurrection process, assigning them to the relevant resources, managing the resources on a regular basis, appraising the director (resurrection champion) of

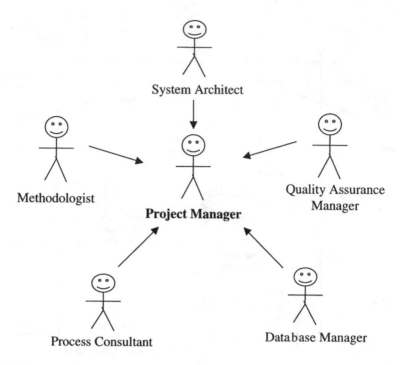

FIGURE 9.2   The methodological actors.

the status of the project, and ensuring that the design and development of the system proceeds in a formal way. The advantages in using a formal methodology discussed in the previous chapter are realized by the work of this actor. Effectively, the project manager is responsible for integration of a formal object-oriented methodology in the resurrection work.

9.2.2   ACTOR: ARCHITECT

In a large Y2K resurrection effort, it will be essential to separate the activities of managing the project from those of putting together the high-level technical aspects of the solution. This is the job performed by the architect who puts together the various infrastructure and application aspects of the solution. This role is further enhanced in a distributed solution, wherein there are many opportunities to salvage the "good" bits from the existing system that can be plugged in the newly designed processes. Furthermore, in a distributed solution it is important to design the overall database, hardware and applications in a way that will make a good use of the available resources. This overall architecture is the responsibility of the actor architect.

9.2.3   ACTOR: QUALITY ASSURANCE MANAGER

The quality assurance manager plays the important role of ensuring that the resurrection process follows the principles and techniques of quality in software development. Quality has to be carefully planned and executed in the overall resurrection process. This would involve formal documentation, setting of standards and metrics, and performing all quality-related activities discussed in the previous chapter and described here within the methodological framework. Compared with the Y2K prevention effort, wherein quality assurance work concentrated on testing the Y2K bugs in a resurrection effort, it is not only testing of dates, but also of the overall resurrected system.

During the activities of quality assurance, this actor may have to interact with the technological actors called programmers and test programmers. The quality assurance manager would manage writing of test cases and test harnesses. Thus, the quality assurance manager deals with the technological activities of quality assurance (TA10).

9.2.4   ACTOR: USER

The actor user, although is a part of the overall resurrection process, is mentioned specifically in the methodological dimension. There are two main reasons why the user plays an important role in the resurrection process:

1. The higher computer literacy among the users enables them to pass informed comments during the dissection and salvage activities, as well as during the modeling for the new system.
2. Because of the small semantic gap between the user models and the physical designs of the system, users can directly identify their business objects within the solution.

However, because the resurrection process is technologically driven, the user appears in the background in the process dimensions.

9.3   METHODOLOGICAL DELIVERABLES

9.3.1   SOFTWARE WITH DEVELOPMENT PROCESS

The software produced at the end of the methodological process is the prime deliverable of the methodological process. However, if a development process is followed in a formal way as prescribed in this book, the result is not only good quality software, but also a well-documented process that may be used to enhance the system in future. The process itself may simply be used to produce future systems within the organization, as seeds of these systems can be found in the formal specifications of the resurrection process itself. The documents that form part of the methodological deliverables and the role they play in producing a quality software is described below (Figure 9.3).

9.3.2   BUSINESS SCENARIOS

Business scenarios are a set of nontechnical description of what the user wants. This deliverable can be made up of the scenarios and use cases discussed in the previous chapter. They can contain both the textual description as well as the graphical pictures

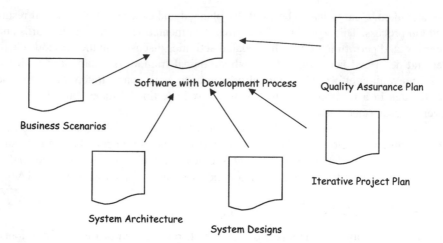

FIGURE 9.3 Variation of the methodological deliverables.

showing how the scenario will work. The user guide and/or the Y2K-hit system that is still executable form the starting point for the business scenarios in the resurrection process. However, care should be taken to ensure that the scenarios of the new system are not restricted by the technology and mind set of the Y2K-hit system. The resurrected system is a superset of the existing system. It contains all the necessary functionality of the Y2K-hit system and also the new functionality that adds value to the organization's business.

Business scenarios also can be a useful tool in determining the flow of control in the Y2K-hit system. Creating scenarios of the affected system would be one good way of identifying the problem areas of the system as well as identifying the salvageable options.

The object-oriented methodological tools discussed in the previous chapter can be used in documenting these business scenario deliverables.

9.3.3   SYSTEM ARCHITECTURE

The prime function of the system architecture deliverable in a software development process is to show how the major modules of the solution fit together. In a resurrection process, though, it can serve a duel purpose. In addition to creating the architecture of how the new system should be put together, this deliverable also can provide an understanding of the system architecture of the existing (hit) system. This can greatly assist in the technological activity of dissection. This is precisely the advantage of modeling as discussed in Section 4.1, wherein we mentioned that models enable us to understand reality as well as create new reality. This is the duel purpose of a good system architecture within the resurrection process.

9.3.4   SYSTEM DESIGNS

System designs derive from the system architecture, and are the lower level designs that can be used in order to produce the resurrected system. These are the object-oriented designs that can be documented using the CASE tools described in the previous chapter. They deal with the object-oriented concepts of classes and their relationships. In a large system, the system designs may be further subdivided into components from which the final code is produced. However, the techniques of creating system designs and component designs are essentially the same.

9.3.5 ITERATIVE PROJECT PLAN

The iterative project plan is the overall resurrection plan containing all the activities and tasks that need to be performed during the resurrection process. To start with, the project plan only contains the three iterations and the relevant activities and tasks within each of these iterations. This may be termed the iteration plan. The activities and tasks within the iteration plan are then assigned to resources and a corresponding timeline making it into a complete iterative project plan. The iterative project plan continues to remain a dynamic document, updated on a regular basis and especially at the end of each iteration — through the activity of project management (MT03-5) and quality management (MT11-3). These updates are based on (and influenced by) the productivity factor for the group arrived at by using the metrics described in the Section 5.12.

9.3.6 QUALITY ASSURANCE PLAN

The quality assurance plan is another "dynamic" deliverable from the methodological process. It contains details of the quality assurance activities within resurrection, the sequence and timing of how the activities will be executed, and the resources to complete the quality assurance and testing tasks. While it encompasses the three major activities within the methodological process: standards, metrics, and testing, it also has details of the quality planning activity. It is important to note that the quality assurance plan does not work independently, but is a document that is read in conjunction with the project plan. Alternatively, for a small-scoped resurrection, it may be a part of the iterative project plan.

9.4 METHODOLOGICAL ACTIVITIES AND TASKS WITH ITERATIONS

The following table (Table 9.1) lists the methodological activities and tasks that are described in more detail in the remainder of the chapter.

9.5 MA01: ALTERNATIVE EVALUATION

This is a major methodological activity in which the project manager, the technical, and business staff is involved. When the date problem occurs, both the data and the software are affected. In order to bring the organization back to its feet, it will be essential to convert the data that are still relevant and to correct the software. The organization has a number of options to achieve this end. At the business level some of these alternatives that need to be evaluated before the resurrection work can

TABLE 9.1
Methodological Activities and Tasks with Iterations

Methodological Activities	Methodological Tasks
MA01: Alternative evaluation Iteration: initial	MT01-01: Background thinking MT01-02: Prioritizing high-level requirements MT01-03: Technological feedback MT01-04: Budgetary feedback MT01-05: Selecting alternative MT01-06: Methodology decision
MA02: Project planning Iteration: initial	MT02-1: Formalize process elements MT02-2: Create iteration plan MT02-3: Assign resources to tasks MT02-4: Assign checkpoints
MA03: Project management Iteration: all	MT03-1: Promote methodology MT03-2: Review technical demos MT03-3: Conduct user demos MT03-4: Track activities and tasks MT03-5: Update project plan MT03-6: Watch out for road factors MT03-7: Contain scope MT03-8: Manage user representatives
MA04: Requirements modeling Iteration: initial–major	MT04-1: Formalize salvageable requirements MT04-2: Identify date specific requirements MT04-3: Specify new requirements MT04-4: Prototype user interfaces MT04-5: Describe business objects
MA05: Architecture Iteration: initial	MT05-1: Identify architectural elements MT05-2: Slice large and complex elements MT05-3: Relate the architectural elements MT05-4: Consider distributed architecture MT05-5: Produce system architecture
MA06: Solution design Iteration: major	MT06-1: Produce component designs MT06-2: Design DATE component MT06-3: Reuse designs MT06-4: Design database tables MT06-5: Consider database distribution MT06-6: Design user interface
MA07: Quality planning Iteration: initial	MT07-1: Identify quality elements MT07-2: Estimate quality resources MT07-3: Create quality plan MT07-4: Review quality plan
MA08: Standards Iteration: initial	MT08-1: Identify needs for standards MT08-2: Map to existing standards MT08-3: Create local standards MT08-4: Publicize standards MT08-5: Upgrade standards MT08-6: Review activities based on standards

TABLE 9.1 *(continued)*
Methodological Activities and Tasks with Iterations

Methodological Activities	Methodological Tasks
MA09: Testing	MT09-1: Create test plan
Iteration: major–final	MT09-2: Identify test approach
	MT09-3: Create test environment
	MT09-4: Create test designs
	MT09-5: Conduct testing
	MT09-6: Review test results
MA10: Metrics	MT10-1: Identify measurement needs
Iteration: initial–major	MT10-2: Locate historical data
	MT10-3: Make "ball park" estimates
	MT10-4: Measure designs
	MT10-5: Measure code
	MT10-6: Measure quality
	MT10-7: Measure processes
MA11: Quality management	MT11-1: Manage quality resources
Iteration: all	MT11-2: Manage documentation
	MT11-3: Update quality plan

proceed are related to how the senior management (including the resurrection champion) sees the resurrection work proceeding. This can be evaluated from the following alternatives:

- The software system should be built in-house.
- Third-party package should be used in implementing the new solution.
- Entire resurrection work to be outsourced.
- External consultants and contract staff should be invited to perform the resurrection or join the in-house teams for the development process.
- A combination of any of the above.

The tasks within this activity provide guidance on how the various alternatives related to resurrection can be evaluated. The result of this activity will influence other methodological activities such as project planning (amount of resources to be allocated), requirements modeling (how do we specify requirements), etc. Decisions taken during the alternative evaluation activity would also influence the technological activities (like dissection).

9.5.1 MT01-1: BACKGROUND THINKING

The task of background thinking is perhaps one of the first tasks within the overall resurrection process. Organizations (except the ones at the red preparedness level) have already started with this task, albeit in varying formats. This task is undertaken in a group with representation from the project manager as well as the resurrection champion.

The format of this task can be brainstorming sessions using a chalk board. All the systems that are affected by the Y2K bug are noted. The areas in which the problem is affecting (data, GUI, etc.), if known, are also noted. More importantly, though, the corresponding business repercussions are noted. The kind of output resulting from the background thinking task includes:

- The list of systems affected by Y2K.
- Areas of the system affected by the problem.
- Likely subsystems and tables that still have data worth salvaging.
- The extent of available functionality from the Y2K-hit system that is still valid.
- Is the new enterprise to be rebuilt by using off-the-shelf, third-party libraries that can provide same/similar functionality?
- Is the work to be performed in-house or outsourced

9.5.2   MT01-2: Prioritizing High-Level Requirements

The results from the brainstorming sessions within the task of background thinking are placed in the order of priority during this task. It is futile to pursue resurrection for a redundant process or convert data that is no longer relevant once we are over the Year 2000 hump. This task is performed by asking a number of business (and technical) questions that help in prioritizing the resurrection requirements. Typically, these questions include:

- What was the business purpose of this system or module?
- What is important and worth salvaging from the system that is hit — the data, the logic, or both?
- The cost benefit of outsourcing the work or buying a third-party package to do the job.
- Time to complete resurrection — the bare minimum time needed to bring the systems back. Some systems that have only served peripheral business purpose can take more time for resurrection or may not ever be resurrected.

Priorities are assigned to the choices that the organization had, depending on the aforementioned factors. Time and budget continue to provide major input into the activity of prioritizing. Thus, this task of prioritizing may iterate with the tasks of technological and budgetary feedback or may continue in parallel with them.

9.5.3   MT01-3: Technological Feedback

The technological feedback may be sought from the project manager and the architect of the solution. They, in turn, may contact the corresponding technical team members regarding their opinion on two topics:

1. The areas and extent of Y2K hits within the existing systems.
2. The manner in which the systems can be technically resurrected.

Although the Y2K prevention exercises have been a specialized area of identifying and correcting date, the people who provide technological feedback on the resurrection process will have to be the ones who understand the Y2K-hit systems from the user's perspective. Therefore, this feedback has to come from the people who belong to the company. However, additional input from external groups may be required. For example, vendors of new hardware, operating systems, development environment, etc. may have their own views on the capability of their technology. Feedback from these parties, especially as we hope to resurrect with newer technology, may be essential. A third party solution may require input from the corresponding software vendors on the functionality of the product, and whether it can function well on the company's platform. For example, a 16-bit application may not work well on a 32-bit NT platform. Alternatively, a 32-bit application may not work on a 16-bit Windows 95 platform without the corresponding drivers or some such translation mechanism.

9.5.4   MT01-4: BUDGETARY FEEDBACK

The budgeting activity takes place during the preliminary work that is done before the core resurrection processes commence. This was discussed in detail in Section 5.5 on budgeting. The resurrection champion, who is involved in that preliminary budgeting work, uses that information in the evaluation of technical and business alternatives. Do we have enough money to get external consulting help for resurrection? Do we have the resources to retrain all personnel in the use of the new applications? Answer to questions like these need budgetary feedback. Thus, providing the budgetary feedback is another important task within the alternative evaluation activity. The project manager provides input on the budgetary amounts and their availability in terms of timings and manner. This feedback will influence the prioritizing of the high-level requirements of resurrection.

9.5.5   MT01-5: SELECTING ALTERNATIVE

This is the task of finally selecting from the alternatives available for resurrection. These alternatives were brainstormed and prioritized in the previous tasks. Although the options and their priority may appear well defined, in reality one would expect to select either one alternative or a combination of alternatives. When a specific course of action (e.g., buying and implementing a third-party package for the areas hit by Y2K) or a combination of actions (partly rewriting and partly converting existing Y2K-hit systems) are selected, they need to be noted and made known to the organization. Selection of alternatives also implies provision for backups. Thus, on selection of a particular alternative, it would also be essential to specify the possible backup alternatives, if the chosen approach fails.

9.5.6   MT01-6: METHODOLOGY DECISION

One of the important tasks of the evaluation activity is to decide on the object-oriented methodology to use during resurrection. After the unification effort of methodologists (described in the previous chapter) and the creation of an object-oriented meta-model, we have, mercifully, a sensible number of methods to choose from. Currently, this choice may be limited to UML and OPEN or a combination of both. In this task, we decide on the use of one such formal methodology in resurrection.

This methodology forms one important aspect of the methodological dimension of the overall resurrection process. It will help us use common notations to understand and document lower level designs for the new system. Furthermore, the choice of a methodological tool will follow on from the decision to use a particular methodology — further facilitating the task of documenting the designs. Since this decision-making process is likely to be influenced by a number of factors within the organization, not excluding the available budgets, the politics within the organization, and the particular preferences of the developers, this task may have to iterate more than once during the evaluation activity.

9.6 MA02: PROJECT PLANNING

The activity of project planning provides major input into the project plan deliverable. This activity is undertaken after the major tasks within the evaluation activity are completed. This is because only after completing the evaluation can we start with detailed project planning. However, as represented by our three-dimensional "white cloud" model, activities can go on in all three dimensions of the resurrection process. Furthermore, some tasks within one activity may precede (or follow) tasks from other activities. For example, after some of the alternative evaluation tasks have been undertaken, we may come to this activity of project planning and enter all the evaluation tasks in detail here. However, project plan may have a higher level entry for the evaluation activity at the initial iteration of the project plan. Thus, we may undertake the evaluation activity without the detailed project plan, but the initial project plan may contain an entry for evaluation.

9.6.1 MT02-1: FORMALIZE PROCESS ELEMENTS

A number of process elements make up the resurrection process. These comprise the actors, activities, tasks, and deliverables from all three process dimensions. However, based on the alternatives evaluated and selected in the previous activity, we may not require all elements in the overall resurrection. The formalization of process elements to be used in *a particular resurrection* process rather than describing them in general within a resurrection process, results in the creation of a process-thread. For example, in an outsourced resurrection process, the task of "selecting methodology" (or methodology decision described in MT01-6) may not be relevant as it is the vendor's methodology and not the methodology used in-house, that matters.

9.6.2 MT02-2: CREATE ITERATION PLAN

The purpose of this task is to create an iteration plan that will enable the resurrection effort to derive the benefits of the iterative nature of object-oriented development. Each iteration of the resurrection process will encompass tasks from all three dimensions of the process. The task of creating iteration plan can be undertaken when the process elements are formalized so that the project manager is aware of the tasks to be performed during the resurrection process-thread. The project manager will be the main actor involved in creating the iteration plan. At the early stage of project planning, it is not essential to put "timings" in the iteration plan. This is because the main purpose of creating the iteration plan is to list the activities and tasks within each of the process dimensions that will be completed during each iteration. Furthermore, the estimate on the timings for each of the iterations can vary depending on the size and complexity of the resurrection project. However, as a rule of thumb, an iteration within a typical development project lasts 3 months. Therefore, one would expect to complete a typical project in 9 months. There are wide variations to these estimates which delve into the area of metrics and measurement. The number of people on the project, their skill level, their motivation, and the availability of budget, all influence the iteration plan. The tasks related to these measurements (described by MA10) may be performed during the later part of the iteration. At this stage, it is only essential to start with an iteration plan wherein the focus is on the tasks to perform and not on when these tasks will be performed and who will exactly perform them. It is worth noting that the creation of the iteration plan itself is a part of the first iteration of the resurrection process.

9.6.3   MT02-3: Assign Resources to Tasks

Once the process elements are formalized in process-threads and an iteration plan is created, it will be essential to assign the people to perform the tasks within the process. This task (MT02-3) assigns the resources to tasks. Herein, we also decide on the number of resources. For example, the project manager and architect performing some of the methodological activities appear against these activities as the assigned resources. However, in a large resurrection process, more than one project manager would be required. Furthermore, other variations of the project manager may make up the numbers that describe the resources. Resources from the technological and the sociological process dimensions are considered and assigned to their respective tasks. Finally, some of the sociological activities like Team Formation (SA02) and Motivation (SA05) will influence how the resources are assigned to their respective tasks.

9.6.4   MT02-4: Assign Checkpoints

It is essential to assign checkpoints within the resurrection process in order to monitor its progress. The checkpoints perform the important task of enabling the project manager to know the status of her project and to enable reporting of the status to the senior management. Although a project manager may be aware of the project status, checkpoints make it mandatory for everyone in the project to complete their tasks before the reporting date. Checkpoints are publicized dates when the reporting and review of the project takes place. The end of each iteration is an ideal checkpoint, but they can be assigned anywhere during the project. Apart from providing the management with the understanding of the project status, checkpoints also provide a metric on the "speed of resurrection" (or "productivity in resurrection") which can be used to update plan.

9.7 MA03: PROJECT MANAGEMENT

The activity of project management forms part of all dimensions of the resurrection process. It also is an activity that happens in all iterations of the process. However, within the methodological dimension of the resurrection process, the focus is on promoting the object-oriented methodology selected in task MT01-6 (methodology decision), controlling and promoting the resurrection work, containing its scope, and updating the project plan based on the work accomplished thus far.

9.7.1 MT03-1: PROMOTE METHODOLOGY

Once an object-oriented methodology is selected for the resurrection work, it is important that the project manager promotes the use of the methodology within the resurrection team, as well as outside the team. Many software projects start with a particular methodology but without the promotion of the approach, they lose track of the life cycles and models suggested by the methodology. Having sufficient literature on the selected methodology, organizing training courses (although formally a sociological activity, SA03), and supporting the approach with relevant CASE tools, all form part of promoting the methodology.

9.7.2 MT03-2: REVIEW TECHNICAL DEMOS

One of the important project management tasks of the project manager is to see the system as it is being developed. Once the technical activity of rewrite–modify–customize (TA03) starts, it is essential to maintain a working demo of the resurrecting system. This task ensures that the project manager gets the technical team to demo the product to her on a regular basis. There is a potential for loss of time due to the effort required to produce the demos, but most IT experience seems to suggest that the effort is worth it.

9.7.3 MT03-3: CONDUCT USER DEMOS

During the entire resurrection process, the project manager should be in a position to show the system to others. This is true especially of the potential users and business sponsors of the resurrection work. Thus, this task requires the project manager to be in charge of the demo version of the software throughout the resurrection process and be in a position to conduct the demo for the users at any point in time.

9.7.4 MT03-4: TRACK ACTIVITIES AND TASKS

Tracking of activities and tasks is a standard project management task that is performed by following the project plan. However, it is suggested that during the resurrection process, the project manager should create a few process diagrams corresponding to her process-threads (using the process discipline notations used in this book) and place them in a prominent place within the development area. Highlighting the tasks that are completed is a technique of making the tracking task visual. This highlighting of completed tasks can be performed at the designated checkpoints, like the end of each iteration. Because of the iterative nature of the resurrection process, the tasks within the process are likely to appear more than once within the process-threads.

9.7.5 MT03-5: UPDATE PROJECT PLAN

This is a task similar to updating the project plan (TT10-5) that was performed in the technological dimension of the resurrection process. In the technological dimension, though, the focus is on updating the technological activities and tasks within the project. Updating the project plan in the methodological dimension encompasses activities and tasks in all dimensions of the resurrection process.

While the project plan is put together during the initial iteration of the project, the continuous activity of project management keeps the project plan updated throughout the life of the resurrection project. During this task, it is essential that the dynamics of the initial iteration are incorporated in the estimation for subsequent iterations. Thus, the update of the project plan would follow the example provided in Section 5.12 on updating the project plan at the end of each iteration.

9.7.6 MT03-6: WATCH OUT FOR ROAD FACTORS

With some variations, tracking the activities and tasks within the resurrection project (MT03-4) and updating the project plan (MT03-5) are tasks that are part of traditional project management. However, these tasks need to be performed with an understanding of the "road map approach" discussed in the previous chapter. In following the road map approach, it is important to watch out for the road factors that will influence the efficiency and effectiveness of the team in carrying out the assigned tasks.

9.7.7 MT03-7: CONTAIN SCOPE

Since the resurrection of the organization depends on the resurrection of the system, it is vital that the project manager contains the scope of the project so that it doesn't "blow out." During the preliminary activities of the process, the scope of resurrection would be identified. This may be small, medium, or large, depending on many factors provided by the intensity of the hit. Having once identified the scope, it is essential to stick to it until the system is delivered. The users of the system can play a very helpful role in the dissection activity as well as in specifying the requirements. It is essential to baseline these requirement as the resurrection project starts. This task of containing scope is especially important at the end of each iteration when the project plan is being updated and when the users are likely to provide additional requests for enhancement of the system.

9.7.8 MT03-8: MANAGE USER REPRESENTATIVES

Users will support the resurrection team during the dissection as well as the requirements modeling activities during resurrection. In the new millennium, one would expect more computer literate users. Furthermore, because of the small semantic gap in object orientation between the problem and the solution domain (Figure 8.2), the users are able to appreciate and make sensible contributions to the modeling process. The project manager needs to derive maximum benefit from this understanding of the users, as well as manage their expectations. This is achieved through the task of managing users.

9.8   MA04: REQUIREMENTS MODELING

The requirements modeling activity is meant to provide a formal set of statements that describe the resurrected business. In the previous chapter we discussed the various techniques used in specifying the requirements (e.g., usecases, scenarios, class diagrams). Because of the seamlessness of the object-oriented approach, some of these requirements would flow through to the architecture and design activities. We write the requirements for the resurrection system by means of formal tasks described in this activity.

While the chief architect bears the major responsibility for the requirements (as they affect the architecture of the solution), the technical members of the team, with support from the users of the system, write the formal requirements. The users of the system may be able to provide considerable input into the requirements modeling for the new system — initially as participants in the dissection process of the Y2K-hit application and later, based on their experience, in specifying what more functionality can be added to the new system. The output of the dissection activity (TA01) plays a significant role in understanding and salvaging the current requirements or functionality of the product and then producing the new requirements. Thus, the activity of requirements modeling also provides the crucial link between the current and potential users of the system and the developers.

9.8.1   MT04-1: FORMALIZE SALVAGEABLE REQUIREMENTS

The technological activity of dissection (TA01) produces a shortlist of salvageable options (task TT01-5). These options are a list of entities from the Y2K-hit system that can be salvaged and reused in the new system. This task of formalizing the salvageable requirements (MT04-1) attempts to convert requirements of the existing system into formal requirements for the new system. The new requirements are made up of the salvageable requirements as well as the requirements for the new processes within the resurrecting system.

The challenge in formalizing the salvageable requirements is that these requirements may not have been stated formally in a Y2K-hit organization in the first place. The applications that are hit by the date problem are likely to be legacy systems written years/decades ago. The very early (1960s) era of legacy code did not necessarily use formal software engineering processes for modeling the requirements. However, when structured methods appeared on the scene in the 1970s, designs were expressed in those methods (e.g., SSADM, Structured System Analysis and Design Method; or even the primitive HIPO, Hierarchical Input–Process–Output charts). Therefore, in formalizing the shortlist of salvageable options from the Y2K-hit application, one may come across data flow diagrams (DFD), entity-relationship (E-R) diagrams or the simple flowcharts. These diagrams are understood and formalized during this task — mainly to provide a starting point for the requirements of the new system.

9.8.2 MT04-2: IDENTIFY DATE SPECIFIC REQUIREMENTS

Because of the emphasis of date in the problem domain of Y2K, it is only reasonable that we consider it as an important entity in the solution as well. Results of the dissection and salvaging operation would provide important date specific requirements of the current system. During this task (MT04-2), we go a step farther in identifying how much of the current date requirements still hold for the new system.

In modeling the date specific requirements for the new system, it is essential to consider *implicit* need for conversion of date. The interesting situations from the requirements point of view is that the users of the system, while fully aware of the cause of the problem and while eager to comply with the 4-digit requirement in the database, may still be interested in a *2-digit expression* of the date. When the 2-digit problem was coded, it was not just an error. Many users had a 2-digit standard, including, I am told, the U.S. Department of Defense. This required all associated activities (such as testing) to *enforce* the 2 digits.

It is essential to discourage the users from specifying a 2-digit field for dates. However, as discussed in the psychological effect of the Year 2000 (Section 1.5), a 2-digit expression is not just a computer phenomena. We have used 2-digit year to express our birth dates, and marriage dates, and convocation dates, and so on. If these "date expressions" still exist or if there is a need to maintain a 2-digit GUI, then they will formally appear in the requirements during this task.

Furthermore, there may be additional need of users to express the days related to dates or to display the Year 2000 as leap year. A financial market system may be interested in the holiday calendar for the new year, as settlement of many trades takes place after 2 working days. The holidays and the leap year would also influence check clearance in banks that usually takes 5 working days. Tellers may have specific requirements to express dates and days in a format suitable for the transactions they are conducting.

Dates are expressed in different sequence around the world. For example, in the U.S. we express it as month–day–year, whereas in Australia it is day–month–year. When year–month–day is the mode of expression, results of sorted dates need to be given careful consideration. If the date specific requirements for the transaction with the latest date to be shown first, then the sorting key will have to be year–month–day; however, the display requirement may be month–day–year, requiring further conversion after the rows have already been sorted.

9.8.3 MT04-3: SPECIFY NEW REQUIREMENTS

This is a task that directly influences the business scenario deliverable, as that is where the new requirements get formally recorded. While the two previous tasks (formalizing the salvageable requirements and identifying date specific requirements) were related more to the Y2K date issue, the writing of new requirements is not limited to the dates. New requirements are written by concentrating on the re-engineered process for the new business and keeping the date-related issues in the backdrop. Thus, apart from solving the issues related to Y2K-date, the resurrection process produces a new system that is also re-engineered. There are a number of ways new requirements can be recorded and quite a few standards exist for the same. The fact that we are going ahead with a re-engineered organization means that we have to use the process-based approach to writing of new requirements. The techniques of specifying the requirements using scenarios and usecases (discussed in the previous chapter) are used in accomplishing this task.

9.8.4   MT04-4: Prototype User Interfaces

After using the salvageable requirements from the Y2K-hit system and specifying newer requirements, it is essential to experiment with the requirements by using the prototyping approach. The task of prototyping enables the requirements modeling team to extract comprehensive requirements from the user. Furthermore, when it comes to the date fields in the new user interface, this task ensures that the date field specifications are sufficiently understood by the users who specify it and the developers to produce it. This includes the consideration of whether it is a 4-digit field or whether it is still a 2-digit field with implicit conversion as also the manner in which date is specified (day–month–year or month–day–year and so on).

There are a few ways that the user interfaces can be prototyped. Initially, they can be a simple pencil sketch or they may be hand-drawn and photocopied from a chalk board. The second stage is to put them on a screen using a prototyping tool. Once the user has time to play around with the prototype look and feel, a walkthrough of the sequence or flow of events can be done. Prototyping tools can be used to then provide a working prototype that the users can play with, navigate, and then refine further.

9.8.5   MT04-5: Describe Business Objects

The final task in the requirements modeling activity is to describe the business objects. By the time we reach this task, it is expected that the resurrection process will have gone through the initial iteration. Although for a small resurrection exercise the business objects may be described during the initial iteration, for a medium- to large-sized project, it is likely that the business objects are only identified during the initial iteration. They are then described in greater detail including all their attributes and their relationships during the major iteration. CASE tools described in the previous chapter can be used to specify the business objects and their relationship here.

9.9   MA05: ARCHITECTURE

The activity of architecture within the methodological process deals with two major aspect of resurrection:

1. Providing some understanding of the way in which the existing Y2K-hit system was put together which assists in the dissection work.
2. Specifying how the new system should be put together.

This activity deals with the system at a building block level, avoiding the lower level details at this stage. Thus, primarily the architect of the system performs this activity with input from other technical team members. This activity iterates with the previous activity of requirements modeling. Sometimes, the architecture of the new system is influenced by the requirements and at other times a good architecture may indicate problems in implementing the requirements, forcing a change in them. In a resurrection attempt, it is important to keep only those parts of the existing system that need no change. If the existing system needs even slight modification because of the date problem, it will be important to produce new requirements and corresponding new architecture for them.

9.9.1   MT05-1: IDENTIFY ARCHITECTURAL ELEMENTS

The first task within the architecture activity is to identify architectural elements that will comprise the new system. However, in order to perform this task effectively, it is also essential to identify the architectural elements of the existing Y2K-hit system. By understanding the current architecture, it will be easier to understand the current requirements and then design the new architecture.

The architectural elements within a system include the databases, the communication mechanisms between systems, the network, the operating system, and the application. Within the application, the systems are divided into subsystems. These subsystems together with their reusable design are part of the architecture of the system and are identified within the existing system and documented at this stage. When the new system is considered, the potential architectural elements of the new system are documented here. Note that this is only an exploratory task and, therefore, it is only concerned with listing the major elements of the system. This task of how these architectural elements are put together is considered separately.

9.9.2   MT05-2: SLICE LARGE AND COMPLEX ELEMENTS

Having identified the architectural elements, it is important to review them from the size and complexity angle. One of the essential aspects of the architectural tasks is to ensure that the system is manageable during development. This is possible only when the large and complex elements of the system are further divided into smaller and manageable chunks. The result of this division is varyingly called subsystems, components, or packages. This task also has correlation with the activity of team formation (SA02, Chapter 11).

There are two major ways in which systems can be sliced at architectural level:

1. The system can be divided into subsystems based on the functionality of the application. This happens when a large application like banking is divided into smaller chunks like accounts and customer information.

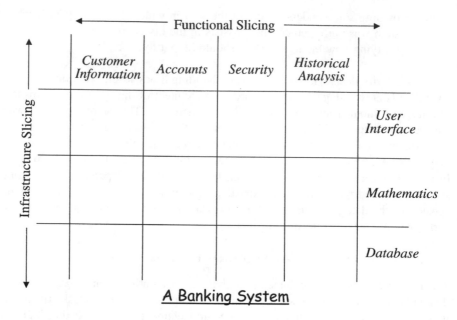

FIGURE 9.4   Functional vs. infrastructure-based slicing in architecture.

2. The system can be divided based on its infrastructure. For example, a system
   is divided into database, mathematical calculation, and user interface.

When large and complex systems are sliced, they result in both types of subdi-
visions. For example, both accounts and customer information subsystems may deal
with database and user interface. This is shown in Figure 9.4.

9.9.3   MT05-3: Relate the Architectural Elements

Figure 9.4 also shows how the sliced elements of the architecture relate to each
other. This task of relating the architectural elements ensures that the relevant
subsystems are placed next to each other in the system architecture. Being part of
an iterative and exploratory activity, this task is not going to produce the final
architecture. However, an attempt to relate the architectural elements of the solution
will clarify any potential problems at an early stage.

For example, when we try and relate the database system to the mathematical
calculations of an interest-bearing account, the role of a third-party library for interest
calculation may become clear. A subsystem relates to many other subsystems and
infrastructure elements within the architecture. This task ensures that the relationship
is making sense in the overall architecture.

9.9.4   MT05-4: Consider Distributed Architecture

Distribution is considered at a very high level during this task. There are two main
reasons why distributed architecture is considered in detail in the resurrection process:

1. It has the potential of salvaging some of the existing part of the system — parts that are not affected by the date problem and parts that are able to serve some purpose in the new requirements.
2. It ensures that the architecture of the solution is flexible and that it is able to incorporate different subsystems on varied platforms.

By distributing the solution, we ensure that the subsystems have minimum dependence on each other. This comes closer to making the architecture "pluggable." Some subsystems from the existing application that are still functioning may continue to be used until such time that we can redesign and implement the new subsystem.

Y2K resurrection aims to bring the organization back on its feet as quickly as possible. Distributed architecture enables the resurrection team to make early releases of subsystems that are ready for deployment rather than wait for the entire development to be completed. Distribution also enhances reuse (especially at run time) as subsystems and components can be executed across the network. Distribution is considered in greater detail in Chapter 12.

9.9.5   MT05-5: PRODUCE SYSTEM ARCHITECTURE

This, the final task within the architecture activity, produces the architecture diagram that contains the infrastructure and application slices, as well their relationships in providing the basis for the new system. Having considered the existing architecture, the subsystems and infrastructure for the new system, and the issues of distribution, this task produces a system architecture that is complete and consistent and which shows clearly the major elements within the solution and how these elements are related to each other. This "produce system architecture" task results in a one- to two-page document that provides a valuable source of reference to the development team throughout the resurrection effort. The final architecture considers all issues that ensure maximum reuse, minimum interdependence of subsystems, and judicious use of middleware platforms wherever relevant. If the task of system architecture is carried out with due diligence and by an architect with knowledge and experience of what she is doing, then the resulting architecture will be stable but flexible. It will be able to absorb changes to the designs without changing itself.

Figure 9.5 shows a simple banking architecture. Relationship between application and infrastructure elements is shown in the figure. The savings, check, loans, and credit cards are the vertically sliced business applications. These applications need to interface with the common module of CIS (Customer Information System). The user interface is shown as a separate system. These applications deal with the database, and all these key entities depend on the infrastructure module within the overall system.

9.10 MA06: SOLUTION DESIGN

This solution design activity flows on from both the requirements modeling (MA04) and the architecture (MA05) activity. The scenarios from the requirements modeling

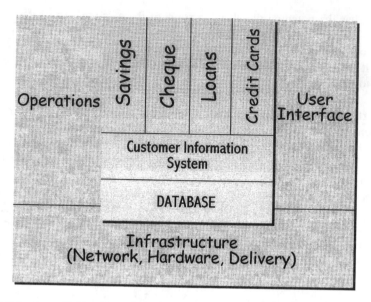

FIGURE 9.5   A typical banking system architecture.

can be used to produce solution level designs. They are influenced by the architecture of the new system, as provided by the architecture activity. The architect is still involved in this activity, but with considerable input from senior team members and the project manager (note that the actors architect and project manager *may be* the same person in real-life resurrection attempts). This is a more "hands on" activity within the methodological process. It is followed by the tasks related to coding and implementation within the technological process. Some of the tasks within the solution design activity may use the CASE tools to draw and document the designs.

9.10.1 MT06-1: PRODUCE COMPONENT DESIGNS

This task results in the production of component level designs. The inputs to this task are the requirements and business objects from the requirements modeling activity and the system architecture from the architectural activity. The component level designs are made up of a group of cohesive classes that serve a common purpose. For example, in a banking solution, the component designs would include designs for customer, accounts, and interest calculation. This would happen if the elements sliced during the architecture activity were smaller in size (as a rule of thumb, a component can be made up of 15 +/– 5 classes). If the subsystems are large and complex, they may be further subdivided into smaller components. Component designs use the object-oriented concepts of inheritance and association in describing relationship between the classes within the component.

9.10.2 MT06-2: DESIGN DATE COMPONENT

Because of the sensitivity of the date within resurrection, it is worth considering the design of the DATE component within the new system. This component would ensure that all storage and retrieval, as well as all date manipulations (such as adding and subtracting dates) within the system are performed by one common and reusable date component. The DATE component would also perform any implicit date conversions. This means that the calling subsystems or components get a 4-digit CCYY year field even if the data stored is in a 2-digit field. Holiday functions related to ascertaining the number of working days (e.g., for a bank check clearance) also can be performed by this component.

9.10.3 MT06-3: REUSE DESIGNS

We discussed the various aspects of reuse in the previous chapter. This task implements the designs so as to maximize reusability during resurrection. The date component produced during the previous task (Figure 9.6) is a component that can be reused throughout the new system. Furthermore, the component designs produced during the current iteration should also be sufficiently generalized (for reuse) so that they can be easily reused in subsequent iterations. Also note the finer granularity of the DATE component, wherein the date class is an aggregation of days, month, and year. It is always possible *not* to have an aggregation but, instead, place the days, month, and year as attributes within the DATE component. That would be

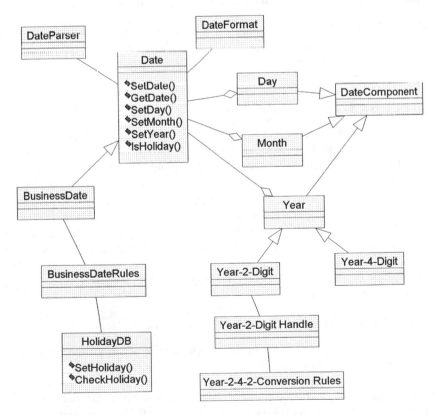

FIGURE 9.6 A comprehensive DATE component in a banking system.

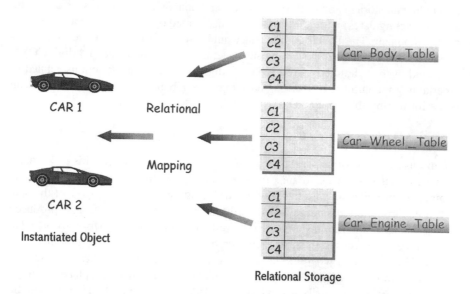

FIGURE 9.7   Mismatch between OO designs and back-end relational tables.

comparatively a coarser granular solution (not advisable if we were building for reuse over a large number of projects). Finally, reuse of designs will happen only after due consideration is given to sociological factors like team formation (SA02) that handle the human side of reuse.

9.10.4 MT06-4: DESIGN DATABASE TABLES

This is a task that presumes that the architecture has a backend relational database that has tables, and that the data is stored in rows and columns. The design of relational database structures is a matured discipline, already discussed at great length within the IT literature. Data tables can be designed with due consideration to the normalisation techniques which would prevent redundancy of data . However, in a large and complex system, redundancy is usually introduced in order to simplify the job of retrieving and displaying data. There is also going to be a mismatch between the backend relational database and the front-end application designed using OO techniques. This is shown in Figure 9.7, wherein a car object is stored in three separate tables (body, wheel, and engine). Every instantiation and storage of car object will necessitate translation.

9.10.5 MT06-5: CONSIDER DATABASE DISTRIBUTION

This task comes into play if distributed architecture is a part of the resurrection solution. This task ensures that the database supporting the system architecture is designed to support distribution. While the database tables are distributed (as a part of the distributed design), this task also ensures that these tables are available to the front-end application through a consistent interface. These interfaces can be a combination of solution-specific interfaces which apply to a particular database, and ready-made database interfaces (such as ODBC). Database access through consistent interfaces ensures that even if the backend database changes, the applications that access the database remain unaffected by the changes. This provides the necessary stability to the front-end system that is missing from a system where the application directly accesses the database. These interfaces also provide additional opportunities to convert the date field in a resurrecting system. For example, if the backend database stores the date in a Y2K-compliant 4-digit field but the front-end GUI application still wants it to be represented in 2-digits (sociological reasons), the database interface can be made to do this conversion. Finally, the need to sort and represent the date in a different format to the one in which it is stored in the database, is solved by using an interface and integrating the application through that interface.

9.10.6 MT06-6: Design User Interface

Following on from the prototyping user interface activity (MT04-4) where the major focus was on creating a prototype to understand the feasibility of the system, this task of designing user interface ensures that the user interface produced as a part of the solution domain is user-centered. This means that the GUI design is not only providing information to the user in a consistent and friendly way, but is intelligent enough to scale its behavior based on the knowledge and skill of the user. For example, the format in which the date is entered in a screen (day–month–year), is carried forward to other screens within the system without asking the user for a format every time a new screen is shown to the user.

Furthermore, navigation models of the user interfaces can be built at this stage. Navigation models simply indicate the easy way in which a user can navigate between screens in order to accomplish his task. Different type of users may use different navigation paths for the same set of screen. For example, a branch manager may view the control totals for a set of transactions first, before going to the individual transactions. However, a teller may be interested in his individual transactions first before looking at the control totals. These essential elements of navigating within the GUI are sorted out in this task, ensuring a user-centered resurrected system. Because of the sociological aspect of a user-interface, this task is closely related to the tasks from the usability activity (SA07) from the sociological dimension.

9.11 MA07: QUALITY PLANNING

The activity of quality planning, performed essentially by the quality assurance manager, results in the deliverable: quality plan. The format of a quality plan is the same as that of the project plan, except that a quality plan concentrates on the activities and tasks related to software quality within the resurrection process. Therefore, the quality plan will contain detailed tasks and timelines for the activities of standards, metrics, and testing. A quality plan provides separate responsibility to the quality assurance manager in ensuring that the new system is produced by following standards and metrics, and is well tested. However, in a small resurrection attempt, the quality plan can well be a part of the overall project plan. It is still advisable to keep the responsibility of quality away from the project manager. This will ensure that the quality assurance work is carried out in an independent manner and is not influenced by the developers themselves.

9.11.1 MT07-1: IDENTIFY QUALITY ELEMENTS

This task identifies the elements that make up the quality of the resurrecting system. They are derived from the existing understanding of quality within the software engineering world. The basic elements that make up quality include: standards, testing, and metrics.

- Standards enable formality and aid people on the project to understand each other's activities. Standards such as ISO9001 are responsible for improving processes across many development organizations.
- Metrics enables measurement with an aim of understanding and improving the quality of the software being developed. Metrics also enables quantification of effort, thus helping in arriving at productivity factors and estimating and refining time to completion. In identifying quality elements, we also identify that which we want to measure and record, and how it is going to improve the software developed and the process of developing software.
- Testing forms a major aspect of quality assurance, especially so in a Y2K resurrection attempt. Therefore, the areas of testing are identified at a very high level during this task.

9.11.2 MT07-2: ESTIMATE QUALITY RESOURCES

The quality assurance manager ensures that quality resources required are specified during this task. The number of test designers, testers, and reviewers who will form part of the overall quality assurance team are estimated. It is essential to consider the skills and experience required of the testers and identifying the skills within the existing quality assurance team, if available.

In addition to the people, it is important to describe all other resources that would comprise the overall quality effort. This includes separate testing environment for the testing effort, separate hardware required to create the test environment, automated testing and measurement tools to be used, separate databases with corresponding test data, copies of publicized standards and their availability, and so on.

9.11.3 MT07-3: CREATE QUALITY PLAN

Having considered the quality elements that make up quality within the resurrection process and the resources required in order to perform the quality related tasks, we put it all together in the quality plan. The quality plan is similar to the project plan, and it also contains a timeline on the quality activities and tasks. This timeline provides information about the tasks, the people who will perform the tasks, as well as the iteration in which the tasks will be performed. The quality assurance manager is responsible for the creation of the quality plan.

9.11.4 MT07-4: Review Quality Plan

After the quality assurance manager produces the quality plan, it is subject to the same review procedure that is applied to other documents. Thus, the quality plan is checked for its completeness and accuracy. This review may be conducted at the end of each iteration, ensuring that the quality plan is updated to reflect the road factors within the project.

9.12 MA08: STANDARDS

Standards activity lasts throughout the resurrection process. The main aim of the standards activity is to ensure that the development progresses in an organized way and that it is a repeatable process that can be applied to subsequent developments within the site. The standards activity also performs the valuable task of enabling reuse of previous work, as well as documenting the current work for future reuse.

9.12.1 MT08-1: Identify Needs for Standards

There are a number of areas where standards need to be applied during the resurrection process. These include the design, coding, quality, testing, and documentation activities, to name just a few. During this task of identifying the need for standards, we list all areas that require standardization. These areas for standards may be prioritized depending on the specific needs of the project.

9.12.2 MT08-2: Map to Existing Standards

During this task, the quality assurance manager relates the existing and accepted standards to the need for standards within the resurrection process. For example, the need for test documentation standard within the organization can be satisfied by the AS4006 standard for testing. After matching the external standards with the need for standards, the external standards are purchased or licensed for use within the organization. Another example would be the use of ISO9000 series of standards for quality within the organization.

9.12.3 MT08-3: Create Local Standards

For some purpose within the resurrection effort, none of the external or public standards may apply. Consider the routine issue of class-naming standards. Development teams usually find that there are no suitable standards for class naming that would readily apply to their development effort. These are the situations where we will have to create local standards and apply them during the development process. For example, all classes within a banking application for a particular bank may start with BANK (wherein the date class would be called BANK-DATE). This also can help identify the subsystems to which the classes belong just by looking at the class name.

9.12.4 MT08-4: PUBLICIZE STANDARDS

Having accepted external standards as well as having created our own standards, it is essential to publicize them. This can be done by providing a standards manual which can be referenced by the developers and all other personnel who need to use the standards at any point in time. The manual may be available on paper as well as in electronic form. During regular discussion sessions, these standards can be applied. For example, the date class would also be referred to as BANK-DATE in all discussions and documentation.

Publicizing standards is a continuous task that ensures that standards evolving along with the development effort are made known to all parties concerned. Furthermore, this task plays an important role when standards themselves *change*. Although the changing of standards is a contradiction of terms in itself, it is still essential to provide a mechanism by which the standards are upgraded to absorb newer ways of managing versions of designs or of incorporating new design tools, etc. These upgrades to standards need to be publicized by performing this task.

9.12.5 MT08-5: UPGRADE STANDARDS

The previous task of publicizing standards iterates with this task of upgrading and versioning of standards. As the development activity proceeds, it becomes essential at times to upgrade the standards because of new ways of doing things, or when the designers are more experienced in producing application specific designs. When relying on third-party products for routine functions (such as storing and retrieving of data) or when using off-the-shelf packages, it is possible that the standards of the supplier have changed. In those cases, it will be essential to upgrade the internal standards as well, and then publicize them through the previous task.

9.12.6 MT08-6: REVIEW ACTIVITIES BASED ON STANDARDS

The development activities carried out during the resurrection process are reviewed during this task based on the standards that are already published. This continuous review ensures that the standards that are publicized are followed during the development process. Activities, which do not conform to standards, are examined for their nonconformance. This task of reviewing the activities for standards conformance ensures that the resurrection process is also a quality process.

9.13 MA09: TESTING

Testing is one of the most important activities within the overall quality assurance framework of the resurrection project. Within the technological dimension of resurrection, it is concerned with issues like writing of test harnesses and test scripts by the developers. In the methodological dimension, the testing activity concentrates on the overall structure of testing including creation of the test plan, the approach taken for testing, creating the environment, conducting the testing, and collating and understanding the results. Because of its sheer importance in a Y2K resurrection project and the detailed nature of the testing work, it is described in detail in Chapter 14. Here we briefly describe the testing tasks within the methodological dimension.

9.13.1 MT09-1: CREATE A TEST PLAN

This task includes creation and writing of overall test plan for the resurrection effort. Effectively it goes hand in hand with the test planning that was mentioned as a part of quality assurance activity in the technological process. However, as compared with the quality assurance activity in the technological process, the testing activity in the methodological process includes not only the unit-level testing of software, but aspects of managing the testing effort. Furthermore, unlike the quality plan that may form part of the project plan, the test plan is a textual description of what is required in the overall testing effort and how the testing effort will be conducted.

9.13.2 MT09-2: IDENTIFY A TEST APPROACH

From the variety of approaches for testing, like black–white box or manual–automated approaches as discussed in Chapter 14, it is essential to identify the type of approach and the applicability of that approach to the respective subsystem or components. A combination of approaches is usual.

9.13.3 MT09-3: CREATE A TEST ENVIRONMENT

During the testing activity it is important to create a complete test environment for the overall testing. The test environment includes the database and the data that goes in the database as well as the application. While we may duplicate the production environment, in many situations it may not be necessary to have the complete production data. However the test environment might include more variation in the data than the production environment, ensuring testing of a wide range of scenarios.

9.13.4 MT09-4: CREATE TEST DESIGNS

This task of creating test design follows from that of identifying the testing approach. The test designs, made up of a group of test cases, provide the approach to test the system at the component levels. The designs are meant to test all aspects of the components in both a positive and negative way.

9.13.5 MT09-5: CONDUCT TESTING

After all aspects of planning the tests and creating the test designs are over, we proceed with conducting the actual testing. This is done by means of conducting the tests within the test environment by the people involved and by use of the corresponding test tools. Some tools are important in GUI testing as well as in regression testing. Sufficient time and effort should be allotted to conduct this task of testing. Since the actual tests can be conducted only after the unit test plans have been written, this task will iterate with the writing of unit test plans within the technological process.

9.13.6 MT09-6: Review Test Results

As the task of testing progresses, various types of software incidences will be found. These will be discovered at all levels of testing including unit, system, and overall acceptance testing. It is essential to continually review the test result so that the technical team can be provided with detailed feedback on the progress. Review of test results also provide opportunities to narrow down the possibilities of finding errors in components or subsystems (as discussed in Chapter 14).

9.14 MA10: METRICS

Metrics and measurements play a key role in all aspects of software development. In a Y2K-hit system, they play the duel role of identifying the extent of damage and identifying and predicting the extent of effort required in resurrection. These measurements will enable the project manager to have sufficient understanding and control of the resurrection project, and enable her to report on the progress to the resurrection champion.

9.14.1 MT10-1: Identify Measurement Needs

This task would be carried out during the initial iteration of the methodological process. It is essential to list what needs to be measured so that the effort can be focused on measuring these elements. For example, if lines of code are the measure of productivity, then it will be essential to identify LOC as a measure. Note that date is not necessarily the most important measure in resurrection. However, in the resurrection process, measuring the size of the process itself can be a measurement need.

9.14.2 MT10-2: Locate Historical Data

The activity of metric not only deals with the current measurement but also with the measurements in similar situation from the past. Historical data provides the ability to understand the behavior of a particular project in the past and, therefore, judge its trends and directions. Thus, this task, by analyzing the historical measurements, provides a much better idea of the trends. This trend-related information can be used in making further educated estimates.

With respect to the data within a Y2K-hit application, it is important to know the extent of importance of the data in the new application. During the prevention effort, organizations used to aim at converting all of their data. However, after a system has already suffered a Y2K hit, it is important to consider only the data that is relevant to the new millennium. For example, from a set of historical closed accounts within a bank, only the dormant account may be converted. Metrics on the historical accounts (including closed, dormant, etc.) will provide valuable insight in the resurrection effort.

9.14.3 MT10-3: Make "Ballpark" Estimates

Once we have identified our needs of measurement and located historical data (if available and if relevant), we can then try and make ballpark estimates on the effort required to resurrect. This would primarily involve budget estimates to produce system level designs and classes and their corresponding implementation. Ballpark estimation is considered a better way of estimating software development effort in comparison with wild guesswork.

9.14.4 MT10-4: MEASURE DESIGNS

Measurement of designs provides information on not only the number of classes but also their quality. The relationships between classes provide the information on coupling and cohesion of classes. In a resurrection attempt, it would be desirable to have a highly cohesive date component which can be reused throughout the system. However, it should not be very tightly coupled with the database or with other subsystems, so that it can be transported easily to other systems. Design metrics like fan-in and fan-out provide information on complexity rather than just the size of the design.

9.14.5 MT10-5: MEASURE CODE

We have already discussed the limitations of the measures of LOC. However it still remains a popular way of arriving at the size of code. In all Y2K projects, the budgeting is based on cost per line of code. If LOC is still a measure that will be used in estimating the resurrection effort, then we do need to measure the lines of codes produced. If some other metrics are to be used to measure the size of the code, then this task will use those metrics and arrive at the productivity figures.

9.14.6 MT10-6: MEASURE QUALITY

In addition to measuring quality of design it is important to measure the overall reliability and the ability of the system to satisfy the functionality specified in the requirements. Thus, measuring quality is a task that spans from measuring the number of software incidences found during a unit testing effort right through to measuring the usability of the system.

9.14.7 MT10-7: MEASURE PROCESSES

This task within the metrics activity is specific to the resurrection process. We have discussed a metric for measuring the effort during the resurrection process in Chapter 4. This metric provides an estimate in a typical resurrection process for all three dimensions of the resurrection. It includes a measure for the four basic elements in a resurrection process: actors, activities, tasks, and deliverables. Depending on an actual process-thread, this metrics can change the weighting factor. By performing this task, the overall size of all three process dimensions can be estimated. The size of the methodological process dimension is described in Section 9.16.

9.15 MA11: QUALITY MANAGEMENT

The methodological process encompasses the quality-related activities of quality planning, standards, testing, and metrics. These activities form the quality group of activities that are usually specified during the initial iteration of the resurrection process. The day-to-day management of the quality group of activities is carried out by means of this activity of quality management conducted by the quality assurance manager. Thus, it is an ongoing activity that will be performed through all iterations of the resurrection process as against the quality planning activity whose focus would be on the initial iteration. The quality assurance manager is responsible for managing the team of testers, the test environment and database, understanding the test results, keeping the standards and documentation (including technical documentation and deliverables) up to date, and updating the quality plan on a regular basis. These tasks, performed during the activity of quality management are discussed next.

9.15.1 MT11-1: MANAGE QUALITY RESOURCES

The activities related to quality assurance are performed with the help of resources. These include the testers who will do the testing as well as the machines and the applications that will be used for the purpose of testing. These resources require careful monitoring. When a testing program is short of resources, sociological activities of staffing (SA01, discussed in Chapter 11) will come into play. Managing and monitoring of the quality resources is carried out during this task on a continuous basis.

9.15.2 MT11-2: MANAGE DOCUMENTATION

Managing documentation produced by the processes, maintaining their correct iterations, and ensuring that they are easily available to people when required is an essential part of quality management performed by this task. This task may result in the documents being put on the Web for easier access across the development sites, or transferred by other electronic means. These include all document deliverables produced during the resurrection process.

9.15.3 MT11-3: UPDATE QUALITY PLAN

At the end of the first iteration, the quality plan is able to provide the productivity factor for the quality effort. This can be fed back into the quality plan to estimate the remaining effort for quality. Furthermore, as the quality assurance activity supports the development, changes to the development environment (e.g., a delayed task) need to be reflected in the quality plan.

9.16 SIZE OF THE METHODOLOGICAL PROCESS

The measuring of the methodological process is a task carried out under the activity of metrics. However, as methodology is one of the three dimension of resurrection, we have shown it separately here to enable us to arrive at the overall size of the resurrection process.

The total units need to be modified based on the level of preparedness of the organization. For example, a red level organization may need a full strength effort at resurrection, whereas the one at yellow may require less effort. Since the level of preparedness in Y2K is a specific instance of a process, this weighting of the process

TABLE 9.2
Size of the Methodological Process

Description of the Element	Number of Elements in the Process	Weighting per Element	Total Strength: Units for the Element
Actors	4	100	400
Deliverables	5	100	500
Activities	11	10	110
Tasks	60	20	1200
Total Units	**80**		**2210**

metrics is described separately in Section 8.8, Table 8.2. In here we simply arrive at the figure for the methodological process based on the weighting per element provided in the technological process. Note that the weighting per element is different from the weighting we assign to the level of preparedness of the organization.

Some of the caveats that were mentioned in measuring the technological process apply to the methodological process. In addition to the technological assumption, there are some additional assumptions in measuring the methodological process. The overall consideration in measuring the methodological process as shown in Table 9.2 are listed below.

9.16.1 CAVEATS AND ASSUMPTIONS

- I have considered each of the actors: project manager, architect, and quality assurance manager. I have also considered the user as an actor. The user may not permanently belong to the development team, but may be a part of the team during the resurrection process.
- The actors within the methodological dimension shoulder senior responsibilities within the process. Therefore, their weighting may be more than the one I have shown (I have kept it the same).
- Other actors within the methodological process also will appear during a process-thread and their appearance will change the values of the number of actors.
- The weighting also may change depending on the number of roles played by one person.
- I have considered the five major variations to the software deliverable. These numbers also may change depending on the specific process-thread.
- The activities and tasks may be repeated more than once in each iteration.
- An update of this metric or creating variation of this metric per process-thread is left up to the project manager who creates the process-threads.

9.17 KEY POINTS

1. The methodological dimension of the resurrection process deals with the "how to" of resurrection. This includes the use of a formal object-oriented methodology in resurrection.

2. The elements that make up the methodological process are actors (project manager, architect, quality assurance manager, and their variation, as well as the user in the background), activities (evaluation, requirement modeling, architecture, designs, project planning, quality planning, testing metrics, standards, project management, and quality management), their corresponding tasks, and the resultant deliverables.

3. The activities and tasks within the methodological process iterate with the activities and tasks from the other two dimensions of the resurrection process.

4. The basic deliverable of the methodological process is the "software with process." This software with process is made up of deliverables like the business scenarios, system architecture, solution designs, and project plan.

5. Quality forms an important aspect of the methodological dimension. The quality group of activities are quality planning, standards, testing, and metrics. They are managed by the activity of quality management.

6. Measuring the resurrection process is the responsibility of the methodological dimension, including the measurement of the methodological dimension itself.

7. Date specific work forms only a small aspect of the overall resurrection activities.

9.18 NOTES

Various aspects of object-oriented methodologies discussed in the previous chapter were put in a formal process in this chapter. The details of the specific OO methodologies were not discussed. For example, the solution designs were discussed, but the detailed techniques of how to produce those solution designs were not discussed. This is because we want to leave the choice of individual techniques up to the users of this resurrection process.

9.19 REFERENCES

1. Gandhi, R., *Quotes of Rajiv Gandhi,* 1994, UBS Publisher, New Delhi.

10 Sociology in Year 2000

The final outcome of any effort is more a function of "who" does the work than of "how" the work is done.

DeMarco and Lister, 1987[1]

Abstract This chapter discusses the sociological dimension of the Y2K resurrection process. Bringing in new technology and modifying the method of development may not be enough to successfully resurrect a Y2K-hit company. In fact, the chances of success in any effort are significantly reduced if the sociological dimension in the effort is not studied and applied in the process. During a Y2K resurrection effort, it is essential to keep in mind that the trigger for the company's problem was technological, not sociological. In other words, people did not cause the problem. Therefore, radical changes to the "people element" of a Y2K-hit company is not recommended. What we discuss in this chapter is the current thinking in the sociological aspect of a software development process. The aim is to fine tune the sociology of the company and put it to good use in the Y2K resurrection process. One such use is the ways in which teams can be organized (especially for object-oriented development) based on people issues or "soft factors." The usability issues are considered in the development of the new system. Communications is discussed with an aim of forging and maintaining relationship with customers and suppliers. Discussion on factors like these would help create the personality of the new organization that would be far removed from the possible schizophrenic personality discussed in Chapter 2. Creating this new and healthy personality of the organization in the new millennium is the essence of the sociological challenge in the Y2K resurrection as discussed here.

10.1 ESSENCE OF SOCIOLOGICAL CHALLENGE IN RESURRECTION

The Y2K resurrection process is essentially technologically driven. However, sociology plays a crucial supportive role in the redevelopment. Technology itself can be quantified to a certain extent. However, what influences the people who work in a technological environment are the sociological factors. These sociological factors are nonmodular and nonquantifiable in nature. Furthermore, sociology did not play a role in creating the Y2K disaster. Therefore, it is not worth spending the time and effort directing the Y2K dissection activity towards sociological factors. Sociology has not caused the problem, but it certainly helps in the resurrection solution. An understanding of the nature of the technical development (that will take place during the resurrection effort) and the role played by sociological factors in this development forms the essence of the sociological challenge the Y2K resurrection process.

10.1.1 Nature of Technical Development

Technical development has often been likened to the construction industry.[2] This can be justified to a certain extent, mainly because construction is one of the most mature branches of engineering and other disciplines like software engineering have a lot to gain from the mature construction approaches. The Y2K resurrection process has tried to be as modular as possible by placing its activities and tasks within the framework of the process discipline. However, the process discipline is still three-dimensional and represented by the white cloud model, indicating that it is not going to be as clear cut and modular as the construction work. As Lanier[3] puts it:

> *The easiest predictions to make about the next 50 years of computer science are those centering on the computers, not the people. It's when people are brought into the equation, however, that the business of prediction becomes difficult.*

We are considering the sociological dimension in great detail in the Y2K resurrection process mainly because of this difficulty in making prediction about human behavior. The nonmodular and creative nature of people means that it will never be possible to make absolute predictions on the sociological nature of the development process. The essence of the challenge lies in creating a road map for the sociological behavior and using it as a reference or a street directory as the resurrection work proceeds.

It was interesting to listen to Constantine[4] during the panel discussion on these "soft issues" at OOPSLA'96, wherein he stated:

> *It is easier to communicate with machines and solve the problems; but with people, it is difficult. This is mainly so because people are very difficult to "generalize."*

However, handling this "difficulty" is precisely at the heart of the sociological dimension of the resurrection process. With the falling costs of hardware, a software shop can be assured of sufficient hardware. Third-party software for customizing the resurrection solution and methodologies for dissecting systems for Y2K problems can be purchased off the shelf. When the technology and methodology have become commonly available, the real discriminators, as Kreindler[5] puts it, "are the skills and abilities of a company's work force and the quality of their development processes."

And it is the responsibility of the management to ensure that these assets are put to their best use. The skills and ability of the workforce can come to fruition depending on the way people are handled and the way they are organized and managed in teams. The quality of the process as well as the product of the process (in our case it is the resurrecting company) can be improved by considering the soft or sociological factors within the development process. This consideration of the human factor in Y2K resurrection process permeates all aspects of the technological, methodological, as well as the sociological dimension of the process, including activities like project planning, analysis and design, testing, and quality assurance, to name but a few.

10.1.2 Relevance of Sociological Factors in Development

Results from a survey of over 250 companies[6] for failure of their IT projects indicate that in 32% of the cases it was inadequate project management that led to the failure of projects. Other major factors were failure to define objectives (17%) and inadequate communication (20%). Less than 7% of the projects were reported to have failed due to technical factors such as languages or databases used. This situation is not going to be much different for the Y2K resurrection process. Thus, one of the potentials for failure of a resurrection process can be inadequate consideration o these sociological factors.

The overall influence of the sociological factors on the development activity in resurrection can be summarized as follows:

- Software development is nonmodular in nature. Therefore, the Y2K resurrection process based on software development will also be nonmodular in nature. This implies it will not be easy to measure the progress of the resurrection process in a linear fashion. Thus, the metrics provided for measuring the resurrection process (Sections 7.16, 9.16, and 11.8) will have to be applied with extreme caution. Unlike the easily quantified activities of sales and production, these metrics will only be indicative.

- Policies and practices of management that are considered sound in a "linear effort" (such as construction activity) may not be appropriate for a software development organization. For example, bonuses, leave availability, working hours, etc. are not very well organized in a software development environment. This would be especially true of the Y2K resurrection effort, wherein the urgency of rebuilding the company's system would mean a completely nonmodular structure to the working hours, recreational leaves, and so on.

- Project management of a Y2K resurrection project has to be astute; it should *not* concentrate on fast or cheap solutions. The entire idea of resurrection rests on providing strategic benefits to the resurrecting organization. These benefits will not happen if the goal is to reproduce the software solution without due consideration to the real-life functionality of the hit system that it is trying to replace and enhance.

- Because of the object-oriented nature of the Y2K resurrection process, the productivity of the team cannot be categorized into good or bad by the length of code and the speed with which it was generated.

- Technical development teams should *not* be organized in a traditional hierarchical way, unless a very routine job is to be performed. This applies to the resurrection process more than ever, as it is a nonroutine, unique job. This idea is further developed in the Section 10.5 on team formation, which has a direct bearing on the outcome of the resurrection process.

10.1.3 EXTERNAL SOCIOLOGICAL FACTORS

In addition to considering the relevance of the sociological factors in the internal development process, it is also important to consider its effect on the external actors. When clients deal with an organization, they are effectively dealing with the personality of the organization. When an organization suffers a Y2K hit, the personality of the organization suffers. Customers do not get the quality service that they are used to receiving from the organization. Furthermore, the society in whose context the organization exists (Section 2.1, Figure 2.1) is also negatively influenced by the change in personality of the organization. Therefore, it is essential for the organization to maintain its personality while the resurrection work is in progress.

This is akin to the re-engineering effort wherein the *core values* and *beliefs* of the organization should not change despite the restructuring of the processes. Hammer and Champy[7] discuss the case of re-engineering Hallmark, whose charitable work and stability is well known in Kansas City. During the re-engineering effort, it was decided *not* to change the "external personality" of the organization, as it represented the core values of the organization. The Y2K resurrection work has to ensure that although the organization is changing to a process-based organization, its core values and beliefs are still maintained. The *external* sociology of the organization should remain the same as the internal resurrection effort takes place.

10.2 PERSONAL SOFTWARE PROCESS

The sociological factors in technical development will be influenced by the desire of individuals to strive for excellence and their personal motivation to achieve that goal. Humphrey[8] has given a well-recognized framework for individuals to strive and reach the best of their own abilities. This framework is called *Personal Software Process* (PSP). The PSP and the personal motivation of an individual in driving and participating in the Y2K resurrection process is a "soft factor," as against the pure technical factors in the resurrection process. Therefore, it is discussed here in the sociological context of a Y2K resurrection team.

10.2.1 PROCESSES WITHIN PSP

The PSP approach takes the following progression:

- The baseline process that includes simple measurement of time and defect recording in personal performance.
- The planning process that deals with estimating the size of programs and the time taken by individuals to develop them; and the planning of tasks in future and scheduling them.
- The personal quality management process that deals with code and design reviews of individual work and strategies to manage them.
- The cyclical personal process that enables a complete software development cycle of designing, coding, compiling, and testing on a base module of a very large piece of software.

These processes provide the necessary tools for individuals to excel by providing due considerations to the soft factors in a software development process. Although the PSP approach has become quite popular, it is still important to consider additional factors in measuring software productivity.

10.2.2 MEASURING PRODUCTIVITY

As discussed in Section 8.8 (on metrics and measurements), although lines of code (LOC) is the starting point for measuring software productivity, still it is not the ideal way to measure an activity that requires creative approach to solutions. LOC does not value a complex piece of code any higher than a simple addition on a single line.

Furthermore, the productivity of an individual in a software development shop cannot be ascertained the way it is arrived at for, say, a sales or a production job. Software development efforts continue to be necessarily nonlinear in the sense that it is difficult to establish a clear one-to-one relationship with productivity and the number of hours spend in designing and coding a system. Sometimes the productivity may be very high and at other times the productivity chart may be going down. Furthermore, in typical cases such as object-oriented software development, it is not possible to ascertain the productivity of an individual or a team by looking only at the final product. Reusing someone else's design and code requires maturity and understanding — the subject of the soft factors rather than pure technical factors. Project management in such situations requires understanding of the nature of software development before productivity metrics and measurements can be applied and judgement about "good" or "bad" can be made.

10.3 LEADERSHIP IN Y2K

There are two aspects to the leadership in a Y2K-hit company. First, providing the leadership to resurrect the company. The second aspect is to provide ongoing leadership to the organization in the next millennium. During resurrection, the leader is involved in crises and the job is to bring the organization back on its feet at the earliest possible opportunity. Once the resurrection has been achieved, the job of the leader is to ensure that the initiative gained by the process is maintained and utilized for other projects. This leadership will primarily come from the "resurrection champion" nominated by the company. However, many of these ideas also will apply at the project manager level, where the manager is dealing with technical and methodological aspect of the resurrection process.

10.3.1 COMMUNICATION

One of the prime responsibilities of the leadership during the resurrection process is to keep everyone informed. This has always been an essential requirement of any leadership, but more so when a company is trying to resurrect from a Y2K disaster. During this period, the leadership will have to face up to real, as well as perceived, fears of the employees and those of the clients and suppliers of the organization. These fears associated with the future of the company and, therefore, of its workforce, will have to be dealt with by continuous communication at regular and casual intervals. Some of the ways the resurrection process can be communicated to the employees as well as to the external actors of the company are

- Posting a copy of the higher level plan and progress of the resurrection on the company's Web site. This will enable both insiders and outsiders dealing with the company to get an idea of how the resurrection process is progressing.
- Framing the high-level resurrection plan and hanging it at a prominent place within the development (and associated social) areas. For example, a framed resurrection plan in the coffee area would not only provide everyone with a visual picture of what the company is doing, but also will initiate discussion on the resurrection activity resulting into valuable insights for the employees themselves.
- Producing a regular internal newsletter to describe the challenges faced by the company as a result of the Y2K hit and the details of how it is carrying out the resurrection process.
- Sending occasional emails from the resurrection champion (usually the CEO) about the status of the resurrection work.
- Producing an internal company video to provide a history of the company, its systems, the areas where it faced problems, and the steps taken for resurrection. This should bring the new members of the resurrection team up to speed and heighten the employee awareness as discussed in Section 3.12. Perhaps it is essential for the CEO to stress here that the problems experienced by the company are *not* the fault of the people, but arising out of a technical problem.
- Producing a similar video for external viewing depicting the company's progress in correcting the date problems, as well as introducing new technology and processes in dealing with its customers and suppliers.

Putting the communication technology available in the new millennium to its best use will be an essential characteristic of leadership. For large organizations, it will be essential for the resurrection champion to reach all its employees, perhaps spread out globally in a uniform and regular manner. Adopting to regular use of e-mails, Internet, video conferencing, and so on will be imperative to achieve the task of communicating the process, as well as maintaining the impetus once the resurrection process is over.

10.3.2 Flattening the Pyramid

One of the essential characteristics of leadership in the next millennium is to lead without appearing to be the leaders. Leadership will have to be subtle and unassuming. This is due to increasing awareness of the final outcome of the work performed at all levels of employment. The employee is no longer going to accept the directives given out without sufficient justification for them. Furthermore, discussion of the merit or otherwise of the work given out is inevitable at personal level.

Another major reason for the need to provide an unassuming style of leadership in the new millennium is the fact that the traditional way of working in a job is disappearing. During the resurrection work that takes place beyond the Y2K hump, at least 30% of the people involved in the resurrection process may *not* be employees of the company. Contracting and independent consulting work is on the rise, and more and more people are taking on the challenges of staying on their own and performing freelance work. These individuals are not performing "jobs." Their commitment is limited to the contracts signed by them. This is particularly true of Y2K-related work as the shortage of people with Y2K skills is well known in the industry. The resulting relationship between the outside consultant and the internal leader is on equal footing and not the traditional hierarchical relationship.

Nevertheless, the resurrection leader still has the challenging task of providing directions and guidelines as well as getting work done from these "equal" workers on the resurrection project. Leadership has to strike a balance between providing openness and discussions within the group vs. exercising control and getting the work done.

Resurrection process can benefit by viewing the team organization from the top because it does not carry the hierarchical notion of traditional team structures. This is a flat *circular* arrangement with many advantages in terms of organization and communication (Figure 10.1). For example, communication is now facilitated between not only the leader and members (L-P1, L-P2, etc.), but also among members (P1-P2, P2-P3, P4-P5, and so on). The position of the leader is not seen as superior, but is seen at the same level as the other members of the team. The leader is the *facilitator* in this case. Thus, this model of team structure caters to the static as well as the dynamic aspect of its functioning. A technical term to describe this social relationship would be *client-server.* The reporting structure within such a team would also be process based rather than structure based. Therefore, if person P1 is

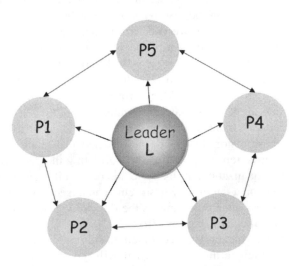

FIGURE 10.1 Top view of a team organization.[9]

working on an insurance claim process, she will report to the process owner of that claim process. Leadership provided by L will be supportive rather than directive. Thus, this view of the team structure would improve the communication between all members of the team as well as the resurrection champion and help avert one of the major causes of project failures (vis-à-vis inadequate communication, 20%) discussed earlier on.

10.3.3 MORALE AND MOTIVATION

One of the recognized jobs of a leader is to maintain high morale and provide the necessary motivation to a team. Innovative thinking has been applied to ensure that teams remain motivated in performing their tasks. One of the major ways to maintain motivation is to ensure that the team knows what its doing or in other words maintains its focus. The motivational aspect of the resurrection process is going to be extremely interesting because, contrary to normal understanding, the Y2K resurrection teams are expected to be highly focused. The usual expectation from a Y2K hit would be disarray within the employee ranks. In fact, everyone in the company is affected by the problem. A business failure will imply involvement of every employee in the process of explosion as well as of resurrection.

In many situations organizations and teams within organizations do not know what their problems are. Therefore, people are unable to relate how their work is going to provide benefits to the goals of the organization. In case of a Y2K hit, the problem will be obvious from the word go. "We have a date problem" provides a simple and easily understood definition of what everyone is working on within the organization.

A Y2K hit is like an organization going to war with its date fields. The equivalent troops or the people working on resurrection don't have to wait much longer for the work to begin. If the people are available and if they are doing any work, it will be effective for them to work on the resurrection. The Y2K firecrackers are going to hurt the organization enough for everyone within the organization to focus on the resurrection attempt from the moment the decision to resurrect is made.

Thus, one expects the resurrection teams to be focused during the resurrection process. However, the leadership will face the challenge of providing motivation *after* the resurrection effort is over. Many professionals who were working in the company as outsiders are likely to leave the organization or their specialized services (as would have been used in the dissection activity TA01) may no longer be required. This is going to cause major changes to the interpersonal relationships within the team. Also, the resurrection work focused on correcting the date problem, as well re-engineering the organization, is likely to be much different from the task of running the company on a day-to-day basis. One can expect a vacuum at the end of the resurrection process, much the same as the direction vacuum that existed at the end of major historical events (e.g., WWII).

If the organizations had only concentrated on solving the date problem without considering the re-engineering ideas, then it will have spent all its regular and extra IT budget without accruing any functional or strategic benefit. However, if the strategic value of the resurrection process is kept in mind, then the directions required for motivational purposes will become obvious. The company that has resurrected itself can provide similar expertise to other organizations (if it is not too late for the others to resurrect), or it can continue its re-engineering effort with the newer technologies that will appear in the next millennium.

10.4 STAFFING IN Y2K

There are a number of ways in which teams can be staffed for the resurrection effort. This will partly depend on the results of the "alternative evaluation" activity within the methodological dimension of the resurrection process. Although the recommendation is to retain the current employees of the company and to get them to work on the resurrection process, still there may be a need to bring in specialist staff from outside, as well as to replace the people who leave due to a number of reasons. The staffing effort for the resurrection work within the organization can be broadly divided into two segments: (1) employing people on a permanent basis within the company and (2) external consultants working on the project. In both cases, since people are going to work in teams within the organizations, the factors that need to be considered in staffing the teams (apart from the usual technical factors) are

- The type of people selected to join the existing teams.
- The cost of people leaving the teams.
- Deriving benefits from people exiting Y2K teams.

10.4.1 BEST FIT APPROACH

Many recruitment philosophies are based on "only the best." This is understandable, as we would always want to go for the best people for the job. However, in a Y2K resurrection process, we are not going for a brand new team. We expect to make the best use of the people we already have (Figure 10.2). When a need arises to replace one of these people who have already been working on the resurrection project, the philosophy should be "the best fit" person for the team. It is imperative to maintain the homogeneity of the team. This would be maintained only if the new recruit is able to adapt and merge with the working conditions and work ethics of the team. Technically brilliant people who are highly individualistic and who are not able to work well in a team may be productive in a situation that requires creative solutions from a single person. However, the resurrection process is a team effort. Therefore, the person who works well with others will help the overall productivity of the team. This will result in a "utopian team" discussed in the Section 10.5 on team models.

10.4.2 COST OF TURNOVER

When a member from a functioning team leaves, replacing that person and bringing the team back to its original performance level incurs costs that are occasionally

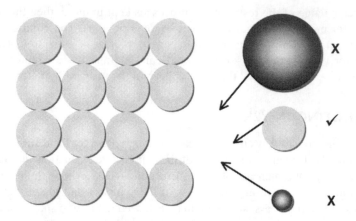

FIGURE 10.2   Recruitment in Y2K resurrection — the best fit approach.

hidden from sight. The costs associated with advertising, scrutinizing, and inter-
viewing are well known and documented. Organizations usually have means of
working out these costs, which are then factored into the overall development
process. However, there are many hidden costs of a person leaving and another
taking her place. This is because people are not modules and their influence on the
team cannot always be quantified. Therefore, replacing a person with another is not
the same as replacing the motherboard of a machine and pressing the button.

The hidden costs of turnover include:

- *The risks of taking a new person on board.* This, as mentioned at the start
  of this chapter, cannot be easily quantified and, therefore, we are unable
  to measure or predict the risk factor associated with new members joining
  the team.
- *The learning curve of the person.* Every new member will take time to
  learn the way the team functions. This is notwithstanding the fact that the
  person may be technically adept and may not need any training at the
  technical level. He has to still understand the applications as well as the
  technical (log-ins, compiler locations, usercodes–passwords) and methodological (checkin–checkout, versions, standards) environment of the
  organization.
- *The learning curve of the team.* It is not only the newcomer that has to
  learn the environment and the functioning of the team, the team itself has
  to stop briefly in order to figure out how to absorb the newcomer and
  understand his style of working.

This "gelling" effort is time consuming, and usually one would expect a short
dip in the performance seismograph of the resurrection team when a person leaves
and another joins the group. The "best fit approach" discussed in the previous section
is extremely beneficial in reducing these hidden costs of turnover.

10.4.3 Gaining from Exit

Just as there are two broad categories of people who join the resurrection effort (employees, consultants), there are two broad ways in which these people can leave the group. The external contracting or consulting group can leave at the end of their contract when either they or the company to which they were contracted decides not to renew their contracts. The internal groups (e.g., employees) can leave when they find better opportunities in terms of salary or working conditions. Due to acute shortages of Y2K-skilled staff, the chances of employees being pinched by competitors or headhunters are very high. Strategies to retain employees start from the recruitment process itself, wherein the person who fits well in the group is recruited. This can be followed by above-average wages and good working conditions. Despite all these attempts, when an employee or a consultant moves on, it is important (especially in a Y2K project) to leverage advantages from such an exit.

An exit interview by a senior person, other than the one to whom the employee was reporting to, is essential. During the exit interview, a person is not under the pressure to remain silent on issues that she clearly sees as wrong, because the concern for the next raise or promotional opportunities or contract renewal is not there. People are more vocal when they leave and this should be formally recorded and put to good use. Designing an exit interview form, which would enable the exit interviewer to record the results of the interview, would be extremely beneficial.

Furthermore, a policy of providing reference letters stating the role played by the person within the resurrection team, the specific contribution, and timings of the contribution within the resurrection process also carries a good impression of the company with the employee. The departing person is, in an indirect way, the ambassador of the company. She carries all the memories of the work she did within her head, and it is beneficial to the company to let every individual leave the organization with a smile. Exit lunches are an important part of the staffing aspect of the resurrection team and should find a place in the sociological budget of the Y2K resurrection.

10.5 TEAM FORMATION

Once we have the right people, and we have put sociological strategies in place to retain them, it is still essential to *organize* them in a way that will be most productive for the Y2K resurrection effort. Simply dividing the people into teams will not provide the benefit in terms of time and effort. In many ways, the software produced reflects the personality of the teams that produced it. The resultant software also reflects the way the teams were organized. The various models on which the Y2K resurrection teams can be built and how that will help object-oriented development is discussed.

10.5.1 Constantine Team Models

Constantine has provided an excellent description of the various ways in which teams could be organized in a software development project. This is shown in Figure

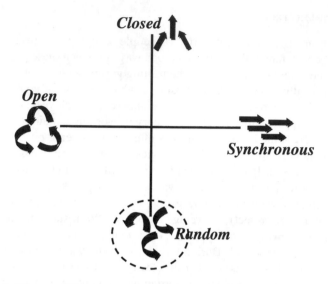

FIGURE 10.3   The possible team structures (based on Constantine, 1989[10]).

10.3. Each of these team models provides an insight into the ways in which teams are structurally organized and how they behave functionally to achieve their goals. Understanding of these team structures and behavior is important in forming the Y2K resurrection teams. However, it is important to note that the real life resurrection teams may not be easily classified into one of these team models. This is because people are continually changing their behavior and, therefore, teams continue to reflect different organizational behavior at different times. The aim is to bring together people in teams that would exhibit one primary model of behavior, but supported by other models.

The team structures are briefly described below.

10.5.1.1 Closed

This team follows the traditional hierarchical structure and is good for traditional development and maintenance such as payroll or accounting systems. For example, there is not much to be innovated in the area of general ledger accounting. Routine applications which are well known and which are taught right from the university level are the ones that can be developed using a closed team model. A closed team model is also helpful where development training is to be provided. These are the situation where information is already known or where information is to be passed on to every member of the team in a concise time-constrained manner. These are the situations where the closed team functions well.

A Y2K resurrection project is unique in the history of computing. Although we understand the basics of the problem conceptually, we have *never* encountered Year 2000 before. The kind of problems and challenges that will surface during this project are unknown. Therefore, a closed model may not be appropriate for the resurrection effort. Furthermore, with the kind of people that will work on the project (e.g., external consultants and contractors), the closed model may not carry any significance. The relationship you have with the external consultants is horizontal and flat, which may not be based on the closed model.

10.5.1.2 Open

These teams perform as collaborators. There is very little hierarchy and no tradition, and people have come together as collaborators to solve a technical problem. This group is loosely hanging, and the lack of hierarchy is particularly appealing to new programmers who have more enthusiasm and who are less likely to follow a tradition.

When a Y2K resurrection specific team is formed, it is likely to be a collaborative team that has come together with the specific goal of solving the date-related problem in the organization, and then going away. However, if the teams are organized entirely on this model, then there will be no strategic advantage derived from the resurrection exercise. It will be essential to extend this model to a model that works for a longer period of time, as we want to leverage the resurrection exercise for the long term.

10.5.1.3 Random

People who are innovators form these teams. The random teams are chaotic and their purpose is to bring innovative answers to the problem at hand, and then disbanding themselves. Typically, the random team model has very few people (three to four), and their life span is only a few months. Thus, they are models for task forces that are put together to achieve a short-term breakthrough goal. Obviously, due to lack of structure, they cannot be expected to perform in a cohesive manner for a long time.

As far as Y2K resurrection process is concerned, the random team model does not provide any advantage. It requires an organized and disciplined approach rather than a unique innovative answer. Some small companies have tried to solve their Y2K problems by innovative solutions provided by third-party tools which help them push their date back by 20 years (see Section 1.4). These, however, are not long-term solutions and these are not the solutions that provide us with the strategic advantage that we are looking for.

10.5.1.4 Synchronous

These are the teams that come together based on a shared common goal. The remarkable thing about a team formed on the basis of alignment is that the need for a leader sitting on top of the hierarchy is not there. Everyone is committed to a shared vision and a known goal, and the work proceeds almost without any apparent pressure. These are alternatively called *utopian*[11] teams, as they are literally "out of the world." This is a team model that would be ideal not only for the resurrection process, but also for the ongoing business of running a re-engineered company in the next millennium.

10.5.2 TEAM MODEL WITHIN OO

One of the important sociological challenges within an object-oriented development environment is that of reuse. The dimension of "for" and "with" reuse in reusability (Section 8.5) indicates that object-oriented development should not be considered as a single project, but rather as an enterprise with ongoing development which feeds the designs into one another. This is different from the traditional team structures, wherein organizations tend to consider a project as a single entity. Considering the Y2K resurrection process as a single project as against a series of small iterative developments would not enable granularity considerations and would also not provide the advantages of reuse.

However, considering more than one projects within (or after) the resurrection process leads to the sociological problems of rewarding accomplishments of reusability. Henderson-Sellers and Edwards[12] report Thomsett discussing the management questions arising regarding the interface between two project teams in a reusable environment. For example, if you are the project manager of one team, you presumably want your team to succeed, even perhaps at the expense of your colleague's team. Within such a competitive corporate culture, how is one team encouraged to build generalized classes useful not for its own future projects, but for an alternative team's next projects? Pant et al.[13] have proposed four models of team organization which assist in the incorporation of reuse into the business plan. These models provide valuable insight into the problems of reuse and how to solve them. Essentially, the models consider additional roles within a software development organization that is emphasizing reuse. These can be the role of a "linchpin" person who is responsible for both "for" and "with" reuse within the organization.

Meyer[14] has discussed in great detail the *non* technical role of a project manager who essentially deals with formation and management of teams. When OO techniques are applied in the resurrection process, the role of reuse influences this formation and management of teams. It becomes essential to organize teams in OO development that enable reuse of both design and code. Formation and operation of teams, however, is not an easy task. As discussed earlier, it does not always follow logic. Therefore, it is not easy to predict the results (or the behavior) of teams based on theoretical understanding of team structure.

It is also important to consider the productivity measurements used for measuring performance of project teams. If the productivity is measured in terms of lines of code written, then obviously this is going to discourage people from reusing code. Reuse of code produces *lesser* lines of code than programs written *without* reuse. A better measure of productivity is required in order to encourage code reuse.

Furthermore, development of the entire system is, in fact, made up of development of individual subsystems that may interact with each other only through an interface. Since the systems are developed as modules or subsystems, teams can be assigned to each of the modules with minimum dependencies on each other. This is called a parallel team structure and it enables multiple modules to be developed simultaneously.

Thus, for overall success in organizing teams, it is essential to consider the context in which they will operate. In case of object-oriented Y2K resurrection work, this context is provided by the need to reuse design and code, as well as to iterate and increment development cycles. This viewpoint is supported by Goldberg and Rubin:[15]

> *Objects are not new. They were tested, were found to work, and are still around. But they continue to be used successfully only where appropriate organizational and management contexts are created.*

10.5.3 TEAM FOR Y2K RESURRECTION

An ideal Y2K resurrection team will be modeled based on the understanding of team structures of Constantine, as well as the particular nuances of OO development. It is assumed that the members of the Y2K resurrection team will be well versed with the object-oriented approach to software development. The members responsible for programming will be knowledgeable and trained in the particular language of choice. It is worth noting that many of these requirements of the resurrection team hold true even if the approach for system development is not object oriented.

A synchronous team with common understanding of goals will be easy to form as the Y2K hit will be a well known fact within the company, and that everyone working in the team will have the prime task of bringing the organization back from the brink. What will benefit a synchronous utopian team is the knowledge that they are not merely fixing the date problem, but actually recreating the organization.

Since an object-oriented approach is being followed, it will be essential to consider the question of reuse in the formation of teams. For example, a third-party package implementation will result in maximum reuse, and teams will be required to only test and implement the package. However, if a large amount of development is taking place in-house, then the Y2K resurrection teams will have to be organized in parallel. This parallel organization results after the entire resurrection project is divided into subsystems. These subsystems could be the front end user-interface subsystem, the database subsystem, the calculations subsystem (if it is a banking application), and so on. Each of these subsystems would relate to the other subsystems through a well-defined interface. Therefore, the teams that handle the development of these subsystems can be organized and made to work in a parallel arrangement.

10.6 ETHICS IN Y2K

We considered the nature of technical development, the kind of leadership we need in a resurrection process, and the formation and management of teams to extract maximum benefit for the chosen approach to development. During this discussion the people who are involved in the resurrection process remain the same, only the environment in which they work and the way they are organized for work, is being fine tuned. One important sociological aspect to consider in this fine tuning process is that of professional ethics. This is important for two reasons:

1. In the short term, since the organization is affected by the Y2K problem, it is possible that the employees are affected by it in their day-to-day lives.

Some of them may not have received their salaries for a month or they may have voluntarily taken a cut in their salaries. Although everyone may not face these extreme situations, it is still reasonable to assume that the employees who are going to work in the resurrection process are in some way inconvenienced due to the Y2K hit. These are the same employees who, as a part of the technological revolution running through the company, may be getting exposed to sophisticated tools and machines that were not available earlier on. For example, it might be worth considering the work ethics of an employee who has recently taken a pay cut, but who has the latest model laptop that can be used to connect to the office from anywhere.

2. In the longer term, technological advances are going to influence more and more of the working world. As discussed in Section 2.1, even the rate of change of these advances is increasing. The work place is going to be influenced by the Internet, video and phone conferencing, and all the multimedia gadgetry that one is able to gather within the home. This is because once the equipment is available at home, the potential for tele-commuting will increase. This will result in only a conceptual work place requiring different ethics and code of conduct than what we have today.

Let us consider some of these ethical questions with respect to the Y2K resurrection process and, thereafter, when the team functions in the next millennium.

10.6.1 PRODUCTIVE TIME

Estimates on how much time a person spends on social and hygiene needs during a working day vary from 30 to as high as 60%. Assuming that these estimates do not apply to every IT shop, it would still be reasonable to consider the additional factors in Year 2000 that are going to influence the average productive day of a person. The major influence on productive time is of Internet browsing and e-mails. Strong work ethics will require the team members to restrict their netbrowsing to work-related activities. However, some organizations may encourage this activity, as they may derive spin-off benefits such as increased employee awareness and improved personnel networking.

10.6.2 TELECOMMUTING

Telecommuting is becoming popular as it saves time and effort in reaching the place of work. It is especially effective during the development work that does not require all members of the team to be present at the same time. For example, after all the design decisions are made, the coding of individual classes doesn't require the entire team. These are the situations where telecommuting will be extremely beneficial to both the individual and the company. In Year 2000 and beyond, it should be expected that at least one or more days per week (20 to 50%) of the job content of an employee who is involved especially in system development effort will be performed by telecommuting. This raises the important questions of work ethics while working from home. Telecommuting has the advantage of enabling people to work in a relaxed way without the pressure of dress code or of social behavior. However, people will have to be more responsible in describing the tasks and the amount of time they think the tasks will take.

10.7 DIRECTIONS ORGANIZATIONS TAKE

Having discussed the major soft factors that will influence the resurrection effort, it is worth considering the results of this effort on the organization. The organization is very well represented by the "white cloud" model, and so is the resurrection process for the organization. The processes within the organization can have multiple dimensions. This also is true of the people who work within the organization and who will be involved in the resurrection effort. The end result is that the final direction of the organization is very difficult to predict. Many times it does not seem to follow what has been advertised and promoted and put on the mission statement of the company. The overall direction of growth of an organization is a complex sum of the individual objects, their influence within the organization, and the directions of the organizational objectives. Thus, considering only the corporate objectives gives a wrong sense of direction for the company and for the resurrection effort. In considering soft factors, we also give a thought here to the individual objectives and their influence on the corporate ones.

10.7.1 INDIVIDUAL OBJECTIVES

The MBO (Management By Objective) approach is based on the assumption that the overall objective for the organization should be set at the top level and this should then percolate down to the grass roots. In case of a Y2K resurrection, it would be easy to set an MBO for the organization. Stated simply, it would be "resurrect." However, what this MBO approach should consider is that the organizations and the individuals that make up the organizations, do not have one single purpose and that their objectives may be in conflict — not only with each other or with the organization, but also with their own selves.

This case of conflicting objectives can be further explained by an example. Jann, the technical writer, has an overall objective to produce the user documentation (e.g., user guides for the resurrecting system) on time so that she may progress professionally. However, Jann as a person is made up of other objectives. She may have a personal objective of relaxing by taking time off which may be in conflict with the professional one of delivering the documentation on time. Alternatively, she may have the social objective of maintaining a strong circle of friends in the new millennium. She may satisfy this objective by ringing her friends from work; something that may go against her professional objective. These different conflicting objectives can be shown as in Figure 10.4.

Observe that the overall direction in which the individual will move will be a *vector sum* of the individual objectives that she has set for herself. Thus, if her personal objectives are *in the same direction* as her professional objectives, *both* stand a high chance of fulfilment and they will, in fact, feed off each other. If they

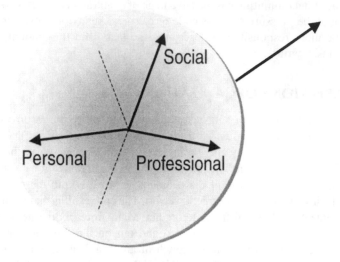

Overall Individual Objective :
Vector sum of all Objectives

FIGURE 10.4   Overall individual objective.

are in opposite directions, they will nullify each other, and the stronger they are the greater will be the nullifying effect. If all objectives are crossing each other out such that the vector sum comes to zero, then the individual will not move in any direction and will experience a kind of *frozen* state. In extreme cases, where the professional vector is *big* and overrides the personal one that is in the opposite direction, a family split may occur. However, if it is the other way round and the personal vector is big, then a resignation may occur.

10.7.2 CORPORATE OBJECTIVES

Since the organizations are made up of individuals, the overall directions that they take is a sum total of their own directions *plus* the sum total of the direction of the individuals (not just employees) that make up the organization. However, while taking a sigma of individual vector sums, the scalar factor is proportional to the position of the individual within the organization. For example, if the personal vector of the senior executive is in the opposite direction to his professional vector, then it will have a major negative influence on the professional (business) objective vector of the company. The overall corporate objective is shown in Figure 10.5.

The above concept could be further clarified with an example. If a PC manufacturing company has sent out PCs with faulty electronic chips, then its social vector will be in a direction opposite to its business one. If the social objective is greater, the company will withdraw its products and pay compensation. However, if the business objective persists, the company will continue to populate the market

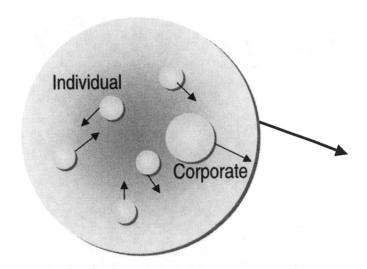

Overall Individual Objective :
Vector sum of all Individual + Corporate Objectives

FIGURE 10.5   Overall corporate objective.

with its product. This decision, however, will be a combination of the social status of the company (goodwill) and the thinking of its senior executives. Thus, the overall direction in which the organization will move will be a *vector sum* of the *net* directions of the individual *plus* the *net* direction of the organization.

Thus, the overall direction of a team or an organization could be arrived at in three steps:

1. The vector sum of the objectives of individuals within the organization.
2. The vector sum of the corporate objective on its own.
3. The vector sum of the individual and corporate objective.

This has been shown in the following figure (Figure 10.6).

10.8 USABILITY IN Y2K

Issues related to usability of software systems will be crucial in the resurrection process. This is because the literate users of the system would want more user-centeredness from the systems they will use in their business processes. Advances in Web technology has fueled the debate on usability further — as providing usability within a Web-based solution is not an easy task because of the balance required between the response time and the ease of using the system. We consider two studies that point us in the direction of user-centered software.

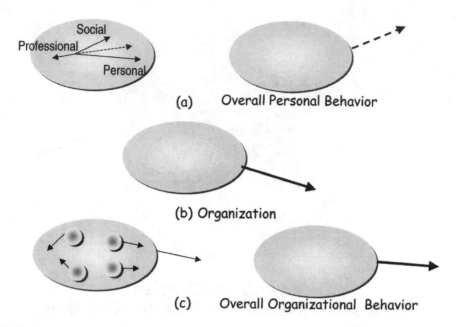

FIGURE 10.6 Summarizing the influence of individual and corporate objectives on the direction of the organization.

10.8.1 User Centered Development

Good and bad software, both come from people. Therefore, providing usability in the software is a question of enabling the developer to understand the needs of the user as if he is the user. Understanding the people element (sociological dimension) in the resurrection process will be crucial in providing user-centered software. Usability of system software can be summarized in the following two laws by Constantine.[16]

The Great Law of Usability — "The system should be usable by a user with knowledge and experience in the application domain but no experience with the system, without help or instruction." This law is aimed at the novice user of the system and we will have many novice users in a resurrected system.

The Lesser Law of Usability — "The system should not interfere with or impede efficient use by a skilled user having substantial experience with the system." As the resurrected systems mature and more and more users get to know and use them, there will be less need for the system to "hold the hands" of the user. These are the situations where the user-centered system should step back and let the user do what he wants to do, without providing unnecessary helps and undue restrictions.

10.8.2 Principles of Usability

In addition to the two laws on usability, Constantine has proposed seven principles of user-centered software.[17] Consideration of these principles can provide significant advantage in the resurrection process. These principles are

Principle of Support — Understand and support the real objectives of the user by making work easier, simpler, and faster.

Principle of Structure — Organize the user interface purposefully by putting related things together.

Principle of Simplicity — Make common tasks simple to do, communicate in the user's own language, and introduce good shortcuts for longer procedures.

Principle of Visibility — Keep all options and materials for a given task visible without distracting with extraneous or redundant information.

Principle of Reusability — Reduce the need to rethink and remember by reusing internal and external components and behaviors. Maintain consistency with purpose, not arbitrary.

Principle of Feedback — Keep users informed of actions, changes of state, and errors using clear, concise, and unambiguous language familiar to users.

Principle of Tolerance — Be flexible, prevent errors by tolerating inputs, interpreting reasonable actions, as well as reducing cost of mistakes by allowing undoing and redoing.

10.9 THE ENVIRONMENT

The physical environment in which the resurrection process is taking place will have a bearing on the quality and the success of the process. It is now accepted that having a larger and comfortable physical space is somehow correlated to the kind of code that programmers produce. This is true of the programmers, designers, and managers who will be involved in the resurrection effort. The quality of code is related to the teams that produce this code and the environment in which the code is written. We consider the physical environment within the resurrection process.

10.9.1 E-FACTOR

One of the major responsibilities of the management of the resurrection process is to provide an *uninterrupted environment* where the resurrection work can proceed. The ratio of the amount of uninterrupted time that is available to the developer compared with the overall time spent at work is a metric presented by DeMarco and Lister.[18] It is called the *environment factor* or *E-factor.*

There are a number of factors that can influence the E-factor. These range from small nuances like chat from a colleague passing by or sounds from the neighboring cubicle, through to the ear-piercing shrill of the fire alarm followed by a cacophonous voice announcing that "this is only a test." It is essential to accept and understand these environment factors and effort put by the management in improving the factors so that the resurrection work can be performed unhindered.

10.9.2 UTILIZING THE TECHNOLOGY

Apart from the role of the technical environment in software development, resurrection work in the new millennium also needs to make good use of the "office technology." This technology includes facilities like video conferencing, mobile phones, Internet access, and so on. For example, placing recruitment ads on the Internet will be one more option available to the resurrection project manager when she deals with the staffing activity (SA01).

10.9.3 POTS AND PLANTS

Sociological issues that never figured in discussions on software development until now are the issues related to the aesthetics of the development place. The E-factor can be improved by soft decisions like placing pots and plants, paintings, and cartoons* and things that are more art oriented rather than engineering oriented.

10.10 GAMES IN A RESURRECTION PROJECT

Unhelkar[19] has further developed the theory of sociological "games"[20] and applied it to an IT shop doing object-oriented development. The work on IT games derives from the Berne's[21] original work on Transactional Analysis. Simply stated, "games" in sociology are a way of structuring, or killing, time. Games are not necessarily productive and are almost always ulterior in nature. Therefore, games are not considered in positive vein and the aim of project management is to stop these unproductive games so that the real project may get under way. Gaming behavior during the Y2K resurrection process needs to be identified and corrected. Some of the games in an object-oriented development environment are briefly considered here from the resurrection viewpoint.

10.10.1 USE IT OR LOSE IT

Some programmers have a need to use every available feature of the language, resulting in a highly complex code. The classes produced by these programmers have features and functionality *only because* the language used in writing the class supports that feature. There is a need to actively discourage the need to use every technical feature supported by the technology within the resurrection process. Since the resurrection process is technologically based and, as discussed in Chapters 6 and 7, we are encouraging the use of new technology, the attraction of using new features of the technology will be high. Conscious effort should be made by the project manager in ensuring that the focus of the resurrection effort is the functionality agreed to and specified by the users, and no more. Additional features can be put to good use after the resurrection process is over or in subsequent iterations.

10.10.2 COWBOY PROGRAMMING

Cowboy programmers are the programmers who disregard methodologies. These are the technical people who couldn't be bothered about methodologies and sociology so far away on the horizon. Typically played by newcomers to the programming world (and we expect a few of them during the object-oriented based resurrection), this game can create problems for a medium- or large-scoped resurrection process.

---

* I wonder by how much my productivity goes up when I am surrounded by Dilbert?

The antidote to this game is described in Section 8.2, wherein the "road map" approach to the use of methodologies was discussed.

10.10.3 FLOUR MIX

The flour mix is a game resulting from the creep factor that results from the increase of a small functionality, not only by the user who has specified the system, but also by the desire of the developer to satisfy "just one more functionality" before releasing the product. The developer wants to add one more functionality before delivering the system and, then to satisfy that functionality, he needs one more resource. The development goes on like mixing the flour/dough for bread. Just as a "gamy" bread mixing would end up with some more flour and then some more water and then some more flour in a vain attempt to reach a balance; similarly the developer playing this game wants to add one more functionality followed by one more resource, ad infinitum.

The time boxed approach to development[22] advocated by Graham can be used as one of the possible antidotes to this game. The technologically driven resurrection team is made to deliver by "time boxes" rather than by functionality. Thus, if closer to correct estimates are made, the technical team does not have the opportunity of playing the flour-mix game.

The Next Release Maybe (NRM) approach proposed by Meyer[23] in which the requirement of the functionality is accepted, but only on the condition that it will be provided *not* in this release but the next one, can also be utilized to help break up this game.

10.10.4 MEETINGITIS

Meyer also discusses the problem in which the development team is plagued by hours and hours of meetings and planning that seems to lead nowhere. This is called meetingitis. It is a game that provides tools to structure time for employees who don't know what to do with their time, but is unproductive and self-defeating. Within the resurrection process, all meetings should be assigned a set time before hand. This will provide help in stopping the meetingitis game.

10.10.5 DEADLINE

The resurrection team will indeed have the pressure of delivering the new system within the specified time. However, in many situations the deadlines are phoney. The Y2K resurrection process, being iterative and incremental, provides a good opportunity to avoid playing this unproductive game. Realistic delivery dates should be set while drawing the resurrection plan, and these dates should be updated based on the results of the initial iteration of the process. Finally, deadlines should not be used in order to avoid the formal activities and tasks of the resurrection process.

10.11 KEY POINTS

1. The essence of the sociological challenge in Y2K resurrection comes from the nature of technical development which is nonlinear.

2. Because of the nonlinearity of the sociological factors, many projects cannot come to grips with the soft issues in management leading to their failures.

3. The personal software process (PSP) approach provides a good tool for the individuals striving for excellence.

4. Leadership in the resurrection project will follow a looser and flatter "client-server" structure rather than the hierarchical structure — this is driven by the need for a process-based organization as well as the new style of working and new work ethics in the new millennium.

5. The resurrection project staffing should be based on best-fit approach, wherein individuals who fit well with the existing team are taken on board — this maintains the homogeneity of the team, so crucial for resurrection.

6. A person leaving the project is, in many ways, an ambassador of the project. Should people leave the resurrection project, their exit should be graceful and properly managed.

7. Constantine's team models (closed, open, random, and synchronous) provide an excellent base on which to model the resurrection teams.

8. The way teams are organized within an OO development shop has a bearing on the reuse achieved.

9. The direction of the organizations (or teams within the organizations) is influenced by individual as well as corporate objectives. Even within one individual there may be conflicting objectives which may prevent him from contributing fully to the project.

10. It is essential to follow the principles of usability in designing and developing user-centered software systems. These principles ensure that the software system helps the novice but does not hinder the work of an expert user.

11. The physical environment (E-factor) has a bearing on the quality of software produced. Therefore the development environment should be carefully prepared with artistic orientation.

12. Games within the workplace have the potential for hurting projects. They should be carefully monitored and individuals and teams should be discouraged from gamy behavior.

10.12 NOTES

The discussion on individual and corporate objectives derives from my study of the HR issues in object-oriented software development with granularity that was a part of my Ph.D. thesis.

The discussion of team formation as well as on usability is influenced by Larry Constantine's involvement with my work at Dow Jones.

10.13 REFERENCES

1. DeMarco, T. and Lister, T., *Peopleware: Productive Projects and Teams,* Dorset House Publishing Co., New York, 1987, 93.

2. Jacobson, I., Christerson, M., Jonsson, P., and Overgaard, G., *Object-Oriented Software Engineering: A Use Case Driven Approach,* Addison-Wesley, Reading, MA, 1992.
3. Lanier, J., The frontier between us, *Communications of the ACM,* 40:2, 55–66, Feb. 1997. (Special Anniversary issue on 50 years of computing.)
4. Constantine, L., "Soft Issues and other Hard Problems in Software Development," Panel including Cunningham, W., Hohmann, L., and Kerth, N., OOPSLA '96, San Jose, CA, Oct. 1996.
5. Kreindler, J., Cultural change and object-oriented technology, *J. OO Prog.,* 5:9, 6–8, Feb. 1993.
6. Greatrex, C. (KPMG Director) Achieving excellence through effective management of your IT project, *Proc. IT Project Management by AIC Conferences,* Auckland, NZ, April 1996.
7. Hammer, M. and Champy, J., *Reengineering the Corporation,* Allen and Unwin, St. Leonards, NSW, Australia, 1994, 163.
8. Humphrey, W., *A Discipline for Software Engineering,* Addison-Wesley, Reading, MA, 1995.
9. Unhelkar, B., Effect of granularity of object-oriented design in modelling an enterprise and its applications to financial risk management, Ph.D. thesis, University of Technology, Sydney, 1997.
10. Constantine, L., Teamwork paradigms and the structured open team, *Proc. Embedded Systems Conference,* San Francisco, Miller Freeman, 1989.
11. Constantine, L., *Constantine on Peopleware,* Prentice-Hall, Upper Saddle River, NJ, 1995, 75.
12. Henderson-Sellers, B. and Edwards, J. M., *BOOKTWO of Object-Oriented Knowledge: The Working Object,* Prentice-Hall, Upper Saddle River, NJ, 1994, 422.
13. Pant, Y., Henderson-Sellers, B., and Verner, J., Generalisation of object-oriented components for reuse: measurements of effort and size change, *J. OO Prog.,* 1995.
14. Meyer, B., *Object Success,* Prentice-Hall, Upper Saddle River, NJ, 1995.
15. Goldberg, A. and Rubin, K., *Succeeding with Objects: Decision Frameworks for Project Management,* Addison-Wesley, Reading, MA, 1995, 5, 280.
16. Constantine, L., Persistent usability: A multiphasic user interface architecture for supporting the full usage life cycle, *OzCHI 94 Proc.,* S. Howard and Y. K. Leung, Eds., Melbourne, Australia, 1994.
17. Constantine, L., General Principles of Software Usability, white paper by Constantine & Lockwood, Ltd., 72067.2631@compuserve.com.
18. DeMarco, T. and Lister, T., *Peopleware: Productive Projects and Teams,* Dorset House Publishing Co., New York, 1987.
19. Unhelkar, B., Transactional analysis (TA) as applied to the human factor in object-oriented projects, *Handbook of Object Technology,* CRC Press, Boca Raton, FL, 1999.
20. Berne, E., *Games People Play,* Penguin, 1964.
21. Berne, E., *Transactional Analysis in Psychotherapy,* Grove Press, First Evergreen ed., 1961, 23–24.
22. Graham, I., *Migrating to Object Technology,* Addison-Wesley, Reading, MA, 1995.
23. Meyer, B., *Object Success,* Prentice-Hall, Upper Saddle River, NJ, 1995.

11 A Sociological Process

The circle is closed now that one of the icons of software engineering has come to focus squarely on the human issues in computing.

Bill Curtis on Larry Constantine, 1995[1]

Abstract The understanding of the sociological factors in the resurrection process developed in the previous chapter is placed in the process discipline in this chapter. The activities and tasks belonging to the sociological dimension are described in detail here. It is this sociological dimension that makes the resurrection process an ideal process for development in the new millennium. Soft issues such as staffing, training, motivation, usability, and so on, all contribute towards creating the resurrected company. It is a company that is based on software processes with aesthetics. The actor director gets involved in the resurrection process by performing activities like advertising, managing corporate relations, and managing litigious activities directed at the organization. Caveats and assumptions related to the process metrics measuring the sociological dimension are described so that the sociological process metrics is used in the context of the process threads. As is the case with the other two dimensions of the resurrection process, the activities of project management and quality assurance also are performed in this dimension — albeit with a different focus of reporting to the business sponsors of the resurrection process.

11.1 DESCRIBING THE SOCIOLOGICAL PROCESS

The sociological process within the Y2K resurrection process plays the crucial role of dealing with the "people" aspect of resurrection. During the resurrection, the sociological process is instrumental in bringing together the people who will work on the project, organizing them in teams that reflect the techniques to be followed during the resurrection, and ensuring that the organization is on the right growth path as a result of resurrection.

It is important to note that the sociological process does not work independently of other dimensions of a process. In fact, all three process dimensions are simultaneously at work during resurrection and, as reflected by the white clouds model, their directions are orthogonal to each other. The sociological process also encompasses all other aspects of a development project that are not included in the technological and methodological dimensions.

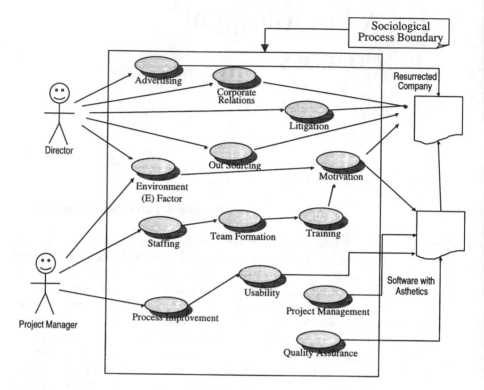

FIGURE 11.1   The sociological process in Y2K resurrection.

11.1.1 THE PROCESS FIGURE

Figure 11.1 describes the sociological process. There are 13 well-defined activities within this process that are made up of a total of 58 tasks. The director and the project manager constitute the two main variations to the actor director within the sociological dimension of the resurrection.

The sociological process deals with the activities that concentrate on "who" resurrects the company. These activities also have significant interface with the society in which the business exists. This is because the activities in the sociological process recreate the business image of the company. Thus, the deliverable from this process is a system that not only has quality and aesthetics, but also a company that relies on this software solution for its business activities after resurrection.

11.1.2 A HIGH-LEVEL PROCESS FLOW

The project manager within the sociological process primarily deals with the issues of team formation and its motivation. The project manager starts the activity of staffing by ensuring that she has enough staff to complete the project. This means there should be people with the right skills for the tasks, and they should have sufficient knowledge and experience to back their skills when they take up the tasks.

Once the right number of such people is available, the teams are formed. As discussed in the previous chapter, these teams are organized to derive advantage of quality and reuse, as is possible by using the object-oriented approach to software development. Sufficient training of the team members to enable them to perform their tasks follows this. The activity of motivating these well-trained teams is continuous and ongoing. Another important activity of the project manager is to focus on the usability aspect of the resurrecting software.

The project manager and the director are together involved in handling the activity of the environment factor which ensures that the physical environment is conducive to good software development. The director is involved in this activity from a budgetary viewpoint. A good development environment should also lead to good motivation. In addition to the environment factor, the director is responsible for the sociological activities of advertising, corporate relations, litigation, and outsourcing which are the external interfaces of the organization.

11.2 Sociological Actors

The two primary actors shown in the process diagram (Figure 11.1) for the sociological process are the project manager and the director. We have discussed variation of the actor project manager in our discussion of the methodological process. Here we present variation of the actor director and his involvement in the sociological activities. Figure 11.2 shows the variations of the actor director. These variations include all actors who are responsible to the owners or shareholders of the company. The role of a director includes the role of a Chief Executive Office (CEO), the Chief Financial Officer (CFO), the Chief Information Office (CIO), the Program director, the Human Resources (HR) director or the General Manager (GM).

11.2.1 Actor: Director

The actor director is the primary sponsor for the project. Therefore, this actor has the prime budgetary and related financial responsibilities in ensuring that the company is on its way to smooth resurrection. This role may be performed by more than one person and it is essentially the "resurrection champion" nominated during the preliminary activities of the resurrection process. The director will deal with the soft activities that represent the organization in the external business world. As mentioned before, the director is responsible for the activities of advertising, maintaining corporate relationships, handling litigation as a result of the Y2K-hit, taking decisions related to outsourcing, and, if outsourced, monitoring the progress of the outsourced project. This actor also associates with the actor project manager to ensure that the resurrection environment is ideal for the technical work that will be carried out during the process.

11.2.2 Actor: Project Manager

The actor project manager has already appeared once in the methodological dimension of the process. In that role the project manager was dealing with the "how to"

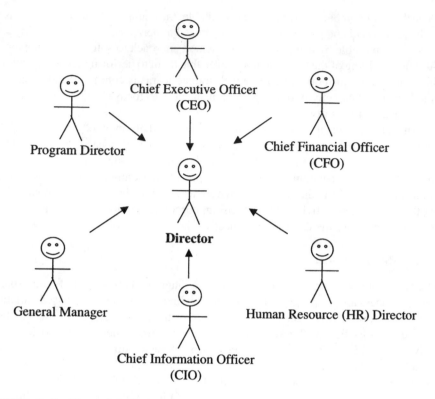

FIGURE 11.2 The sociological actors.

or the methodological aspect of the resurrection work. Here, the project manager deals with the "soft" or "people" issues of the project. These issues include activities such as staffing and team formation, training and motivation, improving the development process, and dealing with the actor director in order to create the ideal environment for resurrection. This actor also is responsible for updating the project plan and monitoring the progress of the resurrection project. A variation of this actor from the methodological dimension is the quality assurance manager. This actor, quality assurance manager, would report the results of quality audits to the board in an independent manner.

11.3 SOCIOLOGICAL DELIVERABLES

The sociological aspect of the resurrection process deals with the soft issues that are not easily quantifiable. Therefore, we don't have the same concrete measures for the sociological deliverables as we have for the technological ones. Thus, the output of the sociological process cannot be measured like the lines of code (or even the design measures) produced from the programming work. There are two main deliverables of this sociological process: (1) a software solution that has something more than quality, it has aesthetics; and (2) the complete resurrected company.

11.3.1 Software with Aesthetics

In the early days of computing, it was sufficient for the system to be technologically sound. However, when we discuss resurrection we are talking about software solutions in the new millennium. We increasingly want our system to not only be technologically robust, but also want it to look and feel good. These aesthetics of the resurrecting system will get translated in the look and feel of the resurrected business as well. We want the system to be more than just friendly, we want it to be centered on the user. The activities within the sociological process play an important role in producing software that has "beauty" in it. It is a system that recognizes the principles of usability and user-centered designs. Thus, one of the major deliverable from the sociological process is software with an aesthetic sense to it.

11.3.2 The Resurrected Company

The entire effort of all activities in the resurrection process is directed towards producing a new organization. Thus, the resurrected company is the overall deliverable of all processes. However, when we say that this resurrected company is a deliverable of the sociological process, we mean that the activities conducted within the final iteration of the resurrection process deal with the external view of the company — the activities like advertising, litigation, and outsourcing. These activities performed by the actor director of the process deal with the entity called *company*. This sociological dimension deals with many aspects of the resurrection process that are at the closing-off stage. The activities within this dimension result in providing shape to the resurrecting company. Therefore, the resurrected company also is described as a formal deliverable from the sociological process within resurrection.

11.4 SOCIOLOGICAL ACTIVITIES AND TASKS WITH ITERATIONS

The following table (Table 11.1) lists the sociological activities and tasks that are described in more detail in the remainder of the chapter.

11.5 SA01: STAFFING

The activity of staffing begins with the need to provide personnel who will be involved in the resurrection process. We have mentioned that the Y2K problem has been technological. People had very little to do with the problem. Therefore, it is essential that we hold onto the people we have, and utilize their skills in the resurrection as well as in the running of the company after resurrection. The aim should be to maintain as many people in-house as is possible, and should there be a shortfall, complete it by getting people from outside.

11.5.1 ST01-1: Identify Staffing Need

Staffing needs can be many fold. They can be based on the need to replace people who have left the team or the organization, or they can be because the organization

TABLE 11.1
Sociological Activities and Tasks with Probable Iterations

Sociological Activities	Sociological Tasks
SA01: Staffing Iteration: initial	ST01-1: Identify staffing need ST01-2: Identify sources ST01-3: Evaluate candidate ST01-4: Negotiate remuneration ST01-5: Offer written letter
SA02: Team formation Iteration: initial	ST02-1: Understand individual objectives ST02-2: Understand system architecture ST02-3: Assign teams to modules ST02-4: Fine tune teams
SA03: Training Iteration: major	ST03-1: Identify training needs ST03-2: Decide training types ST03-3: Initiate training program ST03-4: Obtain feedback ST03-5: Monitor technology trends
SA04: Environment (E) factor Iteration: major	ST04-1: Monitor environment ST04-2: Initiate survey ST04-3: Introduce controls ST04-4: Manage physical layout ST04-5: Beautification
SA05: Motivation Iteration: major	ST05-1: Shortlist motivational factors ST05-2: Correlate with company objectives ST05-3: Manage remuneration ST05-4: Undertake teambuilding ST05-5: Support achievement
SA06: Process refinement Iteration: major–final	ST06-1: Baseline process ST06-2: Organize reviews ST06-3: Set priorities ST06-4: Implement process change ST06-5: Publicize process improvement
SA07: Usability Iteration: major	ST07-1: Awareness of HCI issues ST07-2: Design user centered interfaces ST07-3: Conduct collaborative usability inspection (CUI) ST07-4: Manage usability standards
SA08: Outsourcing Iteration: initial–major	ST08-1: Identify outsourcing needs ST08-2: Evaluate outsourcing partners ST08-3: Outsource projects ST08-4: Manage and review projects
SA09: Advertising Iteration: initial–major	ST09-1: Identify areas for advertisement ST09-2: Advertise resurrection externally ST09-3: Promote resurrection internally ST09-4: Manage advertising contract
SA10: Corporate relations Iteration: initial	ST10-1: Manage board relationship ST10-2: Nominate Y2K experts on board

TABLE 11.1 *(continued)*
Sociological Activities and Tasks with Probable Iterations

Sociological Activities	Sociological Tasks
	ST10-3: Liase with business partners
	ST10-4: Liase with society
SA11: Litigation	ST11-1: Manage documentary evidence
Iteration: major–final	ST11-2: Budget for litigation
	ST11-3: Claim on insurance
	ST11-4: Manage settlement
SA12: Project management	ST12-1: Track activities and tasks
Iteration: all	ST12-2: Report to board
	ST12-3: Publish and present
	ST12-4: Manage HR issues
	ST12-5: Manage games
	ST12-6: Update project plan
SA13: Quality assurance	ST13-1: Manage internal/external audits
Iteration: all	ST13-2: Post audit review
	ST13-3: Post iteration review
	ST13-4: Independent reporting

has a shortage of particular skills. The staffing needs for Y2K resurrection can fall in both these categories. Some of the work in resurrection is routine — data maintenance, backups, LAN administration, parts of documentation, etc. However, when we salvage from the ashes and when we try to re-engineer the new organization, the skill requirements are likely to be different, and more specialized. Since object orientation is the way to go when we resurrect the organization, we will be in need of skills that are related to architecture, design, and process of object orientation. We also need skills related to quality assurance including those of testing, standards, and metrics.

Furthermore, we need to identify the number of people that will be required for the project. These numbers can change depending on the iteration we are performing. We may make an estimate on the number of people needed within the process and we may then revisit these numbers based on the reviews conducted at the end of each iteration. These are some of the staffing needs that should be identified at the start of and during the resurrection process.

11.5.2 ST01-2: IDENTIFY SOURCES

There are a number of sources from which staffing needs can be satisfied. Depending on the skills we seek and the number of people we need, we can source the staff using the following options:

- *Employment agencies* — providing the quickest way to match the skills we seek with those available on the market. However, cost of recruitment needs to be considered, as the agency costs are likely to be higher than direct costs of recruitment.

- *Newspaper advertisement* — which provides another popular means of recruiting.
- *Internal advertisement* — enable opportunities for people within the organization to grow. Since the candidates already know the environment in which they are working, the time spent on induction and the initial learning curve is reduced.
- *Networking* — this can be achieved within the organization itself by encouraging people to locate suitable candidates to fill the skill requirement and providing them financial rewards in return. Networking by people with similar skills is common. This networking can be tapped into for the benefit of the resurrection work.
- *Business partner* — occasionally, a business partner who is interested in seeing the resurrection work proceed smoothly will lend consulting skills for the purpose.
- *Advertising on the Web* — when people with similar interest get together through news groups and chat sessions, they provide an opportunity for advertising jobs with skills in the area of interest.
- *University projects* — although it is less likely that a university would be involved in teaching Y2K skills, the newer skills from the teaching institutions can be utilized for non-Y2K work within the organization. This would free up senior and specialized technical staff who can concentrate on the resurrection effort. Also, the resurrection effort is not entirely related to date fixing. It aims to re-engineer the organization based on the *future* needs. University courses and projects provide a valuable source of semi-skilled personnel who can be trained and brought up to speed quickly.
- *Special Interest Groups* often of professional computer societies — both formal and informal groups of people with special interests, meeting on a regular basis, provide opportunities for organizations to attract relevant technical and project management skills to be used within the resurrection process.

11.5.3 ST01-3: Evaluate Candidates

Traditionally, evaluation of candidates is based through a formal test, an interview, or a combination of both. When the organization utilizes the services of an employment agency, it is expected that the initial matching of the candidate for the Y2K work will have been done by the agency. Apart from the knowledge and experience of the candidate, it is also important to ensure that the candidate fits well into the resurrection team. The approach for such evaluation (i.e., the "best fit" approach) was discussed in the previous chapter. In evaluating a candidate it is important to inform them about the status of the company. Working in a Y2K-hit company may not be the choice of everyone. However, once the prospective candidates are aware of the possibilities that resurrection provides, they may find the challenge and the opportunities to learn quite interesting.

11.5.4 ST01-4: NEGOTIATE REMUNERATION

Remuneration is important in any job, but more so when a person is employed or contracted to work on Y2K resurrection. This is because many candidates believe that working on a date-related problem is not necessarily challenging. It is not seen as a career enhancing move. Therefore, it may be important to highlight the fact that in resurrection we plan to do more than simply fix the date problem. Plans to use new technology and OO approach to resurrection should be highlighted in balancing the work with the remuneration expected.

11.5.5 ST01-5: OFFER WRITTEN LETTER

In case of both permanent and contract positions, it is essential to provide a written letter of offer to the selected candidates. This enables the candidate to plan his or her departure from the current position. A consulting role also needs to plan the number of days she is expected to be working in the role offered. Usually, a senior Y2K consultant working on a resurrection project may not be involved full-time. In that case, the written contract must specify the time she is supposed to be spending each week, the rates for the time (daily, hourly), and so on.

11.6 SA02: TEAM FORMATION

In the previous chapter we described the various team models that can be used in an object-oriented resurrection effort. These team models include the closed, open, random, and synchronous models. The team models have a bearing on the quality of the final output, as well as amount of reuse achieved during development. The theoretical understanding of team formation developed in the previous chapter is put in practice during this activity.

11.6.1 ST02-1: UNDERSTAND INDIVIDUAL OBJECTIVES

Technical people have been reluctant to work on Y2K, as it is not seen as providing enough of a technical challenge to them. In this task, we concentrate on understanding the needs of the people who will form the resurrection team. These needs are essentially the "individual objectives" we talked about in the previous chapter. Understanding these individual objectives has an important bearing on the way in which teams should be formed. These objectives also correlate with the motivational activities that will be performed later on.

Apart from the needs for technical challenge, or higher remuneration, it also may be necessary to know the areas within the development in which the team members are interested. For example, some designers are eager to work on the backend — designing database tables and writing queries and programs to access the data. Others are interested in the GUI and the way the fields and buttons sit on the front-end. It is only when the vector sum of the individual objectives relate to the objectives of the resurrection team that we can have a successful resurrection. Thus, an understanding of people needs at this stage can greatly assist the team formation activity.

11.6.2 ST02-2: UNDERSTAND SYSTEM ARCHITECTURE

The methodological activity of architecture (MA05) that results in the production of system architecture, should be revisited in this task. This will ensure that a higher level understanding of the architecture is reflected in the team formation process. The number of teams, their composition, and sequencing the work these teams will be performing, will be positively influenced by the understanding of the architecture of the resurrecting system. It can only be a very high level understanding of the architecture, as the final architecture would be put in place during the later part of the iteration. However, that understanding is enough to start thinking along the lines of infrastructure team, database team, business team, and so on.

11.6.3 ST02-3: ASSIGN TEAMS TO MODULES

Once the staff is grouped into teams based on their own choices and the needs of the company and once we have a general idea of the solution architecture, then it is possible to assign teams of the larger modules of the solution. For example, in banking architecture, if we have identified customer information system (CIS) and accounts as the two major modules and organized the architecture around these two modules, then it is possible to assign teams to these modules during the resurrection work. However, architecture can go further down to the horizontal level of database and user-interfaces for each of the two modules. Thus, we may have teams that are only working on the front-end of the system, whereas other teams might be capable of handling the database issues. This assignment of teams to the modules is completed during this task. Note that this is not a water tight assignment and those team members can (and do) move between teams. However, this segregation makes it possible to organize and follow the resurrection process keeping the needs of the development (corporate objectives) and the interest of the individuals (individual objectives) aligned with each other (see Figures 10.4, 10.5, and 10.6).

11.6.4 ST02-4: FINE TUNE TEAMS

As mentioned earlier, teams are not watertight. Once people are assigned to teams and when teams are assigned to modules, work can start on the resurrection process. Although the team formation activity may start with the initial iteration of the resurrection process, the fine-tuning of the teams takes place as the resurrection process proceeds. It is an ongoing activity which will be performed depending on the changing needs of people, the technical progress of the project and the road factors that will keep appearing during the project. Individual and corporate objectives can also change. Changes to the vectors representing these objectives can have an influence on the success of resurrection. Thus, it is essential to continuously monitor and fine-tune the team formation process, as mentioned in this task.

11.7 SA03: TRAINING

The training activity is an ongoing activity that starts with the resurrection process, continues throughout the process, and exists even after the company has resurrected. A Y2K-prevention exercises had no major need for training as, technically, the problem was well known. Perhaps training on the tools used for prevention would have been helpful. In case of resurrection, though, detailed training program will be essential. This training program would usually be the responsibility of the project manager or the training manager in a large project. Specifically, the training activity is directed towards the teams and, therefore, it is advisable that the more focused aspect of the training activity is conducted after the teams have been formed.

11.7.1 ST03-1: IDENTIFY TRAINING NEEDS

This first task of the training activity starts with the identification of the training needs. In a resurrection project this will include:

- Need to train in the tools used for resurrection/conversion if they are still used in the project.
- Training in the new technologies (languages, databases) used in the resurrection.
- Training in the methodologies (e.g., object-oriented) for resurrection.
- Training in understanding the existing products — this need for training will depend on whether an external person (a consultant) is brought in to help with resurrection. She may not be aware of the systems and applications of the Y2K-hit company and may need some training in them.
- Training the personnel in the new systems — this would be closer to the completion of resurrection.
- Training in use of new date formats — this would only require an awareness campaign and not necessarily a rigorous training.

11.7.2 ST03-2: DECIDE TRAINING TYPES

There are various types of training that can be used in order to satisfy the training needs of a company. Some types of training require considerable time, effort and budgets — for example, training programming staff in the use of a new language. However, if the training were only to promote the use of a new date format (MM-DD-YYYY or YYYY-MM-DD and so on) then it would be relatively easy and cheap to conduct the training. The type of training would thus depend on the need that it is supposed to satisfy. Some of the training options available are

- Organizing internal training programs — these could be done through regular weekly meeting and informal workshop type discussions.
- External training — this is the formal aspect of training, essential for training technical staff in languages and methodologies. A regular budget is required for the purpose

- University course — staff can be encouraged to undertake university courses (part-time, remote, net-based etc.) to upgrade their skills. If the skills are relevant to the project, compensation for the courses can be provided.
- Conferences — conference programs encourage exchange of ideas across the industry and should be encouraged as a part of training. Encouraging staff to present their work externally (within the confidentiality scope of the organization) can also help in promoting the image of the organization. This is also a project management task (ST12-3) described later on.
- Video and audio courses — these courses save time for the organization and effort on behalf of the employee. These courses can provide input on a certain topic (such as date format, or use of a new telephone code) in a short and concise way. For a complex topic, the video and audio course provide backup to the original course, or can be backed up by a formal course.

11.7.3 ST03-3: INITIATE TRAINING PROGRAM

Once the training needs are identified and the type of training to be provided is shortlisted, the training program can be initiated. Note that the overall training program can be made up of a combination of types of training. Initiating the training program requires the project manager to ensure that employees are free from their regular tasks during the training. It is also essential to sequence the training correctly. For example, it is essential to send the designers on an architecture and design course before they can attend a programming course to appreciate the nuances of a new programming language. Also, training on the 'hit' system will be relevant to the dissection activity for those staff who are responsible for arriving at the salvageable options. Finally, training programs for sales and marketing staff in the new systems of the organization are essential to successfully resurrect the new organization.

11.7.4 ST03-4: OBTAIN FEEDBACK

A training course is not complete unless formal and informal feedback is obtained from the participants of the course. This feedback is essential in order to evaluate the quality of the course, and whether the organization has derived value for money by sending its employees to the course. In case of internal training programs, such feedback would provide opportunity to justify the expense and time incurred in organizing the internal training workshops. Maintaining a record of the feedback and occasionally analyzing the results is essential in forming partnership with training institutions. Formal feedback can be obtained through well-designed forms. It is essential to encourage feedback by continuous reminders during the course. Informal feedback by chatting over the breaks is an invaluable source of information for the course organizers (in this case the training manager) or the course sponsor.

11.7.5 ST03-5: MONITOR TECHNOLOGY TRENDS

Training has to be relevant to the project. In case of resurrection, training on the existing system may be required only from the user's viewpoint in order to know what to dissect and how much of the existing system can be salvaged. This is followed by training for resurrection that involves training developers in the use of new technology and the potential users in the best use of the process-based system can be used. To fulfil this function on a continuous basis, it is also essential for the project manager to continue to monitor the technology trends outside the organization. For example, going from 16-bit programming to 32-bit programming requires an initiative on the part of the management — depending on the environment in which new technology development is going to take place, the technology direction of the company, and the particular initiative and interests of the individual. Thus, this task ensures that training remains an initiative of the management as much as of the staff.

11.8 SA04: ENVIRONMENT (E) FACTOR

The IT world was made aware of the environment factor and the effect it has on the overall development by the work of DeMarco and Lister (discussed in the previous chapter). The project manager is the initiator of this activity, but it has to be supported by the director in terms of budgets, as well as rules and regulations required to implement an undisturbed environment. As shown in the process diagram for sociology, the environment factor has an eventual effect on the motivation of the employees. Here we formalize the process of creating and maintaining the environment factor during the resurrection effort.

11.8.1 ST04-1: MONITOR ENVIRONMENT

The first task in relation to the environment in the resurrection project is monitoring the existing environment. Direct observation of the work environment and the manner in which it is carried out is the best way a project manager can monitor the environment. The factors that cause disturbance in the routine and smooth functioning of the resurrection team are noted during this task. These include the disturbances due to phone rings, meetings and meeting rooms, and so on.

11.8.2 ST04-2: INITIATE SURVEY

If, in the view of the project manager, the environment needs to be controlled and improved, then it is essential to get the feedback from the employees who are affected by the environmental disturbances as to how the environment can be improved. These surveys include two parts:

1. Questions related to the actual disturbances — is the environment as bad as the project manager thinks?
2. Opinions as to how the environment can be controlled.

If formal surveys are not possible, informal querying should be performed.

11.8.3 ST04-3: INTRODUCE CONTROLS

Introduction of formal controls (i.e., rules and regulations) in a workplace should be considered only after the employees themselves feel that such controls are necessary for their efficient working. This is so because without the initiative coming from the people who work, the controls are going to have a detrimental effect on the overall activity of creating a good working environment. Controls will work only when those affected by the controls want them. Once the project manager is convinced that the controls are necessary and that they will be beneficial to the majority of employees working on the project, then it will be necessary to get the director involved in the process. Therefore, the results of the survey should back up the arguments for controls within the workplace. These controls can include judicious use of telephones, Internet, meeting rooms, etc.

11.8.4 ST04-4: MANAGE PHYSICAL LAYOUT

This task involves creation and maintenance of physical layout that is relevant to the kind of work being conducted. In the resurrection environment, the technical activities are related to software design and development. The physical layout should be conducive to these activities. This task is affected by the number of people that are on the project and the way in which they relate to each other. The earlier activity of team formation (SA02) correlates with the way the task of physical layout is conducted. For example, the team involved in the graphical user interface (GUI) design may find it useful to sit next to the potential users or the usability experts, rather than the team working on data models and data delivery mechanisms.

11.8.5 ST04-5: BEAUTIFICATION

The debate on whether software development is an art or an engineering discipline has no hope of ending, for a process that is both art and science cannot be categorized into any one of them. The problem until now has been that although software started off as art form (complete freedom to write 5000 lines of COBOL), it was the engineering image that was more charming to the programming community. As a result of this, the engineering image came to be the accepted image — taking a leaf straight out of the mechanical or construction workshop where oil and grime and dust and noise are an accepted part of life. However, this need not be the case with development teams working on the resurrection process. As the software development thinking progresses towards the new millennium, the softer aspect of software development is gaining more recognition and acceptance. This acceptance has come without the loss of the disciplined approach of engineering so essential for rigorous software development. Thus, we can use the words *beautification* and *beautiful program* without the fear of being labeled non-engineers. This thinking also flows through in creating a beautiful environment for software engineers. It includes things like painting and music and potted plants as a part of the overall environment to work in. Since these tasks do require budgets, either the project manager has sufficient mandate to spend, or she gets the director involved. For larger expenses such as shifting offices, etc., the involvement of the director may be essential.

11.9 SA05: MOTIVATION

Motivation is extremely important in a Y2K-hit organization that is trying to resurrect. A normal Y2K prevention exercise was not technically challenging. Therefore, it did not attract the talent that thrives on challenges. However, resurrection will be different from simple prevention. We try to bring together different aspects of technology and methodology in order to resurrect. The project manager, with support from the director, can manage the motivational factors in resurrection by combining the technical challenges of resurrection with the financial rewards from Y2K-related work.

11.9.1 ST05-1: SHORTLIST MOTIVATIONAL FACTORS

The first of the motivational tasks, creating a shortlist of motivational factors, enables the project manager to understand the driving force behind the resurrection team. A simple list of motivational factors may include:

- New technology — using a high-end distributed architecture is obviously a big motivational factor for many technically minded people.
- A growth path *after* resurrection. One of the main factors that has deterred many computing professionals from getting involved in the Y2K problem is the fact that it provides no career growth for professionals after the Y2K problem is over. During resurrection that problem is overcome by making it known to the people working on the team that resurrection provides opportunities for new development, not only of technology, but also of business.
- Belonging to a Y2K-hit company might be demotivating in itself. There is a need to understand and assuage the feelings of the development team in order to be able to provide the much needed motivation.

This list can keep growing, but more important than the motivational factors provided here are the motivational factors specific to the Y2K-hit organization. The motivational activity will be effective when the vector sum of the individual objectives finds support from the organization. Furthermore, it is also essential to align the vectors representing the individual and corporate objectives. This is performed by the next task.

11.9.2 ST05-2: CORRELATE WITH COMPANY OBJECTIVES

While the management may be able to identify the motivational factors of individuals (based on their individual objectives), simply motivating people for their individual objectives may be counterproductive if those objectives are not aligned with each other and with those of the company. This task ensures that the management pursues the objectives of the employees that are in line with the objectives of the company. For example, if use of a particular new technology serves no particular purpose in the resurrection process, then there is no point in using such technology even if it motivates employees. Typically, a resurrecting organization will find that bringing in new technology may not happen in one go. It will be a phased approach, requiring critically hit areas to be resurrected first, followed by the less crucial ones. Thus, it will be essential to keep the company objectives in mind, and ensuring that they align with those of the individuals.

11.9.3 ST05-3: MANAGE REMUNERATION

As in case of the staffing activity (SA01) where the initial salary packages are offered, we have to consider the effect of Y2K-related work in managing the remuneration on an ongoing basis. Professionals working on prevention of the problem have earned phenomenally high compensation. This was due to a dearth of people wanting to work on the date problem, a narrowed career focus due to work on specific legacy systems and lack of challenge that is derived in building new systems.

If the same professionals who attempted prevention of Y2K problem still continue to work in the resurrection (which they are very likely to do), then it will be necessary to manage their financial expectations. This is so because with the newer technologies being applied in the resurrection process, it is primarily the functionality and the data of the older system that remain important. If the functionality can be captured through the user interfaces, and the user guides (see MA04), then the demand for people who understand the language and the technology of the Y2K-hit system is considerably reduced. Apart from the less demand for the older technology, the professionals dealing with the newer technologies are likely to be available in larger numbers. Thus, Y2K professionals will have to be prepared to work for lesser salaries than what they were used to during the prevention effort.

11.9.4 ST05-4: UNDERTAKE TEAMBUILDING

Apart from managing the motivational factors that relate to the technical work and the financial compensation, it is also essential to make sure that the team continues to function well together during the resurrection effort. We have discussed the initial modeling of the teams in activity team formation (SA02). This task ensures that the team remains cohesive and continues to function well until the resurrection exercise is complete. Therefore, occasionally, it may be advisable to provide teambuilding exercises for the resurrection team. It is essential to continue to stress that the teams are not merely fixing the date problem, but are rebuilding the enterprise based on processes. This theme can provide motivation together with the teambuilding exercises.

11.9.5 ST05-5: SUPPORT ACHIEVEMENT

The date problems will be investigated, the areas from where it is occurring will hopefully be located, and the dissection process will reveal what needs to be salvaged and what can be thrown away. This would be followed by the redevelopment effort. Each of these stages in the resurrection process needs to be recognized and supported, for each of these stages provides a major achievement in the resurrection process. Motivation during the early stages of resurrection will play a crucial role as the team is still recovering from the effect of the Y2K hit to the business, and at the same time it has not yet started the redevelopment effort. Therefore, all work during the earlier stages of resurrection (dissection and salvaging) needs more than normal support in order to keep the resurrection teams motivated.

11.10 SA06: PROCESS REFINEMENT

Y2K prevention was a one-off effort. Y2K resurrection is not. During resurrection exercise, the organization is learning new technology and is fine tuning its methodological approach to software development. This entire process of resurrection can provide a valuable backbone for the future development activities of the organization in years to come. Therefore, simply providing a documented process for resurrection is not enough. It also is important to continue to improve that process, and this activity enables improvement of the process of software development from the sociological viewpoint.

11.10.1 ST06-1: BASELINE PROCESS

The first task within any process refinement effort is to baseline the current process. Although we expect the resurrection process to be "once only," there are still quite a few aspects within a resurrection process that can be baselined. These would be the resurrection activities related to the methodological dimensions, wherein the object-oriented approach used for resurrection can be baselined and improved. Metrics and measurement of the resurrection process can provide valuable input into baselining the process for further improvement. Thus, all relevant activities within the resurrection process that have a potential for being repeated in subsequent development work can be included in the baseline.

11.10.2 ST06-2: ORGANIZE REVIEWS

The entire resurrection process can be reviewed during this task. Once again, the focus will be on reviewing the repeatable activities that can be performed more efficiently and effectively in subsequent development work. If reviews can be organized earlier on in the resurrection process* then there is a possibility of using the results of process refinement within the same resurrection process, but during a later iteration.

The reviewing techniques that can be used during this task are standard quality assurance review techniques.

11.10.3 ST06-3: SET PRIORITIES

As a result of the review of the resurrection process, we are in a position to set priorities on the areas within the process that can be improved. For example, a resurrection process that is run with heavy emphasis on the technological dimension can be improved by balancing it with the sociological needs of the project, as discussed in this chapter. Another example is the lesser need to improve activities

---

* Though not always easy, as the focus during the initial iterations is on getting the resurrection process going rather than improving the process.

like dissection which may not be repeated within the organization. However, for consulting organizations (that have a need for repeatable process even in resurrection), prioritizing activities like dissection is still important.

11.10.4 ST06-4: Implement Process Change

This task implements the process refinement that is prepared in the previous tasks. The task ensures that changes to the various activities and tasks, changes to their flow, and the results of measuring the productivity and estimation processes, etc., all change as the process change is implemented. Implementation of the process change will require procurement of new tools (e.g., work-flow tools) that support the change process.

11.10.5 ST06-5: Publicize Process Improvement

After process improvement takes place within the development environment of the organization, it is vital that this change is communicated to everyone involved within and outside the organization. If process improvement influences the way in which a third-party vendor deals with the organization, it is essential that the vendor is informed of the process change. Publicizing the process improvement also ensures that everyone within the organization knows that a checkpoint has been reached and that that checkpoint can be the baseline for further process refinement in the future.

11.11 SA07: USABILITY

We discussed the principles of usability in the previous chapter. Here, we apply those principles to the resurrection process. By undertaking these tasks, we aim to produce a new user-centered system.

11.11.1 ST07-1: Awareness of HCI Issues

It is essential to create an awareness of the human computer interaction (HCI) issues within the resurrection team. Demonstrating the need for producing user-centered interfaces can generate this awareness. Awareness of HCI issues also derive from the understanding that the computer system is able to generate a range of responses within its users that other "people" can. Therefore, software systems have a personality of their own and we promote this understanding in this task.

11.11.2 ST07-2: Design User Centered Interfaces

The user interface of a software system is a system on its own. Therefore, it should be specified, designed, and developed as a system. The design of user-centered interfaces can follow a range of techniques, starting from paper-based prototypes and Visual Basic mock-ups through to detailed navigation models that deal with the screen navigation of the system. Appropriate helps and "bells and whistles" features can be incorporated here.

11.11.3 ST07-3: Conduct Collaborative Usability Inspection (CUI)

Collaborative usability inspections are formal inspections of the user interface by the prospective users of the system. An "average" user, who is not an expert in the functionality being provided by the system, is asked to start using the system (or its prototype) and make comments on its usability. All comments are recorded in a predetermined format. While the designers and implementers of the system will be present during the inspections, they are not allowed to defend their designs at this stage. Results from the inspections are analyzed and relevant corrections made to ensure that the system is user-centered. Not only are individual screens inspected, but the navigation between screens, their relevance to the work being performed through the interface, and the tolerance of the user interface for errors are inspected.

11.11.4 ST07-4: Manage Usability Standards

Each organization has its own standards for usability. These may not be formally documented. However, things like the logo of the organization and the acronym of the system, etc. are usually standardized. This task ensures that all aspects of the user interface appearing in the resurrecting system are standardized. For example, if colors are used in a bank user interface to indicate status of the account, they will have to be standardized across the application (e.g., does red mean the bank account is overdrawn, or does it mean that it is a very important account needing further attention?). Similarly, audio signals from the user interface may also need standardization. Resurrecting from a Y2K hit, the resurrecting system will certainly have to concentrate on standardizing the date display. For a system deployed across various countries (which have different date standards), date-display standards will have to be customizable. This task will have to consider all possible formats that can be used and the caveats associated with the date display. The usability standards should have considerable input from the users of the system. These standards should only be modified after the user representatives accept the changes.

11.12 SA08: OUTSOURCING

This is an activity performed by the actor director. In Chapter 3, we had discussed *in*sourcing as a possible strategic advantage to resurrection. This is the counter-side of the insourcing advantage. Organizations that have already resurrected successfully or that were not hit by Y2K because of a good level of preparedness are the ones that can help this resurrecting organization.

11.12.1 ST08-1: Identify Outsourcing Needs

The director or the resurrection champion may have to decide on the need to outsource. There are a number of areas within the resurrection process that may be outsourced. For example, once the designs for the new system are completed, the programming work can be outsourced. Once the dissection activity is completed, the salvaging of relevant data can be outsourced. Or if there is a need to enter data, then the data entry work can be outsourced. Finally, if the entire focus of the organization is on resurrection and all its software teams are involved in the resurrection work, then the mundane (and unaffected) operational work on software systems can be outsourced. The director together with the project manager has to identify whether there is a need for, and an area of work, that can be outsourced.

11.12.2 ST08-2: EVALUATE OUTSOURCING PARTNERS

It is important for the director to ensure the technical as well as business strengths of the potential outsourcing partners. This is essential because once a part of work is outsourced, it will be essential for the outsourcing vendor to deliver the work. If any of the resurrection activities are being outsourced, then the potential partner should be conversant with the resurrection process. There is a possibility that the work being outsourced is to a senior business partner of the organization that is already Y2K compliant.

11.12.3 ST08-3: OUTSOURCE PROJECTS

Outsourcing of projects/work related to Y2K resurrection has the same checks and balances that a normal outsourcing work has. Therefore, it is essential to have properly defined timelines, deliverables, and signed contracts for the work to be performed. Outsourcing may be on a module-by-module basis if it is related to the development work, or it may be on an ongoing basis for routine work.

11.12.4 ST08-4: MANAGE AND REVIEW PROJECTS

Outsourced work needs continuous review. While this is true of the routine out-sourced work (e.g., let the outsourcing vendor run my payroll while I concentrate on resurrection), it is even truer of any work that a business partner performs for the resurrection process. The outsourced work can be monitored and reviewed on a regular basis by means of the well-defined activities and tasks within the resurrection process. The iterations within the process should provide the necessary checkpoints at which the outsourcing contracts can be reviewed based on performance and delivery.

11.13 SA09: ADVERTISING

This is the first of the activities in which the director-level actor is directly involved in the resurrection process. The activity of advertising spans the need to advertise the resurrection process through to the commercial business advertisement for the customers and external organization with which the Y2K-hit company was dealing before the hit. Since the fact that the organization was affected by Y2K problem will be well known to the external world, this activity concentrates on recovering and promoting the image of the organization as it attempts to resurrect.

11.13.1 ST09-1: IDENTIFY AREAS FOR ADVERTISEMENT

This task involves identifying the areas of technology and business that are likely to benefit by the advertisement. The use of new technology in the organization has obvious strategic advantages. For example, the use of object-oriented approach to software development carries value in the technical circles. This can provide advantage in terms of retaining technical people on the resurrection team, as well as alluring potential developers to the Y2K resurrection work. The areas in business that need advertisement include:

- Acceptance of the Y2K problem.
- The work being done within the organization.
- The likely dates when the services can be restored.
- The additional advantages that the customers will derive from resurrection.

11.13.2 ST09-2: ADVERTISE RESURRECTION EXTERNALLY

External advertisement primarily concentrates on the business advertisement. After having identified the business areas that can benefit by external advertisement, this task concentrates on actually carrying out the promotional work. This task can be carried out by:

- Advertising the Y2K work carried out through the relevant media.
- Highlighting the resulting advantages to the customers and suppliers.
- Showing how the process-based systems will enable faster and cheaper deals, compensating the customers and suppliers for the Y2K-related losses.
- Expanding on newer lines of business opening up as a result of the resurrection.

This promotion is essential for the effect it is likely to have on the share price of a publicly listed company. Thus, the purpose of external advertisement is not only to maintain relationships with customers and suppliers, but also keep up the share value of the company — which, one presumes, will have been adversely affected by the Y2K hit.

11.13.3 ST09-3: PROMOTE RESURRECTION INTERNALLY

Promoting resurrection internally concentrates on the employees, especially the resurrection team. This task can be performed in conjunction with the motivational activities (SA05), wherein the resurrection work is promoted internally by means of in-house notices, notice boards, newsletters, e-mails, and the company intranet/Internet site.

11.13.4 ST09-4: MANAGE ADVERTISING CONTRACT

When dealing with a large-scale resurrection project, it might be essential to contract the work to external advertisement agencies. If an advertisement company was already dealing with the promotional work for the Y2K-hit company, it would be advantageous to continue with the same company, only with added emphasis on promoting the resurrection work.

11.14 SA10: CORPORATE RELATIONS

The Y2K problem is likely to affect the organization at all levels including the board of directors who are responsible for the external value of the company. Therefore, it will be essential for the resurrection champion to manage the relationship of the organization with the external world. This activity provides for management of corporate relations while the resurrection is on its way.

11.14.1 ST10-1: MANAGE BOARD RELATIONSHIP

The resurrection champion who is entrusted with the job of resurrecting the organization has the task of updating the board continuously with the progress of the work. Furthermore, the resurrection champion has to ensure that relations between the representatives of the various groups within the company are also functional. For example, directors from the finance (from budget), information technology (from technical viewpoint), and the personnel (from the motivational viewpoint) departments will have to work together in order for resurrection to succeed.

11.14.2 ST10-2: NOMINATE Y2K EXPERTS ON BOARD

People who have already worked on the Y2K problem are likely to provide valuable insight into the dissection process. They can help in identifying areas which are hit, which is a big step in moving towards resurrection. Furthermore, these experts are also in a position to throw light on how data affected by Y2K can be salvaged for the new system. Finally, a person with Y2K experience can provide the much needed bridge within the board between members of the business and technology community.

11.14.3 ST10-3: LIAISE WITH BUSINESS PARTNERS

In managing the corporate relationships, it is important to manage the relationships with business partners including clients and suppliers in a professional manner while the resurrection is progressing. Those affected by the breakdown in service need to be provided a regular update (this can be done through advertisements as well) on how long their services will be disrupted before the Y2K problem is solved. Since the aim of resurrection exercise is to provide a new system, it might be important to stress the business advantages to the business partners. Furthermore, at the end of the resurrection process, it might also be essential to share the expertise of dissecting a hit system and salvaging requirements with the business partners. The task of maintaining good corporate relations is with the resurrection champion.

11.14.4 ST10-4: Liaise with Society

We had discussed the relationship of business with society in Chapter 2 (Figure 2.1). The activity of corporate relations has to ensure that the company liaises with the society in a positive way. This interaction should be considered as an integral requirement of the resurrection process. The image the company presents to the society is vital for its survival and prosperity in the new millennium. Technology will enable resurrection only from a technical viewpoint. The sociological aspect of resurrection is handled by liaising with the society. This task also is an antidote to the organization for its possible schizophrenic behavior when it was hit by Y2K.

11.15 SA11: LITIGATION

The Y2K problem is expected to provide a rich field for litigations. For a Y2K-hit company, the legal aspects need to be managed from the following angles:

1. The organization may be defaulting on its contract to provide services or to provide a problem-free date.
2. Alternatively, the organization itself is affected because its business partners did not comply with the Y2K date requirements.

In both cases, it will be essential to consider the legal aspects of a Y2K hit. This activity, typically carried out by the legal director(s) of the company, provides for the legal protection as well as compensation for possible losses.

11.15.1 ST11-1: Manage Documentary Evidence

If the organization has already attempted a Y2K prevention effort (i.e., red level and above), it is important to maintain evidence of all aspects of this Y2K effort. This can be

- In the form of documents dealing with investigation and fixes of the date problem.
- Budgets sanctioned and spend on the Y2K effort.
- Software backups and audit trails of the databases that were used in the prevention effort.

If the contract with the business partner reads "compliance with Y2K," the hit organization is not left with much choice but to take responsibility for the Y2K problem. However, a Y2K software contract is not going to be so general. Instead, the emphasis on a software contract is whether due diligence has been taken by the organization in order to prevent the Y2K problem. If evidence of such effort can save the organization from getting dragged to the courts for lengthy legal battles, then the energy thus saved can be focused on the actual resurrection effort. Therefore, managing the evidence of Y2K effort — both before and after the hit — is essential from legal viewpoint.

11.15.2 ST11-2: Budget for Litigation

If an organization realizes that it is hit by the Y2K problem and that there is little or no provision for it to escape responsibility, it may be necessary for the resurrection champion to budget for potential legal battles. Although not an ideal scenario, it might be necessary to legally prove the effort undertaken by the organization in prevention of the Y2K problem, and then resurrecting from the problem once it hits the company. A prudent approach to overall resurrection requires the organization to budget for litigation during Year 2000.

11.15.3 ST11-3: Claim on Insurance

Quite a few insurance companies have made a business out of the Y2K problem. If the Y2K-hit organization has already insured itself against the problem, it may be necessary to place claim on the insurance for the possible losses due to the Y2K problem. Care needs to be exercised to show the dissection and salvaging of requirements, as well as conversion of relevant data as a part of the Y2K problem, rather than a totally new development activity.

11.15.4 ST11-4: Manage Settlement

The area of litigation needs careful management and, finally, careful settlement. This task requires the resurrection champion to ensure that all litigation is settled as quickly as possible so that the main technical work of resurrection does not suffer. If, as a result of the Y2K insurance, the organization is due for insurance returns, then it is important to chase that settlement. This task ensures responsible management of the legal settlement process so that monies recovered from such settlement can be immediately put in the resurrection effort.

11.16 SA12: PROJECT MANAGEMENT

11.16.1 ST12-1: Track Activities and Tasks

While this same task is performed in the methodological dimension (MT03-4), the focus in the methodological dimension is the information the project manager needs herself in order to follow the project. The focus within the sociological dimension is to track the activities and tasks within all dimensions of the resurrection process with an aim of reporting them to the business sponsors of the project, which is the board of the company. This is not to say that the task of tracking activities and tasks is performed twice. Like all other tasks within the project management and quality assurance activities, this task has double focus. Also, if there is only one person managing the project, then the same task will carry the duel significance of tracking the resurrection activities and tasks for both internal and external purposes.

11.16.2 ST12-2: Report to Board

Reporting the progress of the resurrection project is a vital task that ensures that the board, which has funded this resurrection in the first place, is aware of the milestones achieved by the resurrection team. The reporting resulting from this task may influence the scope of the project at the end of each iteration. The points of interest to the board are the amounts spend and the time remaining for the resurrection activities to be completed. Refinement of the plan will be carried out to ensure that the project remains on track. However, lower level details such as the progress of individual tasks may not be of interest to the board.

11.16.3 ST12-3: Publish and Present

The resurrection work is likely to be technically challenging. The senior management of the organization should ensure that the success achieved during this process is made known to the technical and business community. This can be achieved by means of conference presentations and journal publications. The information disbursed as a result of these publications can be a valuable source for the other organizations that are facing similar problems.

11.16.4 ST12-4: Manage HR Issues

The sociological task within project management requires the project manager to handle the human relations (HR) issues. These issues include remuneration packages, internal promotions, individual contract negotiations, and so on.

11.16.5 ST12-5: Manage Games

If the resurrection process gets embroiled in unproductive yet seemingly frantic work, then it will be essential for the project manager to identify and control this behavior of the resurrection team members. Various games and their antidotes were mentioned in the previous chapter. This task ensures that the project manager is aware of the need to control this sociological factor that has an influence on the outcome of the process.

11.16.6 ST12-6: Update Project Plan

Updating the project plan is a continuous task throughout the three dimensions of the resurrection process. Although it is a routine task, it is important that this task is performed carefully as the results from the updates will be used in projecting the progress of the remainder of the resurrection process. Updated project plan is an important source of project reports that are used by senior managers and the board is gauging the progress of the resurrection work.

11.17 SA13: QUALITY ASSURANCE

Similar to the activity of project management, the activity of quality assurance forms part of all three dimensions of the resurrection process. The quality assurance manager (a variation of the project manager from the methodological dimension) will be involved in this activity.

11.17.1 ST13-1: MANAGE INTERNAL/EXTERNAL AUDITS

Auditing the process as well as the result of the process of resurrection should be conducted at a specified time within the resurrection process. These audits can be performed on the dissection activity to ensure that the salvageable data is indeed relevant to the organization's work. More importantly though, the audits can ensure that no data that is still important and is legally binding is left behind as a result of the salvaging operation.

11.17.2 ST13-2: POST AUDIT REVIEW

Results from the formal audits carried out need to be logged and analyzed in order to understand areas for improvement. Furthermore, post audit reviews may indicate new areas within the resurrecting system that need further audits.

11.17.3 ST13-3: POST ITERATION REVIEW

The end of each iteration within the resurrection process is a checkpoint where the reporting of most of the work takes place. It is also a point where the scope of the resurrection plan is revisited. Therefore, at the end of each iteration, after all the activities related to reporting are completed, it will be essential to conduct a post iteration review. The purpose is to provide clues as to which areas are going wrong and how they can be improved in the next iteration.

11.17.4 ST13-4: INDEPENDENT REPORTING

This task requires an independent report from the quality assurance manager to the board on the quality of the resurrecting system. The reporting should include studied opinion on the resurrection process itself. It is important to have an independent report from the QA manager, as it will enable the person reporting to present an unbiased view of the process.

11.18 MEASURING THE SOCIOLOGICAL PROCESS

It will be presumptuous to state that the following process metrics measures the size of the sociological process as it is implemented during the resurrection project. This metrics only indicates the way in which the sociological process can be measured. There are a number of caveats and assumptions that need to be considered in reading the following figures.

11.18.1 CAVEATS AND ASSUMPTIONS

- The director and the project manager are considered as the two actors within this metrics. In a real process-thread, there will be more actors than just these two.
- The weighting of these two actors is kept at 100, the same as that of the programmer in the technological process. Needless to say that the

TABLE 11.2
Size of the Sociological Process

Description of the Element	Number of Elements in the Process	Weighting per Element	Total Strength: Units for the Element
Actors	2	100	200
Deliverables	2	100	200
Activities	13	10	130
Tasks	58	20	1160
Total Units	**75**		**1690**

weighting of the actors within this dimension can be increased to reflect the higher costs associated with these actors.

- The two deliverables included in Table 11.2 are abstract. Resurrection teams may be able to work out more deliverables within the sociological dimension. These deliverables still may be abstract (e.g., a highly motivated team), but they should not be ignored in the overall metrics for the process.
- The activities and tasks may have the same weighting as the activities and tasks in the other two dimensions. However, they may be executed in different sequences and may be performed more than once depending on the importance of sociology in the resurrection process.

These caveats and assumptions will change the total strength of the sociological process measured above. However, these changes do not invalidate the model. As "indicative" metrics, they serve the purpose of providing guidance and benchmarks in the estimation process.

11.19 KEY POINTS

1. The sociological dimension of the resurrection process deals with the people who are involved in the resurrection.
2. This dimension is involved in the external interfacing of the company with the society in which it exists.
3. The elements that make up the sociological dimension are actors (project manager, director, and their variations); and activities (staffing, team formation, training, environment factor, motivation, process refinement, usability, outsourcing, advertising, corporate relations, litigation, project management, and quality assurance and their corresponding tasks).
4. The deliverables from this process of the resurrected company and the software with aesthetics are abstract.
5. The activities and tasks within the sociological process iterate with the activities and tasks from the other two dimensions of the resurrection process.

6. Project management and quality assurance continue to be a part of all dimensions of the process, including the sociological dimension. However, the focus here is on reporting the results to the board (internally) and promoting the work externally.

11.20 REFERENCES

1. From foreword by Curtis, B., *Constantine on Peopleware,* Yourdon Press, 1995.

12 Distributed Architecture in Y2K Resurrection

Beyond Year 2000 it is all a global village. And within the high-tech huts of this village lie many artifacts, objects. Some objects are there because they are too big to move, others are small yet play a significant role in maintaining the village. Some are worn out and eaten by a "bug." They are being renovated. The thread that unites these disparately placed objects is distribution. Therefore, call it unification, if you like.

S.D.Pradhan, CEO, Tata Technologies India Ltd.

Abstract   The resurrection process discussed so far presents an approach to recovering from Y2K hits by recreating the affected business. However, process-based business cannot be re-engineered for the new millennium without due consideration to the distributed aspect of processes. Distribution is an integral part of all new system architectures. Distribution of processes has been facilitated by standardized "gluing" tools such as CORBA and DCOM. In this chapter we discuss the importance of distribution with object technology and the role it plays in Y2K resurrection. Distribution is discussed in the context of the architecture of the business solution. A formal architecture is essential in providing not only a system that replaces the Y2K-hit system, but also a system that has the vision of the future. This means the system is able to absorb new technology as well as changing business requirements without breaking the infrastructure of the solution. Finally, some thoughts are presented on distributing components, patterns in distribution, and measuring distribution.

12.1 DISTRIBUTION WITH OBJECTS

Discussion of distribution is fundamental to the architecture of an enterprise in the new millennium. Distribution in the resurrection process was briefly mentioned in Chapter 6. Distribution also appeared as part of activities within the methodological dimension of resurrection. For example, we considered distribution in the architectural activity (Activity MA05, Task MT05-4). At design level we considered Task MT06-5. Thus, we see that activities and tasks related to distribution continue to play an important role in resurrecting the new system by providing the ability to unify the various and disparate elements of a Y2K-hit system. We look at the background of distribution and its advantages in this section, followed by its specific role in Y2K resurrection.

12.1.1 BACKGROUND OF DISTRIBUTION

Distributed computing essentially deals with distributing the functionality of a system across a network. This aspect of computing has become popular and widely accepted by the adoption of a set of specifications for distributed object computing by the Object Management Group (OMG). Applications developed in the new millennium will be based on self-managing components or objects that can operate across disparate networks and operating systems. This has been made possible due to ease and availability of powerful communications infrastructure. The component-based, distributed-object computing model enables the resurrection teams to build an infrastructure that is adaptive to ongoing change and responsive to market opportunities appearing in the new millennium.

12.1.2 DISTRIBUTED OBJECTS

Distributed objects enhance the contribution of object-orientation in the resurrection process. Structurally, the distributed object need not be much different from a nondistributed one. The difference is in the accessibility of the object. A distributed object can be accessed remotely from anywhere on the network. Objects within a distributed application may run on multiple machines and platforms within a network. The user of the object is not concerned with the physical location of the object, he has a unified view of the rest of the network. The object he is using may be on his own machine or on the server or on some other machine. As described later, this characteristic of distributed objects leads to its application in resurrection, wherein the DATE object can be made to reside on a separate server and the rest of the system accesses this object from anywhere on the network.

12.1.3 DISTRIBUTING COMPONENTS

While we have discussed distributing objects, it would be more pertinent to discuss distribution of components rather than objects. Components are able to maximize reuse by combining a set of objects that can be reused as a group and can satisfy a certain business functionality. Distributing the components on a network goes a step farther, in that it encourages dynamic use of a set of objects. The date component that we have discussed in Chapter 9 is not one object, but a set of objects collaborating together to satisfy the date requirements of the system. Instead of simply using the component as a library of classes (amounting to static reuse), if the date component can be kept as an independent executable on a separate machine, the resulting distributed architecture will provide substantial modularization that will increase the quality and amount of reuse. This is true of other business components within the system as well; components that are a set of objects collaborating together to satisfy business functionality.

Distributed components add value to the solution architecture by providing a way of managing complexity and maximizing reuse. This is accomplished by encapsulating the business concepts more completely and placing the final executable components on separate machines depending on the anticipated load and complexity of the components.

12.1.4 ADVANTAGES OF DISTRIBUTION

Distributed applications provide an opportunity to establish and maintain competitive advantage by creating a flexible IT infrastructure. This flexibility enables architects to delineate the applications from their support mechanisms. Since the data is distributed, it is possible to access and update it from anywhere on the network. Furthermore, the hardware capabilities of the organization also are well utilized with the distributed architecture.

Distributed applications also bring together the heterogeneous computing environments of a business, enabling it to leverage its older systems while progressing with the newer applications at the same time. This is important for the resurrecting system that will have the need to integrate salvaged entities with newer development.

Some of the specific advantages of distributed applications include:

- Ability to bring together applications on varied machines and operating systems (e.g., connecting a PC application with a UNIX process or linking it to a mainframe database).
- Share data and information across physically separate machines, as will be the case when businesses are spread globally.
- Synchronize applications running on several machines, especially where a common set of data are being updated from multiple sources.
- Enable changes within areas of an existing application without affecting the rest of the system.
- Maximum utilization of the computing resources across the network by sharing the computing load.

12.1.5 CAVEATS IN DISTRIBUTION

Although distribution has a significant role to play in Y2K resurrection, considerable care needs to be exercised in incorporating distribution in the architectural solution. For example, if all objects within the application are distributed, then the system may encounter performance-related problems. Therefore, a formal requirements modeling exercise is a must before arriving at the distributed architecture for the system. Distribution considerations are expected to contribute in a Y2K resurrection that is experiencing medium to severe hits and where the resurrection team has the time and budgets to produce a detailed architecture. Smaller Y2K problems that can be easily fixed (perhaps due to higher level of preparedness of the organization) need not include distribution.

12.2 ROLE OF DISTRIBUTION IN Y2K

Having briefly mentioned distribution, we now look at the role it plays in Y2K resurrection. First, the business of a resurrecting organization itself may be distributed with the production facilities in one location, the sales and marketing in another location, or country and the accounting function controlled globally from yet another location. It is appropriate to consider distributing the computing processes associated with such physically distributed organization.

However, distribution of a software application need not be restricted to the physical distribution of the organization. There also are a number of technical advantages (e.g., incorporating salvaged entities within the solution, ability of different users to share the same information, leveraging of processing power over the network, and collection of information from disparate sources) in considering distribution in medium to large resurrection exercises. The distributed "way of thinking" can help in the dissection activities. Thus, the ability of distributed approach to isolate the Y2K-affected parts of the system and bring newer solutions together with the salvageable options means that distribution has a vital role to play in completing the resurrection process.

12.2.1 Dissecting a Y2K Hit Using Distribution

In explaining the core philosophy of dissection (Figure 5.1), we discussed the treatment of data and logic for a Y2K-affected application. During the discussion on technology (in Chapter 6), we again considered data and logic separately. During resurrection, we find it beneficial to separate the data from the logic and ascertain the extent of damage to each of these entities within the application. This is shown in Figure 12.1. In practice, the separation of data from logic is not going to be as clear cut as shown in Figure 12.1. However, viewing the Y2K hit separately is a good starting point for taking a distributed approach to dissection itself. Furthermore, by separating the data from the logic, we are able to concentrate on the area of the system where the problem is occurring.

For example, consider the logical problem of incorrect interpretation of data by the system. A date stored in the database as 2000-01-10 may still be read as 1900-01-10. The logic of the system has the problem here. The other problem can be that the date itself may not be stored correctly in the database — it may be stored as

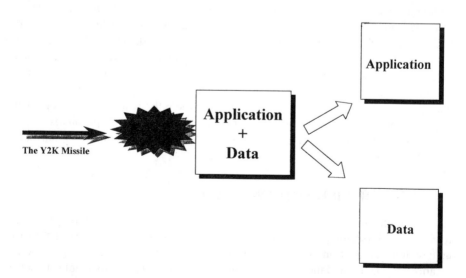

FIGURE 12.1   Y2K hits a system.

00-01-10 (6 digits) instead of 2000-01-10 (8 digits). If the application is "implicitely date conscious" then it will be able to convert the 6-digit date correctly to 8 digits. If it is not, then the data is said to be having a Y2K-related problem.

As shown in Figure 12.1, as soon as the system is hit by the date-related problems, it is essential to start viewing the system from the distribution viewpoint. This involves separating the data from the logic and viewing them independently for the problem. This approach can be extremely helpful when we consider the architecture to the problem. It provides an excellent starting point for the architecture that has to consider the areas of the system that are salvageable, that cannot be converted, and the new applications that need to be integrated with the existing applications. This task concentrates only on the functional aspect of the Y2K problem and does not delve into the hardware or network issues at this stage.

12.2.2 DISTRIBUTING DATE COMPONENTS

Distribution of date component within Y2K resurrection provides the system with the ability to reuse the component from anywhere on the network. Thus, although the actual design and implementation of the date component may be the same as shown in Figure 9.6 (Section 9.10), the difference here is the accessibility of the date component. Since messages are the only means of communication between objects, it is easily possible to distribute the date component anywhere on the system without affecting the resurrecting application that will be accessing this date component.

12.2.3 CREATING "OBJECT WRAPPERS" AROUND LEGACY DATE CODE

In addition to separating the date object and placing it on a separate server, some resurrection work will benefit by simply wrapping the date component as it exists in the "hit" application. Of course, the area of the application that is affected by the Y2K problem will need some modification (Activity TA03). However, the modified code encapsulated by an object wrapper provides a viable alternative in salvaging the affected application and data. The advantage in wrapping the legacy code with objects is that it allows the resurrection team to represent each entity within the legacy code as one object. Thus, an account and a customer entity can be represented as an object, and so can the date entity. Once such wrapping is accomplished, it allows the legacy code to participate in the distributed object environment by providing a "message interface" to the legacy object.

Furthermore, situations in resurrection, wherein the date logic is so tightly bound together with the application that it is impossible to separate the date component from the rest of the application, will benefit by provision of a wrapper around the affected code. When the date logic is wrapped within an object, not only do the existing applications benefit, but the new applications also deal with only the interface of the object and don't have to worry about the underlying code.

Finally, a single object may be able to represent information derived from multiple legacy systems. Therefore, providing object wrappers to Y2K-affected applications and placing those objects on a server provides a common reference

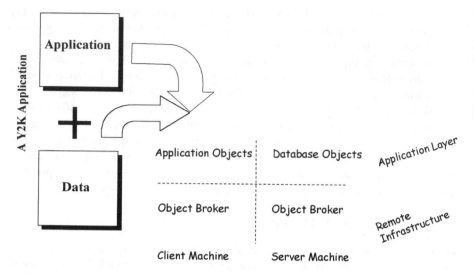

FIGURE 12.2   Distributing a resurrecting application.

point for all applications to access these objects. If the new applications still continue to have date-related problems, it is easier to localize these problems as they will all be restricted to the logic wrapped by the object. A concentrated effort can be launched to either solve the problem or to rewrite the legacy code underneath.

12.2.4 DISTRIBUTING THE APPLICATION

Once the Y2K-hit application has been viewed in two parts (data and logic) and the areas of the system that can be salvaged are identified, the resurrecting application will be bringing the salvaged and new data and application together to form the application objects and the data objects as shown in Figure 12.2. During the initial iteration of a distributed solution, it will be enough to categorize the solution objects as follows:

- Objects that reside on the client machine and primarily deal with the logic of the system.
- Objects that reside on the server machine and primarily deal with the storage and retrieval of data.

12.2.5 FURTHER DISTRIBUTING THE APPLICATION

The client-server approach is a restricted approach to distributed computing. While in a client-server architecture, the application used by the user is on the client machine and the computing-intensive application is on the server. In case of a fully distributed computing architecture, the location of the application is of no consequence. Furthermore, a fully distributed *n*-tiered application will be able to accommodate a large number of external systems, databases, and third-party applications within the overall architecture of the system. An example of a distributed architecture that can be used in the resurrection process is shown in Figure 12.3. While the client applications are shown as being Web-based, it is not essential.

12.3 SYSTEM ARCHITECTURE IN Y2K

In order to incorporate distribution in the Y2K resurrection, it will be essential to consider the architecture of the solution through a rigorous and formal process. Importance of the system architecture in the Y2K solution derives from the fact that the architecture not only encompasses the existing organization of the applications but also the "visionary" aspect of the solution. Therefore, discussion of the system architecture is carried out in further detail here within the context of distribution.

12.3.1 DEFINING ARCHITECTURE

An architecture is a high-level description of the functional responsibilities of a system. Its aim is to capture and convey the general structure of the applications within the organization's software solution. Architecture for a system is different from its design in that it deals with the overall building blocks of the system. It does not go down to the level of class designs or flow charts. Since an architecture defines the relationship between various components of a system, it does not worry about the specific implementation of those components. For example, a system architecture may specify the database component needed for the solution and the place where this component will fit in the overall solution. However, the nitty-gritty of how the table joins are conducted to satisfy a query, which will be of little interest at this stage.

At a technical level, the architecture defines the tools and technologies used and how they are put together in the solution. For example, the architecture will specify the objects that encapsulate various databases and how they are glued together using the middleware components. Architecture also will discuss the tools that can be used in the design and development of the solution.

At the business level, the architecture describes the content, behavior and interaction of business objects. This leads to specification of the framework for the business objects (e.g., the roles, events, and business rules associated with the objects in the solution).

12.3.2 PROGRESS IN ARCHITECTURE

In early designs, where distribution was not a part of the solution, the applications and data resided on the same machine. As the "architecture" of these applications progressed, data and logic got separated. However, the front-end of the old legacy applications was still the "dumb" terminal whose primary responsibility was to display the data being processed by the "intelligent" and capacious back-end machine. With the advances in networking, not only was it possible to keep the data separate from the application that was using the data, but it was also possible to perform certain computations by the front-end of the application. With this ability of separating the data and the application came the era of "client-server." Initially,

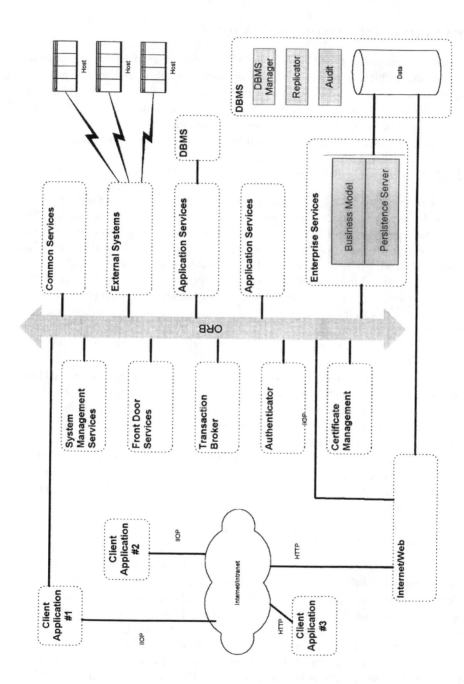

FIGURE 12.3 A fully distributed application.[1]

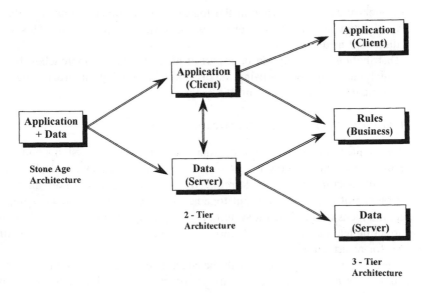

FIGURE 12.4 Progress in system architecture.

we separated only the application and the data, resulting in a 2-tier architecture. This was further followed by separation of the business rules and storing them elsewhere. Essentially, it resulted in a 3-tier architecture, with a glue putting them all together (Figure 12.4). Finally, as shown in earlier Figure 12.3, a fully distributed *n*-tiered architecture could be produced using the middleware glue that would bring together the data and the logic, as well as external applications.

12.3.3 ARCHITECTURAL APPROACH

In order to create a well-defined *n*-tiered architecture, it is essential to follow a formal approach to creating the architecture. During resurrection, this formal approach to creating the system architecture takes place during the methodological dimension of the process. A good architectural approach combines the knowledge of the architect with his practical experience in order to produce the right architecture for the solution. There are a number of ways in which the architectural solution can be approached.

- Top-down vs. bottom-up approach to architecture, wherein the system is viewed from the top and divided into subsystems and components or its components are made up of reusable objects that are already designed and coded. This was discussed in MT05-2.
- Vertical vs. horizontal slicing (or breaking up) of the system — not only from development viewpoint, but also from the maintainability and reusability of the architecture in future developments. This was discussed in MT05-5.

- Logical vs. physical, wherein the logical or conceptual approach to the architecture of the system precedes the physical architecture. This is discussed next.
- Distribution — which can be a part of all of the above approaches, but which puts emphasis on using the distributed technology in order to gain advantages discussed later in this chapter.

12.3.4 LOGICAL VS. PHYSICAL ARCHITECTURE

When the architectural activities are dealing with the major subsystems and components of the system and how they are being put together, they are dealing with the logical architecture. The logical architecture contains details of how the major building blocks of the system are put together. By providing an understanding of the building blocks of the Y2K-hit system, drawing a logical architecture also helps the resurrection team to narrow the location of the date problem and in formulating a strategy for resurrection.

The physical architecture deals with the concrete entities of the solution. Therefore, it translates the logical architecture of the system into building blocks like databases, middleware, and application objects. It also depicts the interfaces that the solution will need with the legacy applications or other existing components. The physical architecture also deals with performance and security issues, as well as operating systems and communication methods that would affect them.

In many cases, the system's logical architecture is heavily influenced by the physical context in which the system must operate. This is particularly true of distributed systems. Hence it is important to consider the physical architecture along with the logical architecture of the system at a high level.

12.3.5 ARCHITECTURAL ISSUES IN Y2K RESURRECTION

Whatever is the architectural approach chosen for the resurrecting system, it will have to consider the following architectural issues in proposing a Y2K architectural solution.

- Consideration of the databases that will be used by the resurrecting system — this would include the size (data storage), speed (performance), multiple simultaneous updates (concurrency), and related issues.
- Reusability of the current architecture in future development — especially considerations of granularity in the architecture that would enable reuse of components over a number of projects.
- Platforms and operating systems that would be used in development as well as in production.
- Communications methods — including interprocess communications and their underlying infrastructure.
- Interfaces with other systems within the domain — especially of importance when only a part of the systems is affected by Y2K and, therefore, the organization is operating two systems for a short time. Interfaces also

are important when the organization is dealing with a business partner that has been hit by Y2K, as it is through the external interfaces that the effect of the Y2K problem travelled from one organization to another.

- Security of the software environment — architecture issues would consider in detail the security and access to the network from inside as well as outside the organization.
- Integration of salvageable data and applications as a result of the resurrection work — once the salvageable data is converted, the resulting output data should be compatible with the new applications.
- Due consideration to the constraints and exclusions within the system — this would include issues like specifying the operating systems or database that should *not* be used, or the communication protocols that are *outside* the organizational standards.

12.3.6 RELATING THE ARCHITECTURE TO THE REQUIREMENTS

Considering the architecture of the system independent of the requirements of the resurrecting system will not lead to a visionary architecture. This is so because the initial attempt at architecting the solution has to consider the requirements at the logical level and the constraints to the solution at the physical level.

The resurrection process specifies the requirements for the resurrecting system through the activities of requirements modeling (MA04) and solution design (MA06). These requirements are the description of what the user wants from the system. However, the user of the system is not concerned about the way in which the system is put together. The architecture of the system is neither the responsibility nor of interest to the user.

The architect of the system, however, ensures that the architecture of the system relates to the requirements. The requirements should be allowed to influence the architecture of the system. One way of relating the architecture of the system to the requirements is by stepping through the use cases and scenarios specified by the users step by step, and ensuring that the system architecture is able to hold itself together as the use cases and scenarios are satisfied. During resurrection, there also would be an additional need to incorporate the salvageable items (resulting from dissection) into the architecture.

12.4 MIDDLEWARE IN DISTRIBUTED ARCHITECTURE

As mentioned in the technology chapter (Chapter 6), middleware is the "gluing" technology that resides between business applications and the underlying layer of heterogeneous platforms and network protocols. It is the middleware standards that have enabled elements of distributed applications to operate across network links despite variations in the underlying communication protocols, operating systems, hardware, system architectures, databases, and application services.

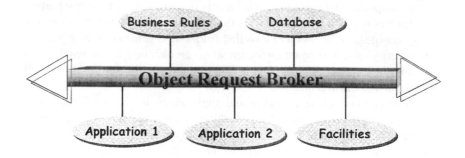

The ORB extends a 3-Tier Architecture to essentially an
open-ended multi-tiered Architecture

FIGURE 12.5   Role of middleware in distributed architecture for Y2K processes.

12.4.1 DESCRIBING AN OBJECT REQUEST BROKER (ORB)

The mechanism that enables objects to interact in a distributed environment is called
the Object Request Broker (ORB). As shown in Figure 12.5, application and database
objects are able to locate and activate each other as well as other objects on the
network, irrespective of the processor and the programming language in which they
have been coded. Since the implementation details of the interacting objects are hidden
from one another, an ORB enables the architectural solution of a resurrecting system
to focus entirely on the messages between objects. The developers are shielded from
the underlying complexity of the messaging system. Objects continue to reside on
their own machines and are oblivious to their users. Thus, using a standardized ORB,
technical and business objects not only interact but also continue to grow with the
growing needs of the business (as is expected of the resurrecting business in the new
millennium). If we are able to successfully segregate the data and the logic problem
of a Y2K-hit system during the dissection work, we may be able to incorporate the
resultant salvageable entities easily within the overall solution using the ORB.

In order to make this interaction between varying objects possible, the OMG
undertook the task of specifying the standards for the ORB. A standardized ORB
would make it possible for objects written by different vendors across the networks
and operating systems to talk with each other easily. This has resulted in the well-
known standard — the Common Object Request Broker Architecture (CORBA) that
is a distributed object computing middleware standard defined by OMG. Thus, the
CORBA standard would be a specialized case of the ORB shown in Figure 12.5.

In addition to the OMG standard, Microsoft has also specified and produced a
Distributed Component Object Model (DCOM). We examine these two middlewares
in the context of a distributed architecture for the resurrecting systems.

12.4.2 CORBA ADVANTAGES IN RESURRECTION

CORBA is a widely accepted standard for distributed computing that can provide
components within the resurrecting system the much needed advantages of location

transparency, activation transparency, language independence, and platform neutrality. CORBA achieves this by providing an Interface Definition Language (IDL). IDL has become an international standard providing common notation for software interfaces that are used by various components across the network. It is the IDL that will provide the mechanism through which integration of salvageable entities within the Y2K legacy systems and the new functionalities of the resurrecting system (implemented using object technology) will take place.

Thus, using CORBA the resurrection architecture can define a combination of new and salvaged software components that can be reused and shared between applications. The internal structure of the component remains encapsulated while the object presents a well-defined interface. This results in reduction of complexity in implementing the newly resurrecting application. This also results in improved quality as once a component is implemented, tested, and accepted in the solution, it can be reused (invoked) without further need for testing from anywhere on the network. Due to corresponding advantages of time saving and leveraging of programming skills, this has a potential of reducing the time for development.

The advantages of distribution and its application to Y2K is further discussed with reference to CORBA standards below.

- CORBA is supported by more than 600 organizations (including hardware, networking and software companies) and is accepted as an industry standard. This enables "compliant" vendors to offer various products that can be used by a large cross-section of users.
- CORBA provides integration with wide-ranging technologies such as languages, databases, messaging systems, user interfaces, and so on. For example, scripting languages such as VisualBasic easily can be used to implement user interfaces that may have a more complex backend database.
- The communication protocol for CORBA, Internet Inter-ORB Protocol (IIOP), ensures that distributed objects built using different CORBA products also are able to communicate with each other. This provides advantages in resurrection, wherein the resurrection teams may want to use different CORBA-based products for their work. Furthermore, software bridges are able to facilitate communications between CORBA objects and objects developed using Microsoft's DCOM technology (discussed next).
- While the core level of CORBA standards are applicable across all types of applications, specialized implementations are provided in areas such as real time and embedded systems. This will be helpful in resurrection situations that combine different implementations in order to provide a complete solution.
- CORBA supports both static and dynamic usage that can be used in the solution architecture for the resurrecting system.
- The Web-based clients and servers can play an important role in a Web-based resurrecting application, wherein they can be used in Java-based implementations of CORBA.
- The IDL of CORBA is mapped separately to each programming language. This allows programmers the ease of usage in the language of their choice.

CORBA supports most popular languages that are likely to be used in resurrection work.

- CORBA is based on an open, published specification. It is implemented on and supported by numerous hardware and operating system platforms. Therefore, it is possible to build the objects on one platform and deploy them on other supported platforms.
- Since the components within CORBA interact only through their interfaces (which remain the same), developers are able to modify their internal implementations without affecting other applications. This has a definite advantage during resurrection, if there is a large amount of salvaged data that can be made accessible through an interface.
- CORBA protects your investment in existing systems. You can encapsulate a legacy application, module, or entry point in a CORBA IDL wrapper that defines an interface to the legacy code. This object wrapper makes the legacy code interoperable with other objects in a distributed computing environment.
- Because of features such as encryption, authentication, and authorization, CORBA is able to offer security by protecting data and controlling access of users to components and their services. Resurrection may occasionally prioritize applications for resurrection. A distributed architecture will enable the resurrection team to recreate the new applications and implement them one at a time. Thus, a CORBA IDL wrapper not only integrates salvaged entities from the Y2K-hit application with the new applications, but also provides integration for new applications as they are being released.

12.4.3 DCOM AND ITS USE IN RESURRECTION

As mentioned in Chapter 6, DCOM is the distributed version of the Component Object Model (COM) that enables objects in a Microsoft environment to interact with each other. If the Y2K resurrection process is taking place in a Microsoft environment, then DCOM will have an edge as a communication protocol between objects, as compared with CORBA.

Some of the issues and advantages related to use of DCOM in a Y2K resurrection process are

- Capitalizing on COM investment. If the organization already has developers who are familiar with COM and the Microsoft environment, then it will be easier for them to start applying this knowledge to distributed applications designed and implemented using the DCOM glue.
- Reusability — All components developed using DCOM will be reusable in all future applications that are produced in similar domain. Thus, although a distributed DATE component may initially be designed to handle the Y2K resurrection, all future applications will be able to reuse that component.

- COM components can be created using many different languages and tools (e.g., Visual C++, Visual Basic, and Micro Focus COBOL). These components are integrated using the DCOM protocol. Thus, DCOM helps in bringing together products of various languages, which is a vitally important feature in resurrection work.
- DCOM is able to provide an efficient and effective mechanism to ensure smooth communication between components on the network (e.g., through DCOM's pinging protocol).
- Resurrection will have to cater to growth in business and, therefore, a corresponding growth in demands on the software systems. As the number of users and their transactions on the system increase, DCOM applications will be able to grow not only from the functionality viewpoint, but also growing in terms of increasing processing power through increased number of processors and their functioning together.
- In producing a distributed architecture using DCOM, if the architect is able to ascertain the components of the resurrecting system that will be heavily loaded or that are likely to be the "bottleneck" for the system, these components can be deployed on powerful and dedicated machines. DCOM also supports dynamic redeployment, wherein a change in the location of the component is all that is required in order to deploy the component on a separate server. While initially we may run many components on the same machine, by using DCOM they can be distributed over multiple machines as the processing demands grow.
- DCOM facilitates sophisticated connection management protocol by providing automatic coordination among many COM-based custom protocols for multiple applications running on the same machine. This means that instead to receiving one control message (or ping) per application, DCOM would allow a single coordinated ping for all applications. This would significantly reduce the network overhead and, as a result, may play an important part in the networking activities (TA08) of the resurrection process.
- DCOM provides network stability by being able to re-establish connection if failed networks recover within a set time-out interval. Thus, DCOM exhibits support from fault tolerance that would be useful in a resurrecting system.
- Using the discretionary security mechanisms that enable developers of the system to configure their own security settings for each of the components developed, DCOM components can be selectively made available to the calling applications. For example, the DATE component might be commonly required by all application users, whereas components that deal with company tax calculations may be required only by a select group of users. The list of users and the corresponding components they can access can be configured using DCOM tools or programs written by the developers.
- DCOM enables access of any transport protocol including TCP/IP, UDP, IPX/SPX, and NetBIOS. Furthermore, it also provides a security

framework on all of these protocols. However, use of this feature would depend on the protocol that is used in the resurrecting system.

- DCOM is able to implement multithreading and concurrency control for distributed components by simply using the services available on multiple platforms. This includes locating and deploying components, invoking methods for components, and providing security-related protocols for the distributed components. Incorporation of these features in the resurrecting system will result in a more sophisticated use of the same functionality that was there in the original system.

12.5 MEASURING DISTRIBUTION

Among other advantages of metrics and measurement in a software system, measuring distribution of the resurrecting system can provide indication of complexity as well as performance. One of the basic measures of a distributed application is the number of objects being handled by the system. However, the count of the number of objects depend on the classes, and the count of the number of classes differ depending on the type of middleware being used. Once the objects per class count is sorted out, we are able to calculate the classes per nodes and class allocation ratio. The usage of a class determines whether it is a frequently used class or not. Hence, by the usage and the class counting rules, we can calculate the frequently referenced class per node metric. These measures can be very helpful in determining the complexity of the distributed architecture as well as the load on the system. Once appropriate figures indicating the complexity and load on the distributed system are arrived at, appropriate action can be taken to redistribute the load by moving components to different servers or by increasing the hardware capacity of the servers and so on.

In order to apply metrics to distribution, we start by considering each machine as a physical node in the distributed object-oriented application. The Nodes Per System (NPS) would provide a physical count of the number of machines used in the system. A distributed application would have two types of nodes: client workstations that are used to communicate with the users and the remaining machines that can are considered as server machines. One of the measures is the ratio of the client nodes/server nodes which indicates the number of "users" of the system compared with the "suppliers."

Measuring the number of objects loaded on a distributed application also is interesting as it does not directly follow from the number of classes deployed on the network. In a distributed application (unlike a normal nondistributed one), the number of objects instantiated depends on how the client classes are requesting the services from the servers. A distributed resurrecting application developed in Java and CORBA will end up with an ORB object for each request of the client application. Thus, a class that uses a remote class will create two objects. The server class that is using CORBA to communicate with the client class will create three objects: the object instance of the server class, the ORB object to handle networking jobs, and the servant object to carry out the services requested by the client. Thus, the relationship of the number of objects to their corresponding classes would be as follows: the class that does not require or provide remote services is counted as 1, the class that requests remote services is count as 2, and the class that provides remote services is count as 3.

There are three types of servers in DCOM: inprocess server, local server, and the remote server. The in-process server is a Dynamic-Link Library (DLL) and is running inside the client application. The client can directly call the server object's method, so the number of class of the client class which uses an in-process server is 1. Since the in-process server will create the server object only, the number of class for the in-process server is 1 as well. However, when a client requests a service from either a local server or a remote server, a client proxy is created, so the number of class for a client which requests services from any server other than in-process is 2. The local server or the remote server requires a server stub to handle the communication with the client, hence the number of class for these types of server is 2.

Since the object-oriented middlewares do not affect the functionality of the server object, the number of methods in a server class are not affected by the underlying middleware. For example, a savings account server class can have three public methods: balance enquiry, deposit, and withdraw. The server class uses this method because it has to provide services for the client to inquire or change the balance of the saving account. Hence, irrespective of the type of middleware being used, these methods must exist in the server class.

The number of objects created from a class depends on the underlying middleware, but, when we consider the relation between two peer classes, we want to know whether or not they have a client/server relation. Even when we are counting the number of request statements in a class, we are counting the number of the client/server relations that exist in the class. Since the existence of the client/server relation depends on the structure of the application system, the coupling/performance metrics does not depend on what object-oriented middleware is chosen to provide the distributed environment.

These metrics mentioned above can be further expanded depending on the way in which they are intended to be used within the resurrection process. Each resurrection process will be unique and will require different types of metrics. However, the underlying theme of measuring distribution within the resurrecting system remains the same, and that is to understand the complexity and load on the system to enable efficient and effective redistribution of the components.

12.6 KEY POINTS

1. Advantages and caveats in using distribution with object technology were discussed.
2. Distribution has a role to play in Y2K resurrection. This role includes dissecting a Y2K-hit application by viewing the data and the logic separately, creating a distributed DATE component, creating "object wrappers" around the legacy date code, and so on.
3. Incorporating distribution in a resurrecting solution requires carefully designed system architecture. A formal architecture was defined and

    described and was especially related to the requirements for the new system.

4. Role of middleware as the "glue" that puts various elements on the resurrecting system together was discussed. Specifically, CORBA and DCOM were described.

5. Some metrics for a distributed object system were described, with an aim of enhancing them further as the actual resurrection process progresses.

12.7 NOTES

Thanks to Cindy Hsiao for her comments on DCOM and CORBA, Richard Cheuk for discussions on distributed metrics, and Kevin Lun for his ideas on distribution and legacy systems. All three individuals have written Master's thesis in the area of distribution at the University of Technology, Sydney.

12.8 REFERENCES

1. From Object Oriented Pty Ltd's Reference Architecture; see www.oopl.com.au.

13 Processes from Ashes

None. I also did not have any previous experience of how to make babies, when I became a father for the first time.

The Author (B. Unhelkar) in reply to a query,
"What's your previous experience of resurrection?"

Abstract   Until now, we have considered in detail the three dimensions of the Y2K resurrection process and the role of distribution in resurrection. In this chapter we discuss how this knowledge and understanding can be applied in creating and following a practical resurrection process from the ashes of the Y2K explosion. Since we have not yet crossed the Y2K hump, we may not know the practicalities of all aspects of the resurrection process beyond the Year 2000. This does not take anything away from the resurrection process, as it is targeted precisely at situations in the new millennium which are new to each and every one of us. In this chapter we identify the business processes that are hit, refer to the relevant resurrection activities and tasks, and create new business processes for the resurrecting organization. We consider example processes from the payroll and banking domain.

13.1 RESURRECTING FROM THE ASHES

The three dimensions of the resurrection process together with the preliminary activities comprise the overall outline for resurrecting from the ashes of a Y2K disaster. Herein, we consider the application of this resurrection framework in practical situations. These practical situations will differ for different business domains. They also will differ in their scope of application of the resurrection process. For example, in some resurrection projects it may be necessary to use only a small number of activities and tasks within a single iteration. Other situations, where the organization has been affected by the Y2K problem in all aspects of its functioning, the entire resurrection process will apply. Furthermore, in a full-scale resurrection, the sequence in which activities and tasks are applied will change depending on the situation. In practice, even the same case studies as described in this chapter may apply the resurrection process in a different sequence. Thus, understanding of and experience with the resurrection process will play a crucial role in the way in which business processes are resurrected from the ashes of Y2K disasters.

In the earlier chapters, we had considered a number of factors that would influence the timing and manner in which an organization will be hit (Chapter 2), and the way in which it will resurrect (Chapter 5). Although January 1, 2000 is meant to be the "crucial" date in the Y2K saga, we accept that many systems will be affected by the problem before (and after) the D-day. Therefore, in this chapter, we concentrate on the application of the resurrection process irrespective of the precise date when the system is affected.

13.2 THE RESURRECTION REPOSITORY

The theoretical aspects of the resurrection process span the three dimensions of the process, as discussed in this book. When we come closer to applying the process, we will be faced with many options to choose from. The resurrection repository provides this "typical" list of options that will be available to the resurrection team during the resurrection process. This repository will include the details of all entities that are discussed during the resurrection process. It also will contain, at more technical level, the details of possible technological entities (such as languages and databases) that the resurrection teams will choose from. Although the repository provides a list of resurrection entities that we have discussed, additional entities from practical resurrection projects can be added to this list.

13.2.1 PROCESS REPOSITORY

The process repository lists the possible options that are related to the resurrection process itself. It provides an indication or a checklist of the various items to be considered by the resurrecting organization. Inspecting the process repository will lead to a complete picture of the enterprise as it is hit by Y2K and at the same time it will also provide a high-level view of the approach to be taken for resurrection. Items can be selected from the example choices provided here (Table 13.1) and, optionally, a separate resultant repository can be created for the specific organization.

TABLE 13.1
The Resurrection Process Entities' Repository

The Resurrection Process Entity	Example Choices (Informative Only)
Self assessment of organization	Ignorant, callous, dependent, rigid, hierarchical, coarse, bulky, unhedged
Level of preparedness	Red, orange, yellow, green, blue, gold
Position in sequence of events	Where was the problem discovered?
Criticality of affected systems	
Intensity of explosion	Mild, medium, severe
Scope	Small, medium, large
Iterations	Initial, major, final
Preliminary activities	Section 5.4, Chapter 5
Technological activities	Table 7.1, Chapter 7
Methodological activities	Table 9.1, Chapter 9
Sociological activities	Table 11.1, Chapter 11

TABLE 13.2
The Resurrection Products Repository*

The Resurrection Domain	Example Choices (Informative Only)
Technology	
Front-end development work	Visual C++, Smalltalk, VisualBasic, Eiffel
Component-based technologies	ActiveX, Java
Middleware technologies	CORBA, COM/DCOM, RPC/DCE
Database products	SQLServer, Oracle, Ingress, Sybase, Access (for small-scoped resurrection)
Connectivity in databases	ODBC, JDBC
Development/deployment platforms	Windows 95/NT, IIP-Unix
ERP solutions	SAP, PeopleSoft, Oracle Financials
Dissection and salvage	CA-Impact/2000, System Vision Inventory, SmartApps/2000, VisualAge for COBOL, etc.
Methodologies	
OO Methodologies (third generation)	UML, OPEN
CASE tools for methodologies	Select, Rational Rose, MetaEdit,
Distributed architectures	IONA Orbix, OLTP/Tuxedo
Testing and QA	SQATeamTest, AutoTester CASE-SIR (test results record/analysis)
Project management	Microsoft Project, Mentor Assistant Tool (MAT), CASE-WhiteClouds
Sociology	
Useability	Collaborative Usability Inspection tools (Constantine and Lockwood)
Communications	LotusMail, Internet Explorer, Netscape Browser
Games	CaseDigital–GameSuite

* All registered trademarks are acknowledged.

13.2.2 PRODUCT REPOSITORY

The product repository (Table 13.2) serves a purpose similar to the process repository. However, instead of providing a status of the organization the product repository provides a technological checklist from which selections can be made for the software solution. Once again, this list is not exhaustive and it will continue to grow as our experience with the resurrection process grows. However, this product repository provides a list of items that may apply to the various technological, methodological and sociological needs of the resurrection process.

13.3 PAYROLL PROCESS

Having considered the process and product repositories for the resurrection process, we now apply our overall understanding of resurrection to a practical situation.

Herein is an example of a payroll process within a large academic institution with more than 5000 employees. This payroll process is affected by the Y2K problem. We consider the Y2K hit and the subsequent actions by the organization within the framework of the resurrection process.

13.3.1 Existing Process

The existing payroll process of the organization is a manual process in which time sheets are inputted using a centralized data entry function and computations and printing is carried out on a mainframe machine. There are two payruns every month — on the 15th of the month followed by the one at the end of the month. During these payruns, a series of batch jobs (overnight) are run in order to calculate various aspects of the payroll for each employee.

The payroll system is written in COBOL and uses a set of indexed files in the background as a database. The programmers have "hand-coded" data storage and retrieval routines. Senior management of the institution had considered upgrading the payroll system many times in the past. However, the application was satisfactorily performing the job of accepting the inputs, calculating the pay and the leave balances, crediting the bank accounts of employees by sending checks to respective banks, and so on. Therefore, the decision making related to upgrading the system did not have the necessary urgency.

The data within the payroll database has two major aspects to it. First is the relatively stable data related to the employee including the name, address (postal, residential), employee ID, bank account details, family status (in order to calculate tax to be deducted), and so on. This data remains relatively stable over many runs of the payroll. The second or dynamic part of the data is related to the specific payroll run. This data include the amount to be paid, the tax deducted, the special payments, the leave accrued to date, and so on. This data continue to change with every payroll.

13.3.2 Effect of Y2K Hit

The effect of Y2K on the application and, hence, on the organization, came in an unexpected way. The organization had undergone considerable Y2K testing and had assured itself that its applications will be able to handle the switching over of the system to the new millennium. While the static data and logic of the payroll remained free from any problems, it was the dynamic part of the data and logic that was affected. The specific way in which the leave balance calculation was affected is described below.

The algorithm for accruing the leave balances would subtract today's date from the date of the previous payroll run. Leave was calculated at the rate of 1/365 per day of work, or 1/366 in case of a leap year. As it crossed the Y2K hump (January 1), not only did the system logic have a problem in subtracting the dates in order to arrive at the number of days in a payroll, it also treated the New Year as turn of the century and, therefore, treated it as not having an extra day in February. However, as discussed in Section 1.4.4, Year 2000 is indeed a leap year. This resulted in the wrong calculation of leave balances and, in many cases, no calculation at all.

The problem with the leave balances escalated as, during the Christmas and New Year holidays, many employees had applied for and taken leaves. This put additional computational load on the batch jobs that were calculating the outstanding leaves. Thus, the end result of the error in calculating the leave balances, especially when many employees had taken leave, meant that the employees could not figure out their leave balances.

Furthermore, because of the industrial relations legislation, the organization was required to keep certain funds aside as a percentage of the leave balances accrued by the employees. Due to incorrect computation of leave balances of a large number of employees, the organization was going to be forced to keep aside an amount larger than legally necessary for the accrued leave balances.

13.3.3 THE RESURRECTION PROCESS

The organization was neither ignorant nor callous (at this stage, these terms can be drawn from the Process Repository) in its approach to Y2K. Sufficient testing had been done in the lead up to the Year 2000 and the application had passed most of the tests. Although the in-house written legacy application had performed well until now, the need to move forward with a new payroll was being felt across the entire organization. As mentioned before, the senior management of the organization had considered many times to move away from the legacy weight of the payroll application. However, it was unable to move forward with a new application because of its "rigidity" in decisionmaking as well as in implementing the decisions.

When hit by Y2K, the first action by the organization was to ascertain its level of preparedness. The management of the organization discovered that it was at a reasonable level of preparedness for the Y2K hit. The Y2K bug had been investigated in detail and the IT department also had attempted detailed testing and fixing of problems related to the bug. Because of its testing and prevention effort, it already had a group of people who were experienced in working with Y2K. Based on this understanding, the organization felt it was somewhere between the yellow and green level of preparedness. The resultant intensity of the explosion was mild to medium, as it was only the leave balance area (within the dynamic data within every payrun) of the application that was affected. Had the main payroll run that calculates the pay amount been affected, the intensity would have been more severe than the current one.

Instead of fixing the leave balance calculation, the organization decided to use the opportunity of being hit by Y2K to resurrect. Following were the considerations in its approach to resurrection:

- The activity of Dissection (TA01) was used in identifying and logging the details of the problem occurring within the application.
- Nomination of the resurrection champion was swift — being aware of the need to resurrect the system, the organization did not loose time in considering the quick fix options.
- All resources that were used earlier during the Y2K prevention exercise were committed to the resurrection work.

- The scope of the resurrection was not large, yet it was detailed enough to enable the organization to derive the strategic benefits from the resurrection exercise.
- Internal sociological factors had to be handled with care.

Dissection of the affected application verified the initial interpretation that the pay amounts were still calculated correctly but the leave balances were in error. The resurrection champion also realized that the holiday season had just passed. The next larger need for holiday calculations was going to be around April (perhaps due to Easter). Thus, it was possible to maintain a manual system for the 3 to 4 months that were needed to get through the major iteration of the resurrection process and get the basic application up and running.

Thus, the organization decided to keep its current payroll going for the time needed to resurrect. The calculation and accrual of leave balances was shifted to a manual approach for the duration of the resurrection. Since the original programs written were large and bulky (the organization was "coarse"), it was not possible to separate the leave balances module as an entity. It was decided to keep the leave balances as they were, but ignore the calculations. The real leave balance calculations were switched onto a manual system. The resurrection champion also ensured that sufficient "temp" staff was brought in to assist the departmental managers to handle the manual leave balance system.

Given the relatively short time that was available for the resurrection, the activities of alternative evaluation (MA01) resulted in the decision to purchase a third-party payroll application. Once again, because of its higher level of preparedness, the organization had already considered a few packages as prospective applications for its payroll. Therefore, it was easier to shortlist and select the application that would suit the requirements of the academic institution. Since the organization already had an existing Web infrastructure, it was decided to purchase and customize a solution that was Web-based. Furthermore, because of the additional capabilities of the package, it was proposed that the package be augmented to include an "interactive" human relations (HR) facility that will accept details and answer many queries related to HR. This would result in a number of strategic benefits to the organization, akin to the ones discussed in Chapter 3.

Thus, with the new technology that was to be used in the customizing and deploying the system, it was envisaged that the resurrecting application would allow direct real time access to, and updating of, data from the core business systems using the Internet. Furthermore, not only were the employees to be allowed to view their salary and personnel information but, for the relatively stable data like the address and the bank account details, they could change it as well. Thus, the system would allow the employees some control over their own information by allowing certain changes to be made.

This approach was in line with the strategy for human resources management to shift toward enabling employees and managers to take greater responsibility for managing their own HR information and processes. The package selected for the purpose would enable the academic institution to deploy a system that would eventually become an "employee self-service" system.

The new application was able to use the hardware (e.g., desktop machines) and network (already being used for intranet and Internet), additional needs for hardware (e.g., for the payroll server) were well within the resurrection budget. Because of the package procurement and customization work, it was not necessary to go through the architecture and solution design activities. Instead, the focus was on the requirements modeling (MA04) activity. These included documenting the existing requirements of the payroll, augmenting it with the newer requirements and describing new business objects. The new database (resulting from the activity TA06) was a part of the package procured. Therefore, the major work related to the database was that of conversion of the salvaged data. A part of the team that was earlier involved in the prevention work, was now involved in converting the data to the new database. Quality assurance and project management activities continued throughout the resurrection process.

One of the major concerns to the senior management was the internal effect the Y2K problem was going to have on the morale of the employees. By organizing judicious training (SA03) for all employees on the use of the new package, ensuring that the employee objectives were in sync with the company objectives (SA05), and highlighting the resultant improvement in the process (SA06), the resurrection champion ensured that the sociological aspect of resurrection was properly handled.

13.3.4 PAYROLL IN THE NEW MILLENNIUM

By resurrecting from a Y2K hit, the organization has now produced a payroll system that has the salvaged data from the previous application and the functionality of the new system. In addition to the efficiency in the business processes, the new application also has brought a culture change within the organization that is advantageous to it in the new millennium. Some of these advantages include:

- Payslips and leave balances are no longer printed and distributed as they used to be before the system was hit. Thus, employees no longer wait for the physical arrival of payslips but, instead, log on to the system and access their payslips.
- Because of the "configurability" of the new package, the original problem of leave-balance calculation was avoided. The calculation of leave accrued per day did not go through the original algorithm of subtracting dates. Instead, a more robust algorithm was available in the new package, which was thoroughly tested to ensure that it did calculate the correct leave balances.
- Employees also are able to access and project their leave balances — this ensures that the employees and their managers have a correct figure for leave balances before leaves are approved. This is highly advantageous when leaves are approved in advance.
- Employees are generally able to access their payslips and leave data from computers in their own offices. Those employees with dialup facilities are able to access and download the data from their homes. Also, Internet

kiosks are provided by the organization at suitable locations (canteen, library, etc.) to enable convenient access, especially for those employees who do not yet have their own computers within the organization.

- Although the data related to the payruns are still updated twice a month (when the payruns are conducted), progressively updated data can be viewed by employees as many times as they want. Furthermore, the net-based access implies that the payroll and leave information is now available at any time of day or night. Thus, employees are able to access their data almost round the clock and on any day (including weekends), resulting in considerable convenience and timesaving.
- Those in need of a printed payslip (e.g., in order to provide proof of income for renting a home) are still able to do so by using the printer setup in the kiosks.
- Employees are able to access current, as well as past, payslips and leave balances through the payroll application. This reduces administrative load on the pay office that is in line with the company objectives of creating a virtual HR facility.
- Direct debits to the payroll from the accounts system has resulted in a much faster payroll.
- The system has found social acceptance and has resulted in a boost to the employee morale.

13.4 BANK LOAN PROCESS

This is an example of a major Y2K resurrection process. A bank's business loan applications system is affected by Y2K. As an example of a severe Y2K hit all databases and applications of the loan system are affected. (e.g., the way they were shown in the example in Figure 5.1). The resurrection process uses most of the activities and tasks described in this book in detail. The process also goes through the initial, major, and final iterations to produce the complete solution.

13.4.1 DESCRIBING THE EXISTING LOAN SYSTEM

A certain bank has an existing client base that comprises personal investors, small businesses, and large corporations. Each of these clients can have various types of accounts with the bank. Examples of these accounts include the credit, savings, check, and loan accounts. Loan accounts for small businesses as well as large corporations are a variation of their credit arrangements with the bank.

The bank had a mainframe system that was performing all the calculations related to acceptance and approval of loan applications. Approval of small business loans is an integral part of the bank's strategy to expand its business in the new millennium. Therefore, the sales and marketing arms of the bank had been vigorously pursuing the small business market throughout 1999.

The purpose of this system is to provide support for the entire process of small business loan approval. Specifically, the system performs the following functions:

- Identifies the potential customers.
- Provides support in managing the information related to the customers.
- Identifies and values their assets (which they plan to use as security against the loan).
- Extrapolates the returns-on-loan to the bank by matching the interest rates on the loan to the external interest rates.
- Accepts and processes the loan applications.
- Monitors the loan throughout its life.

Two of the complex parts of this application (that also depend on date calculations) are

- Extrapolating the returns on loan so that the assets of the customer are balanced with the loan amount and term applied for. This is done by considering the valuation of the asset and ensuring that the valuation is sufficient to cover the loan amount. Historical and future interest rates are a part of this detailed calculation.
- Since the customer is usually going to use the returns from the small business in order to service the loan, it also is essential to determine the potential revenue from the small business. This may be done by comparing the trading results of this business in the past or of similar businesses within the industry.

The system obviously has many more modules that are essential to provide the complete functionality of the system. However, those modules are not described here in great detail as they are less relevant to the Y2K problem experienced by the system. For example, the initial loan application process (which can take place on the phone) may perform some "cursory" calculations, or the final loan application may have to interface with the printing module which would print the loan details in a format suitable for both parties to sign. Fees and government duties are another factor to be considered in finalizing the loan approval.

13.4.2 DESCRIBING THE EFFECT OF Y2K HIT

With the advance of the new millennium, the bank finds to its utter dismay that it is unable to process all the necessary details of a loan application. The mathematicians and the business experts in the bank find that many calculations on the returns on the loans offered are not matching up with their own "spot" manual calculations which they performed on random loan samples. This inaccuracy in many loan application calculations has lead to further errors and confusion in comparisons of loan values with the assets offered as collaterals for the loan.

Initial investigation reveals that the calculations started going wrong only after the date switched over to the new millennium. Although a reasonable amount of Y2K testing had been done for the application, the level of preparedness of the organization as far as the loan application was concerned, was not rigorous. Being a relatively newer application (i.e., not a part of the legacy suite), the bank's management did not expect to encounter Y2K problems with it. Hence, the testing was not that exhaustive.

Switching over to the new millennium highlighted the following issues in the bank's loan application system:

- Sample calculations for short- and long-term loans were correct for all tests before the Year 2000.
- Results were extrapolated in the future to arrive at returns-on-investment.
- Results were also extrapolated in the future in order to ascertain correct collateral values for assets offered.
- In order to extrapolate, the system was using interest rate values from the past.
- After switching over to the new millennium, these values were not coming out correct.

The initial investigation confirmed that the same calculations had returned correct values (i.e., values that matched with the spreadsheet-based calculations of the market experts of the bank) before the millennium. Because the differences in calculation started occurring after the new millennium, it was easier to narrow down the problem to date calculations used in extrapolation, which was based on historical interest rates that had a date stamp of the previous millennium.

The effect of the errors in calculations started becoming serious with every trading day. Although this was not an application that would bring to a halt the entire business, it was still an extremely important strategic application for the bank. Since the bank had been aggressively pursuing the small business loan market, there were detailed sales and marketing activities going on. This was leading to innumerable queries and requests for loan interviews. However, because of the erroneous calculations, customers were no longer able to take out loans. This was also influencing the customers who had already taken loans from the bank. Service to these customers started dropping and the bank started loosing business.

Because the business of the bank was spread out over many different areas of the market, the bank's immediate survival was not threatened. However, it was realized by the senior management of the bank that it had to provide a long-term solution to the loans market. A resurrection of the system was inevitable. Following were the activities and tasks followed by the resurrection team in order to recreate the system.

13.4.3 Preliminary Activities

The preliminary activities of resurrection that were carried are discussed below.

The board of directors of the bank got together and immediately nominated the resurrection champion. Because of the involvement of the "business side" of the bank in the resurrection process, it was decided to assign this task to the CEO of the bank.

An initial attempt at the budgeting activity lead to an understanding that the effect of Y2K was going to cause considerable loss of business to the bank, especially in terms of lost opportunities. It was decided to dedicate significant budget to the resurrection process to not only mitigate the losses but to target the strategic advantages of a resurrecting system. The initial estimate for the time required for resurrection was between 6 to 9 months. During this time it was proposed that the current system would continue to serve the existing customers as best as it could. Existing customers would be immediately appraised of the situation. New customers were to be interviewed by market experts from within the bank and the loans application process was switched over to a manual system supported by spreadsheets.

The scope of the resurrection was large because every aspect of the loan process was affected by the problem. It was obvious to the resurrection champion and to the board that the extent of work required in the resurrection process was large and rigorous. The scoping activity had determined that multiple process-threads were required for the resurrection and that many activities and tasks of the resurrection process were going to be repeated a number of times. Selection and dropping of activities and tasks at this stage are quite normal.

In order to ensure that the resurrection work would be acceptable internally, the resurrection champion immediately started promoting the strategic advantages of resurrection. Strategic briefings for the employees were organized to ensure that they understood and accepted the situation the bank found itself in due to the Y2K problem.

13.4.4 INITIAL ITERATION

The initial iteration of the resurrection process for the bank loan application started with the task of prioritizing high-level requirements (MT01-2) based on the technological feedback (MT01-3) and the budgetary feedback (MT01-4). In the given circumstances, the resurrection champion, together with the senior members of the resurrection team decided that it was going to be beneficial for the organization to resurrect the entire system.

The staff for resurrection was sought from the existing teams that had worked on object-oriented developments. Many members of the resurrection team were drawn from within the IT department (ST01-1 and ST01-2). Hence, there was no detailed recruitment drive required in the process. The teams were assigned to modules (ST02-3) based on the high-level architecture of the system (ST02-2).

The initial iteration also included the creation of the iteration plan (MT02-2) and high-level assignment of resources to tasks (MT02-3). This was followed by the technological activity of dissection (TA01). The scope of dissection (TT01-1) was kept small. Also, dissection of logic and presentation was not considered essential, as both areas of the system were going to be recreated.

Throughout the initial iteration, a list of salvageable options was kept updated (TT01-5). In addition to the data, there were many user procedures regarding loan processing that were documented by the market experts. These comprised salvageable entities. All these salvageable options were formalized (MT04-1) and prioritized. Furthermore, the entire hardware and network were evaluated (TT07-1 and TT08-1) and it was decided to keep them the same, resulting in salvageable entities.

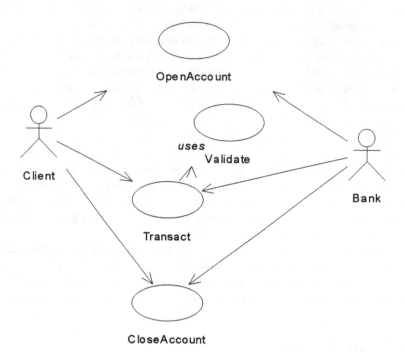

FIGURE 13.1   A use case for bank loan transactions.

The current Windows NT network required some fine tuning, which was carried out as a part of the task of maintaining the network (TT08-3).

The developers were already familiar with the language of choice, so there were only a few additional computers that needed Visual Basic installed (TT02-1). After a few potential databases were evaluated (TT06-1), it was decided to license SQLserver because the use of Visual Basic was facilitated by the database. TT02-3 resulted in the installation and fine tuning of the database.

The activity of requirements modeling (MA04) used many salvageable entities from the hit system. These included the existing help systems, user manuals, and some documented procedures on the use of the hit application. As far as the date-specific requirements were concerned, it was decided to use 4-digit dates in all aspects of the system (database, logic, and presentation: MT04-2). New requirements for the application that related with the architecture of the application were specified using use case diagrams, as shown in Figures 13.1 and 13.2 (MT04-3). The use case diagram for bank loan transactions described the relationship of the client and the bank (or its teller) with the use case for opening and closing of loan accounts with the bank. Additional transactions (e.g., queries, extra payments) are represented by the transact use case which, in turn, uses details from "validate." It is the usage of the application represented by the "open account" use case that was affected by the Y2K problem in the hit application. Figure 13.2 describes in further detail how a small business client is able to register his loan application (as a part of opening

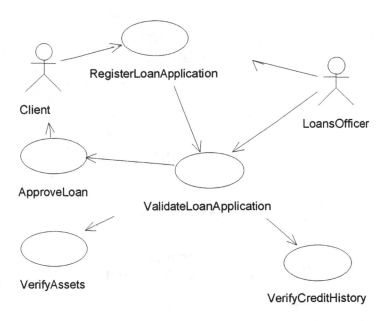

FIGURE 13.2 A detailed use case indicating verification of credit history and assets for loan applications.

his/her accounts with the bank) which is validated in detail (including the credit history of the business, where the date/time stamp becomes very important; and the verification of assets for loan collateral).

Prototypes (using simple whiteboard sketches and powerpoint) of the sensitive areas of these use cases within the resurrecting loans system were created and shown to the users.

The architectural activity (MA05) produced a simple architecture block diagram as shown in Figure 13.3. This diagram identifies the high-level architectural elements (MT05-1) and shows their relationship (MT05-3). It was affected by loan calculations of the system that was using a mainframe subroutine to perform the extrapolations. Hence, the block diagram shows the relationship of the loan application subsystem with the mainframe. The GUI was common to the loan application as well as other modules within the system.

The resurrection team of 20 developers included a quality manager and two testers (MT07-2). The quality manager was responsible for creation of the quality plan (MT07-3) and the review of the plan was carried out on a continuous basis together with the project manager (MT07-4). Furthermore, some initial standards for class names were created (MT08-3) and publicized to the resurrection team (MT08-4).

Once the resurrection was underway, the resurrection champion ensured that the process was advertised to the existing as well as prospective clients (ST09-2). Potential clients were the ones with whom the market experts had had a one-to-one discussion of their loan requirements. These clients had to be apprised of the new

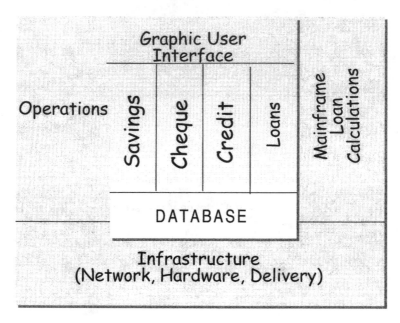

FIGURE 13.3   Loan application architecture.

system that was going to serve their needs in the future. Current loan accounts were consolidated by upgrading them to the new system.

The resurrection champion continued to update the board on the nature of the resurrection process and the manner in which time and budgets were being consumed (ST10-1). A regular effort was made by the project manager to ensure that the resurrection process did not get entangled in the IT games that were nonproductive to the overall effort (ST12-5).

13.4.5 Major Iteration

The focus of the major iteration was to produce detailed designs (shown in Figures 13.4 to 13.7) of the requirements specified in the initial iteration. During this iteration, the resurrection team ensured that each module or component was designed using object-oriented design principles (MT06-1). A detailed date-component was designed as specified in the task MT06-2 that would be able to perform all date calculations in the new application. Database tables were designed after the main class diagrams had been completed, as this would give the database designers a good idea of the persistence requirements of the classes (MT06-4).

Design of the user interfaces was started along with the work on class designs as the resurrection team wanted more feedback from the users on the design of the user interfaces (MT06-6). Furthermore, all principles of useability (activity SA07) were applied to the designs as the tasks related to useability were carried out in great detail. Collaborative useability inspection (CUI — ST07-3) was carried out on most of the screens with special emphasis on the most frequently used screens.

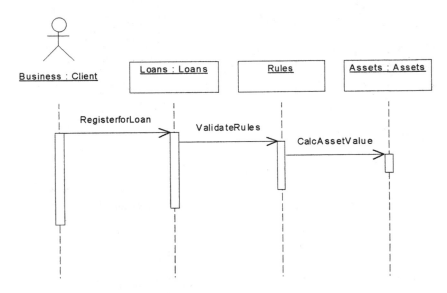

FIGURE 13.4   Sequence diagram for registering for loans.*

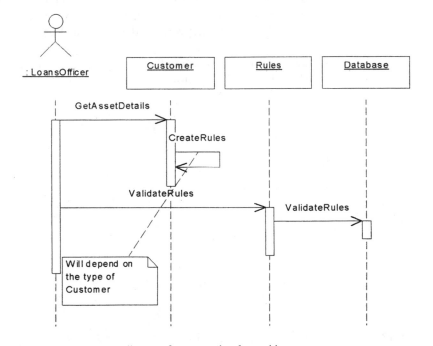

FIGURE 13.5   Sequence diagram for approving loans.**

---

* The Rules object is where the business rules related to calculating assets as stored. For example, 70% of the actual asset value may be used as collateral for the loan.
** Once the assets have been valued, Rules will be used to extrapolate the returns-on-loan. Data will come from the previously Y2K-affected database.

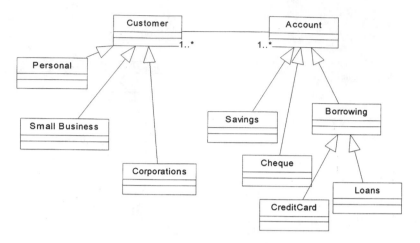

FIGURE 13.6 Class diagram for customer and accounts.*

An investigation into the delivery mechanism (TT09-1) led to the understanding that the current delivery mechanism used by the loans system was not adequate. Once the new system was up and running, the users expected the number of customers to double every 6 months for at least 2 years. Hence, it was decided to upgrade delivery of the data through the network to the distributed users of the system (TT09-2).

Activity of project management started during the initial iteration with focus on the methodological tasks. During this major iteration, project management

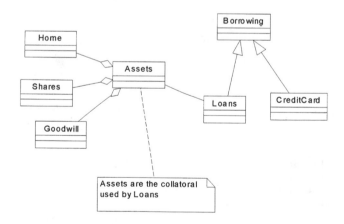

FIGURE 13.7 Class diagram for assets and loans.**

---

* Indicates small business as a variation of customer and loans class as a three-deep hierarchy; a relatively fine granular account.
** Assets can be of various types — each will be revalued by the resurrecting application and used in the extrapolation exercise.

concentrated on the technological tasks of creating and managing the build environment (TT11-1) and keeping the working version current (TT11-2). The focus also was on ensuring that the current system was released in a way that would enable easier configuration management and releases in the future (TT11-3).

During the major iteration, technical demos were carried out on a regular basis (MT03-2) and any errors found during the demos were logged and processed using the Software Incident Reporting (SIR) system. Furthermore, formal demos were organized for the users (MT03-3) to not only elicit responses and refinement from them, but to also update the users on the progress of the project. The project manager was continuously watching for road factors (MT03-6) to ensure that these "unexpected" factors did not affect the schedule of the resurrection project.

While the architectural and requirements modeling activities were carried out during the initial iteration, results from the activities provided input to the detailed activity of rewriting the application logic (TA03). The programming team had the opportunity to make estimates (TT03-2) on implementing the scenarios that were developed during the initial iteration, prototype the solution (TT03-4), and continue with the detailed coding task (TT03-5) that would satisfy not only the current functionality of the application but also possible changes and extensions that were inevitable with growth in the loans business. Solution code was tested (TT03-6) and solved (TT03-7) at individual code level.

The new application and the converted data were being put together (TT04-1) as the development progressed and was being continuously verified against requirements (TT04-3) and performance (TT04-4). New data models were created for the database (TT06-3) and stored procedures were written to handle storage and retrieval of data from the SQLserver database (TT06-4).

Scope of the data creation was kept big (TT05-2) as a large amount of data relating to the existing customers had to be transported across to the new application. However, extreme care was exercised in the conversion of "time stamped" historical interest rate data (TT05-3, TT0505) as that was the data that had caused date-related problems in the first place. This conversion and testing was part of one of the first activities that ensured that the interest calculations were matching up with the manual calculations performed by the market experts.

The activity of metrics and measurements (MA10) was restricted to measuring the designs (MT10-4), code (MT10-5), and measurement of processes (MT10-7). The rest of the measures were evaluated, but it was decided not to extend the measurement requirements beyond the basic measurements of design and code.

The methodological approach to testing required creation of a test environment (MT09-3) and creation of test designs that would reflect the subsystems and modules of the resurrecting application (MT09-4). Technological tasks related to test designs merged with the methodological tasks. Technical test designs were created to handle the major modules of the system (TT10-2) and code walkthroughs (TT10-4) were a regular part of the QA process of the resurrection team. Actual testing of components (MT09-5) was carried out as and when they were ready and available for testing.

Since most of the technical staff had available the technologies used in resurrection, they did not have an urgent need to undergo detailed training. However, the business users of the system required training in the use of the new application (ST03-1). A training program was outlined for the business users (ST03-3) that would train them in utilizing the new application to its full potential.

The project manager ensured that the physical environment was free from distractions (ST04-1) and that issues related to the E-factor were kept in mind as the teams settled down for the resurrection work. Effort also was put in to ensure that the career and motivational objectives of individuals remained in line with those of the organization (ST05-2).

Although the bank was not involved in direct legal action, all documentary evidence related to the prevention effort was formally recorded and stored for future reference (ST11-1). Furthermore, a small sum of money was kept aside for possible Y2K litigation from any of the current clients who had taken out small business loans (ST11-2).

13.4.6 FINAL ITERATION

The focus of the resurrection work was the major iteration where most activities and tasks related to the resurrection project were carried out. However, it was decided to iterate one more time in order to ascertain that the final product of the resurrection work was "polished." During the final iteration, the focus was on the sociological activities of reporting and promoting the work that had been accomplished so far.

For example, the resurrection champion continued to report the progress to the board on a regular basis (ST12-2). As the resurrection process came closer to completion, a detailed review was organized together with the quality assurance manager (ST13-3).

While tracking activities and tasks (MT03-4) was performed during all iterations, it was considered especially important by the project manager to watch out for the road factors during the final iteration (MT03-6). This was the time when there was a possibility of requirement creep and it was essential to contain the scope (MT03-7) and manage user expectations of the resurrecting system (MT03-8).

A regular maintenance of the hardware and network (TT07-3 and TT08-3) was carried out during the final iteration, and procedures were put in place to ensure that both hardware and the network were able to handle the development activities after the product had been released.

13.4.7 BANK LOAN PROCESS IN THE NEW MILLENNIUM

As a result of the resurrection process, which took approximately 6+ months to complete, the bank was able to start processing loans more quickly and efficiently than before. The extrapolation calculations were fixed as new logic was written for them. Since all new designs and code had 4-digit dates in them, there were no problems encountered in date-related calculations. The salvageable data, resulting from the dissection activities, proved to be extremely valuable. Together with the new data that was entered manually, the loan application of the bank had a comprehensive suite of information on current and potential clients for loan application. In conclusion, the bank found it was worth spending the time and effort in resurrecting the application, rather than testing for the Y2K problem and fixing it. However, it was appreciated by the senior management of the bank that without the reserves to carry it through for the 6 to 9 months budgeted for the resurrection process, the bank could not have successfully resurrected.

13.5 KEY POINTS

1. A sample process and product repository for the resurrection process was presented.
2. Two examples of "possible" resurrection processes (payroll and banking) were outlined.
3. An example of the various ways in which activities and tasks from within the three dimensions of the resurrection process would intermingle in order to produce a comprehensive and practical resurrection process within the initial, major, and final iterations was described.
4. Ability of organizations to survive through the resurrection process was shown as important for a successful resurrection exercise.

13.6 NOTES

Both example case studies described here were drawn from "semi-real life" situations. Both case studies were "play acted" by the CASE Digital Inc.'s potential resurrection teams.

14 Testing Strategies for Y2K Processes

I will tell you the golden rule of testing — one who has the gold (the business sponsor) makes the rule.

John Phippen, during a 10-day SQA and Testing Course[1]

Abstract The activity of testing forms part of the overall quality assurance group of activities within the resurrection process. Due to the sheer importance of testing in prevention as well as resurrection exercises in Y2K, it is described here in great detail. Quality assurance activities are spread over all three dimensions of the resurrection process. Therefore, testing and validation work also appears in all three dimensions. Discussion of testing in this chapter starts with the various approaches one can use in testing a resurrecting system. These approaches are also helpful in dissecting a Y2K-hit system in order to find the nature, severity, and area of the hit. The overall architecture of a Y2K testing approach is described next. This involves the types of test elements that comprise the architecture and the way in which they are related to each other. This is followed by the high-level activity of test planning that describes the resources and priorities in testing. The test designs and their format, as well as the individual test cases and their format, is described next. Finally, as the testing effort progresses, it is important to understand the results produced by the tests. This is done by recording the results in a spreadsheet or database, analyzing them, and making estimation of likely errors and the potential areas where they will occur. Test cases from the prevention effort also may be reused. However, one of the important differences between a normal testing effort and the one related to Y2K is the need to revisit all existing test cases which used to "enforce" a 2-digit year.

14.1 TESTING IN Y2K RESURRECTION

Testing has played a major role in the Y2K prevention effort. It would not be wrong to state that testing required more than half the effort in any Y2K fixing before the Y2K hump. Once a date problem was located as a result of detailed testing, converting the date was not that difficult (although the logistics were challenging). After the fixes were effectuated, once again testing played an important part in ensuring that the conversion process did not affect the functionality of the system. The IT industry has accumulated good experience in testing the applications for the Y2K problem which now can be repeated in resurrection.

In testing for Y2K resurrection, we try and bring together the principles of sound testing with the various aspects of preventive Y2K testing in which we are already experienced. Testing plays a crucial role in Y2K resurrection by ensuring that not only are the date problems in the hit system fixed, but also the existing and new functionality of the resurrecting system conforms to the requirements specified by the users. Because of the various ways in which a system can be tested, the activity of testing appears in all three dimensions of the Y2K resurrection process. In this chapter, we discuss the testing in resurrection in greater detail.

Some of the important aspects of Y2K testing are

- It plays an important role in what I have called *dissection* of a Y2K-hit application. As mentioned in the activity of dissection, the dissection of a Y2K-hit application is essentially testing it with the difference that it may no longer be a production application.
- Since resurrection is a lot more than fixing a Y2K date, testing has a major responsibility to ensure that the resurrected application satisfies the functionality of the existing system and any new functionality that has been added by the users during the resurrection process.
- Due to use of distributed architecture and object-oriented techniques, it is essential to consider the nuances of testing within these technologies (e.g., testing inherited classes).
- Since test cases for the Y2K-hit system are likely to be designed to *ensure* 2-digit compliance, reusing these test cases and their corresponding test data would require extra care and perhaps rewrite of the test cases.

With this background discussion on testing within the Y2K resurrection project, we consider all details of testing including its approaches, testing architecture, test management and planning, collating of test results, and so on. It is important to remember that testing is a part of overall quality assurance and, therefore, it is an ongoing activity that takes place not only during the resurrection process, but also after the recreated company is in place.

14.2 TESTING APPROACHES FOR Y2K RESURRECTION

Testing approaches provide an understanding of the various ways in which software can be tested. This understanding is important in a resurrection effort wherein the testing activity is carried out not only to identify the date problem, but also to test thoroughly the resurrected system that has been produced.

Furthermore, the background provided by the testing approaches helps narrow down the dissection process. The scope of dissection (task TT05-2) can be determined as well as influenced by the testing approaches. When a system is affected by Y2K, the end-user is only able to report the problem based on what he or she sees as the problem at the front-end of the system. Unless the problem is specifically related to the GUI, the front-end of the system forms only a small part of the system that needs investigation or correction. In most cases the Y2K problem may be deep inside the code or even in the operating system or hardware. Locating this problem

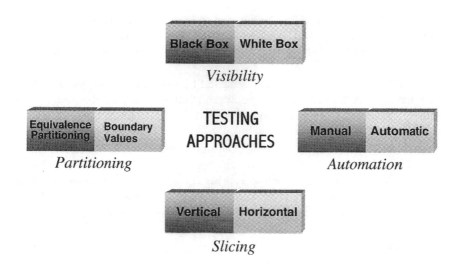

FIGURE 14.1   Testing approaches in Y2K resurrection.

within the software system or its underlying architecture is the aim of dissection. Considering the various approaches to testing facilitates that aim.

Figure 14.1 describes the testing approaches that can be used in testing the resurrecting system. The importance of these approaches is as follows:

- Black — white box testing deals with the openness or closeness of the code.
- Manual — automated testing indicating the type of people and usage of tools in testing.
- Vertical — horizontal slicing indicates how the resurrecting system is to be divided for testing.
- Equivalence partitioning and boundary values indicate how the test data is to be sampled for testing.

In real life testing though, the testing approach would not be a single approach. It would be a combination of these approaches. The following sections describe the detailed approaches to testing.

14.2.1 BLACK BOX

When the testing concentrates only on the input and the output without knowing much about the internals of the system, then such testing approach is called *black box* testing. The aim of the black box testing is to analyze the behavior of the software with respect to the functionality specified in the requirements. It verifies GUI and concentrates on end results without the need for explicitly understanding the application's internal structure.

This is an ideal approach when testing for user interfaces, as well as for the business processes expressed in the requirements model. One of the advantages of this approach to testing is it can be automated by means of scripts that are created using automated testing tools. This reduces the time required in regression testing as entire tests can be left running overnight without manual intervention from the testers.

Typically, this testing would be conducted by the users of the system, who are only interested in the behavior of the system rather than how the system is put together. These users are not worried about the architecture of the system and, therefore, they treat the system as a "black box."

Application in Y2K Resurrection — During the initial stages of dissection, when we can't search the internals of the system because we don't know what to search for, the black box testing comes into play. This is when a whole series of date-related input is provided and the results are verified to see where the problem exists. Black box testing in Y2K will localize the error to a module or a program.

14.2.2 WHITE BOX

The *white box* approach to testing is the opposite of the black box approach and requires detailed examination of the system processes and programs from the technical viewpoint. The white box test design focuses specifically on internal knowledge of the software and seeks to investigate what is inside the "box."

The white box approach is not restricted to code. During the early phases of development, designs and documents can be subjected to white box testing. This would result in detection of problems before too much time has been wasted in coding wrong functionality, etc. Thus, white box testing can result in considerable savings that is realized during the later phases of the project.

Two of the common ways of performing white box testing are walkthrough and inspection. During walkthrough, the person responsible for the work (e.g., programmer, if it is a program, or technical writer, if it is a document) is asked to take the quality assurance and testing team through the work. Thus, in the walkthrough of a technical document, the technical writer will describe the document to the test team and provide sample test cases that would be positive in nature. The aim is not to break the flow of the document, but to understand its flow and pass comments on it. In case of inspection, though, the program or document is divided into its individual modules and is carefully inspected in small steps to ensure that it does not have any logical bugs. Inspection of these modules is assigned to team members who have expertise in their particular area. The experience of the inspector can help not only in finding bugs but also in ensuring that unnecessary bugs are not introduced as a result of the inspection.

These white box tests are conducted not by actual execution of the relevant modules, but by using paper and pencil or describing the flow on the white board or even projecting the designs or code on the wall using transparencies. The result of these tests are not always clear cut (as they would be in a black box testing) and it is common to find problems related to the semantics or logic of the module rather than its syntax.

Since these tests are conducted in the open where the work of the person is up for display, these tests have a sociological angle which has been discussed in the chapter on sociology. Therefore, it is worth considering soft issues like self esteem and sensitivity of people to criticism of their work.

Application in Y2K Resurrection — After the black box testing has localized the module or program that is hit by the Y2K problem, it will be necessary to go inside the code in order to find the problem. The date problem can be within the logic of the program or in the database itself. Either of these areas will need further dissection that is facilitated by the white box approach. However, this approach may not be very convenient if a large amount of data has to be inspected. If there is a need to dissect a large amount of data, perhaps the writing of testing harnesses may be required. To further aid dissection, verification of scenarios and designs for new modules in the resurrecting system also is assisted by the white box approach.

14.2.3 MANUAL TESTING

Manual testing is based on the human intervention with the application that is being tested. In this approach to testing, the software programs are executed manually through their user interfaces and the results are checked manually. Furthermore, system designs and structure of the programs also can be checked by manual intervention. There are many situations where there is a need to write special programs to test sections of data or to replicate code with some variation. This requires the writing of programs which is categorized as manual testing. Many testing situations require writing of test harnesses that are skeletal programs running larger programs that are being tested. These skeletal test programs are called test harnesses, and they run a large amount of testing data with wide variation through the tested programs.

Application in Y2K Resurrection — Although the user has reported a problem in a particular module of the system, a proper dissection during a Y2K hit will require thorough testing of all areas of the system. This would require manual intervention. Test teams comprised of the user and the tester can manually step through the programs. Test programmers also can write test harnesses and users can help create the wide variation in the input data for these kinds of tests.

14.2.4 AUTOMATED TESTING

While manual testing provides depth in testing the systems, automated testing is able to provide the breadth or coverage of a large amount of input which can be passed through the system. Automated testing is conducted by using software test tools to automatically perform one or more testing functions. By using test tools we can record a sequence of user actions that are performed on the system. These sequences are replayed with the varying data without the intervention of the user or the tester. The recording of key strokes and their playback is able to reduce the amount of work to be performed during testing. This is the most efficient way of conducting regression testing which ensures that although a small part of the system has changed, the rest of the system has been tested thoroughly by conducting the automated tests as a part of the routine.

Some of the other advantages of automated testing include:

- Ability to reproduce bugs at any time in order to demonstrate them to the programmer responsible for the module.
- Ability to record the results automatically.
- Comparison of results with a predefined standard set of results and recording the differences and reporting them without manual intervention.
- Reducing the time in conducting regression tests as the tools are able to replay the sequence of events much faster than when they were manually keyed in.

Application in Y2K Resurrection — Automated testing using many of the popular "date search" tools are able to highlight the date problems in logic and data and create a metrics of the programs and date occurrences which were used for fixing the date problems in the prevention effort. The focus of automated testing in Y2K resurrection has shifted from simply locating date problems to ensuring that the new system is able to satisfy the functionality of the existing system. Conversion of salvageable data will also need testing. These are the areas where the automated testing will play a major role in Y2K resurrection. The tools for date location and fixing mentioned earlier will still be useful in the dissection work, but the focus is no longer on fixing of date only.

Finally, since our concentration in resurrection has been on object technology and since many automated tools focus on object technology, it will make it worthwhile using automation in our Y2K resurrection testing. Automated tools are able to verify all properties of the objects from an application including the hidden properties of an object that are not easily tested in manual tests. Thus, automated testing in Y2K will ensure better use of the development as well as testing resources and improve the quality of the resultant code.

14.2.5 VERTICAL SLICING

When a testing approach slices the system vertically, it is essentially dividing the system into subsystems from the application viewpoint. For example, a resurrecting banking application would be divided into customer information subsystem and accounting subsystem. The vertical slicing of a system derives from the vertical slicing of the system that was discussed in detail during the methodological activity of architecture (MA05). The main advantage of vertical slicing is derived in acceptance testing when the users of the system are involved in conducting the tests. Each of the subsystems can form part of an individual's expertise. Therefore, dividing the testing into vertical slices can lead to thorough testing by the people who are experts in a narrow module of the system.

14.2.6 HORIZONTAL SLICING

Horizontal slicing is when the system is divided based on its infrastructure rather than its application. For example, in the banking system mentioned before, if the system is divided into data and logic and operating system and network for the purpose of testing, then the slicing is said to be horizontal. Technical testers who have expertise in the relevant modules that result from the slicing will conduct testing of these modules. One does not expect a large amount of user involvement (except in the front end) in the horizontally sliced tests because the infrastructure is essentially a black box for the users.

This division also derives from the architecture (MA05) activity, wherein the development was divided horizontally into database, logic, and the front-end. This division is helpful during system testing, when developers from a particular area of expertise (such as database, on useability experts) can concentrate on the areas of the system they are totally familiar with.

14.2.7 EQUIVALENCE PARTITIONING

Equivalence partitioning is the partitioning of the target test application and its data in such a way that each of the partitions provide homogeneous test targets. Usually, it is the data that is divided into equivalent partitions and test targets selected from within the partitions. For example, a banking application may be made up of 10,000 accounts, which may be divided among four different account types as shown below.

Account Types	Number of Accounts
Savings Accounts	2000
Check Accounts	4000
Credit Accounts	3000
Business Accounts	1000

If the aforementioned sets of accounts are to be tested, then their equivalence partitioning will result in four partitions. Each of these account types is made up of its respective number (different) of accounts. In equivalence partitioning we do not divide the available data into equal parts by numbers, but in parts that represent a logical entity. For example, if we were to create one test case per equivalence partition for the given banking application, then the first test case for the savings accounts will represent testing of 2000 accounts (1 in 2000), whereas that of the credit accounts will represent testing of 3000 (1 in 3000).

Application in Y2K Resurrection — Equivalence partitioning is applicable to the data as well as to the time. For example, the above accounts are divided according to their numbers so those samples from each of the account partitions can be selected for testing. However, when we divide these accounts by dates (in this case, say, and the account opening dates), then the equivalence partitions will be as shown in Figure 14.2. Although the difference in time between 1/1/1981 to 2/29/1984 (2 years and 2 months), and between 12/31/1990 to 9/9/1999 (9 years and 9 months) is not equal, still if nothing significant is happening in between those times then the partitions will still hold true. We will select randomly from within these dates in order to conduct testing.

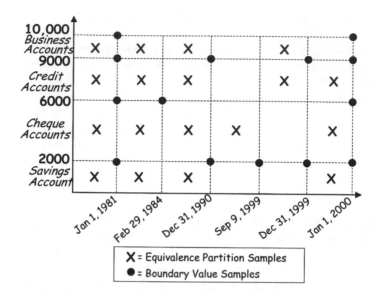

FIGURE 14.2   Applying equivalence partitioning and boundary values to Y2K resurrection testing.

14.2.8 BOUNDARY VALUE

The edges of the equivalence partitions, as shown in Figure 14.2, are the boundary values. Thus, in case of numbers it will be a few accounts from each of the partitions that have boundary values like very high or very low amounts, high or low transactions, and so on. In case of dates, it will be the dates at the edges of the partitions (e.g., 2/28, 2/29, and 3/1/1984; 12/31/1990 and 1/1/1991). The boundary values provide the opportunity to test the extreme cases within an equivalence partition. This leads to concentration of testing effort in the areas where the system is the most vulnerable.

14.3 TESTING ARCHITECTURE FOR Y2K RESURRECTION

The testing approaches feed into the testing architecture. The architecture, as shown in Figure 14.3, depicts the various types of tests and how they are all put together in order to provide comprehensive testing for the resurrecting system. Some elements of this testing architecture will also be used for dissection of the Y2K-hit system. The architecture continues to be influenced by the approaches to testing as described in the previous section.

14.3.1 UNIT TEST

The unit test is the basic testing of the program conducted by the programmer herself. It deals with an individual class or program and is restricted to testing the syntax

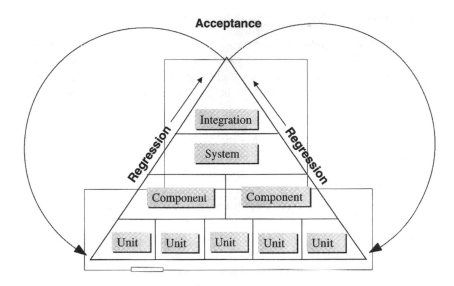

FIGURE 14.3 Testing architecture for Y2K resurrection.

as well as the flow of the program. In unit testing we execute the class being tested by means of another class called the test harness. Alternatively, the class being tested can be executed within the overall test environment.

Testing is continued until the developer is satisfied that the results from the test are matching with the expected results and that all the functionality that the class is supposed to satisfy is indeed being satisfied. During unit testing the programmer may also check the implemented structure of the class against its intended design structure. From this description it is obvious that the unit testing is restricted to the performance of an individual class or program and, therefore, the detailed functionality of the rest of the system may not make much sense at this stage. Recording the results and re-testing the code may not be very formal at this stage. This is so because at the end of a test the programmer may realize the error, correct it, and re-test without recording the error anywhere. However, depending on the importance of the class, formal recording of errors and fixes at unit test level may be carried out.

The testing approaches discussed in the previous section have a bearing on the unit tests. For example, white box testing would be very common when unit tests are conducted. The programmer may step through the code herself and inspect it for syntax of the statements, branching logic, and adequate coverage. While statement coverage only inspects the statements that are executed, inspection of branching logic involves each of the conditional statements within the program and the results from the true–false results at the end of each test. Black box tests would appear when the GUI classes are tested. In these unit tests the programmer would want to ensure that the data content as well as the display from the class she has written is satisfying the requirements of the class.

14.3.2 Component Test

A component test is conducted when a few classes are ready to be tested together. Thus, this test will not only concentrate on the output from the given classes, but also how they behave in relation with each other. For example, a date component that is made up of 10 date classes, will have to be tested for the working of all of the classes together in order to ensure that the right results are produced. The concept of coupling between the component under test and other components, as well as the concept of cohesion for classes within the component will come in to play during the component test. Once again, a component test can be a white box manual test wherein we are stepping through the designs of the component, or a black box test wherein we are writing test harnesses which run a large amount of data through the component in order to test every possible variations to the input.

14.3.3 System Test

The system test is still within the technical domain and is involved with detailed testing of the resurrecting system not only with respect to its functionality, but also with respect to its performance, installation, backup and recovery, security, and stability. System testing involves end-to-end testing of all components within the system in an integrated fashion. System testing would involve both black and white box testing approaches, and the test suites would comprise test harnesses to pass a large amount of data through the system.

The functionality of the system is tested by using the test designs and the test cases within the test designs. These test designs are created by using the use cases and scenarios in the requirements modeling activity. The performance is tested by simulating the real life environment of the resurrecting system. This would involve creating a large amount of test data and loading the system with a large number of transactions by using an automated test simulator. Installing the application (if physically deployed) on a new machine would test out the installation and deployment of the new application. Sociological aspects (like graceful recovery of software from a crash) also are tested within the system test.

14.3.4 Acceptance Test

During acceptance testing the system moves from the technical domain on to the user domain. It is up to the users to accept (or reject) the system by testing its functionality against the specified requirements. This test would decide whether the resurrecting system is ready for deployment or not. Therefore, it is important that the users of the system test out the system using all relevant approaches to testing. Testing and verification of the specified help system and the accompanying user guides, etc. is carried out in this test.

Users may need technical support at this stage. This support would involve creation of databases, installing the application, and providing help in using test harnesses and/or automated testing tools, if relevant.

The acceptance criteria for this testing (acceptance testing) would have some influence on the way the test cases are designed. Discussion on Y2K resurrection acceptance criteria is in the last section of this chapter.

14.3.5 REGRESSION TEST

Regression tests are conducted in the later iterations of a development project. After the system has undergone all the formal testing processes and the errors are recorded *and* fixed, it is essential to ensure that not only are those fixes working okay, but by fixing the errors we have not ended up introducing more errors in other parts of the system. This flow-on effect of the errors is minimized by the object-oriented designs, wherein it is easier to locate the errors because of encapsulation of classes. However, regression tests are still essential after the errors have been fixed. They can be performed by means of the automated tools (black box tests) unless a design or code inspection is deemed necessary, in which case they will be white box manual tests. Regression tests are facilitated by the cyclic approach to testing as the experience as well as the results from the first cycle of testing can be reused in the next cycle. If the results from the initial cycle of the overall tests are errors of minor category, then a smaller number of samples may be selected from within the equivalence partitions. However, it is recommended that all boundary values should be selected in all passes of the regression tests.

14.4 TEST PLANNING FOR Y2K RESURRECTION

Test planning is a part of quality assurance planning or project planning within the resurrection process. The test planning discussion here focuses on the strategy for testing, the resources required for the tests, the risks associated with testing, scheduling of test cases, and the creation and maintenance of the test environment that would be required to conduct the testing. This test plan would provide the necessary background for the overall testing activity within the resurrection process (Figure 14.4).

14.4.1 A GOOD TEST PLAN

A good test plan should involve the objectives, the acceptance criteria, the system and integration test plans, the approaches and methods to be used for testing, and the responsibilities and schedule for testing. A good test plan works out the modules to be tested and the resources available to do so. The plan also decides the order in which modules are to be tested.

A good test plan would ensure that the testing activity starts from the early stages of the resurrection process. This would require the test plan to be developed during the initial iteration of the process. It would result in a thread that would run through all iterations and all dimensions of the process. The focus of the test plan should be towards the higher, integrated system level test approach as that is where the scope of testing, the time and cost of required resources, and other such complexities need to be sorted out.

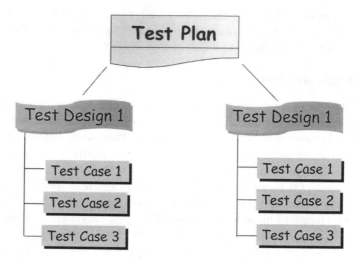

FIGURE 14.4   Organization of testing.

The schedule of the test plan (perhaps within the quality or project plan) also should have a schedule of specific dates on which individual tests are to be completed and tested by the responsible team member. Creating a database in order to record and report software incident reports would be part of a good test plan. Such a database will enable analyzing of the test results and making educated guesses on the risks associated with testing.

14.4.2 ANALYZING RISKS

Since no testing is perfect, it is essential to analyze the risks associated with what has been tested and what has been left out. In addition to the risks associated with choosing the scope of testing, there are also risks associated with the actual testing cycle. This risk includes situations that can hamper the testing effort (like resources, system, or network availability). Hence, proper test planning is required to identify and prioritize these risks. Analyzing risks during initial iterations of the resurrection process can help avoid many problems at a later stage. Early identification of testing risks is essential to minimize the effect on both the resurrection process and the testing itself.

Some of the common examples of risks in Y2K resurrection testing are

- Limited experience of staff in testing object-oriented solutions — most of the effort in the Y2K prevention testing was focused on the existing legacy systems. Object-oriented systems require a different approach to testing because of encapsulated components and inheritance of objects. The experience in prevention testing may not be always helpful in the resurrection testing.

- Unavailability of suitable test environment — it will be essential to create a separate environment in which the resurrecting system will be tested. Creation of this environment and its maintenance is a testing overhead that needs to be considered during test planning. If a suitable test environment is not created early in the testing cycle, then it will be a significant risk to the project.
- Discovery of major errors in the later cycles of the resurrection testing. We plan for regression tests to ensure that the errors detected in the earlier cycle are fixed, and that those fixes have not created problems elsewhere. Significant risks are associated in the assumption that no major problems will be discovered during the later cycles of regression tests.
- Unavailability of test data. If suitable test data is not available for creation of the test database, then we cannot guarantee sufficient and thorough testing. Design and creation of data is a vital element of test planning, without which the testing of the system is at considerable risk.
- Distributed applications need to be tested over a real life network. Unavailability of such networks or their inability to simulate real life situations would lead to inaccurate performance tests.
- Sufficient hardware in terms of machines, memory, and communications should be available for testing.
- Finally, intensity of a Y2K hit would be a good indication of the risks associated with the testing. The higher the intensity of the hit, the greater the risks associated with testing.

14.4.3 Prioritizing Risks

Depending on the criticality of the risks described in the previous section, it will be essential to prioritize these risks so that the test manager can take suitable actions. Prioritizing the risks involves understanding of the risks as well as opportunities that exist at the end of the resurrection process. Once again, depending on the intensity of the hit, it will be essential to decide which systems are crucial and the number of test cases and the test data required for testing.

14.4.4 Test Resources

As a part of test planning, the test manager will have to list all IT resources available for testing. Furthermore, the strengths and skills of testing team and any special training requirements will have to be identified by the test manager. A decision can be made to reorganize these resources to carry out testing successfully. The common resources are

- Hardware
- System (OS)
- Database (including for results)

- Application
- People
- Tools
- Environment

The maximum utilization of these resources can be done for setting a suitable test environment, designing and executing various test cases (e.g., system and acceptance test cases), and finally storing their test results in proper database. The advantage of analyzing and utilizing resources is that it minimizes the vulnerability and cost of the overall testing activity.

14.4.5 TEST ENVIRONMENT

Testing of any application should be done in an environment that matches with the environment of the application's end user. To create such an environment, first identify the equipment, software, and sites where the software will be operating. Establishing an effective test environment takes major planning and implementation efforts. It is easier to analyze a test environment by considering acceptance test cases and test data. Determine the tools and mechanisms required for creating, running, and storing test results. Requirements may include various software and hardware products. The common requirements are

- Separate testing area (physical location)
- Physical movement of testing staff (e.g., in testing large numbers of PCs in Y2K)
- Configuration for testing
- Similar to production environment
- Creation of test-beds in test databases
- Management of test databases (backups, consistency)
- Tools for recording and analyzing results
- Network administration, etc.

14.4.6 TEST TIMELINE

The test timeline before the Y2K hump had to meet the deadline of 1/1/2000. Therefore, the testing to prevent date problem had to be done in a hurry. The timeline for resurrection testing will also be under pressure as the organization will have to ensure that the new system is up and running quickly. However, this resurrection testing should ensure that enough time is available in order to test all aspects of the new system.

Test timelines need not be limited to timing the test cases. The timelines should include the considerable time required in creation of the test environment, loading of test data, designing of test cases, and staffing and managing the test resources. All these aspects of testing are outside the time *per test case* and they should be included in the overall planning for test time. Furthermore, because of the iterative nature of the resurrection process, it will be essential to schedule the test plan such that test cases for the components that are developed in the initial iterations are scheduled first and so on.

14.4.7 TEST CYCLES

The need for test cycles arises because it is neither possible nor worthwhile testing an entire system in a single attempt. Testing a resurrecting system requires a cyclic approach to testing which ensures that the testing is carried out in the most efficient and effective manner. The test cycles achieve the following two purposes:

1. They accumulate the experience and the data resulting from the execution of the tests thereby ensuring that the first broad brush cycle provides input into the next detailed cycle.
2. They also ensure that the tests are scheduled in an appropriate manner so that the results of testing a particular module can be used in testing (or postponing the tests) of another module.

The number of cycles (or passes or iterations) in testing would usually be three cycles. These cycles bring in activities from all three dimensions of the resurrection process. These test cycles ensure that the test cases are sequenced in such a way that the higher level tests (e.g., system test) which depend on the lower level tests (e.g., unit test) appear later on in the test cycles. Thus, the cycles relate to the iterations of the resurrection process. The test cycles ensure the coordination of tests so that the right types of tests are conducted during the right iterations. If all types of tests discussed in this architecture are conducted at the same time then failures will occur from testing of functionality which has not yet been implemented. By testing the functionality within appropriate initial, major, and final releases, problems of testing unimplemented functionality can be avoided. As shown in Figure 14.5,

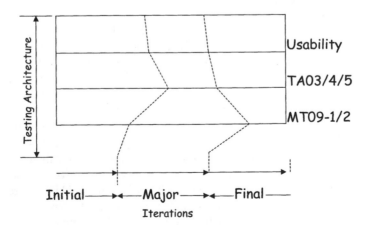

FIGURE 14.5   Considering test cycles in testing planning.

the tasks from technological activities of TA03, TA04 and TA05 are performed to a large extent during the initial iteration of the resurrection process. During the major iteration, though, it is the methodological tasks (MT09-1, MT09-2) that play a major role. Useability from the sociological dimension continues throughout the three iterations.

14.4.8 Reuseability in Testing

Following are the reuseability aspects in Y2K resurrection testing:

- Reusing the large suite of test cases that an organization will have created for its earlier prevention effort. These test cases would require careful study and modifications in order to ensure that they test the system for the various formats of date.
- Reusing the test harnesses and test cases used in the initial iteration of testing components in the later iterations.
- Reusing the test data from the testing effort in prevention in order to ensure that all problems related to the original Y2K date are not appearing in the new system.
- Reusing test harnesses designed by following the object-oriented principles. This can be achieved by inheriting from the existing harnesses in order to test new functionality.

14.5 TEST DESIGN FOR Y2K RESURRECTION

Test design follows from test planning. The various architectural approaches to testing are implemented in test designs are typically prepared for a subsystem or a component, and are made up of a group of test cases.

14.5.1 Description of Test Designs

Designing a suite of test cases for a component is called a test design. Therefore, a test design would make use of the test approaches in order to create the suite of test cases appropriate for a component. The test designs ensure that the right test environment is available for testing the component and that all the classes within the component have been developed and unit tested. Test designs are created within the overall framework of the test plans.

Test design subject areas can be derived from the vertical and horizontal slicing of the system for testing. The vertical slicing will provide the subsystems. If these subsystems are smaller in size, then each of the subsystems will result in a test design. If the subsystems are larger in size, then we will have two or three test designs handling each of the subsystems. Each test design would incorporate a series of test cases handling all aspects of testing the system from the application perspective. Note that as shown in Figure 14.4, test designs are created within the overall framework of the test plan. However, they are not test cases themselves. Instead, the test designs encompass the test cases.

14.5.2 Sources for Test Designs

Test designs can be created based on the understanding of the system at subsystem or component level. The scenarios developed during the activity of requirements modeling (MA04) provide an excellent starting point for the test designs. These test designs give a broad coverage of the required functionality rather than the lower level test cases for each unit of the system. The test designs resulting from the business scenarios ensure that the division of system testing is ideal — the test designs reflecting the need to test the system in a modular fashion. The user also can contribute to these test designs and later on use the same in order to conduct acceptance tests. The test designer would incorporate the requirements, their variations, and their extensions within the test designs.

Test designs would consider the number of classes that have to be tested and their corresponding complexity. For each class there would be a number of test cases that test different functionality of the same classes. Test designs also would incorporate extra test cases that deal with testing the entire component, as against individual classes. For example, a set of test cases within a test design may test the date class and another set of test cases may test the account class. However, a good test design will ensure that there is a third group of test cases that test the working of the two classes together.

14.5.3 Format for Test Designs

A typical test design would contain the following:

Name — this identifies the test design.

Module — this indicates the name of the module within the target system that is targeted by this test design.

Dependency — to indicate the other test designs or test data on which this design depends for its testing.

List of test cases — this is the list of test cases which make up this test design. All test cases belonging to this design are listed together with a brief one-line description of the test cases. Also, indicate any DATE specific test cases that form part of this test design.

14.6 TEST CASES FOR Y2K RESURRECTION

Test cases are atomic or smallest unit of testing. They start from where the test designs are completed. They were described earlier in the technological and methodological dimensions of the resurrection process. They are considered in greater detail here with their applicability for all kinds of testing (including the Y2K testing).

14.6.1 Description of Test Cases

The basic purpose of a test case is to test a single element within a component. This single element can be a class or it can be a function within the class. In order to accomplish this, a test case has to provide a set of input data and parameters, the steps that are needed in order to execute the tests and the expected results.

In large or complex projects, test cases can be generated automatically. They will keep track of configurations and automatically retest changed components. The purpose of generating a large number of test cases automatically is that it ensures that a sufficient number of test cases are available to test every aspect of the software. Auto generation of test cases is associated with auto generation of test data which would otherwise take a long time to generate manually.

Test cases also may be made up of test harnesses, which are test classes that execute a large number of variations of logic within the target class. Although test cases usually are executable, manual testing includes inspection and verification of classes. Thus, a test case may not always include execution of the program.

14.6.2 DESIGNING THE TEST CASES

Designing the test cases follows from the test designs for a component. Each test case should be at an atomic level and should try and test a single element of the system. This will enable good management of the test execution as well as recording and analyzing of the results from the test cases. However, within the element being tested, the test cases should ensure that maximum variations of the input are passed through the class and that all possible outputs are thoroughly verified. A wide area of test coverage is the aim of designing test cases.

Test cases should be properly documented and their repository should be kept current all the time. This is because, with small changes in functionality, it should not be necessary to recreate a new suite of test cases. Existing test cases should be modifiable and reusable. Proper documentation of test cases would enable this to happen.

Test cases also may be generated from the requirements, if those requirements are documented in a proper format. This can considerably reduce the cost of creating test cases.

14.6.3 FORMAT FOR TEST CASES

Depending on the application's input, a format for a test case can be built up. An ideal input for Y2K testing is a series of different key dates covering the century date on either side of the Y2K hump. In general, a test case format would consist of the following three parts.

1. Input — the data that has to be input into the system.
2. Actions — the actions required on part of the tester in order to carry out the test.
3. Expected output — will determine whether the test was a success or a failure.

It is essential to ensure that the input covers a broad range of data and the expected output matches with the corresponding input for the test case. The input may be made up of an input file containing a large number of records and the corresponding output can also be a file. This file can be matched against a predetermined set of records to ensure verification of test results.

14.6.4 VERIFYING TEST CASES

Once the test cases are designed and created in the specified format, it is essential to verify that the test cases are themselves correct. They can be cross-checked against the results from the existing system (as far as nondate-related calculations are concerned). Test cases also can be verified against sample manual calculations performed by expert users of the system. In testing date-related classes, it will be essential to verify that the test cases are not coming up with a "pass" result for a 2-digit date field (remember, test cases for legacy systems used to *ensure* a 2-digit date field).

14.6.5 MODIFYING THE TEST CASES

Once the test cases are verified and accepted within a suite of test repository residing within a test design, they should be placed under a formal change control mechanism. There will be a number of reasons to modify the test cases that have been accepted within the suite. The modules being tested are undergoing change and so are the data being input to the classes. Also, as the testing progresses, new needs for additional testing will be discovered. Therefore, test cases will need modifications and upgrade during the test cycles.

14.7 TEST EXECUTION IN Y2K RESURRECTION

Test execution is a continuous activity throughout the Y2K resurrection process. It takes place in all three dimensions of the resurrection process. It is performed in the technological dimension during the unit tests (TT03-6, TT04-3, TT04-4, TT05-5, and the entire activity of quality assurance TA10), during the methodological dimensions (activity testing MA09), and sociological dimension (usability inspections ST07-3). Herein, we describe the general approach to test execution.

14.7.1 GETTING READY

Preparation is the initial part of executing tests. All test cases need some preliminary preparations before they can be successfully executed. This includes the preparedness of the modules that are to be tested, availability of test data, as well as availability of sample test results against which the results of the test execution can be measured. Getting ready for test execution includes familiarization of the tester with the test cases and the input and output of the test cases. While test data is prepared when the test designs are finalized and the test cases are written, it is not unusual for the test data to be incomplete during the initial cycles of testing. In getting ready for the test execution, this data may have to be augmented by the results of the previous cycle or from any other relevant source. In preparing for the tests, it will be necessary for the tester to familiarize himself with the "associated" test cases. Test cases that test the remaining functions within a class or other classes within the component will have some bearing on the current test case. An overall idea of the test designs is essential for all testers before the formal tests can be executed. Finally, administrative procedures like backing up and recreating test data and test cases also need to be put in place before the test execution can start. It is a part of the getting ready procedures.

14.7.2 ACCEPTANCE CRITERIA

Understanding the criteria that will decide whether the test is a success or not is an important aspect of executing the tests. These criteria may range from the single criteria for a unit test to a broad description of acceptance of the system at the integrated test level. Although the expected results are a part of the acceptance criteria, the acceptance criteria is more than just the results. A user may accept the valid results but with some additional conditions. Also, the acceptance of a test as a "pass" in the initial cycle of testing may not be so in the subsequent cycles of testing. Therefore, it is essential to understand what constitutes a "pass" for a test from the users perspective. A discussion on the Y2K resurrection acceptance criteria follows in the last section.

14.7.3 EXECUTE TEST SUITES

Once the test cases are designed, understood, and their dependencies worked out, it is time to conduct the actual testing. This would require execution of the set of test cases and comparing the results in order to record the success or failure of the test cases. The testing follows the test plans and uses the test cases within the test designs to test the components within the resurrecting system. Depending on the architecture of testing, some test cases will be executed by actual execution of components, others can be white box walkthroughs. Also, depending on the cycle of testing, some test cases will be the "broad brush" runs, whereas the same test cases during the major iteration of testing will be thorough and provide a wide coverage of data and functionality.

14.7.4 RECORD INCIDENT REPORTS

The results of the test cases are normally categorized as pass or fail. However, it is essential to categorize the results in further details. That will facilitate analysis and understanding of not only the system being tested, but also the testing process itself. The results of the test execution are called *incidences* within the resurrection process. Recording and analysis of these results in described in the next section.

14.8 TEST RESULTS IN Y2K RESURRECTION

Test results provide the valuable information on the system under test. They are produced as a result of the test execution. It is important to formally categorize and analyze the results in order to take advantage of the test execution events. The test environment or test project plan can be changed by understanding the results of testing during each cycle of testing. Hence, it is important to collate all test results generated during any phase of testing in a manner which is intuitive and useful.

14.8.1 SOFTWARE INCIDENTS

As the execution of the test suite progresses, results are produced. Although we normally expect the results of the test case to be a pass or fail, in many situations the results are not that clear-cut. Therefore, it is not appropriate to call every recording of problems as bugs. There are three categories of events that result from testing:

1. Problems — which are what we normally call bugs. These are errors in the system and they need fixing.
2. Enhancements — these are not errors. However, they have to be handled in the upgrade of the system.
3. Informative — these are only statements of events that are recorded within the incident database. No action is required on them, but they can provide help in future testing.

This categorization of test results makes it convenient to record them and group them for appropriate action. For example, informative incidences may not need a corrective action, but may have to be published for the rest of the testers and perhaps included in the user guides, etc.

14.8.2 RECORDING TEST RESULTS

Performance of any Y2K project is judged by the results of its testing activity. Hence, time-to-time reporting of results and its maintenance plays a major role in decision-making. All reports should be sorted according to their criticality and date/time of generation. Also, they should be located (stored) at a central place so that project manager and each team member can have easy access to it.

These needs are handled by making a separate database for storage of test results. The database must hold sufficient test details such as date, trial version, problem, its urgency, output results, and remarks of QA and product managers. Once a particular record is sent to the development team for implementation, the database should be updated with rest of the details such as developer's remark, date of modification, date of fix, fix version, etc. Once a bug is fixed, it may appear again in future release because of changes done in related areas. Hence, it is advisable to keep such reports in database for future reference (Figure 14.6).

Comprehensive reporting ensures maximum productivity and utilization of available IT assets. Up-to-date maintenance of results leads to improved quality of the application under test. By using these results, the product development manager can constantly improve the development procedures leading to improved quality of the product.

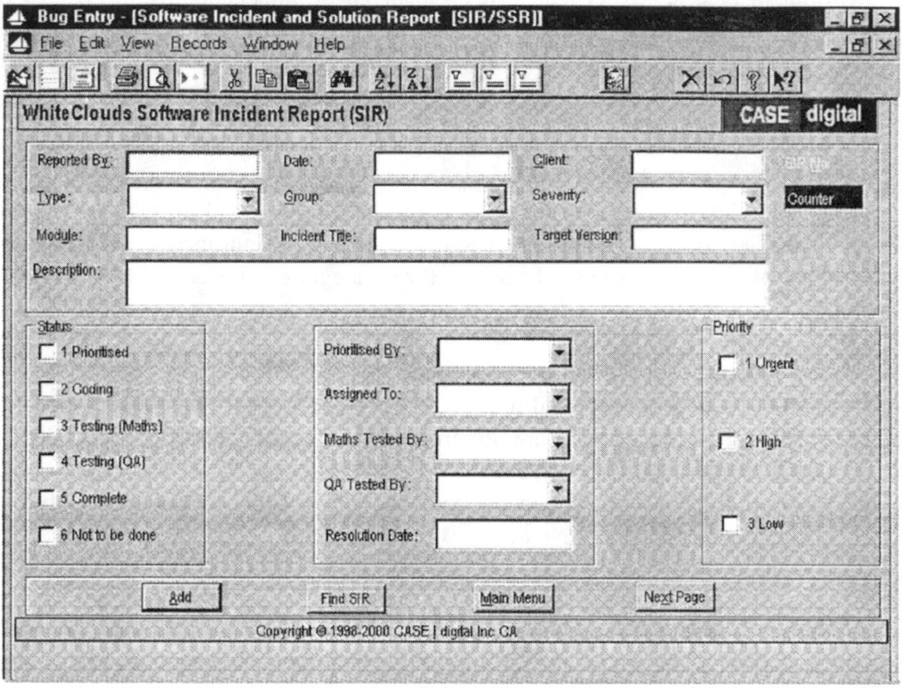

FIGURE 14.6   A typical SIR system (a CASE digital mock-up).

14.8.3 ANALYZING RESULTS

Once the testing is underway and we have started recording results of the tests as described in the previous section, it is important to analyze these results as the testing progresses. Understanding of the test results can be based on a number of metrics like number of incidents found per module (application based), or number of incidents per week (time based). Whatever criteria is used in analyzing the results, those results should be able to provide some confidence in the state of the software solution, i.e., whether the developed software is able to meet the stated requirements in the requirements model.

It is important to continue to monitor the state of the test results as the testing progresses rather than waiting for the testing phase to be completed. This is so because data from the initial testing not only provides information on the state of the software that has been tested, but also it is able to indicate the areas in which there is higher probability of finding bugs. We extend the understanding of Meyers[2] on probabilities of finding software bugs in any software system, to finding bugs in Y2K resurrection testing. In testing the date problem, the possibility of finding more bugs is indicated by the bugs already found, as shown in Figure 14.7.

In case of data, the probabilities of finding bugs increases sharply with bugs already found. For example, if a date in a particular table is corrupted, then the chances of other dates in the same table being corrupt are high. Thus, the data

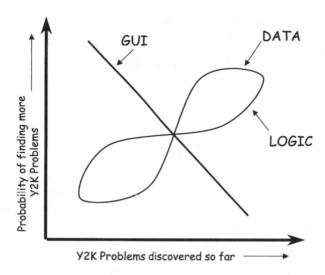

FIGURE 14.7   Probabilities of finding Y2K bugs based on recorded hits.

problems can multiply quickly, based on their existence in the data tables in the first place.

Logic problems do not multiply in the same way as the data problems do. Therefore, the chances of finding logic-related problems increase slowly (as compared with the data-related problems) as more bugs are found in the logic of the software. However, after a certain breakeven point, the probability of finding more bugs grow exponentially. This is because if the software is written in a haste or without following a process or by an inexperienced person, then those characteristics will percolate throughout the entire module for which the person was responsible.

14.8.4 REPORTING

Finally, after the results from the testing cycle have been collated, it will be essential to report them to the person who can make decisions based on them. The test manager (a variation of the project manager actor) would usually perform the reporting function. The results of the initial cycles need not be reported to the senior management of the company, as these initial results may not be a true reflection of the state of the software. The test environment and the testing experience of the tester may skew the initial results. However, once the major testing iterations are performed, it will be necessary to let the resurrection champion know the status of testing. If testing indicates major problems with the system, they should be immediately investigated in further detail. If the architecture, requirements, and designs of the system have been carried out systematically, then the test results should not show any major architectural problems within the system. However, if the requirements have changed since they were first specified, the test results will indicate that the system is not satisfying the new functionality. In such cases, the tests themselves should not be called a failure. Informing all the developers and testers of the results is helpful in providing them with an overall idea of the software status.

14.9 TEST ACCEPTANCE CRITERIA

We discussed earlier on the need for formally stating the acceptance criteria. Acceptance criteria determine the success or failure of a test case. If the results of the test case satisfy the acceptance criteria then the test case is successful. The criteria itself need not be positive. The criteria may specify the requirement of a failure (negative) and, accordingly, the test case should produce negative result. For example, if invalid log-on is supposed to reject the log-on attempt, then a failure to log on is a success as far as the test criteria are concerned. Acceptance criteria also specify more than the simple pass or fail. They specify the understanding of the user of the test case. Thus, acceptance criteria can be specified at the unit test level to indicate a unit level pass or fail; they can also be specified at the system or integration test level, wherein they are described in a more "general" way rather than a precise pass or fail.

Some of the test criteria are as follows:

Output Validation — This is the specific criteria that ensures that the expected results match with the results produced by the system.

Logic Validation — This ensures that if the logical flow is being tested then the flow of the program satisfies the functionality.

Error handling — This criteria deals with handling the errors generated by the system. Thus, by passing the predetermined "wrong" input, the tests ensure that the "correct" error messages are generated.

Recovery — By forcing a system to crash, this criteria tests out the recovery of the system. This is especially important in the transaction based systems where incomplete transactions may corrupt the database.

Performance — Herein, the system is stressed by overloading it with a large number of real life transactions. Thus, testing a banking system for performance will require the testers to load the database with a large number of customers and then passing a typical busy day's load of accounting transactions on the customer's database.

Security — The security of the system is tested by attempting to break in the system. Various attempts at log-ins, physical access to the system, software-aided attempts to get in the system, etc. form part of the security criteria.

Help and user documentation — This criteria ensures that the help and associated user documentation is up to scratch.

Configuration — This criteria ensures that the system operates under different configurations and versions of the environment (i.e., operating system, databases) in which it is supposed to operate.

14.10 KEY POINTS

1. Testing in the Y2K resurrection effort is different from the testing in the date prevention effort. This resurrection testing not only concentrates on the date testing, but needs and utilizes all aspects of testing a new development.

2. However, dissection and salvage activities within Y2K resurrection can still make use of the experience of the organization in testing the earlier date problem.

3. Testing approaches can be categorized as black–white box, manual–automated, vertical–horizontal and equivalence partitioning–boundary value.

4. The testing architecture includes unit, component, system, acceptance, and regression tests.

5. A test plan is made up of test designs that concentrate on testing a component. The test designs are made up of test cases.

6. Testing cycles ensure that the tests are sequenced in such a way that we don't end up testing functionality that hasn't been implemented.

7. Test execution uses test cases and produces test results.

8. Recording and analysis of test results provides immense help in understanding the status of the software as well as the status of testing; certain predictions on the possibilities of finding incidences can be made based on the incidences found already.

9. Acceptance criteria determines the success or failure of a test case as well as the entire testing.

14.11 NOTES

Thanks to Rama Kasbekar who has done a lot of test planning as well as testing while in Dow Jones Markets in Sydney, for her input into the writing of this chapter. Thanks also to Stephan Meyn at Object Oriented P/L and Sanjay Vaidya at Dow Jones Markets for their comments and input.

14.12 REFERENCES

1. Phippen, J., *Certificate in Software Quality,* 10-day course conducted by Australian Computer Society and Software Quality Association (Qld), July 1993.

2. Meyers, G., *The Art of Software Testing,* John Wiley & Sons, New York, 1979.

15 The *Adwait* Enterprise in Year 2000

No story can be beautiful if it is utterly finished. It will be utterly dead. Some of the greatest songs are those which are unfinished. Some of the greatest books are those which are unfinished. Some of the greatest music is that which is unfinished.

Osho, 1994[1]

Abstract   We discussed the resurrection process within the framework of the three dimensions of a process. We expect the result of our effort to be an organization that is based on the resurrected system. It is not only free from the Y2K problem that originally caused it to crash, but it is also a new way of conducting business processes. However, a careful scrutiny of this new enterprise will reveal that it is not so much a combination of various business processes, but is, in fact, a single process. In this final chapter we argue that all processes of an enterprise are derived from a single abstract process which forms the central theme of the enterprise. We also extend the same argument and apply it to the entire business universe, wherein the business does not exist in isolation, but is related to the rest of the business world through its relationships with clients and suppliers. Anything and everything that affects them has the potential of affecting the new enterprise. Thus, at the highest level of abstraction we deal with the business universe as a single entity. A single entity that has no other is what is implied by the Sanskrit word *Adwait*. This chapter discusses this single process and extends the same argument further to the "business universe" which, it argues, is a single process in itself.

15.1 UNDERSTANDING *ADWAIT*

We have resurrected successfully. What next? It would be appropriate to complete this discussion on resurrection by leaving pointers to the various ways in which the newly resurrected system will be required to support the new business. We are arguing during the closing stages of this book that the nature of the new business will be quite different from the way it was in the past millennium. The focus of management in the new millennium will have to expand to encompass many entities that were once considered "outside" the interests of the organization.

FIGURE 15.1   Traditional view of business.

15.1.1 THE TRADITIONAL VIEW OF BUSINESS

We have considered resurrection as an opportunity to rebuild not only a software system but also a new organization. Therefore, it is essential to move away from the traditional view of the business as shown in Figure 15.1. This traditional view of business has restricted itself to its own immediate boundaries. These boundaries were made up of the immediate suppliers and clients. Therefore, these suppliers and clients were important only to an extent that they affected the profitability of the business in the past.

However, our arguments right from the beginning (Chapter 2) have been that the business exists within the broader context of the society. Therefore, it is essential to consider relationships beyond those of the clients and the suppliers. Thus, it is important to consider the fact that these clients and suppliers are themselves business entities that, in turn, have their own clients and suppliers (one of which may be our business). If we consider our business in this global context, it is best described through the framework of *Adwait*.

15.1.2 MEANING OF THE TERM *ADWAIT*

At the end of the resurrection process, we don't want to end up with the same business that we were before. If we were to continue to compete at the same level as before and maintain the same criteria of success (or failure) as we did before the resurrection, we will be back to where we were. We will have achieved very little beyond a technologically sound software system that supports a new business.

By understanding the concept of *Adwait*, business can do a lot more than simply compete. *Adwait* is an ancient Sanskrit term that literally means "no other." It is an appropriate term to describe the highest level of abstraction that businesses (especially resurrected businesses) will have to be aware of in their dealings in the new millennium.

We are not "closing the shop" at the end of resurrection. In fact, by developing an understanding of *Adwait*, we are opening the business (and the supporting software applications) to a different and abstract view of the world. This should lead to many unexpected and unknown opportunities for the resurrecting organization and a cycle of continuous improvement.

It is a view that is likely to be missed if we don't look beyond the need to maintain our account books and see that the new millennium is operating at a much higher and abstract level than we have ever experienced.

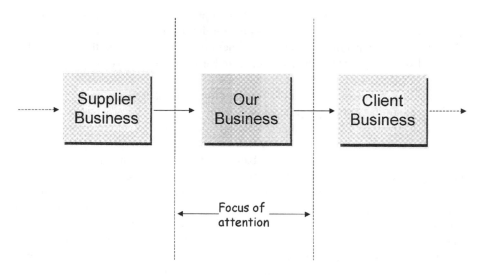

FIGURE 15.2   Management focus during the Y2K saga.

15.1.3 *ADWAIT* — After the Y2K Resurrection

Our goal in resurrecting was to produce a process-based organization that will be flexible enough to handle the rapid changes envisaged in the new millennium. When each business process is scrutinized in detail, it tends to reveal its relationship with other processes within the business (Figure 15.2). For example, a payroll process is related to the accounting process which, in turn, is related to the procurement process. Thus, except for a few theoretical situations (as are encountered during process designs), it is not possible to consider a process in isolation. When all processes for a business are considered together, their scrutiny leads to a higher level process which describes the central theme of the business. This is the reason why it is possible to express an entire business using a single use case. It is not always practical to do so, but its feasibility shows that there is a common theme to a business which can be abstracted to a higher level and may be represented by a single abstract process. This would make that higher level process an *Adwait* process within the organization.

During the initial attempts at fixing Y2K, processes were not considered in great detail. During resurrection, we considered processes as the pillars of the new organization. Here, we are considering the fact that at a high level of abstraction, an organization has a unique process of its own and that the same is true of all other organizations to which it is related.

Y2K-hit organizations will be in a position to ascertain how they were affected and influenced by organizations they were dealing with. As this is being written, the IT community realizes that the effect of the bug is not restricted to a single organization. Effect of noncompliance of business partners is an important aspect of Y2K hits. Organizations at green and above level of preparedness could be hit by Y2K because of the bug-ridden interfaces of their business partners.

Because the problems of its clients and suppliers were influencing even Y2K-compliant organizations, it was not possible for the organization to disassociate itself from issues and concerns of the other business partners. Stretching this idea further can lead to the realization that anything and everything that is happening in the business world is going to affect our business.

The idea of one business (and events within that business) influencing another business is similar to the effect described by the theory of chaos, wherein the cause and effect are far removed in time, space, and magnitude (e.g., fluttering of butterfly wings in Tokyo can cause a hurricane in a Florida). Based on this theory, a Y2K hit to a small business account within a bank has the potential of bringing the entire banking system down, leading to the collapse of the business.

However, by developing an understanding of *Adwait*, we attempt to identify the reverse of the "chaos" theory. If the effect of the Y2K disaster is an explosion, our attempt to handle this explosion should be such that it leads to an understanding of underlying order within the organization. Not only do we attempt to identify the order within the organization, but also within the business world. For example, resurrecting from a Y2K hit in a banking application should create a process-based software that considers issues and concerns of its business partners in valuing loan applications and allocating loan amounts.

15.2 RELATIONSHIPS WITH BUSINESS PARTNERS IN Y2K

15.2.1 RETAINING BUSINESS PARTNERS

An organization with *Adwait* considerations will ensure that it retains relationships with its business partners despite the Y2K problem. Efforts will be made to ensure that the businesses of the clients and those of the suppliers are also performing well. Repeat business from partners that are already used to the sociology and the methodology of our business will be an important part of growth in the new millennium. Therefore, the focus of attention of *Adwait* businesses will not be restricted to their own business, but will encompass the business processes of their clients and suppliers (Figure 15.3). This does not mean an indiscriminate interference in the business processes of the partners, but developing a well-educated and well-informed understanding of the business of the partners and its influence on our own business. The *Adwait* organization should budget for keeping it and its business partners updated on the processes within the industry. It should also budget to ensure that the business partners have been consolidated after the Y2K problem and that they have started generating repeat business.

15.2.2 MOVING ON

Although it is essential to understand their processes and maintain the relationship with the business partners, it is possible that because of a severe Y2K hit, relationships with a business partner may be permanently damaged. If litigation is involved,

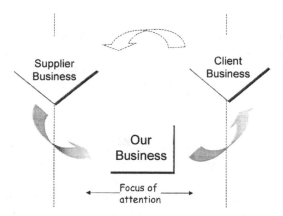

FIGURE 15.3 Focus of attention after *Adwait* considerations.

there is greater possibility of a damaged relationship with a business partner. This will lead to higher cost of retaining business relationships.

When we reach a point where the relationship is resulting in a *negative* effect on the business, it may be advisable to let the relationship "drop," and move on with developing new opportunities. However, keeping in view the *Adwait* considerations, it is essential to understand that while we lose relationship with an individual business, that same business is still a part of the overall business world. Therefore, the industry as a whole has still the need for that business.

15.2.3 RELATIONSHIP WITH BUREAUCRACY

Relationship with the government bureaucracy will be an important aspect of a successful business in the new millennium. With the advance of E-commerce, it is possible for smaller businesses to enter a comparatively leveled field with larger businesses. This has made it possible for smaller businesses to vie for government work that was earlier available to only large organizations. Use of new technology has made it possible for organizations to maintain relationship with bureaucracy, ensure it has the latest information on the rules and regulations within the industry, and continue to compete.

15.3 THE MARTIAN BUSINESS

An *Adwait* organization in the new millennium will be dealing with not only the business that it is used to, but also with work that it had never envisaged. This can be business coming from remote physical locations and of a nature that it did not anticipate. An *Adwait* organization that is aware of the high-level abstraction of its business process will be well placed to take advantage of this "Martian"* business that may be expected in the new millennium.

---

* As coming from beyond Earth — from Mars.

15.3.1 THE STAR BUSINESS

A fully resurrected organization is asked to help with the Y2K resurrection process of a senior business partner. The sociological experience of a banking business is called upon by an insurance organization to help it with the morale and motivation of its claims department. The new millennium brings the need to ask and need to provide work that may not fall within the definition of the "core" business. With individuals and organizations developing multiple skills in many different business domains and the technological growth bringing the world closer together into a global village, the kind of business that the resurrecting organization may deal with can be appropriately called the "Martian business" or "star business." The growth of this business may not be always focused and directed. Organizations will have to consider the "mutation" effect of the opportunities that are being presented to it and combine them with the skills and experience that the organization has internally, in order to move forward. Furthermore, businesses will have to consider not only the skills and abilities but also the effect of massive social networking that will expose the business to "star" work.

15.3.2 GROWTH OF MARTIAN BUSINESS

Adwait moves us from Earthly business to Martian business. It is a business we haven't fully envisaged yet, let alone comprehended. However, it is a business that is less concerned with the red vs. black equation. It is a business that leaves the Earthly plain of red and black and moves in a vertical direction. It has time on its side and, therefore, it knows that it will shift from red to black easily.

An organization that appreciates the concept of *Adwait* will put priority on its movement from "Earthian" to "Martian" direction; this involves accepting and absorbing yearly profits and/or losses but not measuring its success based entirely on these figures. This is what is shown in Figure 15.4. Some characteristics an *Adwait* organization will be

- It will work in parallel with organizations, wherein similar business domains are treated as an opportunity rather than a threat.

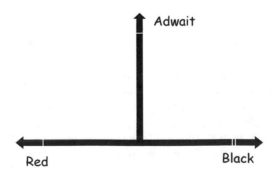

FIGURE 15.4   An *Adwait* enterprise moves in vertical dimension.

- It will reflect the concept of multi-threading in its functioning. It will expect problems *and* solutions to "happen" simultaneously and will have mechanisms put in place to deal with these events effectively.
- Expansion of the business may occur by a combination of strategy and focus as well as by "mutation" and networking.
- The organization's management will have put in place sophisticated feedback loops that provide it with the effect of its action in the business world and, based on the *Adwait* concept, back to its ownself. These would include short-, medium-, long-term feedback of the organization's action on itself.

15.4 KEY POINTS

1. All processes within a business are related to each other, therefore, at a higher level of abstraction the business seems to have a single process.
2. *Adwait* indicates "no other." A single abstract process which forms the backbone of the business, is an *Adwait* process.
3. The same argument of *Adwait* can be extended further to apply to an entire industry or to the entire business world that also is made up of a single process.
4. Y2K effects of business partners will be felt by our business. This is an indication of the underlying *Adwait* nature of the business world.
5. It is essential for management to switch focus from the narrow view of its own business to that of its business partners and beyond.
6. An *Adwait* organization will be ready for the Martian business — a business that is unknown at this stage and that will come in a nontraditional format and from unknown places.

15.5 NOTES

I find the sociological aspect of business very interesting. The problems and the solutions in sociological domain are at a more abstract level than the technological and methodological ones. I also find that the concept of *Adwait* describes this "abstract" view in a much better way than any other concept. Hence, in concluding my work on Y2K resurrection, I decided to describe this abstract view of the new business. These are thoughts beyond resurrection and are not necessarily subject to the same rigors as the rest of the book. Perhaps feedback from the readers will give them a better shape than what they are today.

Reducing the feedback loop for an Adwait organization is enticing a number of researchers. Potential research in utilizing and applying the concept of neural networks can lead to an understanding of the influence of an organization's behavior on the rest of the business universe and then back on itself. Recognizing and extracting complex patterns in the business world will be easier in the new millennium with the availability of abundant computing power. One would expect application of neural networks to be an integral part of the suite of business applications.

15.6 REFERENCES

1. Osho Rajneesh, *The Heart Sutra: Discourses on the Prajnaparamita Hridayam Sutra of Buddha,* 1994, 265.

Appendix A

Sample Y2K Acceptance Criteria

INTRODUCTION

This appendix is a cross-check of some of the standard Y2K tests that were performed for (typically) small- to medium-sized businesses by CASE digital Inc. during its Y2K prevention work. They may be used during resurrection exercises as well. Although the resurrection process that we have discussed applies to all types of businesses, this cross-check is relevant to only small- to medium-scoped resurrection exercises, wherein the end result may be verified against the tests that were performed by the organization during the prevention work (some time ago). This is so because small- to medium-sized businesses and home PC users depend on the smaller applications and packages (e.g., Excel, Word, and Access) to continue their routine activities. Therefore, if the Y2K bug hits them, their resurrection would mostly be small to medium in scope, which may benefit by the same tests that were performed during prevention. Thus, this appendix is a summary of cross-checks for office applications and tools which can be used for resurrection as well as some home-based prevention (!) work.

STANDARD OFFICE APPLICATIONS REMINDERS

Most Microsoft office products rely on the operating system for their date formats and, thus, handle dates well into the next century. Every Microsoft database product including Microsoft Access, Visual FoxPro, and Microsoft SQL Server stores years in 4-digit form. Microsoft provides 2-digit short cuts for people entering years (i.e., "96" instead of "1996"). When a user types in a 2-digit year, the programs store the complete 4-digit year instead of just the 2-digits. However, the industry-wide concern of interpreting 2-digit short cuts continued to influence these office products. For example, if you are importing date fields from older products to the new Office 97 suite of products, interpreting the 2-digit field will be a problem (i.e., a date that was entered as 16 but was meant to be 1916 will be interpreted to be 2016).

Following are more specific situations related to date–field in office applications.

SPREADSHEETS

MICROSOFT EXCEL FOR WINDOWS (OFFICE 97)

- Last recognized 2-digit year format (12/31/19): December 31, 2029.
- Last recognized date in 4-digit year format (12/31/2078): December 31, 9999 (Long Date).

Note: Please note that there has been no confirmation from Microsoft on the following problem.

Excel v7.0 (found in Office 95) uses the following logic to expand 2-digit year dates to 4 digits:

If 2DD < 19 or = 3D19, then 4DD = 3D 20DD else 19DD
So 1/1/18 is 2018, and 1/1/20 is 1920

Excel 97 (found in Office 97) uses the same logic with a different switch date :

If 2DD < 29 or = 3D29, then 4DD = 3D 20DD else 19DD
So 1/1/18 is 2018, 1/1/20 is 2020, 1/1/28 is 2028, and 1/1/30 is 1930

Both applications seem to be fine if you always format and enter in 4-digit years.

Further note: If you open an Excel 7.0 spreadsheet under Excel 97, the cells taken from the older version keep their previous logic. If you reformat the column, the old cells maintain the old logic and newly typed dates *in the same column* take on the new logic.

Conclusion: Importing Excel 7 spreadsheets with 2DD into Excel 97 will have flawed logic unless one actually retypes each 2DD cell entry.

Microsoft Excel for Windows (Office 95)

- Last date not recognized even in 4-digit long/explicit "YYYY" format: 12/31/1899.
- First recognized date in 4-digit year format (1/1/1900): January 1, 1900.
- First recognized 2-digit short/assumed "YY" format (1/1/20): January 1, 1920.
- Last recognized 2-digit year format (12/31/19): December 31, 2019.
- Last recognized date in 4-digit year format (12/31/2078): December 31, 2078.
- First date not recognized in the next century: 1/1/2079.

Microsoft Excel Version 5

This version of Microsoft Excel is currently the most widely used version within the industry. It can manage Year 2000 dates and can display dates containing 4-digit years as long as the cells in which these dates are to be entered are formatted correctly.

In order to format the cells correctly, highlight the appropriate cells that you wish to format, then select "Format\Cells\" from the menu, then from the category box choose "date" and enter in the code box "DD/MM/YYYY" and click "OK." The dates within those cells will now be displayed with a 4-digit year.

If system dates are bought in via functions such as "now" or "today," then these dates will be displayed in whichever format the cells are set to. This version of Excel also recognizes leap years, in particular the Year 2000 leap year and can manage dates up to and including December 31, 2078.

DATABASES

Microsoft SQL Server

- The full 4-digit YYYY year field can handle dates up to the Year 9999.

Microsoft Access (Access 97)

The release of Access, released in January 1997, will interpret "00" to "29" as short cuts for the years "2000" to "2029." The older Access 95 interprets "00" to "29" to be short cuts for "1900" to "1929." However, it is important to note that users can type in all 4 digits of a year to clearly identify the date they want to store.

More specifically:

- The full 4-digit YYYY year field can handle dates up to the Year 9999.
- The 2-digit YY year field can handle dates up to the Year 2029.

If *oleaut32.dll* is the original file that ships with Access 95 (Version 7.0) then:

- YY dates are assumed to be in the 20th century.
- YYYY dates work as entered.

If *oleaut32.dll* is version 2.20.40xx (installed from IE3, O97, or other newer programs) then:

- YY dates from 30 to 99 are considered the 20th century.
- YY dates from 00 to 29 are considered the 21st century.
- YYYY dates work as entered.

Microsoft Access Version 2

This database will allow 4-digit years to be used; however, in order for it to do this, the data field containing the date must first be formatted. This can be done by defining the format you wish to use for the date field when the database is first set up. This can be done via the following steps.

1. When defining the date field date type, click on the arrow and choose "Date/Time."
2. Click on format and then the arrow again.
3. Choose an appropriate format that will allow the dates to be displayed with a 4-digit year, e.g., short date format ("12/31/2000").

This database package is also capable of recognizing leap years in particular the Year 2000 leap year and will not allow dates to be entered into the database that are not valid, for example the date "02/29/1997" cannot be entered, however the date "02/29/2000" can be entered.

If a date is entered in a 2-digit format then Access V2.0 assumes it to be a 20th century year. For example, if there are two dates in a data table, one "12/03/1900" and one "12/03/2000" then if a query is run looking for the date "12/03/00," then only the 1900 date will be returned. It is important to note this especially when the date "02/29/00" is entered, as this will be taken as "02/29/1900" and Access will produce an error as the Year 1900 was not a leap year.

Microsoft Access sorts the data correctly depending on the sort specification even if the dates span over the Year 2000. Data can also be queried using operators such as "<" and ">" and will produce correct answers to queries even if the date spans over the century switch over. It is important to note that in order for Access to do this correctly, all 21st century dates must be entered in a 4-digit format to prevent confusion and invalid query results.

There also are a number of date operations within Microsoft Access, such as "DATEADD," "DATEDIFF," "DATEPART," all these work fine with 21st century dates but again care must be taken to make sure that such dates are entered in a 4-digit format.

MAIL PACKAGES

CCMAIL

The cc:Mail for Windows R6 client manipulates the year as an integer value ACTUAL_YEAR — 1900. We display the year depending on the Windows date display format. If the date is greater than 1999, it is displayed as the year 20xx or truncated to the xx if the display format dictates a 2-digit format. This treatment ensures that both date display and date math will be correctly handled both before and after the Year 2000.

The cc:Mail clients on other platforms will be updated similarly to handle date display and date math correctly for the Year 2000 in either the R6 release or in a subsequent release.

Lotus Notes support for the Year 2000 was architected into Notes from the very beginning of its development. Thus, all Notes releases beginning with Release 1.0 fully support all year 2000 date functions and no human intervention will be necessary for Notes to continue functioning correctly when we move into the Year 2000.

When discussing the impact of Year 2000 dates in Lotus Notes, there are three areas of Notes date functionality to consider. Below are descriptions of each of these areas and explanations of how Notes handles them:

Date entry — Since Release 1.0 of Notes, it has been possible to enter dates for the Year 2000 and beyond simply by typing all 4 digits of the year (e.g., "1/1/2000").

For all Notes releases prior to Release 4.5, if only 2 digits were typed in for the year (e.g., "1/1/20"), Notes assumed that the user means the date within the base century 1900 (e.g., 1920 in the previous example). Beginning in Notes Release 4.5, if a user types in just 2 digits for the year and the 2 digits are a value between 50 and 99, then Notes will assume that the year is within the base century 1900. If the 2-digit year value entered is between 00 and 49, then Notes will assume that the century is base 2000. For example, if the date entered is "1/1/97," Notes will internally store the year as "1997." If the date entered is "1/1/00," Notes will internally store the year as "2000." This new feature in Notes Release 4.5 will allow data entry to be more intuitive for users as we move into the next millennium.

The only place where Notes does not make this assumption is with the @Date function. If you enter an @Date formula with a year as 2 digits, Notes assumes you mean the literal year that is entered. For example, @Date(94;3;16) will evaluate as 03/16/0094, when you probably intended @Date(1994;3;16) which will evaluate as 03/16/94. This is true in all Notes releases, including Notes Release 4.5.

Date calculations — All calculations using pre- and post-year 2000 dates in Notes will execute correctly. Notes' internal TIMEDATE structure stores the dates in such a way that they can be manipulated in formulas in any way, regardless of the year or any other part of the date. Notes internally supports up to the year 32767 on 16-bit operating systems (limited by a 15-bit year quantity in our TIME structure), and the year 41247 on 32-bit operating systems (limited by a 24-bit Julian date quantity in our TIMEDATE structure), so it is well prepared not only for the Year 2000, but for many millenniums beyond that.

Notes server time synchronization — When a Notes server is started for the first time, it picks up the time from the operating system it is running on and then keeps its own time from then on until the server is brought down again. The Notes server already knows how to manage the Year 2000, so it will automatically roll its time from December 31, 1999 at 11:59:59 p.m. to January 1, 2000 at 12:00:00 a.m. The Notes server also knows how to work with leap years and daylight savings time, so both of these also will be handled correctly during the Year 2000.

CALENDAR

MICROSOFT SCHEDULE+

Schedule+ assumes that any 2-digit year number less than 80 (that is, before January 1, 1980) refers to a year that has a value equal to that particular year number plus 2000 (that is, 75 refers to 2075, not 1975). In other words, the dates supported within Schedule+ are January 1, 1980, through December 31, 2079.

ORGANIZER CALENDAR

Organizer 2.x

Organizer 2.x releases will allow an appointment to be scheduled up to and including the Year 2099. Therefore, users of Organizer 2.x will experience no problems with the Year 2000, and users of previous versions should upgrade to the latest edition.

Organizer 1.x

Organizer 1.0 and Organizer 1.1 only support dates that fall within the time frame of December 31, 1990 to January 31, 2001. There is no workaround for booking appointments in the Calendar section that fall outside of this time frame. Users of these versions should upgrade to the latest edition.

MICROSOFT PROJECT

Microsoft Project can handle dates up to 2049. However, if you have a project file with tasks that start in the Year 2000 or later and you save the project file to a database, when you open the database in Microsoft Project you may receive any of the following error messages:

- Constraint date not valid
- Project finish date not valid
- Date not valid

Furthermore, when the project is opened, the dates that are in the Year 2000 or later will have changed to the project start date or the current date. The following steps reproduce the problem:

1. Create a new Project file with the project start date set to a date in the Year 2000.
2. Create two sample tasks.
3. On the tools menu, select multiple projects and then save to database.
4. On the tools menu, select multiple projects and then open from database. Select the database that was just created.
5. You will see error messages about dates not being valid. Click OK through each error message.

When the file is open in Microsoft Project, the project start date and the task start dates will have changed to the current date.

NOTES

Most of the above tests were performed by team members of CASE digital at their Centre for Object Technology Excellence (COTE) in Pune, India. Thanks to the COTE team for sharing their experiences. We recognize the fact that some of the issues mentioned here may have been fixed by the time this work is published. Appropriate acknowledgements will be made by the author for these "fixes" during subsequent publications and presentations.

Appendix B

WhiteClouds™

INTRODUCTION

WhiteClouds™[1] has been developed by CASE digital Inc. in order to Support Iterative Development within the Y2K resurrection process. The tool derives its name from the same arguments that were presented in Chapter 4 for a process; it assists in the three-dimensional tracking of a project. However, WhiteClouds is not meant to be used on its own, but in conjunction with other project management tools. It is a tool that can automate many tedious tasks of project management like creation of uniform documents, tracking the deliverables, and integrating the project management environment that may be made up of different tools like Excel, Word, Visio, and Project. It utilizes the existing tools and components and binds them together to achieve the desired goals. Since a Y2K resurrection project is likely to use all these tools, WhiteClouds is ideally placed to participate in the three-dimensional resurrection process.

TARGET ENVIRONMENT

WhiteClouds is meant for software production houses that are using organized methodological approaches to software development. Examples of these approaches include OPEN, UML, and Process MeNtOR. Currently, WhiteClouds uses the 32-bit Windows platform as its Enterprise OS. However, it can become a cross-platform tool should DCOM be available on other platforms (such as Mac).

WhiteClouds requires the presence of the underlying components, e.g., MS Project, MS Outlook, Rational Rose, etc. WhiteClouds is based on the concept of binary reuse. It doesn't *aim to replace* the functionality of existing components but, instead, WhiteClouds simply binds these components into an integrated system that automates repetitive tasks. It also serves as a single interface for diverse components.

A typical deployment environment for WhiteClouds is shown in Figure B.1.

IN Y2K RESURRECTION

The use of standard project management tools such as Microsoft Project and Microsoft Outlook in Y2K resurrection is vital. However, it is important that these

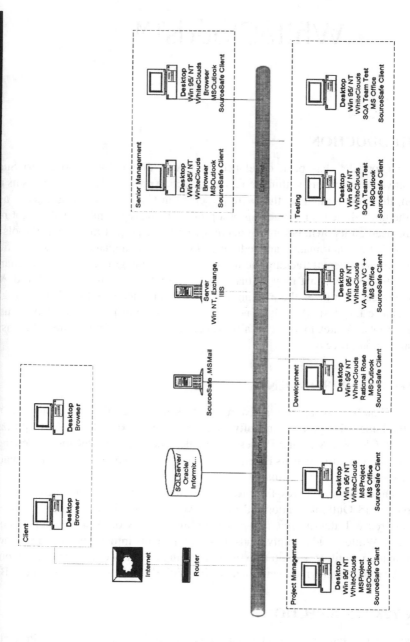

FIGURE B.1 A typical deployment environment for WhiteClouds in a resurrection process.

tools talk with each other so as to preclude manual intervention at every step of the resurrection project.

For example, consider the process of Work Allocation within the resurrection process. This can be performed within MS Project. However, the work allocation templates have to be completed by hand by the concerned project manager. These completed templates are then translated to MS Outlook Calendar entries (since the individuals may have other activities lined up). The scheduling conflicts are noted and resolved after a succession of meetings. A great deal of effort and time would have been saved if the project plan could have been integrated with the MS outlook workgroup calendar. It would have allowed automatic creation of the outlook schedules from the project plan. This is achieved by the use of WhiteClouds.

WhiteClouds uses the basic infrastructure for this intercomponent communication that has already been put into place by Microsoft. It satisfies the need of a controller that can effect this coordination of the components in a controlled manner. WhiteClouds also presents a standard interface to the user, within which the respective project management components operate, resulting in a single "point of call" for all project management activities within the resurrection process.

Finally, WhiteClouds also integrates some additional activities such as logging and analyzing of test results to ensure that the management of the testing activities is properly controlled and coordinated through the Software Incident Reporting System (see Figure 14.6).

NOTES

WhiteClouds has been developed by CASE digital Inc. at their sophisticated software development facilities at Centre for Object Technology Excellence (COTE) in Pune, India. The development was led by the Chief Technical Architect, Rajesh Pradhan, and supported by a team of five programmers. Rajesh is a winner of the young entrepreneur award from the Indian Computer Society.

REFERENCES

1. WhiteClouds is developed by CASE digital Inc. For details see www.casedigital.com.

Appendix C

MeNtOR Assistant Tool (MAT)™

INTRODUCTION

Tasks and deliverables within any project (including the Y2K resurrection project) need careful and continuous tracking. MeNtOR Assistant Tool (MAT)[1] has been developed in order to assist the tracking of tasks and deliverables within the Process MeNtOR methodology by Object Oriented Pty Ltd. MAT is a tool that integrates project tracking, issue/defect tracking, time tracking, and testing across all activities within an organization. Thus, MAT is able to track all aspects of a resurrection process by means of project tasks and/or deliverables together with an integrated single "timesheeting" system. Furthermore, MAT may also be used in conjunction with other project management tools like Microsoft Project or Timeline, which are more conducive to a waterfall development lifecycle.

Because of its ability to handle the iterations in a process, the MAT tool is ideal for supporting object-oriented methodological processes such as described in Process MeNtOR. Since a Y2K resurrection effort, as described in this book, is also an iterative process, it can derive significant benefits by using the tracking capabilities of MAT.

Y2K RESURRECTION PROCESS IN MAT

ENTERING THE PROCESS ELEMENTS

We briefly describe how the process elements for a Y2K resurrection process can be entered and tracked using MAT. These elements derive from the three-dimensions of the resurrection process vis-à-vis the technological, the methodological, and the sociological dimension. These process elements can be shortlisted based on the example process repository described in Chapter 13.

TRACKING THE PROCESS ELEMENTS

The tool is a top-level slice across the whole software life cycle, integrating the best, most widely used features of the best of existing commercial tools. The tool uses terminology that can be mapped to Y2K terms as follows:

- Y2K Scope is termed Lifecycle in the Tool.
- Y2K Dimension is termed Process Unit in the Tool.
- Y2K Activity is termed Tracking Item in the Tool.

DEFINE THE DIMENSIONS

We start the use of MAT in Y2K resurrection project tracking by defining "what" has to be tracked. At a higher level, whatever is done in the resurrection project is derived from the three separate dimensions representing technological, methodological and socialogical groups of activities. These dimensions are entered as "Process Units" in MAT together with an optional description for each. The activities within each of the dimensions of the resurrection process are then defined, as shown in the Figure C.1.

Once the activities within the dimensions are described, MAT will let you enter the tasks for each of the activities. These tasks are defined together with their optional brief description in MAT as shown in Figure C.2.

DEFINE THE SCOPE OF RESURRECTION

Once the activities and tasks have been entered with MAT, the next step is to create the scope (or lifecycle) that defines "when" to perform the activities and tasks. Multiple scopes can be defined (e.g., for different size projects). In Figure C.3 are defined the iterations for the scope (also referred to as segments, phases, or stages in MAT). They can be nested any number of levels deep. The activities to be performed during each iteration are selected by clicking on the "Tracking Items" button and ordered.

CREATING A Y2K RESURRECTION PROJECT

A project can now be created that uses the default dimensions and scope that were described earlier on. Herein, the project is named and described with its default scope. Management details such as the resurrection champion and cost center are defined (in the management tab) and all staff and nominal people working on the project are selected from an organizational hierarchy (within the resourcing tab). Nominal people may be used for planning when the name of the actual person(s) is as yet unknown. Details of the person are entered and shown using the Details tab. This has been shown in Figure C.4.

Once defined, the project is planned (by clicking Project Plan). The plan is created from the default scope that can then be tailored to the specific project. Multiple occurrences of the same activity may occur, each being specifically

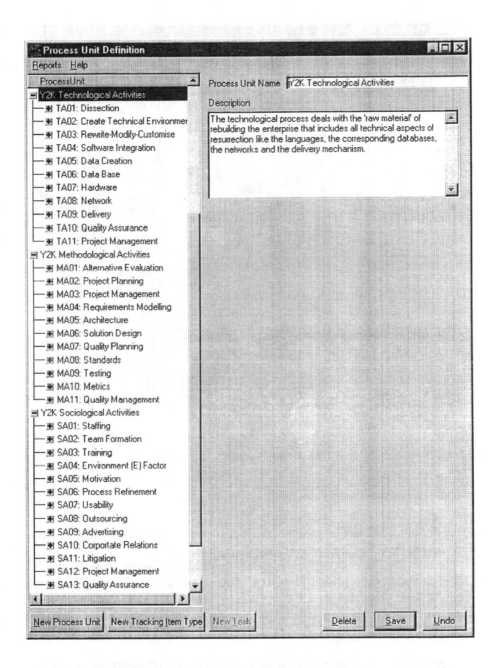

FIGURE C.1 Defining the dimensions of the resurrection process.

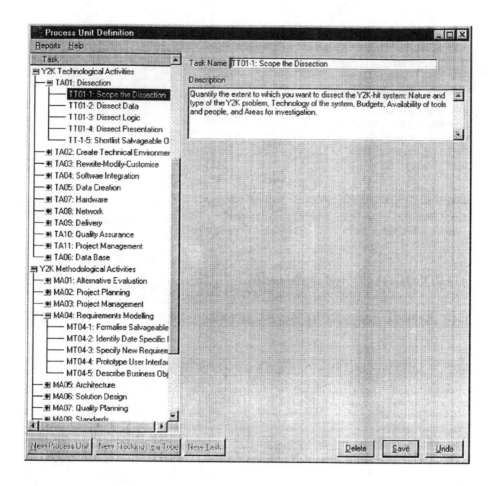

FIGURE C.2   Defining tasks within MAT.

renamed. Additional project specific activities may also be created. This has been shown in Figure C.5.

The tasks for each activity are copied from the default scope that can also be tailored to the specific project. Tracking of the activity (e.g., TA01: Dissection) within MAT is shown in Figure C.6.

SCHEDULE THE PROJECT

For each activity, select the resources to do the work, the scheduled dates, and the estimated effort to complete, as shown in Figure C.7. All the resulting information can be exported to Microsoft Project where dependencies and resource leveling can be performed as well as a Gantt chart printed. Updates to schedule dates resulting from defining dependencies, etc. can be imported back into the tool.

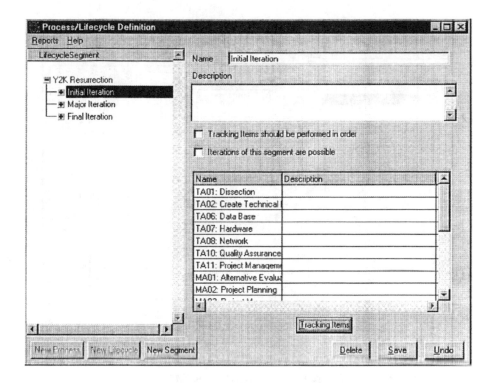

FIGURE C.3 Defining the scope by iterations in MAT (initial, major, final).

TRACKING EFFORT AGAINST THE PROJECT ACTIVITIES

As work is performed, project members record their own time against the project activities as part of completing a weekly timesheet. All entries are displayed in a timesheet dialog that can be printed or interfaced to the companies accounting package. Each entry in the timesheet is recorded by entering the effort spent in the week on the activities. Figure C.8 shows a time sheet entry for the scoping task within dissection activity (with comments seeking help for the work).

The project members then re-estimate the estimate to completion (ETC) or percentage complete by clicking the "View" button to display the planning details dialog (with the actual effort automatically updated). An updated version of the dissection activity with time details of the resources is shown in Figure C.9.

NOTES

MeNtOR Assistant Tool (MAT) has been developed by John Warner, who is a senior consultant with Object Oriented Pty Ltd. He also is a Master's student at the University of Technology, Sydney. His areas of expertise (as well as research interests) include requirements modeling, project management, and project tracking, to name but a few.

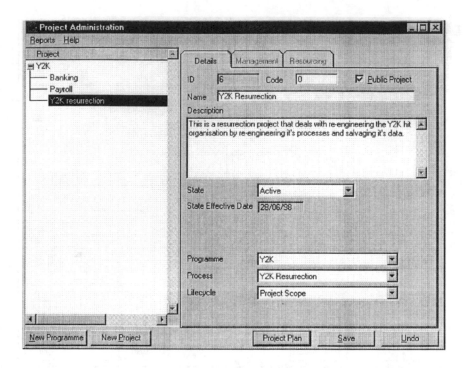

FIGURE C.4   Creating a Y2K resurrection project within MAT.

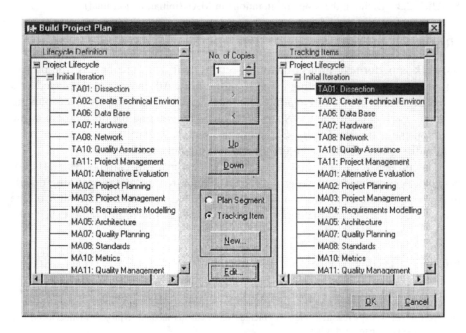

FIGURE C.5   Building a project plan.

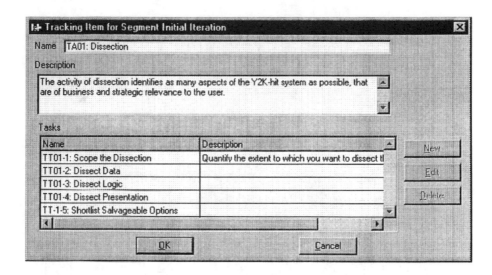

FIGURE C.6 Tracking activity dissection (TA01) within MAT.

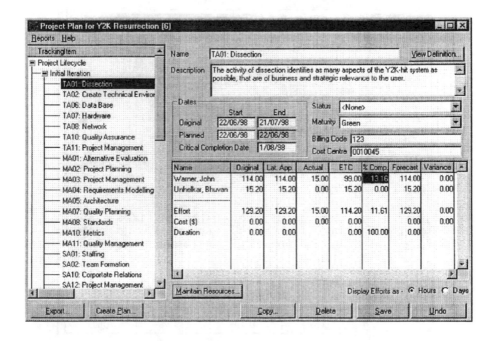

FIGURE C.7 A typical resurrection project plan with resources in MAT.

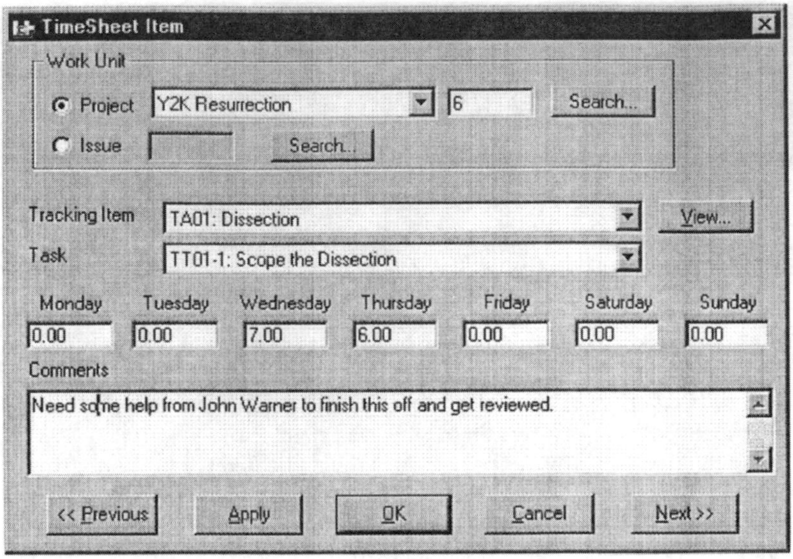

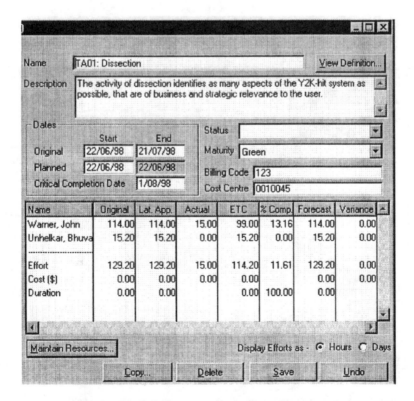

FIGURE C.8   A typical timesheet item in MAT.

FIGURE C.9   Further details on the timesheet item used in tracking TA01 activity.

REFERENCES

1. By Objcct Oriented Pty Ltd, North Sydney, Australia. See www.oopl.com.au for further details.

Index

A